More praise for *Wilderness and the A*

"When Roderick Nash's *Wilderness*
peared in 1967, it was justly praised as 'the first real idea book in environmental history'—indeed a classic study greatly influencing other scholars and the public down to the present. This revised edition not only demonstrates his ongoing concern for the environment with new chapters and a needed coverage of recent developments, it also conveys a spirit of optimism about the future."
—Howard R. Lamar, Yale University

"One of those rare works that combines exemplary scholarship with readability."—*Washington Post Book World*

"This book is a mandatory prelude to any modern treatment of conservation problems. It does not purport to tell us where we go from here. But it reports in telling fashion how we got where we are and the nature of the forces that have driven us pell-mell toward a leveling of the wilderness."—William O. Douglas, *Natural History*

"A masterly study of the wilderness mystique."—*Pacific Historian*

"A classic, unique in its field."—William E. Shands, *American Land Forum*

"Should be on every conservationist's bookshelf."
—*Living Wilderness*

WILDERNESS AND THE AMERICAN MIND

Wilderness and the American Mind

RODERICK FRAZIER NASH

Fourth edition

Yale University Press New Haven and London
Nota Bene

NB

First published as a Yale Nota Bene book in 2001.

For information about this and other Yale University Press publications, please contact:

U.S. office sales.press@yale.edu
Europe office sales@yaleup.co.uk

Printed in the United States of America

TITLE PAGE ILLUSTRATION: *Leaving the Grove,* by Richard Claude Ziemann.

The Library of Congress cataloged the previous edition as follows:

Nash, Roderick.
Wilderness and the American mind.
Bibliography : p.
Includes index.
1. United States—Civilization. 2. Frontier and pioneer life—United States.
3. Nature conservation—United States. I. Title.
E169.1N37 1982 973 82-4874
ISBN 0-300-09122-2 (pbk.)

A catalog record for this book is available from the British Library.

10 9 8 7 6 5 4

Contents

Preface to the Fourth Edition

TIMING, it is often said, is everything. The axiom is a reminder to me that while this book may be a good one, even "a classic," it is indisputably lucky. I caught the wilderness wave as it began to crest and became the beneficiary of the very intellectual revolution I described.

Think about the timeline. In the fall of 1960, as a first-year graduate student in history at the University of Wisconsin, I approached the intellectual historian Merle Curti with the idea of a dissertation about wilderness. Assuming, quite logically, that wilderness had nothing to do with human beings, the Pulitzer Prize winner gently suggested that I take my plans to the geology or biology department. But in the few minutes left in our interview, I managed to make a case for the concept that if wilderness was really a state of mind, a perceived rather than an actual condition, why not a history of the wilderness idea?

Four years later, when I slipped the completed thesis into its binder and went off to teach history at Dartmouth College, the American fascination with wilderness was gaining momentum. Pushing it were broad changes in American values and priorities that we know as 1960s environmentalism, the ecological perspective, and the counterculture. Rachel Carson published *Silent Spring* in 1962, Aldo Leopold's *A Sand County Almanac,* largely ignored since its 1949 publication, became a best-seller, and Bob Dylan sang about changing times. The Wilderness Act became law in 1964, the same year I finished the dissertation.The biggest preservation fight of the century was shaping over the proposal to dam the Grand Canyon. Suddenly it seemed that wilderness was "relevant." When, in 1967, Yale University Press published the first edition of this book, readers were ready. Marketing was easy in a generation that watched Neil Armstrong walk on the moon (1969), celebrated the first Earth Day (1970), and accepted the radical political changes implied by both the National Environmental Policy Act (1970) and the Endangered Species Act (1973). This was a period of growing criticism of American culture; it followed that the antipode of civilization, namely wilderness, would attract attention. "Ecology" and "environment" became household words between the first (1967) and second (1973) editions of the book. My pride in its early success is frequently tempered with the realization that I was very fortunate in my selection of a subject. If, as *Outside* magazine said in 1996, *Wilderness and the American Mind* was one of the books that changed our world, then it must be recognized that the world was ready to be changed.

The first edition of this book concluded with a discussion of the then-new Wilderness Act. In the 1973 edition, I extended this treatment of legislated wilderness preservation with special attention to the climactic battle over dams in the Grand Canyon. A new chapter explored the significance of wilderness for ecology and for the counterculture, and I treated the new problems that popularity posed for wilderness. The third edition (1982) did not alter the core of the book, but I added chapters on contemporary concepts of wilderness value, on Alaska, on wilderness management, and on the international significance of the American inventions of national parks and legal wilderness protection.

Several reviewers faulted the 1982 book for focusing too sharply on the anthropocentric significance of wilderness to the exclusion of ethical or biocentric values. There is no defense for my omission of what was becoming a major part of the discussion of wilderness. I can only state that it required a rather heavy book to present just the outlines of the revolution in thought that underlay wilderness appreciation and that for most of the last two centuries this *was* an anthropocentric story. Wilderness was valued and preserved *for people.* Twenty years ago, I dismissed the intrinsic value of wilderness, or what I called "the rights of nature,"[1] much too quickly. I did, however, pick up that phrase in the title of a later book, *The Rights of Nature: A History of Environmental Ethics.*

In that study, which is in many ways a sequel to *Wilderness and the American Mind,* I traced the idea that ethics could and should be extended to the human relationship to nature. This time around I did focus on the intrinsic value of nature. I recognized that wilderness should be thought of as more than just a concept, and in Henry David Thoreau's words, as "a civilization other than our own."[2] A state of mind was involved, but so was an environmental condition.

1. See below, p. 271.
2. As quoted in Roderick Frazier Nash, *The Rights of Nature: A History of Environmental Ethics* (Madison, Wisc., 1989), p. 37.

In *The Rights of Nature* (1989), I was curious if American natural rights ideology, taken to its logical limits, could lead some philosophers and activists to the rights of nature. Although I did not recognize it fully in 1982, wilderness plays a critical role in environmental ethics; it is the best place to learn that humans are ecologically and ethically involved in the larger community of life. Wilderness preservation is a gesture of planetary modesty and a badly needed exercise of restraint on the part of a species notorious for its excesses. No wonder, I finally understood, that such seminal wilderness philosophers as Henry David Thoreau, John Muir, and Aldo Leopold also pioneered ethical extension.

This fourth edition also lets the core of the earlier books stand—although I wish I could have changed all those "mans" to "humans"! What is new in this book is the epilogue, and there I use the past to explore the future of wilderness. I am interested in the scenarios that could maximize, minimize, or even eliminate wildness on this planet.

My other major concern in the epilogue is to fill those 1982 holes by reflecting on the ethical and biocentric relevance of wilderness. In doing this I will veer away from the hallowed (if always somewhat hollow) traditions of academic objectivity. I have tenure now; in fact, I'm retired! I don't have to conform to those canons of impartiality that my graduate school mentors valued so highly. So I can come out of the closet. I like wilderness, and although I wrote as a scholar about its history, I'm also a fan and an advocate; I want to see wilderness have a future as well! I think it is both an ecological and a moral resource, critically important to maintaining a sustainable civilization into the new millennium and beyond. It should also be said that wilderness is the essential habitat of most of those other "civilizations": the millions of species that have a right to share the evolutionary endeavor of this planet. Their future is just as morally and ecologically important as ours.

In making this updated case for the ecocentric importance of wilderness, I will be responding in part to recent criticisms of wilderness preservation as an outdated, elitist, even dangerous, component of environmental thought. In the epilogue I will give a twenty-first-century spin to Thoreau's old argument about wildness being the preservation of the world.

It is appropriate here, once again, to recognize the late Merle Curti for taking a gamble forty years ago on a graduate student's dream of a "big picture" dissertation that initially did not even seem to be a part of "history." Thanks to Chester Kerr, John Ryden, and Edward Tripp for supporting the early editions, and to Larisa Heimert, the present Yale University Press history editor, for proposing this new edition. I am also grateful to the many students, colleagues, and general readers, both in academic and in activist circles, who have valued this book over many years.

Crested Butte, Colorado
January 2001

Introduction

WILDERNESS was the basic ingredient of American culture. From the raw materials of the physical wilderness, Americans built a civilization. With the idea of wilderness they sought to give their civilization identity and meaning. The subject of this study is the changing American conception of wilderness.

Wild places and wild things currently enjoy widespread popularity. Indeed, the preservation of wilderness is now threatened as much from enthusiastic visitation as from economic development. Unbelievably, wilderness is in danger of being loved to death. From the perspective of intellectual history, this appreciation is revolutionary.

The roots of the story lie in the fact that civilization created wilderness.[1] For nomadic hunters and gatherers, who represented our species for most of its existence, "wilderness" had no meaning. Everything natural was simply habitat, and people understood themselves to be part of a seamless living community. Lines began to be drawn with the advent of herding, agriculture, and settlement. Distinctions between controlled (domesticated) and uncontrolled animals and plants became meaningful, as did the concept of controlled space: corrals, fields, and towns. For the first time humans

1. New scholarship on this subject includes Max Oelschlaeger, *The Idea of Wilderness: From Prehistory to the Age of Ecology* (New Haven, Conn., 1991), esp. chs. 1 and 2, and Oelschlaeger, ed., *The Wilderness Condition: Essays on Environment and Civilization* (San Francisco, 1991). See also the work of Paul Shepard, particularly *Thinking Animals: Animals and the Development of Human Intelligence* (New York, 1978); *Traces of an Omnivore* (Washington, D.C., 1996); *Nature and Madness* (San Francisco, 1982); and *Man in the Landscape: A Historic View of the Esthetics of Nature* (College Station, Tex., 1991). Also relevant are Hans Peter Duerr, *Dreamtime: Concerning the Boundary Between Wilderness and Civilization* (New York, 1985); Neil Evernden, *The Natural Alien: Humankind and Environment* (Toronto, 1985); Calvin Luther Martin, *In the Spirit of the Earth: Rethinking History and Time* (Baltimore, 1992); David B. Rothenberg, ed., *Wild Ideas* (Minneapolis, 1995); Mark Nathan Cohen, *The Food Crisis in Prehistory: Overpopulation and the Origins of Agriculture* (New Haven, 1977); Edward O. Wilson, *Biophilia: The Human Bond with Other Species* (Cambridge, Mass., 1984); and Stephen Kellert and E. O. Wilson, eds., *The Biophilia Hypothesis* (New York, 1995). An interesting popularization of the impact of civilization on human-nature relationships is Daniel Quinn, *Ishmael: An Adventure of the Mind and Spirit* (New York, 1992).

saw themselves as distinct from and, they reasoned, better than the rest of nature. It was tempting to think of themselves as masters and not as members of the life community. The conceit even extended to the idea that they "owned" it.

The intellectual consequence was the application of the concept of "wild" to those parts of nature not subject to human control. The concept of wilderness emerged as a way of thinking about nature with the beginnings of a pastoral style of life some twelve thousand years ago.[2] This was, of course, also the start of the remarkable upswings in the growth curves of population, technological prowess, wealth, and environmental deterioration.

The dawn of civilization created powerful biases. We had settled down, developed an ecological superiority complex, and bet our evolutionary future on the idea of controlling nature. Now there were survival-related reasons to understand, order, and transform our environment. Wilderness became the unknown, the disordered, the dangerous. The largest portion of the energy of early civilization was directed at conquering wildness in nature and eliminating it in human nature.

It followed that dogs were superior to wolves, wheat to wild grass, cows to deer, and the controller to the controlled. And since civilized people tended to prevail over wilder ones (witness the histories of Africa, Australia, and the Americas), a flood of tempting ideas swirled up with the village smoke. A little seemed good; why not modify nature some more? Make the crooked straight and the rough places plain; force the desert to blossom like a rose. The capstone of these civilized dreams was the idea of "paradise"—an environment perfectly suited to human interests. The opposite of paradise was, of course, wilderness.

Civilization severed the web of life as humans distanced themselves from the rest of nature. Behind fenced pastures, village walls, and, later, gated condominiums, it was hard to imagine other living

2. In earlier editions of this book I suggested that historically the word "wilderness" means the place of wild beasts: see below, pp. 1–2. In 1983, Jay Vest read a paper at the Third World Wilderness Conference which adds the idea that in early Celtic tradition, "wilderness" also signified land that is possessed of its own "will power" and could be thought of as willful or "self-willed": Jay Hansford C. Vest, "Will of the Land: Wilderness Among Primal Indo-Europeans," *Environmental Review*, 9 (1985), 323–29. The essential idea in both etymological versions is that "wilderness" signified a place that was uncontrolled by the settled civilization that developed after the end of hunting and gathering.

things as brothers or nature as sacred. The remaining hunters and gatherers became "savages." The community concepts, and attendant respect, that had worked to curb human self-interest in its dealings with nature declined in direct proportion to the rise of civilization. Nature lost its significance as something to which people belonged and became an adversary, a target, merely an object for exploitation. Uncontrolled nature became wilderness.

We should pause to recognize that at the time of European colonization, there were already hunting and gathering people in the New World who did not recognize the wilderness/civilization distinction. Indeed, "wilderness" may, in retrospect, be the wrong word to characterize North America at the time of European contact. But the colonists *did* use it, and they carried the full set of pastoral prejudices. Living on the edge of what they took to be a vast wilderness, they re-experienced the insecurities of the first farmers and town builders. There was, initially, too much wilderness for appreciation. Understandably, the wild people of the New World seemed "savages," and their wild habitat a moral and physical wasteland fit only for conquest and transformation in the name of progress, civilization, and Christianity.

Evidence that civilization created wilderness is found in the attitudes of the so-called Indians that the European settlers found in the New World. It made no sense for them to distinguish wilderness from civilization or to fear and hate what they did not control in nature. Chief Standing Bear of the Ogalala Sioux explained that by tradition his people "did not think of the great open plains, the beautiful rolling hills and the winding streams with their tangled growth as 'wild.' Only to the white man was nature a 'wilderness' and . . . the land 'infested' with 'wild animals' and 'savage' people."[3] The "wild West" and the "frontier" were products of the pioneer mind; so was the idea of wilderness.[4]

3. Standing Bear, *Land of the Spotted Eagle* (Boston, 1933), p. 38. See also p. 196, where he says of the beliefs of pre-contact Indians, "there was no wilderness; since nature was not dangerous but hospitable." The statement is conveniently reprinted in T. C. McLuhan, ed., *Touch the Earth: A Self-Portrait of Indian Existence* (New York, 1971), p. 45. For more on early human relationships to the environment of the New World see William Cronon, *Changes in the Land: Indians, Colonists and the Ecology of New England* (New York, 1983).

4. Relevant here are parts of the "New Western History," for example Patricia Nelson Limerick, *Legacy of Conquest: The Unbroken Past of the American West* (New York, 1987).

This book is concerned with the transformation in thought that has gradually, but still incompletely, replaced the old pastoral biases with appreciation of wilderness. After the psychologically important "ending" of the American frontier in 1890, the scarcity theory of value began to work on behalf of wilderness. Americans were becoming civilized enough to appreciate wilderness. They could begin to understand it as an asset rather than as an adversary. Perhaps uncontrolled nature could be beautiful; maybe it was more appropriate for worship than churches; certainly it had a lot to do with American character and tradition and, possibly, with mental health in an increasingly complex civilization. Some even began to reason that since the wilderness had been conquered, now it was time to conquer the self-destructive tendencies of civilization. Wilderness might be useful in that task as a symbol of restraint, an environmental base on which to build a legacy of limitation and sustainability. By the end of the twentieth century a vanguard of philosophers, intellectuals, and activists were even testing the deep ethical waters that accorded wilderness, and nature in general, existence rights totally independent of their utility to people.

The point is that the American attitude toward wilderness is much older and more complex than we customarily assume. The idea of wilderness was created in a context of fear and opposition, and the ancient and powerful biases against it have died hard. American wilderness appreciation and preservation must be understood as recent, revolutionary, and still incomplete. Rather than being discouraged at the lingering public distrust of what relatively little wild country remains, contemporary wilderness advocates might remember that in terms of history, they are riding a very recent intellectual wave. Time, in other words, is on their side.

Santa Barbara, California
January 2001

PROLOGUE

The Condition of Wilderness

Wild-dēor . . . n. A wild animal, wild beast

An Anglo-Saxon Dictionary

"WILDERNESS" has a deceptive concreteness at first glance. The difficulty is that while the word is a noun it acts like an adjective. There is no specific material object that is wilderness. The term designates a quality (as the "-ness" suggests) that produces a certain mood or feeling in a given individual and, as a consequence, may be assigned by that person to a specific place. Because of this subjectivity a universally acceptable definition of wilderness is elusive. One man's wilderness may be another's roadside picnic ground. The Yukon trapper would consider a trip to northern Minnesota a return to civilization while for the vacationer from Chicago it is a wilderness adventure indeed. Moreover, the number of attributes of wild country is almost as great as the number of observers. And over time the general attitude toward wilderness has altered radically. Wilderness, in short, is so heavily freighted with meaning of a personal, symbolic, and changing kind as to resist easy definition.

The etymology of the word itself offers one approach to understanding. In the early Teutonic and Norse languages, from which the English word in large part developed, the root seems to have been "will" with a descriptive meaning of self-willed, willful, or uncontrollable. From "willed" came the adjective "wild" used to convey the idea of being lost, unruly, disordered, or confused. In Old Swedish, for instance, wild derived from the figure of boiling water; the essential concept was that of being ungoverned or out of control. Applied initially to human conduct, the term was extended to other life forms. Thus the Old English "dēor" (animal) was prefixed with wild to denote creatures not under the control of man. One of the earliest uses was in the eighth-century epic *Beowulf,* where wildēor appeared in reference to savage and fantastic beasts inhabiting a dismal region of forests, crags, and cliffs.[1]

1. *Beowulf and the Fight at Finnsburg,* ed. Fr[iedrich] Klaeber (Boston, 1922), p. 54.

From this point the derivation of wilderness is clear. Wildēor, contracted to "wilder," gave rise to "wildern" and finally "wilderness." Etymologically, the term means "wild-dēor-ness," the place of wild beasts.[2]

A more precise meaning of wilderness as forested land is defensible in view of the restriction of the term's etymological roots to the languages of northern Europe. In German, for example, *Wildnis* is a cognate, and *Wildor* signifies wild game. Romance languages, on the other hand, have no single word to express the idea but rely on one of its attributes. Thus in Spanish, wilderness is *immensidad* or *falta de cultura* (lack of cultivation). In French the equivalents are *lieu désert* (deserted place) and *solitude inculte*. Italian uses the vivid *scene di disordine o confusione*. This restriction of wilderness to the Teutonic tongues links it to the north of Europe, where uncultivated land was heavily forested. Consequently, the term once had specific reference to the woods. Wild beasts certainly favored them, and the forest, rather than the open field, was the logical place to get lost or confused. Further evidence comes from the possibility that wild is in part related to "weald" or "woeld," the Old English terms for forest. Although later extensions of its meaning obscured the word's original precision, the initial image wilderness generally evokes is that of a forest primeval.

Wilderness, of course, also had significance in human terms. The idea of a habitat of wild beasts implied the absence of men, and the wilderness was conceived as a region where a person was likely to get into a disordered, confused, or "wild" condition. In fact, "bewilder" comes from "be" attached to "wildern." The image is that of a man in an alien environment where the civilization that normally orders and controls his life is absent.

The first known use of wilderness was in the early thirteenth century in *Layamons Brut*,[3] but the word did not gain general recognition until late in the fourteenth century when John Wycliffe inspired the first English translation of the Latin Bible. He and his associates used wilderness to designate the uninhabited, arid land

2. James A. H. Murray et al., *A New English Dictionary on Historical Principles* (10 vols. Oxford, 1888–); Eric Partridge, *Origins: A Short Etymological Dictionary of Modern English* (London, 1958); Ernest Weekley, *An Etymological Dictionary of Modern English* (London, 1921); Hensleigh Wedgwood, *A Dictionary of English Etymology* (2nd rev. ed. London, 1872).

3. *Layamons Brut*, ed. Frederic Madden (3 vols. London, 1847), *3*, 217.

of the Near East in which so much of the action of the Testaments occurred. William Tyndale followed this practice in 1526 in translating the Greek and Hebrew versions of the Scripture, and the compilers of the King James Bible further publicized the term. Through this Biblical usage the concept of a treeless wasteland became so closely associated with wilderness that Samuel Johnson defined it in 1755 in his *Dictionary of the English Language* as "a desert; a tract of solitude and savageness." Johnson's definition remained standard for many years in America as well as England.

Today dictionaries define wilderness as uncultivated and otherwise undeveloped land. The absence of men and the presence of wild animals is assumed. The word also designates other non-human environments, such as the sea and, more recently, outer space. Of equal importance to these actualities are the feelings they produce in the observer. Any place in which a person feels stripped of guidance, lost, and perplexed may be called a wilderness. This usage, with its rich figurative possibilities, has extended the meaning of the word far beyond the original applications. Large and disordered collections of things, even if man-made, may qualify. Thus a wilderness is also that part of a formal garden which is deliberately planted with hedges in the form of a labyrinth. And, for the Christian, wilderness has long been a potent symbol applied either to the moral chaos of the unregenerate or to the godly man's conception of life on earth.

Henry Adams completely reversed the original significance of the term when he wrote in an 1880 novel about a "wilderness of men and women."[4] The rise of the city opened still another field. It became commonplace to speak of a wilderness of streets or of ships' masts in a crowded harbor. Authors discussed slum conditions and urban degeneracy under such titles as *The City Wilderness* and *The Neon Wilderness*.[5] A recent study of metropolitan areas refers to "this new 'wilderness' that has grown up in Megalopolis."[6] The implication is that modern man feels as insecure and confused in an urban setting as he once felt in the forest among wild beasts. The word has even been extended to ideologies regarded as mis-

4. Adams, *Democracy* (New York, 1880), p. 2.

5. Robert A. Woods, *The City Wilderness* (Boston, 1898), and Nelson Algren, *The Neon Wilderness* (New York, 1960).

6. Jean Gottmann, *Megalopolis: The Urbanized Northeastern Seaboard of the United States* (New York, 1961), p. 216.

guided or sinister: a chapter heading in an American history book refers to Herbert Hoover during the Franklin D. Roosevelt administrations as a "Voice in the New Deal Wilderness."[7]

The usual dictionary sense of wilderness implies hostility on man's part, but the term has also developed a favorable connotation. Although English dictionaries avoid the dual meaning, the chief German work confronts it directly. According to Jacob and Wilhelm Grimm and their revisers, *Wildnis* has a twofold emotional tone. On the one hand it is inhospitable, alien, mysterious, and threatening; on the other, beautiful, friendly, and capable of elevating and delighting the beholder. Involved, too, in this second conception is the value of wild country as a sanctuary in which those in need of consolation can find respite from the pressures of civilization.[8]

While the definition of wilderness is complex and partly contradictory, at least lexicographers have the advantage of dealing with the idea in general. When it becomes necessary to apply the term wilderness to a specific area, the difficulties are compounded. There is the problem of how wild a region must be to qualify as wilderness, or, conversely, how much of the influence of civilization can be admitted. To insist on absolute purity could conceivably result in wilderness being only that land which the foot of man has never trod. But for many persons minimal contact with man and his works does not destroy wilderness characteristics. The question is one of degree. Does the presence of Indians or range cattle disqualify an area? Does an empty beer can? How about airplanes overhead?

The question of size is an additional frustration. Here too the mental criteria for wilderness are as important as the physical. In theory, if a person does not see, hear, or smell civilization, he is in wilderness. But most people require the additional knowledge that a soft-drink dispenser is not quietly humming around the trail's next bend. Some want it to be miles away. The explorer and crusader for wilderness preservation, Robert Marshall, demanded an area so large that it could not be traversed without mechanical means in a single day.[9] Aldo Leopold, ecologist and philosopher,

7. *The New Deal at Home and Abroad, 1929–1945,* ed. Clarke A. Chambers (New York, 1965), p. 103.

8. Jacob and Wilhelm Grimm et al., *Deutsches Wörterbuch* (2nd ed. Leipzig, 1960).

9. Robert Marshall, "The Problem of the Wilderness," *Scientific Monthly, 30* (1930), 141.

set as his standard a region's ability to "absorb a two weeks' pack trip."[10]

Recently land managers and politicians have struggled without marked success to formulate a workable definition of wilderness. In the 1920s and 1930s the United States Forest Service experimented with a variety of terms in an effort to categorize the land under its supervision but found that "primitive," "roadless," and "natural" were no clearer than the broader category.[11] What, after all, is a road? The Outdoor Recreation Resources Review Commission's report of 1962 defined wilderness as areas over 100,000 acres "containing no roads usable by the public." The land was also supposed to show "no significant ecological disturbance from on-site human activity" yet, under certain circumstances, the grazing of livestock and evidence of earlier lumbering would be tolerated.[12] The authors of the act of September 3, 1964, which climaxed a century-old movement to protect wild country in the United States with the creation of a National Wilderness Preservation System, also attempted a definition. According to the legislators, "a wilderness, in contrast with those areas where man and his own works dominate the landscape, is hereby recognized as an area where the earth and its community of life are untrammeled by man, where man himself is a visitor who does not remain." The act went on to require that a wilderness retain "its primeval character and influence" and that it be protected and managed in such a way that it "appears to have been affected primarily by the forces of nature."[13] The old difficulties, however, persisted. What actually constitutes an untrammeled or primeval condition? And how much visiting can a wilderness stand?

Given these problems, and the tendency of wilderness to be a state of mind, it is tempting to let the term define itself: to accept as wilderness those places people call wilderness. The emphasis here is not so much what wilderness is but what men *think* it is. The obvious advantage is an accommodation to the subjective nature of

10. Aldo Leopold, "The Wilderness and its Place in Forest Recreational Policy," *Journal of Forestry, 19* (1921), 719.

11. James P. Gilligan, "The Development of Policy and Administration of Forest Service Primitive and Wilderness Areas in the Western United States" (unpublished Ph.D. dissertation, University of Michigan, 1953), pp. 122–30, 196–203.

12. Wildland Research Center, *Wilderness and Recreation—A Report on Resources, Values, Problems,* Outdoor Recreation Resources Review Commission Study Report, 3 (Washington, 1962), pp. 3–4, 26.

13. U.S., *Statutes at Large, 78,* p. 891.

the concept. And the focus on belief rather than actuality is especially useful to the historian of ideas who wants to study the thought of the past on its own terms. The limitation of this procedure, however, is the way it makes definition an individual matter and hence no definition at all.

A possible solution to the problem is the conception of a spectrum of conditions or environments ranging from the purely wild on the one end to the purely civilized on the other—from the primeval to the paved. This idea of a scale between two poles is useful because it implies the notion of shading or blending. Wilderness and civilization become antipodal influences which combine in varying proportions to determine the character of an area. In the middle portions of the spectrum is the rural or pastoral environment (the ploughed) that represents a balance of the forces of nature and man.[14] As one moves toward the wilderness pole from this midpoint, the human influence appears less frequently. In this part of the scale civilization exists as an outpost in the wilderness, as on a frontier. On the other side of the rural range, the degree to which man affects nature increases. Finally, close to the pole of civilization, the natural setting that the wild and rural conditions share gives way to the purely synthetic condition that exists in a metropolis.

As a basis for definition, the spectrum of environments puts a premium on variations of intensity rather than on absolutes. The necessity of finding the watershed where wild becomes civilized is made less pressing. Yet the spectrum idea can permit distinctions to be made between wilderness and such related concepts as scenery, country, outdoors, frontier, and rural. Depending on the context, for instance, "nature" might be synonymous with wilderness, or it could refer to a city park. The scale also suggests a general definition of wilderness as the range closest to the wilderness pole. According to the individual the end of the band to be included could be located at various points, but a consensus might certainly be expected for some distance along the scale. Land in this category

14. Leo Marx, *The Machine in the Garden: Technology and the Pastoral Ideal in America* (New York, 1964), especially pp. 73–144; Charles L. Sanford, *The Quest for Paradise: Europe and the American Moral Imagination* (Urbana, Ill., 1961), pp. viii, 135–54; John William Ward, *Andrew Jackson: Symbol for an Age* (New York, 1955), pp. 30–45, 78; and Henry Nash Smith, *Virgin Land: The American West as Symbol and Myth* (Cambridge, Mass., 1950), pp. 51–120 have used a related concept.

would be predominantly the environment of the non-human, the place of wild beasts. The presence of an occasional beer can, cabin, or even road would not disqualify an area but only move it slightly toward the civilized pole. Vast, largely unmodified regions would be very close to absolute wilderness: the North American continent prior to settlement serves as an example. It was immense in area, and its Indians were regarded as a form of wildēor whose savageness was consistent with the character of wild country. The New World was also wilderness at the time of discovery because Europeans *considered* it such. They recognized that the control and order their civilization imposed on the natural world was absent and that man was an alien presence.

CHAPTER 1

Old World Roots of Opinion

> The land is the Garden of Eden before them, and behind them a desolate wilderness.
>
> Joel 2:3

EUROPEAN discoverers and settlers of the New World were familiar with wilderness even before they crossed the Atlantic. Some of this acquaintance was first-hand, since in the late Middle Ages a considerable amount of wild country still existed on the Continent. Far more important, however, was the deep resonance of wilderness as a concept in Western thought. It was instinctively understood as something alien to man—an insecure and uncomfortable environment against which civilization had waged an unceasing struggle. The Europeans knew the uninhabited forest as an important part of their folklore and mythology. Its dark, mysterious qualities made it a setting in which the prescientific imagination could place a swarm of demons and spirits. In addition, wilderness as fact and symbol permeated the Judeo-Christian tradition. Anyone with a Bible had available an extended lesson in the meaning of wild land. Subsequent Christian history added new dimensions. As a result, the first immigrants approached North America with a cluster of preconceived ideas about wilderness. This intellectual legacy of the Old World to the New not only helped determine initial responses but left a lasting imprint on American thought.

The value system of primitive man was structured in terms of survival. He appreciated what contributed to his well-being and feared what he did not control or understand. The "best" trees produced food or shelter while "good" land was flat, fertile, and well watered. Under the most desirable of all conditions the living was easy and secure because nature was ordered in the interests of man. Almost all early cultures had such a conception of an earthly paradise. No matter where they were thought to be or what they were called, all paradises had in common a bountiful and beneficent natural setting in accord with the original meaning of the word in Persian—luxurious garden. A mild climate constantly prevailed. Ripe fruit drooped from every bough, and there were no thorns to prick reaching hands. The animals in paradise lived in harmony with man. Fear as well as want disappeared in this ideal state of nature.[1]

If paradise was early man's greatest good, wilderness, as its antipode, was his greatest evil. In one condition the environment, garden-like, ministered to his every desire. In the other it was at best indifferent, frequently dangerous, and always beyond control. And in fact it was with this latter condition that primitive man had to contend. At a time when there was no alternative, existence in the wilderness was forbidding indeed. Safety, happiness, and progress all seemed dependent on rising out of a wilderness situation. It became essential to gain control over nature. Fire was one step; the domestication of some wild animals another. Gradually man learned how to control the land and raise crops. Clearings appeared in the forests. This reduction of the amount of wilderness defined man's achievement as he advanced toward civilization. But progress was slow. For centuries the wild predominated over the precarious defenses thrown up against its influence. Men dreamed of life without wilderness. Significantly, many traditions located paradise on an island or in some other enclosed area. In this way the wild hinterland normally surrounding and threatening the first communities was eliminated. Wilderness had no place in the paradise myth.

The wilds continued to be repugnant even in as relatively advanced civilizations as those of the Greeks and Romans. The celebrations of nature, which abound in classical literature, are restricted to the cultivated, pastoral variety. The beautiful in nature was closely related to the fruitful or otherwise useful.[2] The Roman poet of the first century B.C., Titus Lucretius Carus, spoke for his

1. Mircea Eliade, "The Yearning for Paradise in Primitive Tradition," *Daedalus, 88* (1959), 255–67; Loren Baritz, "The Idea of the West," *American Historical Review, 66* (1961), 618–40; Arthur O. Lovejoy and George Boas, *Primitivism and Related Ideas in Antiquity* (Baltimore, 1935), pp. 290–303; George Boas, *Essays on Primitivism and Related Ideas in the Middle Ages* (Baltimore, 1948), pp. 154–74.

2. Lovejoy and Boas, pp. 222–42; Henry Rushton Fairclough, *Love of Nature Among the Greeks and Romans* (New York, 1930); Archibald Geikie, *The Love of Nature*

age in *De Rerum Natura* when he observed that it was a serious "defect" that so much of the earth "is greedily possessed by mountains and the forests of wild beasts." Apart from the areas man had civilized, it "is filled full of restless dread throughout her woods, her mighty mountains and deep forests." Yet Lucretius took hope because "these regions it is generally in our power to shun."

Turning to history, Lucretius drew a grim portrait of precivilized life in the wilderness. Men lived a nightmarish existence, hounded by dangers on every hand and surviving through the ancient code of eat or be eaten. With obvious satisfaction, Lucretius related how the race escaped this miserable condition through the invention of clothing, metals, and, eventually, "ships, agriculture, city walls, laws, arms, roads." These enabled man to control wild nature and achieve relative security. Cultural refinements and "all charms of life" followed the release from the wilderness.[3]

When Lucretius, Horace, Virgil and their contemporaries confessed their love of "nature" and expressed a desire to leave the towns for a "natural" way of life, they meant the pastoral or rural environment. Lucretius, for one, applauded the efforts of the first farmers whose labor "forced the forests more and more to climb the mountain-sides." This made room for the cultivated landscape that was so highly prized. It consisted of "fields, . . . crops, and joyous vineyards, and a gray-green strip of olives to run in between and mark divisions, . . . adorned and interspersed with pleasant fruits, and fenced by planting them all round with fruitful trees."[4] If this was the ideal, wilderness could only be forbidding and repulsive.

While inability to control or use wilderness was the basic factor in man's hostility, the terror of the wild had other roots as well. One was the tendency of the folk traditions of many cultures to associate wilderness with the supernatural and monstrous. There was a quality of mystery about the wilderness, particularly at night, that triggered the imagination. To frightened eyes the limbs of trees became grotesque, leaping figures, and the wind sounded like a weird

---

Among the Romans during the Latter Decades of the Republic and the First Century of the Empire (London, 1912); Charles Paul Segal, "Nature and the World of Man in Greek Literature," *Arion, 2* (1963), 19–53.

3. *Titus Lucretius Carus on the Nature of Things,* trans. Thomas Jackson (Oxford, 1929), pp. 155, 160, 184ff., 201. Lovejoy and Boas, pp. 192–221, present other instances of "anti-primitivism" among Greek writers.

4. *Lucretius,* pp. 198–99.

scream. The wild forest seemed animated. Fantastic creatures of every description were thought to lurk in its depths. Whether propitiated with sacrifices as deities or regarded as devils, these forest beings were feared.[5]

Classical mythology contained a whole menagerie of lesser gods and demons believed to inhabit wild places. Pan, the lord of the woods, was pictured as having the legs, ears, and tail of a goat and the body of a man. He combined gross sensuality with boundless, sportive energy. Greeks who had to pass through forests or mountains dreaded an encounter with Pan. Indeed, the word "panic" originated from the blinding fear that seized travelers upon hearing strange cries in the wilderness and assuming them to signify Pan's approach. Related to Pan were the tribe of satyrs—goat-men of a demoniacal character devoted to wine, dancing, and lust. They were thought to appear only at night and then solely in the darkest parts of the forest. According to Hellenic folklore, satyrs ravished women and carried off children who ventured into their wilderness lairs. Sileni and centaurs completed the Greek collection of forest spirits. These monsters had the torso and head of a man and the body and legs of a goat or horse. Usually, they were represented as carrying a club in the form of an uprooted tree which also served as a reminder of their favorite habitat. In Roman mythology satyr-like figures appeared as fauns and also lurked in thickly wooded regions.[6]

In early folk belief, the wildernesses of central and northern Europe also swarmed with supernatural beings. Some were worshipped, but generally with the fear characteristic of the attitude of the unsophisticated toward the incomprehensible. Others received classification as demons and cohorts of the devil. In the Scandinavian countries, for instance, it was thought that when Lucifer and his followers were expelled from heaven, some landed in the forests and became Wood-Sprites or Trolls. Many of the medieval Euro-

5. Edward B. Tylor, *Primitive Culture* (2nd ed. 2 vols. London, 1873), *2*, 214–29; Willhelm Mannhardt, *Wald- und feldkulte* (2 vols. Berlin, 1904–05); James Frazier, *The Golden Bough: A Study in Magic and Religion* (3rd rev. ed. 12 vols. New York, 1935), *2*, 7–96; *9*, 72–108; Alexander Porteus, *Forest Folklore, Mythology, and Romance* (New York, 1928), pp. 84-148.

6. Porteus, pp. 114–19; J. H. Philpot, *The Sacred Tree: The Tree in Religion and Myth* (London, 1897), pp. 55–58; Thomas Keightley, *The Mythology of Ancient Greece and Italy* (2nd ed. London, 1838), pp. 229–35, 316–18; Robert Graves et al., *Larousse Encyclopedia of Mythology* (New York, 1959), pp. 182–85.

pean monsters were lineal descendants of the man-beasts of classical mythology. Russian, Czech, and Slovak folklore spoke of a creature living in forests and mountains with the face of a woman, body of a sow, and legs of a horse.[7] In Germany, when storms raged through the forests, it was widely believed that the ghostly Wild Huntsman was abroad with his pack of baying hounds, riding furiously and killing everything in his path. Man-eating ogres and the sinister werewolves were also identified with wild, remote regions. While in certain circumstances forest beings, like the elves, could be helpful to men, most were considered terrifying and added to the repulsiveness of wilderness.[8]

Among the Anglo-Saxons, from whom most of the first Americans descended, there were long traditions of locating horrible beasts in the wilderness. The *Beowulf* epic of the eighth century brought together many of these legends. The heart of the story is the conflict between two gigantic, blood-drinking fiends and the tribes that Beowulf led. As the action unfolds it is apparent that wilderness was a concept loaded with meaning for the early Middle Ages. Throughout the poem the uninhabited regions are portrayed in the worst possible light—dank, cold, and gloomy. The fiends are said to live "in an unvisited land among wolf-haunted hills, wind-swept crags, and perilous fen-tracks." Bravely Beowulf advanced into this wilderness and below "a dismal grove of mountain trees" took his revenge on the monsters.[9]

The most important imaginary denizen of the wildernesses of medieval Europe was the semi-human Wild Man. His naked figure, covered completely with thick hair, appeared widely in the art, literature, and drama of the period.[10] Immensely strong, he was frequently portrayed in the tradition of the classical sileni and centaurs, grasping an uprooted tree. According to folk tradition, the Wild Man lived in the heart of the forest as far as possible from civilization. He was regarded as a kind of ogre who devoured children

7. Porteus, p. 84; Jan Machal, *Slavic Mythology: The Mythology of All Races,* ed. Louis Herbert Gray (13 vols. Boston, 1916), *3,* 261–66.

8. The folk traditions of the Teutonic and Nordic peoples, which contain numerous references to wilderness-dwelling spirits, are discussed extensively in Mannhardt; Jacob Grimm, *Teutonic Mythology,* trans. James Steven Stallybrass (4 vols. London, 1880); H. R. Ellis Davidson, *Gods and Myths of Northern Europe* (Baltimore, 1964); and Benjamin Thorpe, *Northern Mythology* (3 vols. London, 1851).

9. *Beowulf,* trans. David Wright (Harmondsworth, Eng., 1957), pp. 59, 60.

10. The definitive study is Richard Bernheimer, *Wild Men in the Middle Ages: A Study in Art, Sentiment, and Demonology* (Cambridge, Mass., 1952).

and ravished maidens. The character of his mate varied from place to place. In the Austrian Tyrol and Bavarian Alps, the Wild Woman was imagined to have enormous size, tough bristles, immense pendulous breasts, and a hideous mouth that stretched from ear to ear. Further north in Germany, however, she was thought to be smaller and somewhat less fearsome in appearance. Her principal offense was stealing human babies and leaving her own offspring in their place. Along with the other forest demons, the Wild People invested the gloom of the wilderness with a terrifying eeriness that proved difficult to dispel.

The Judeo-Christian tradition constituted another powerful formative influence on the attitude toward wilderness of the Europeans who discovered and colonized the New World. The authors of the Bible gave wilderness a central position in their accounts both as a descriptive aid and as a symbolic concept. The term occurs 245 times in the Old Testament, Revised Standard Version, and thirty-five in the New. In addition there are several hundred uses of terms such as "desert" and "waste" with the same essential significance as "wilderness" and, in some cases, the identical Hebrew or Greek root.[11]

Uninhabited land where annual rainfall was less than four inches dominated the geography of the ancient Near East. Such area included a strip of land beginning just west of Jerusalem and paralleling the Jordan River and Dead Sea. From here the desert sprawled southward into the Sinai Peninsula and Arabia.[12] Without advanced technology, men could not survive for long in such an inhospitable environment. In order to distinguish it from the "good" land which supported crops and herds, the ancient Hebrews used a number of terms which have been translated "wilderness."[13]

Even in places where the rainfall was above the crucial four

11. John W. Ellison, *Nelson's Complete Concordance of the Revised Standard Version Bible* (New York, 1957).

12. Denis Baly, *The Geography of the Bible: A Study in Historical Geography* (New York, 1957), pp. 34–36, 252–66; Robert W. Funk, "The Wilderness," *Journal of Biblical Literature, 78* (1959), 205–14.

13. James Hastings, ed., *Dictionary of the Bible* (rev. ed. New York, 1963), p. 1037; Thomas Marland Horner, "A Study in the Terminology of Nature in Isaiah 40–55" (unpublished Ph.D. dissertation, Columbia University, 1955), pp. 41–49; Ulrich W. Mauser, *Christ in the Wilderness*, Studies in Biblical Theology, 39 (Naperville, Ill., 1963), pp. 18–20.

inches, existence was precarious. An unusually dry season could wither crops and turn arable land into desert. In these circumstances men naturally hated and feared the wilderness. Moreover, since the amount of rain was beyond human influence or understanding, it was reasonable to give its variance a religious explanation. Drought and the resulting wilderness were thought of as the curse dispensed by the divine power in order to show his displeasure.[14] God's approval, on the other hand, meant an abundance of life-giving water. The baptismal rite, for instance, was a symbolic ceremony that the climate and geography of the Near East made meaningful.

The Old Testament reveals that the ancient Hebrews regarded the wilderness as a cursed land and that they associated its forbidding character with a lack of water. Again and again "the great and terrible wilderness" was described as a "thirsty ground where there was no water." When the Lord of the Old Testament desired to threaten or punish a sinful people, he found the wilderness condition to be his most powerful weapon: "I will lay waste the mountains and hills, and dry up all their herbage; I will turn the rivers into islands, and dry up the pools. . . . I will also command the clouds that they rain no rain upon it."[15] The cities of Sodom and Gomorrah became parched wastes of salt pits and thorny brush as a penalty for the sins of their citizens.

Conversely, when the Lord wished to express his pleasure, the greatest blessing he could bestow was to transform wilderness into "a good land, a land of brooks of water, of fountains and springs." In the famous redemption passage in Isaiah, God promises that "the wilderness and the dry land shall be glad . . . for waters shall break forth in the wilderness and streams in the desert." To "give water in the wilderness" was a way God manifested his care.[16] It was a fitting image for a people so fearful of the desert.

The identification of the arid wasteland with God's curse led to

14. Johannes Pedersen, *Israel: Its Life and Culture* (2 vols. London, 1926, 1940), *1*, 454–60; Eric Charles Rust, *Nature and Man in Biblical Thought* (London, 1953), pp. 48 ff.; Alfred Haldar, *The Notion of the Desert in Sumero-Akkadian and West-Semitic Religions.* (Uppsala, 1950); George H. Williams, *Wilderness and Paradise in Christian Thought* (New York, 1962), pp. 10–15.

15. Deut. 8:15; Isaiah 42:15, 5:6. These and subsequent wordings are according to the *Holy Bible: Revised Standard Version* (New York, Thomas Nelson and Sons, 1952).

16. Deut. 8:7; Isaiah 35:1,6; Isaiah 43:20. See also Isaiah 41:18–19 and 32:15.

the conviction that wilderness was the environment of evil, a kind of hell. There were several consequences. Like that of other cultures, the Hebraic folk imagination made the wilderness the abode of demons and devils. Among them were the howling dragon or *tan,* the winged female monster of the night called the *lilith,* and the familiar man-goat, *seirim.* Presiding over all was *Azazel,* the arch-devil of the wilderness. He was the key figure in an expiatory rite in which a live goat was brought before the chief priest of a community who symbolically laid upon it the sins of the group. The animal was then led to the edge of the cultivated land and "sent away into the wilderness to Azazel."[17] The ritual has significance not only as the origin of the conception of a "scapegoat" but as a demonstration of the Hebrews' opinion of wilderness.

This idea of the immorality of wild country is also evident in the Old Testament treatment of the paradise theme. From what little we are told about the Garden of Eden it appears to have been, in the tradition of other paradises, the antipode of wilderness. "Eden" was the Hebrew word for "delight," and Genesis represents it as a pleasant place, indeed. The Garden was well watered and filled with edible plants. Adam and Eve were relieved of the necessity of working in order to survive. Fear also was eliminated, since with one exception the creatures that shared paradise were peaceable and helpful. But the snake encouraged the first couple to eat the forbidden fruit and as a punishment they were driven out of the Garden. The world Adam and Eve now faced was a wilderness, a "cursed" land full of "thorns and thistles." Later in the Scripture, Eden and the wilderness are juxtaposed in such a way as to leave no doubt about their original relationship. "The land is like the garden of Eden before them," wrote the author of Joel, "but after them a desolate wilderness." And Isaiah contains the promise that God will comfort Zion and "make her wilderness like Eden, her desert like the garden of the Lord."[18] The story of the Garden and its loss embedded into Western thought the idea that wilderness and paradise were both physical and spiritual opposites.

The history of the Israelite nation added another dimension to the Judeo-Christian understanding of wilderness. After the Exodus

17. Deut. 16:10. On Hebrew folklore regarding the wilderness see Williams, p. 13; Frazier, *9,* 109 ff.; and Angelo S. Rappoport, *The Folklore of the Jews* (London, 1937), pp. 39 ff.

18. Genesis 2:9, 3:17; Joel 2:3; Isaiah 51:3.

from bondage in Egypt about 1225 B.C., the Jews under the leadership of Moses wandered in the wilderness of the Sinai Peninsula for an alleged forty years. The Old Testament account emphasizes the hardships encountered in this "howling waste of the wilderness,"[19] yet the desert experience was immensely important to the tribes of Israel. During these years the God their fathers had worshipped revealed himself as Yahweh and promised to be their special protector. In the heart of the wilderness on Mount Sinai, Moses received the Ten Commandments which created a covenant between Yahweh and Israel. Thereafter the Lord demonstrated his protective power by the miraculous provision of water and food. He also promised that if the Israelites remained faithful to the covenant, he would allow them to escape the wilderness and enter Canaan, the promised land of milk and honey.[20]

The Israelites' experience during the forty-year wandering gave wilderness several meanings. It was understood, in the first place, as a sanctuary from a sinful and persecuting society. Secondly, wild country came to signify the environment in which to find and draw close to God. It also acquired meaning as a testing ground where a chosen people were purged, humbled, and made ready for the land of promise.[21] Wilderness never lost its harsh and forbidding character. Indeed, precisely *because* of them it was unoccupied and could be a refuge as well as a disciplinary force. Paradoxically, one sought the wilderness as a way of being purified and hence delivered from it into a paradaisical promised land. There was no fondness in the Hebraic tradition for wilderness itself.

The Exodus experience established a tradition of going to the wilderness for freedom and the purification of faith. When a society became complacent and ungodly, religious leaders looked to the wilderness as a place for rededication and refuge. This is the meaning behind Jeremiah's plea: "Oh that I had in the desert a wayfarers' lodging place, that I might leave my people . . . for they are all adulterers, a company of treacherous men." When Elijah

19. Deut. 32:10.

20. Martin Noth, *The History of Israel* (New York, 1958), pp. 107–37; W.O.E. Oesterley and Theodore H. Robinson, *A History of Israel* (2 vols. Oxford, 1932), *1*, 67–111.

21. For amplification see Williams, pp. 15–19; Mauser, *Christ in the Wilderness*, pp. 20–36; and Robert T. Anderson, "The Role of the Desert in Israelite Thought," *Journal of the Bible and Religion*, 27 (1959), 41–44.

sought inspiration and guidance from God, he went into the wilderness a symbolic forty days and received it, like Moses, on a deserted mountain.[22] Sometimes an entire group left the settled parts of Israel for the wilderness with the intention of achieving a degree of purity and simplicity that would in fact prepare the way for the Messiah's coming. The most famous of these apocalyptic communities was that of the Essenes, who lived in caves near the Dead Sea in the second century before Christ. They hoped their sojourn, like the one of their ancestors in the Sinai desert, would lead to another and better promised land.

The importance of wilderness as a sanctuary was perpetuated in Christianity. John the Baptist was the New Testament counterpart of Moses, Elijah, and the Essenes. He sought the wild valley of the Jordan River to revitalize faith and make ready for the Messiah.[23] Each one of the Gospels connected John with the prophet mentioned in Isaiah whose voice would be heard crying "in the wilderness" to prepare God's way. When Jesus went to John in the Judean Desert for baptism the prophecy was fulfilled. Immediately thereafter Christ "was led up by the Spirit into the wilderness to be tempted by the devil."[24] This experience, complete with forty days of fasting, alluded to the testing of Israel during the Exodus. And wilderness retained its significance as the environment of evil and hardship where spiritual catharsis occurred. Jesus emerged from the wilderness prepared to speak for God.

In early and medieval Christianity, wilderness kept its significance as the earthly realm of the powers of evil that the Church had to overcome. This was literally the case in the missionary efforts to the tribes of northern Europe. Christians judged their work to be successful when they cleared away the wild forests and cut down the sacred groves where the pagans held their rites.[25] In a more figurative sense, wilderness represented the Christian conception of the situation man faced on earth. It was a compound of his natural inclination to sin, the temptation of the material world, and the

22. Jeremiah 9:2; I Kings 19:4–18.

23. John H. Kraeling, *John the Baptist* (New York, 1951), pp. 1–32. The uses of wilderness in the New Testament are discussed in full in Mauser, pp. 62 ff.

24. Isaiah 40:3–5; Matthew 4:1.

25. Philpot, *Sacred Tree*, p. 18; Jacob Burckhardt, *The Civilization of the Renaissance in Italy* (New York, 1954), p. 218.

forces of evil themselves. In this worldly chaos he wandered lost and forlorn, grasping at Christianity in the hope of delivery to the promised land that now was located in heaven.

Yet Christianity also retained the idea that wild country could be a place of refuge and religious purity. A succession of Christian hermits and monks (literally, one who lives alone) found the solitude of the wilderness conducive to meditation, spiritual insight, and moral perfection. Saint Anthony's lifelong retirement in the third century to the desert between the Nile and the Red Sea was the classic example. Subsequently monasticism flourished, and numerous zealots sought solitary retreats.[26] In the fourth century Saint Basil the Great established a monastery in a wilderness south of the Black Sea and proudly reported, "I am living . . . in the wilderness wherein the Lord dwealt." Basil's description of the forested mountain on which he lived even suggested some recognition of beauty in wilderness,[27] but his virtual uniqueness in this respect dramatizes the general indifference in his time. On the whole the monks regarded wilderness as having value only for escaping corrupt society. It was the place in which they hoped to ignite the flame that would eventually transform all wilderness into a godly paradise.

The tradition of fleeing into uninhabited country to obtain freedom of worship persisted strongly into the Middle Ages. Late in the twelfth century, for instance, Peter Waldo, a merchant of Lyons, began advocating a form of Christian asceticism that included the surrender of all worldly wealth and pleasure. The established Church took a dim view of Waldo's implied criticism of its materialism. Excommunication followed in 1184, and Waldo and his followers were hounded as heretics. Refusing to surrender their beliefs and facing death at the hands of the Inquisition if they remained in society, several thousand Waldensians elected to flee into the Piedmontese Alps on the border between France and Italy. In the caves and secluded valleys of this wilderness they

26. Walter Nigg, *Warriors of God: The Great Religious Orders and their Founders*, ed. and trans. Mary Ilford (New York, 1959), pp. 19–49; Charles Kingsley, *The Hermits* (London, 1891), pp. 21–82; Helen Waddell, *The Desert Fathers* (London, 1936), pp. 41–53; Williams, pp. 28 ff.; Kenneth Scott Latourette, *A History of Christianity* (New York, 1953), pp. 221–35; Herbert B. Workman, *The Evolution of the Monastic Ideal* (London, 1913), pp. 29 ff.

27. *Saint Basil: The Letters*, trans. Roy J. Deferrari (4 vols. London, 1926), *1*, 261; 107–11.

found escape from religious persecution as well as an environment conducive to their philosophy of self-abnegation.[28]

Among medieval Christians St. Francis of Assisi is the exception that proves the rule. He stood alone in a posture of humility and respect before the natural world. Assuming that birds, wolves, and other wild creatures had souls, St. Francis preached to them as equals. This challenge to the idea of man as above, rather than of, the natural world might have altered the prevailing conception of wilderness. But the Church stamped St. Francis' beliefs as heretical. Christianity had too much at stake in the notion that God set man apart from and gave him dominance over the rest of nature (Genesis 1:28) to surrender it easily.[29]

The belief that good Christians should maintain an aloofness from the pleasures of the world also helped determine attitude toward wilderness. The ideal focus for any Christian in the Middle Ages was the attainment of heavenly beatitudes, not enjoyment of his present situation. Such a point of view tended to check any appreciation of natural beauty. Thus during the Renaissance, Christianity offered considerable resistance to the development of joy in perceiving wild landscapes. Petrarch's 1336 ascent of Mount Ventoux provides an example. He initially had no other purpose in climbing than experiencing some of the "delight" he found in wandering "free and alone, among the mountains, forests, and streams." After an all-day effort, Petrarch and his brother gained the summit. "The great sweep of view spread out before me," Petrarch wrote to a friend, and "I stood like one dazed." Clouds floated beneath his feet, and on the horizon he could see the snow-covered Alps. Had he descended from the mountain at this point Petrarch might have retained an undiminished sense of enjoyment in the view, but it occurred to him to look at the copy of Saint Augustine's *Confessions* he was accustomed to carry. By chance he

28. Emilio Comba, *History of the Waldenses of Italy* (London, 1889); Alexis Muston, *The Israel of the Alps: A Complete History of the Waldenses,* trans. John Montgomery (2 vols. London, 1875).

29. For this interpretation of St. Francis I am in debt to Lynn White, Jr.'s "The Historical Roots of Our Ecologic Crisis," a paper read December 26, 1966 to the American Association for the Advancement of Science and scheduled for publication in a forthcoming issue of *Science*. The general problem of the conception of the man-land relationship in Western culture is considered in Clarence J. Glacken's monumental *Traces on the Rhodian Shore* which, at the author's kindness, I read in manuscript before its publication by the University of California Press.

opened to the passage that admonished men not to take joy in mountains or scenery but rather to look after their salvation. Petrarch responded as a Christian: "I was abashed, and . . . I closed the book, angry with myself that I should still be admiring earthly things who might long ago have learned . . . that nothing is wonderful but the soul." After this he hurriedly left the peak, "turned my inward eye upon myself," and returned to his inn, muttering imprecations at the way the world's beauty diverted men from their proper concerns.[30]

With the cases of St. Francis and Petrarch in mind, a comparison of early Western attitude toward wilderness with that of other cultures dramatizes the great influence of the Judeo-Christian tradition in arousing and nourishing antipathy. In the Far East, by way of contrast, the man-nature relationship was marked by respect, bordering on love, absent in the West. India's early religions, especially Jainism, Buddhism and Hinduism, emphasized compassion for all living things. Man was understood to be a part of nature.[31] And wilderness, in Eastern thought, did not have an unholy or evil connotation but was venerated as the symbol and even the very essence of the deity. As early as the fifth century B.C., Chinese Taoists postulated an infinite and benign force in the natural world. Wilderness was not excluded. Far from avoiding wild places, the ancient Chinese sought them out in the hope of sensing more clearly something of the unity and rhythm that they believed pervaded the universe.[32] In Japan the first religion, Shinto, was a form of nature worship that deified mountains, forests, storms, and torrents in preference to fruitful, pastoral scenes since the wild was thought to manifest the divine being more potently than the ru-

30. James Harvey Robinson and Henry Winchester Rolfe, eds., *Petrarch: The First Modern Scholar and Man of Letters* (2nd rev. ed. New York, 1914), pp. 297, 313–14, 317–20. A relevant secondary discussion is Alfred Biese, *The Development of the Feeling for Nature in the Middle Ages and Modern Times* (London, 1905), pp. 109–20.

31. Albert Schweitzer, *Indian Thought and Its Development,* trans. Mrs. Charles E. B. Russell (New York, 1936), passim; A. L. Basham, *The Wonder That Was India* (New York, 1954), pp. 276 ff.

32. Joseph Needham, *Science and Civilization in China* (4 vols. Cambridge, 1962), 2, 33–164; Arthur Waley, *The Way and Its Power: A Study of Tao Te Ching and Its Place in Chinese Thought* (Boston, 1935), pp. 43 ff.; Maraharu Anesaki, *Art, Life, and Nature in Japan* (Boston, 1933), pp. 3–28.

ral.[33] In linking God and the wilderness, instead of contrasting them as did the Western faiths, Shinto and Taoism fostered love of wilderness rather than hatred.

Largely as a result of their religious views but possibly also because their relatively advanced and populous civilizations had tamed most of their countries, Chinese and Japanese landscape painters celebrated wilderness over a thousand years before Western artists. By the sixth century, canvasses which hoped to capture the spiritual significance of nature, were a major art form. Frequently the artist-philosopher made a pilgrimage into the wilderness and remained there many months to meditate, adore, and penetrate, if possible, to inner harmonies. Wild vistas dominated this genre, while human figures, if they appeared at all, took secondary importance to cliffs, trees, and rivers.[34]

Kuo Hsi, the eleventh-century Chinese master of landscapes, expressed his artistic philosophy with pen as well as brush. His *Essay on Landscape Painting* began by asking, rhetorically, "why does a virtuous man take delight in landscapes?" The answer was that away from civilization man "may nourish his nature." Expanding on this, Kuo Hsi continued: "the din of the dusty world and the locked-in-ness of human habitations are what human nature habitually abhors; while, on the contrary, haze, mist, and the haunting spirits of the mountains are what human nature seeks, and yet can rarely find." According to him the purpose of landscape painting was to make it possible for men to experience the delights and absorb the lessons of nature when they could not do so directly. That Kuo Hsi had wilderness in mind rather than the pastoral is evident from his lengthy opening section in the *Essay* where the emphasis was entirely on streams, rocks, pine trees, and, especially, mountains.[35]

Freed from the combined weight of Classicism, Judaism, and Christianity, Eastern cultures did not fear and abhor wilderness.

33. G. B. Sansom, *Japan: A Short Cultural History* (rev. ed. New York, 1962), pp. 46–63; J.W.T. Mason, *The Meaning of Shinto* (New York, 1935).

34. Hugo Munsterberg, *The Landscape Painting of China and Japan* (Rutland, Vt., 1955), pp. 3 ff.; Michael Sullivan, *The Birth of Landscape Painting in China* (Berkeley, Cal., 1962); Arthur de Carle Sowerby, *Nature in Chinese Art* (New York, 1940), pp. 153–60; Otto Fischer, "Landscape as Symbol," *Landscape, 4* (1955), 24–33; Benjamin Roland, Jr., *Art in East and West* (Cambridge, Mass., 1954), pp. 65–68.

35. Kuo Hsi, *An Essay on Landscape Painting*, trans. Shio Sakanishi (London, 1935), p. 30.

Nor did they feel the conflict between religion and appreciation of natural beauty which caused Petrarch's anguish on Mount Ventoux. But Western thought generated a powerful bias against the wilderness, and the settlement of the New World offered abundant opportunity for the expression of this sentiment.

CHAPTER 2

A Wilderness Condition

> Looking only a few years through the vista of futurity what a sublime spectacle presents itself! Wilderness, once the chosen residence of solitude and savageness, converted into populous cities, smiling villages, beautiful farms and plantations!
>
> Chillicothe (Ohio) *Supporter*, 1817

ALEXIS DE TOCQUEVILLE resolved to see wilderness during his 1831 trip to the United States, and in Michigan Territory in July the young Frenchman found himself at last on the fringe of civilization. But when he informed the frontiersmen of his desire to travel for *pleasure* into the primitive forest, they thought him mad. The Americans required considerable persuasion from Tocqueville to convince them that his interests lay in matters other than lumbering or land speculation. Afterwards he generalized in his journal that "living in the wilds, [the pioneer] only prizes the works of man" while Europeans, like himself, valued wilderness because of its novelty.[1] Expanding the point in *Democracy in America,* Tocqueville concluded: "in Europe people talk a great deal of the wilds of America, but the Americans themselves never think about them; they are insensible to the wonders of inanimate nature and they may be said not to perceive the mighty forests that surround them till they fall beneath the hatchet. Their eyes are fixed upon another sight," he added, "the . . . march across these wilds, draining swamps, turning the course of rivers, peopling solitudes, and subduing nature."[2]

The unfavorable attitude toward wilderness that Tocqueville observed in Michigan also existed on other American frontiers. When William Bradford stepped off the *Mayflower* into a "hideous

1. Alexis de Tocqueville, *Journey to America,* trans. George Lawrence, ed. J. P. Mayer (New Haven, Conn., 1960), p. 335. For the circumstances of the Michigan trip and a slightly different translation see George Wilson Pierson, *Tocqueville in America* (Garden City, N.Y., 1959), pp. 144–99.

2. Tocqueville, *Democracy in America,* ed. Phillips Bradley (2 vols. New York 1945), 2, 74.

and desolate wilderness" he started a tradition of repugnance. With few exceptions later pioneers continued to regard wilderness with defiant hatred and joined the Chillicothe *Supporter* in celebrating the advance of civilization as the greatest of blessings. Under any circumstances the necessity of living in close proximity to wild country—what one of Bradford's contemporaries called "a Wilderness condition"—engendered strong antipathy. Two centuries after Bradford, a fur trader named Alexander Ross recorded his despair in encountering a "gloomy," "dreary," and "unhallowed wilderness" near the Columbia River.[3]

Two components figured in the American pioneer's bias against wilderness. On the direct, physical level, it constituted a formidable threat to his very survival. The transatlantic journey and subsequent western advances stripped away centuries. Successive waves of frontiersmen had to contend with wilderness as uncontrolled and terrifying as that which primitive man confronted. Safety and comfort, even necessities like food and shelter, depended on overcoming the wild environment. For the first Americans, as for medieval Europeans, the forest's darkness hid savage men, wild beasts, and still stranger creatures of the imagination. In addition civilized man faced the danger of succumbing to the wildness of his surroundings and reverting to savagery himself. The pioneer, in short, lived too close to wilderness for appreciation. Understandably, his attitude was hostile and his dominant criteria utilitarian. The *conquest* of wilderness was his major concern.

Wilderness not only frustrated the pioneers physically but also acquired significance as a dark and sinister symbol. They shared the long Western tradition of imagining wild country as a moral vacuum, a cursed and chaotic wasteland. As a consequence, frontiersmen acutely sensed that they battled wild country not only for personal survival but in the name of nation, race, and God. Civilizing the New World meant enlightening darkness, ordering chaos, and changing evil into good. In the morality play of westward expansion, wilderness was the villain, and the pioneer, as hero, relished its destruction. The transformation of a wilderness into civiliza-

3. William Bradford, *Of Plymouth Plantation, 1620–1647*, ed. Samuel Eliot Morison (New York, 1952), p. 62; Edward Johnson, *Johnson's Wonder-Working Providence, 1628–1651* (1654), ed. J. Franklin Jameson, Original Narratives of Early American History, 7 (New York, 1910), p. 100; Alexander Ross, *Adventures of the First Settlers on the Oregon or Columbia River* (London, 1849), pp. 143, 146.

tion was the reward for his sacrifices, the definition of his achievement, and the source of his pride. He applauded his successes in terms suggestive of the high stakes he attached to the conflict.

The discovery of the New World rekindled the traditional European notion that an earthly paradise lay somewhere to the west. As the reports of the first explorers filtered back the Old World began to believe that America might be the place of which it had dreamed since antiquity. One theme in the paradise myth stressed the material and sensual attributes of the new land. It fed on reports of fabulous riches, a temperate climate, longevity, and garden-like natural beauty.[4] Promoters of discovery and colonization embellished these rumors. One Londoner, who likely never set foot in the New World, wrote lyrically of the richness of Virginia's soil and the abundance of its game. He even added: "nor is the present wildernesse of it without a particular beauty, being all over a naturall Grove of Oakes, Pines, Cedars . . . all of so delectable an aspect, that the melanchollyest eye in the World cannot look upon it without contentment, nor content himselfe without admiration."[5] Generally, however, European portrayers of a material paradise in the New World completely ignored the "wildernesse" aspect, as inconsistent with the idea of beneficent nature. Illogically, they exempted America from the adverse conditions of life in other uncivilized places.

Anticipations of a second Eden quickly shattered against the reality of North America. Soon after he arrived the seventeenth-century frontiersman realized that the New World was the antipode of paradise. Previous hopes intensified the disappointment. At Jamestown the colonists abandoned the search for gold and turned, shocked, to the necessity of survival in a hostile environment. A few years later William Bradford recorded his dismay at finding Cape Cod wild and desolate. He lamented the Pilgrims' inability to find a vantage point "to view from this wilderness a more goodly coun-

4. Loren Baritz, "The Idea of the West," *American Historical Review, 66* (1961), 618–40; Charles L. Sanford, *The Quest for Paradise* (Urbana, Ill., 1961), pp. 36 ff.; Howard Mumford Jones, *O Strange New World* (New York, 1964), pp. 1–34; Louis B. Wright, *The Dream of Prosperity in Colonial America* (New York, 1965); Leo Marx, *The Machine in the Garden: Technology and the Pastoral Ideal in America* (New York, 1964), pp. 34–72.

5. E[dward] W[illiams], *Virginia . . . Richly and Truly Valued* (1650) in Peter Force, *Tracts and Other Papers* (4 vols. New York, 1947), *3*, No. 11, 11.

try to feed their hopes."[6] In fact, there was none. The forest stretched farther than Bradford and his generation imagined. For Europeans wild country was a single peak or heath, an island of uninhabited land surrounded by settlement. They at least knew its character and extent. But the seemingly boundless wilderness of the New World was something else. In the face of this vast blankness, courage failed and imagination multiplied fears.

Commenting on the arrival of the Puritans some years after, Cotton Mather indicated the change in attitude that contact with the New World produced. "Lady Arabella," he wrote, left an "earthly *paradise*" in England to come to America and "encounter the sorrows of a wilderness." She then died and "left that *wilderness* for the Heavenly *paradise*."[7] Clearly the American wilderness was not paradise. If men expected to enjoy an idyllic environment in America, they would have to *make* it by conquering wild country. Mather realized in 1693 that "Wilderness" was the stage "thro' which we are passing to the Promised Land."[8] Yet optimistic Americans continued to be fooled. "Instead of a garden," declared one traveler in the Ohio Valley in 1820, "I found a wilderness."[9]

How frontiersmen described the wilderness they found reflected the intensity of their antipathy. The same descriptive phrases appeared again and again. Wilderness was "howling," "dismal," "terrible." In the 1650s John Eliot wrote of going "into a wilderness where nothing appeareth but hard labour [and] wants," and Edward Johnson described "the penuries of a Wildernesse."[10] Cotton Mather agreed in 1702 about the "difficulties of a rough and hard wilderness," and in 1839 John Plumbe, Jr. told about "the hardships and privations of the wilderness" in Iowa and Wisconsin.[11] Invariably the pioneers singled out wilderness as the root cause of their difficulties. For one thing, the physical character of the primeval forest proved baffling and frustrating to settlers. One chronicler of

6. Bradford, p. 62.

7. Mather, *Magnalia Christi Americana* (2 vols. Hartford, Conn., 1853), *1*, 77. The original edition was 1702.

8. Mather, *The Wonders of the Invisible World* (London, 1862), p. 13. Alan Heimert, "Puritanism, the Wilderness, and the Frontier," *New England Quarterly, 26* (1953), 369–70, has commented on this point.

9. Adlard Welby, *A Visit to North America* (London, 1821), p. 65.

10. Eliot, "The Learned Conjectures" (1650) as quoted in Williams, *Wilderness and Paradise*, p. 102; Johnson, p. 75.

11. Mather, *Magnalia, 1*, 77; Plumbe, *Sketches of Iowa and Wisconsin* (St. Louis, 1839), p. 21.

the "Wildernesse-worke" of establishing the town of Concord, Massachusetts portrayed in graphic detail the struggle through "unknowne woods," swamps, and flesh-tearing thickets. The town founders wandered lost for days in the bewildering gloom of the dense forest. Finally came the back-breaking labor of carving fields from the wilderness.[12] Later generations who settled forested regions reported similar hardships. On every frontier obtaining cleared land, the symbol of civilization, demanded tremendous effort.

The pioneers' situation and attitude prompted them to use military metaphors to discuss the coming of civilization. Countless diaries, addresses, and memorials of the frontier period represented wilderness as an "enemy" which had to be "conquered," "subdued," and "vanquished" by a "pioneer army." The same phraseology persisted into the present century; an old Michigan pioneer recalled how as a youth he had engaged in a "struggle with nature" for the purpose of "converting a wilderness into a rich and prosperous civilization."[13] Historians of westward expansion chose the same figure: "they conquered the wilderness, they subdued the forests, they reduced the land to fruitful subjection."[14] The image of man and wilderness locked in mortal combat was difficult to forget. Advocates of a giant dam on the Colorado River system spoke in the 1950s of "that eternal problem of subduing the earth" and of "conquering the wilderness" while a President urged us in his 1961 inaugural address to "conquer the deserts." Wilderness, declared a correspondent to the *Saturday Evening Post* in 1965, "is precisely what man has been fighting against since he began his painful, awkward climb to civilization. It is the dark, the formless, the terrible, the old chaos which our fathers pushed back. . . . It is held at bay by constant vigilance, and when the vigilance slackens it swoops down for a melodramatic revenge."[15] Such language animated the wilder-

12. Johnson, pp. 111–15; For a dramatic portrayal of the forest as obstacle, see Richard G. Lillard, *The Great Forest* (New York, 1947), pp. 65–94.

13. General B. M. Cutcheon, "Log Cabin Times and Log Cabin People," *Michigan Pioneer Historical Society Collections, 39* (1901), 611.

14. George Cary Eggleston, *Our First Century* (New York, 1905), p. 255. The representation in late-nineteenth century literature of evil, menacing nature has been discussed in Carleton F. Culmsee, *Malign Nature and the Frontier,* Utah State University Monograph Series, 8, (Logan, Utah, 1959).

15. Ashel Manwaring and Ray P. Greenwood, "Proceedings before the United States Department of the Interior: Hearings on Dinosaur National Monument, Echo

ness, investing it with an almost conscious enmity toward men, who returned it in full measure.

Along with the obstacle it offered to settlement and civilization, wilderness also confronted the frontier mind with terrifying creatures, both known and imagined. Wild men headed the menagerie. Initially Indians were regarded with pity and instructed in the Gospel, but after the first massacres most of the compassion changed to contempt.[16] Sweeping out of the forest to strike, and then melting back into it, savages were almost always associated with wilderness. When Mary Rowlandson was captured in the 1670s on the Massachusetts frontier, she wrote that she went "mourning and lamenting, leaving farther my own Country, and travelling into the vast and howling Wilderness." The remainder of her account revealed an hysterical horror of her captors and of what she called "this Wilderness-condition." A century later J. Hector St. John Crevecoeur discussed the imminency of Indian attack as one of the chief "distresses" of frontier life and described the agony of waiting, gun in hand, for the first arrows to strike his home. "The wilderness," he observed, "is a harbour where it is impossible to find [the Indians] . . . a door through which they can enter our country whenever they please." Imagination and the presence of wild country could multiply fears. Riding through "savage haunts" on the Santa Fe Trail in the 1830s, Josiah Gregg noticed how "each click of a pebble" seemed "the snap of a firelock" and "in a very rebound of a twig [was] the whisk of an arrow."[17]

Wild animals added to the danger of the American wilderness, and here too the element of the unknown intensified feelings. Reporting in 1630 on the "discommodities" of New England, Francis Higginson wrote that "this Countrey being verie full of Woods and

Park and Split Mountain Dams," (April 3, 1950), Department of the Interior Library, Washington, D.C., pp. 535, 555; John F. Kennedy, "For the Freedom of Man," *Vital Speeches, 27* (1961), 227; Robert Wernick, "Speaking Out: Let's Spoil the Wilderness," *Saturday Evening Post, 238* (Nov. 6, 1965), 12.

16. Roy Harvey Pearce, *The Savages of America: A Study of the Indian and the Idea of Civilization* (rev. ed., Baltimore, 1965); Jones, *O Strange New World*, pp. 50 ff.

17. Mary Rowlandson, *Narrative of the Captivity and Restauration* (1682) in *Narratives of the Indian Wars, 1675–1699*, ed. Charles H. Lincoln, Original Narratives of Early American History, 19 (New York, 1913), pp. 126, 131–32; Crevecoeur, *Letters from an American Farmer* (London, 1782), 272; Gregg, *Commerce of the Prairies or the Journal of a Santa Fe Trader* (2 vols. New York, 1845) *1*, 88.

Wildernesses, doth also much abound with Snakes and Serpents of strange colours and huge greatnesse." There were some, he added, "that haue [have] Rattles in their Tayles that will not flye from a Man . . . but will flye upon him and sting him so mortally, that he will dye within a quarter of an houre after." Clearly there was some truth here and in the stories that echo through frontier literature of men whom "the savage Beasts had devoured . . . in the Wilderness," but often fear led to exaggeration. Cotton Mather, for instance, warned in 1707 of "the *Evening Wolves,* the rabid and howling *Wolves* of the *Wilderness* [which] would make . . . Havock among you, *and not leave the Bones till the morning.*" Granted this was a jeremiad intended to shock Mather's contemporaries into godly behavior, but his choice of imagery still reflected a vivid conception of the physical danger of wild country. Elsewhere Mather wrote quite seriously about the "Dragons," "Droves of Devils," and "Fiery flying serpents" to be found in the primeval forest.[18] Indeed, legends and folktales from first contact until well into the national period linked the New World wilderness with a host of monsters, witches, and similar supernatural beings.[19]

A more subtle terror than Indians or animals was the opportunity the freedom of wilderness presented for men to behave in a savage or bestial manner. Immigrants to the New World certainly sought release from oppressive European laws and traditions, yet the complete license of the wilderness was an overdose. Morality and social order seemed to stop at the edge of the clearing. Given the absence of restraint, might not the pioneer succumb to what John Eliot called "wilderness-temptations?"[20] Would not the proximity of wildness pull down the level of all American civilization? Many feared for the worst, and the concern with the struggle against barbarism was widespread in the colonies.[21] Seventeenth-

18. Higginson, *New-Englands Plantation* (1630) in Force, *1,* No. 12, 11–12; John Lawson, *Lawson's History of North Carolina* (1714), ed. Frances L. Harriss (Richmond, Va., 1951), p. 29; Cotton Mather, *Frontiers Well-Defended* (Boston, 1707), p. 10; Mather, *Wonders,* pp. 13, 85.

19. Richard M. Dorson, *American Folklore* (Chicago, 1959), pp. 8 ff.; Jones, pp. 61 ff. The European precedent for this practice has been noted in Chapter 1.

20. Eliot as quoted in Williams, *Wilderness and Paradise,* p. 102.

21. Oscar Handlin, *Race and Nationality in American Life* (Garden City, N.Y., 1957), p. 114; Louis B. Wright, *Culture on the Moving Frontier* (Indianapolis, 1955), esp. pp. 11–45. Edmund S. Morgan, *The Puritan Dilemma* (Boston, 1958) has used the example of John Winthrop to demonstrate how the Puritan emphasis on the organic community was in part a response to the license of the wilderness. Roy Har-

century town "planters" in New England, for instance, were painfully aware of the dangers wilderness posed for the individual. They attempted to settle the northern frontier through the well-organized movement of entire communities. Americans like these pointed out that while liberty and solitude might be desirable to the man in a crowd, it was the gregarious tendency and controlling institutions of society that took precedence in the wilderness.

Yale's president, Timothy Dwight, spoke for most of his generation in regretting that as the pioneer pushed further and further into the wilds he became "less and less a civilized man." J. Hector St. John Crevecoeur was still more specific. Those who lived near "the great woods," he wrote in 1782, tend to be "regulated by the wildness of their neighborhood." This amounted to no regulation at all; the frontiersmen were beyond "the power of example, and check of shame." According to Crevecoeur, they had "degenerated altogether into the hunting state" and became ultimately "no better than carnivorous animals of a superior rank." He concluded that if man wanted happiness, "he cannot live in solitude, he must belong to some community bound by some ties."[22]

The behavior of pioneers frequently lent substance to these fears. In the struggle for survival many existed at a level close to savagery, and not a few joined Indian tribes. Even the ultimate horror of cannibalism was not unknown among the mountain men of the Rockies, as the case of Charles "Big Phil" Gardner proved.[23] Wilderness could reduce men to such a condition unless society maintained constant vigilance. Under wilderness conditions the veneer civilization laid over the barbaric elements in man seemed much thinner than in the settled regions.

It followed from the pioneer's association of wilderness with hardship and danger in a variety of forms, that the rural, controlled, state of nature was the object of his affection and goal of his labor. The pastoral condition seemed closest to paradise and the

---

vey Pearce contends that "the Indian became important for the English mind, not for what he was in and of himself, but rather for what he showed civilized men they were not and must not be": Pearce, *Savages of America,* p. 5.

22. Timothy Dwight, *Travels in New-England and New-York* (4 vols. New Haven, Conn., 1821–22), 2, 441; Crevecoeur, *Letters,* pp. 55–57, 271.

23. LeRoy R. Hafen, "Mountain Men: Big Phil the Cannibal," *Colorado Magazine, 13* (1936), 53–58. Other examples may be found in Ray A. Billington, *The American Frontiersman: A Case-Study in Reversion to the Primitive* (Oxford, 1954) and Arthur K. Moore, *The Frontier Mind* (Lexington, Ky., 1957), pp. 77 ff.

life of ease and contentment. Americans hardly needed reminding that Eden had been a garden. The rural was also the fruitful and as such satisfied the frontiersman's utilitarian instincts. On both the idyllic and practical counts wilderness was anathema.

Transforming the wild into the rural had Scriptural precedents which the New England pioneers knew well. Genesis 1:28, the first commandment of God to man, stated that mankind should increase, conquer the earth, and have dominion over all living things. This made the fate of wilderness plain. In 1629 when John Winthrop listed reasons for departing "into . . . the wilderness," an important one was that "the whole earth is the lords Garden & he hath given it to the sonnes of men, and with a general Condision, Gen. 1.28: Increase & multiply, replenish the earth & subdue it." Why remain in England, Winthrop argued, and "suffer a whole Continent . . . to lie waste without any improvement."[24] Discussing the point a year later, John White also used the idea of man's God-appointed dominion to conclude that he did not see "how men should make benefit of [vacant land] . . . but by habitation and culture."[25] Two centuries later advocates of expansion into the wilderness used the same rhetoric. "There can be no doubt," declared Lewis Cass, soldier and senator from Michigan, in 1830, "that the Creator intended the earth should be reclaimed from a state of nature and cultivated." In the same year Governor George R. Gilmer of Georgia noted that this was specifically "by virtue of that command of the Creator delivered to man upon his formation—be fruitful, multiply, and replenish the earth, and subdue it."[26] Wilderness was waste; the proper behavior toward it, exploitation.

Without invoking the Bible, others involved in the pioneering process revealed a proclivity for the rural and useful. Wherever they encountered wild country they viewed it through utilitarian spectacles: trees became lumber, prairies farms, and canyons the sites of hydroelectric dams. The pioneers' self-conceived mission

24. Winthrop, *Conclusions for the Plantation in New England* (1629) in *Old South Leaflets* (9 vols. Boston, 1895), *2*, No. 50, 5.

25. White, *The Planters Plea* (1630) in Force, *Tracts*, *2*, No. 3, 2. For a discussion of similar rationales which the Puritans used in taking land from the Indians see Chester E. Eisinger, "The Puritans' Justification for Taking the Land," *Essex Institute Historical Collections*, *84* (1948), 131–43.

26. Cass, "Removal of the Indians," *North American Review*, *30* (1830), 77; Gilmer as quoted in Albert K. Weinberg, *Manifest Destiny: A Study of Nationalist Expansionism in American History* (Baltimore, 1935), p. 83.

was to bring these things to pass. Writing about his experience settling northern New York in the late eighteenth century, William Cooper declared that his "great primary object" was "to cause the Wilderness to bloom and fructify." Another popular expression of the waste-to-garden imagery appeared in an account of how the Iowa farmer "makes the wilderness blossom like the rose." Rural, garden-like nature was invariably the criterion of goodness to this mentality. A seventeenth-century account of New England's history noted the way a "howling wilderness" had, through the labors of settlers, become "pleasant Land." Speaking of the Ohio country in 1751, Christopher Gist noted that "it wants Nothing but Cultivation to make it a most delightful Country." Wilderness alone could neither please nor delight the pioneer. "Uncultivated" land, as an early nineteenth-century report put it, was "absolutely useless."[27]

At times the adulation of the pastoral became charged with emotion. On a trip to the fringe of settlement in the 1750s Thomas Pownall wrote: "with what an overflowing Joy does the Heart melt, while one views the Banks where rising Farms, new Fields, or flowering Orchards begin to illuminate this Face of Nature; nothing can be more delightful to the Eye, nothing go with more penetrating Sensation to the Heart." Similarly, on his 1806 journey of discovery Zebulon M. Pike conceived of the wild prairies near the Osage River as "the future seats of husbandry" and relished the thought of "the numerous herds of domestic cattle, which are no doubt destined to crown with joy these happy plains." Several decades later, in the Sierra, Zenas Leonard anticipated in a few years even those mountains being "greeted with the enlivening sound of the workman's hammer, and the merry whistle of the ploughboy."[28]

27. Cooper, *A Guide in the Wilderness or the History of the First Settlements in the Western Counties of New York with Useful Instructions to Future Settlers* (Dublin, 1810), p. 6; John B. Newhall, *A Glimpse of Iowa in 1846* (Burlington, 1846), ix; Anonymous, *A Brief Relation of the State of New England* (1689) in Force, *Tracts, 4,* No. 11, 4–5; *Christopher Gist's Journals*, ed. William M. Darlington (Pittsburgh, 1893), p. 47; Gabriel Franchere, *Narrative of a Voyage to the Northwest Coast of America,* ed. and trans. J. V. Huntington (New York, 1854), p. 323.

28. Thomas Pownall, *A Topographical Description of . . . Parts of North America* (1776) as *A Topographical Description of the Dominions of the United States of America,* ed. Lois Mulkearn (Pittsburgh, 1949), p. 31; Zebulon Montgomery Pike, *The Expeditions of Zebulon Montgomery Pike,* ed. Elliott Coues (3 vols. New York, 1893), 2, 514; *Adventures of Zenas Leonard: Fur Trader,* ed. John C. Ewers (Normal, Okla., 1959), p. 94.

Frontiersmen such as these looked through, rather than at, wilderness. Wild country had value as potential civilization.

Enthusiasm for "nature" in America during the pioneering period almost always had reference to the rural state. The frequent celebrations of country life, beginning with Richard Steele's *The Husbandman's Calling* of 1668 and continuing through the more familiar statements of Robert Beverley, Thomas Jefferson, and John Taylor of Caroline, reveal only a contempt for the wild, native landscape as "unimproved" land.[29] When wilderness scenery did appeal, it was not for its wildness but because it resembled a "Garden or Orchard in England."[30] The case of Samuel Sewall is instructive, since his 1697 encomium to Plum Island north of Boston has been cited[31] as the earliest known manifestation of love for the New World landscape. What actually appealed to Sewall, however, was not the island's wild qualities but its resemblance to an English countryside. He mentioned cattle feeding in the fields, sheep on the hills, "fruitful marshes," and, as a final pastoral touch, the doves picking up left-over grain after a harvest. In Plum Island Sewall saw the rural idyll familiar since the Greeks, hardly the American wilderness. Indeed, in the same tract, he singled out "a dark Wilderness Cave" as the fearful location for pagan rites.[32]

Samuel Sewall's association of wild country with the ungodly is a reminder that wilderness commonly signified other than a material obstacle or physical threat. As a concept it carried a heavy load of ethical connotations and lent itself to elaborate figurative usage. Indeed, by the seventeenth century "wilderness" had become a fa-

29. American attraction to the rural is fully discussed in Marx, *Machine in the Garden;* Sanford, *Quest for Paradise;* Henry Nash Smith, *Virgin Land: The American West as Symbol and Myth* (Cambridge, Mass., 1950), pp. 121 ff.; and A. Whitney Griswold, *Farming and Democracy* (New York, 1948).

30. George Percy, "Observations" (1625) in *Narratives of Early Virginia, 1606–1625,* ed. Lyon Gardiner Tyler, Original Narratives of Early American History, 5 (New York, 1907), p. 16. The same rhetoric was employed when pioneers emerged from the heavy, Eastern forest onto the open, garden-like prairies of Indiana and Illinois: James Hall, *Notes on the Western States* (Philadelphia, 1838), p. 56.

31. Perry Miller, in *The American Puritans: Their Prose and Poetry* (Garden City, N.Y., 1956), pp. 213, 295, and in *The New England Mind: From Colony to Province* (Boston, 1961), p. 190, contends that Sewall's "cry of the heart" marked the moment at which the Puritan became an American "rooted in the American soil" and took "delight in the American prospect."

32. Sewall, *Phaenomena . . . or Some Few Lines Towards a Description of the New Haven* (Boston, 1697), pp. 51, 59–60.

vorite metaphor for discussing the Christian situation. John Bunyan's *Pilgrim's Progress* summarized the prevailing viewpoint of wilderness as the symbol of anarchy and evil to which the Christian was unalterably opposed. The book's opening phrase, "As I walk'd through the Wilderness of this World," set the tone for the subsequent description of attempts to keep the faith in the chaotic and temptation-laden existence on earth. Even more pointed in the meaning it attached to wilderness was Benjamin Keach's *Tropologia, or a Key to Open Scripture Metaphor.* In a series of analogies, Keach instructed his readers that as wilderness is "barren" so the world is devoid of holiness; as men lose their way in the wilds so they stray from God in the secular sphere; and as travelers need protection from beasts in wild country, so the Christian needs the guidance and help of God. "A Wilderness," Keach concluded, "is a solitary and dolesom Place: so is this World to a godly Man."[33]

The Puritans who settled New England shared the same tradition regarding wilderness that gave rise to the attitudes of Bunyan and Keach. In the middle of his 1664 dictionary of the Indian language Roger Williams moralized: "the Wildernesse is a cleer resemblance of the world, where greedie and furious men persecute and devoure the harmlesse and innocent as the wilde beasts pursue and devoure the Hinds and Roes." The Puritans, especially, understood the Christian conception of wilderness, since they conceived of themselves as the latest in a long line of dissenting groups who had braved the wild in order to advance God's cause. They found precedents for coming to the New World in the twelfth-century Waldensians and in still earlier Christian hermits and ascetics who had sought the freedom of deserts or mountains. As enthusiastic practitioners of the art of typology (according to which events in the Old Testament were thought to prefigure later occurrences), the first New Englanders associated their migration with the Exodus. As soon as William Bradford reached Massachusetts Bay, he looked for "Pisgah," the mountain from which Moses had allegedly seen the promised land. Edward Johnson specifically compared the Puritans to "the ancient Beloved of Christ, whom he of old led by the hand from Egypt to Canaan, through that great and terrible Wildernesse." For Samuel Danforth the experience of John the

33. Bunyan, *The Pilgrim's Progress from this World to That which is to Come,* ed. James Blanton Wharey (Oxford, 1928), [p. 9.]; Keach, *Tropologia* (4 vols. London, 1681–82), *4,* 391–92.

Baptist seemed the closest parallel to the New England situation, although he too likened their mission to that of the children of Israel.[34]

While the Puritans and their predecessors in perfectionism often fled to the wilderness from a corrupt civilization, they never regarded the wilderness itself as their goal. The driving impulse was always to carve a garden from the wilds; to make an island of spiritual light in the surrounding darkness. The Puritan mission had no place for wild country. It was, after all, a *city* on a hill that John Winthrop called upon his colleagues to erect. The Puritans, and to a considerable extent their neighbors in the plantations to the south,[35] went to the wilderness in order to begin the task of redeeming the world from its "wilderness" state. Paradoxically, their sanctuary and their enemy were one and the same.[36]

Recent scholarship has glossed over the strength of the Puritans' intellectual legacy concerning wilderness. Their conception of the American wilderness did not come entirely or even largely "out of that wilderness itself," as Alan Heimert alleges.[37] They realized before leaving Europe that they were, as John Winthrop put it in 1629, fleeing "into . . . the wildernesse" to found the true Church.[38] And their Bibles contained all they needed to know in order to hate wilderness. Contact with the North American wilderness only supplemented what the Puritans already believed. In this sense the colonists' conception of the wilderness was more a product of the Old World than of the New.[39]

34. Williams, *A Key into the Language of America*, ed. J. Hammond Trumbull, Publications of the Narragansett Club, 1 (Providence, R.I., 1866), p. 130; Bradford, *Of Plymouth Plantation*, p. 62; Johnson, *Wonder-Working Providence*, 59; Danforth, *A Brief Recognition of New-England's Errand into the Wilderness* (Cambridge, Mass., 1671), pp. 1, 5, 9.

35. On this point see Perry Miller, "The Religious Impulse in the Founding of Virginia: Religion and Society in the Early Literature," *William and Mary Quarterly*, 5 (1948), 492–522, and Louis B. Wright, *Religion and Empire: The Alliance Between Piety and Commerce in English Expansion, 1558–1625* (Chapel Hill, N.C., 1943).

36. Williams, *Wilderness and Paradise*, pp. 73 ff., explores the meaning of this relationship.

37. Heimert, "Puritanism, the Wilderness, and the Frontier," 361.

38. Winthrop, *Conclusions*, 5.

39. In comparison to the impulse to redeem the wilderness, I am deliberately minimizing as of secondary and ephemeral significance the notion of some Puritans that the Atlantic Ocean was *their* Sinai desert and that Canaan lay across it in New England. Heimert, 361–62, discusses this position briefly.

Without intending to belittle my debt to him, I am also discounting Perry Miller's

For the Puritans, of course, wilderness was metaphor as well as actuality. On the frontier the two meanings reinforced each other, multiplying horrors. Seventeenth-century writing is permeated with the idea of wild country as the environment of evil. Just as the Old Testament scribes represented the desert as the cursed land where satyrs and lesser demons roamed, the early New Englanders agreed with Michael Wigglesworth that on the eve of settlement the New World was: "a waste and howling wilderness, / Where none inhabited / But hellish fiends, and brutish men / That Devils worshiped." This idea of a pagan continent haunted the Puritan imagination. Wigglesworth went on to term North America the region of "eternal night" and "grim death" where the "Sun of righteousness" never shone. As a consequence "the dark and dismal Western woods" were "the Devils den." Cotton Mather believed he knew how it got into this condition: Satan had seduced the first Indian inhabitants for the purpose of making a stronghold. From this perspective, the natives were not merely heathens but active disciples of the devil. Mather verged on hysteria in describing "the Indians, whose chief Sagamores are well known unto some of our Captives to have been horrid Sorcerers, and hellish Conjurers and such as Conversed with Daemons."[40] The wilderness that harbored such beings was never merely neutral, never just a physical obstacle.

As self-styled agents of God the Puritan pioneers conceived their mission as breaking the power of evil. This involved an inner battle over that "desolate and outgrowne wildernesse of humaine nature,"[41] and on the New England frontier it also meant conquering wild nature. The Puritans seldom forgot that civilizing the wilderness meant far more than profit, security, and worldly comfort. A manichean battle was being waged between "the cleare sunshine of the Gospell" on the one hand and "thick antichristian darkness" on

---

contention that the nature of the Puritans' "errand" to the New World changed by the late seventeenth century from leading the Reformation to conquering the American wilderness: *Errand Into the Wilderness* (Cambridge, Mass., 1956), Chapter 1. The latter purpose, I feel, was strong from the beginning and was, moreover, always a necessary part of the former.

40. Wigglesworth, *God's Controversy with New England* (1662) in *Proceedings of the Massachusetts Historical Society,* 12 (1871), pp. 83, 84; Mather, *Magnalia, 1,* 42; Mather, *Decennium Luctuosum: An History of Remarkable Occurrences in the Long War which New-England hath had with the Indian Salvages* (1699) in Lincoln, ed., *Narratives,* p. 242. For elaboration on the idea of Indians as devils see Jones, *O Strange New World,* pp. 55–61, and Pearce, *Savages of America,* pp. 19–35.

41. "R.I.," *The New Life of Virginea* (1612) in Force, *Tracts,* 1, No. 7, 7.

the other.[42] Puritan writing frequently employed this light-and-dark imagery to express the idea that wilderness was ungodly. As William Steele declared in 1652 in regard to missionary work among the Indians, the "first fruits of a barren Wilderness" were obtained when civilization and Christianity succeeded in "shining . . . a beame of Light into the darknesse of another World." Cotton Mather's *Magnalia* concerned the wondrous way that religion "flying . . . to the American Strand" had "irradiated an Indian Wilderness." Those who resisted the "glorious gospel-shine" fled, as might be expected, ever deeper into "forrests wide & great."[43]

In view of the transcendant importance they attached to conquering wilderness the Puritans understandably celebrated westward expansion as one of their greatest achievements. It was a ceaseless wonder and an evidence of God's blessing that wild country should become fruitful and civilized. Edward Johnson's *Wonder-Working Providence* of 1654 is an extended commentary on this transformation. Always it was "Christ Jesus" or "the Lord" who "made this poore barren Wildernesse become a fruitfull Land" or who "hath . . . been pleased to turn one of the most Hideous, boundless, and unknown Wildernesses in the world . . . to a well-ordered Commonwealth." In Boston, for instance, the "admirable Acts of Christ" had in a few decades transformed the "hideous Thickets" where "Wolfes and Beares nurst up their young" into "streets full of Girles and Boys sporting up and downe."[44] Johnson and his contemporaries never doubted that God was on their side in their effort to destroy the wilderness. God's "*blessing* upon their undertakings," the elderly John Higginson wrote in 1697, made it possible that "a *wilderness* was subdued . . . Towns erected, and Churches settled . . . in a place where . . . [there] had been nothing before but *Heathenism, Idolatry,* and *Devil-worship.*"[45] The New England colonists saw themselves as "Christs Army" or "Souldiers of Christ" in a war against wildness.[46]

42. Thomas Shepard, *The Clear Sunshine of the Gospel Breaking Forth upon the Indians in New-England* (1648) in Joseph Sabin, *Sabin's Reprints* (10 vols. New York, 1865), *10,* 1; Mather, *Magnalia, 1,* 64.

43. William Steele, "To the Supreme Authority of this Nation" in Henry Whitfield, *Strength out of Weakness* (1652) in *Sabin's Reprints, 5,* [2]; Mather, *Magnalia, 1,* 25; Wigglesworth, *God's Controversy,* p. 84.

44. Johnson, *Wonder-Working Providence,* pp. 71, 108, 248.

45. Higginson, "An Attestation to the Church-History of New-England" in Mather, *Magnalia, 1,* 13.

46. Johnson, *Wonder-Working Providence,* pp. 60, 75.

One reason why the Puritan settlers portrayed wilderness as replete with physical hardships and spiritual temptations was to remind later generations of the magnitude of their accomplishment. The credit for this feat, of course, went to God, but the colonists could not hide a strong sense of pride in their own role in breaking the wilderness. One of the first explicit statements appeared in the *Memoirs* of Roger Clap. A member of the group who arrived in New England in 1630, Clap decided in the 1670s to write an account of the early days for the instruction of his children. He detailed the distresses of life in the "then unsubdued wilderness" and the many "wants" of God's servants. Then, directly addressing the second generation, he drew the moral: "you have better food and raiment than was in former times; but have you better hearts than your forefathers had?" In 1671 Joshua Scottow used the same theme when he demanded that the initial colonists' "Voluntary Exile into this Wilderness" be "Recollected, Remembered, and not Forgotten."[47] Implied was a relationship between the dangers of the wilderness and the quality of those who faced them. A few years later John Higginson looked back on his long experience as a pioneer and declared: "our *wilderness-condition* hath been full of *humbling, trying, distressing providences.*" Their purpose, he felt, had been to determine "whether according to our professions, and [God's] expectation we would *keep* [*H*]*is* commandments or not."[48] Survival seemed an indication of success in this respect. Portrayed as a harsh and hostile environment, wilderness was a foil that emphasized the predicament and accentuated the achievement of pioneers.

The sinister connotation of wilderness did not end with the seventeenth century. Representatives of later generations, especially those persons who came into direct contact with the frontier, continued to sense the symbolic potency of wild country. While Jona-

47. *Memoirs of Capt. Roger Clap* (1731) in Alexander Young, *Chronicles of the First Planters of the Colony of Massachusetts Bay* (Boston, 1846), pp. 351, 353; Scottow, *Old Men's Tears for their own Declensions Mixed with Fears of their and Posterities further falling off from New-England's Primitive Constitution* (Boston, 1691), p. 1. Roger Williams stressed his agony in the Rhode Island wilderness for a similar purpose: Perry Miller, *Roger Williams* (Indianapolis, 1953), p. 52. Secondary commentary on the question may be found in Kenneth B. Murdock, "Clio in the Wilderness: History and Biography in Puritan New England," *Church History*, *24* (1955), 221–38.

48. Higginson, "Attestation" in Mather, *Magnalia*, *1*, 16.

than Edwards might occasionally derive spiritual joy from, and even perceive beauty in, natural objects such as clouds, flowers, and fields, wilderness was still beyond the pale.[49] For Edwards, as for his Christian predecessors, "the land that we have to travel through [to Heaven] is a wilderness; there are many mountains, rocks, and rough places that we must go over in the way."[50] Following the Puritans, Americans continued to interpret wilderness in Biblical terms. When Eleazar Wheelock founded Dartmouth College on the upper Connecticut in 1769, he took as his motto "Vox Clamantis in Deserto." The use of "desert" to describe a forest in this and so many other accounts suggests that the Old Testament was even more important than New England actuality in determining reaction to the wilderness. The Dartmouth motto also was reminiscent of John the Baptist, and the initial impulse behind the college was similar: spreading the Word into a pagan realm. Later college founders advanced boldly into the west with a comparable idea of striking the spark that would in time transform darkness into light. Joseph P. Thompson, for instance, closed an 1859 speech before the Society for the Promotion of Collegiate and Theological Education At the West with an exhortation: "go you into the moral wilderness of the West; there open springs in the desert, and build a fountain for the waters of life."[51] Wilderness remained the obstacle to overcome.

Much of the writing of Nathaniel Hawthorne suggests the persistence into the nineteenth century of the Puritan conception of wilderness. For him wild country was still "black" and "howling" as well as a powerful symbol of man's dark and untamed heart. In several of Hawthorne's short stories wilderness dominated the action. Its terrifying qualities in *Roger Malvin's Burial* (1831) prompted a man to shoot his son in retribution for a dark deed the father performed earlier in "the tangled and gloomy forest." The protagonist of *Young Goodman Brown* (1835) also found the wilderness a nightmarish locale of both the devil and devilish tenden-

49. For examples of Edwards' appreciation of natural beauty see Alexander V. G. Allen, *Jonathan Edwards* (Boston, 1890), pp. 355–56, and *Images or Shadows of Divine Things by Jonathan Edwards,* ed. Perry Miller (New Haven, 1948), pp. 135–37.

50. "True Christian's Life," *The Works of President Edwards* (4 vols. New York, 1852) *4*, 575.

51. Thompson, *The College as a Religious Institution* (New York, 1859), p. 34. Williams, *Wilderness and Paradise,* pp. 141 ff., discusses the expansion of colleges in terms of the paradise tradition.

cies in man. *The Scarlet Letter* (1850) climaxed Hawthorne's experimentation with the wilderness theme. The primeval forest he creates around seventeenth-century Salem represents and accentuates the "moral wilderness" in which Hester Prynne wandered so long. The forest meant freedom from social ostracism, yet Hawthorne left no doubt that such total license would only result in an irresistible temptation to evil. The illegitimate Pearl, "imp of evil, emblem and product of sin" is the only character at home in the wilderness. For Hawthorne and the Puritans a frightening gulf, both literal and figurative, existed between civilization and wilderness.[52]

The increasing tendency to redefine America's mission in secular rather than sacred terms made little difference in regard to antipathy toward wilderness. Insofar as the westward expansion of civilization was thought good, wilderness was bad. It was construed as much a barrier to progress, prosperity, and power as it was to godliness. On every frontier intense enthusiasm greeted the transformation of the wild into the civilized. Pioneer diaries and reminiscences rang with the theme that what was "unbroken and trackless wilderness" had been "reclaimed" and "transformed into fruitful farms and . . . flourishing cities" which, of course, was "always for the better."[53] Others simply said the wilds had been made "like *Eden*."[54]

This taming of the wilderness gave meaning and purpose to the frontiersman's life. In an age which idealized "progress," the pioneer considered himself its spearhead, performing a worthy cause in the interest of all mankind. While laboring directly for himself and his heirs, pioneers and their spokesmen were ever conscious that

52. References are to *The Complete Writings of Nathaniel Hawthorne* (Old Manse ed. 22 vols. New York, 1903). For instruction in Hawthorne's use of wilderness I am indebted to R. W. B. Lewis, *The American Adam: Innocence, Tragedy, and Tradition in the Nineteenth Century* (Chicago, 1955), pp. 111–14; Wilson O. Clough, *The Necessary Earth: Nature and Solitude in American Literature* (Austin, Texas, 1964), pp. 117–25; Edwin Fussell, *Frontier: American Literature and the American West* (Princeton, N.J., 1965), pp. 69–131; and Chester E. Eisinger, "Pearl and the Puritan Heritage," *College English*, *52* (1951), 323–29.

53. Judge Wilkinson, "Early Recollections of the West," *American Pioneer*, 2 (1843), 161; William Henry Milburn, *The Pioneer Preacher: Rifle, Axe, and Saddle-Bags* (New York, 1858), p. 26; J. H. Colton, *The Western Tourist and Emigrant's Guide* (New York, 1850), p. 25; and Henry Howe, *Historical Collections of the Great West* (2 vols. Cincinnati, 1854), *1*, 84.

54. As quoted from a 1796 account in Jones, *O Strange New World*, p. 212.

greater issues hung in the balance. Orators at state agricultural society gatherings harped on the theme of the beneficent effect of the law of "progressive development or growth" under whose guidance cities sprang "from the bosom of the wilderness." They raised paeans to those who worked "until the wilderness has blossomed with the fruits of their toil, and these once western wilds are vocal with the songs of joy."[55] As the pioneer conceived it, the rewards of this process were far greater than bountiful harvests. Was he not the agent of civilization battling man's traditional foe on behalf of the welfare of the race? After all, it was he who broke "the long chain of savage life" and for "primeval barbarism" substituted "civilization, liberty and law" not to speak of "arts and sciences."[56] Put in these terms, there could be little doubt of the value of destroying wilderness. As Andrew Jackson asked rhetorically in his 1830 inaugural address, "what good man would prefer a country covered with forests and ranged by a few thousand savages to our extensive Republic, studded with cities, towns, and prosperous farms, embellished with all the improvements which art can devise or industry execute."[57] In the vocabulary of material progress, wilderness had meaning only as an obstacle.

The nineteenth-century pioneer's emphasis on material progress did not entirely exclude the older idea of conquering wilderness in the name of God. William Gilpin, an early governor of Colorado and trumpeter of America's Manifest Destiny, made clear that " 'Progress is God' " and that the "occupation of wild territory . . . proceeds with all the solemnity of a providential ordinance." It was, in fact, the "hand of God" that pushed the nation westward and caused the wilderness to surrender to ax and plow. The frontiers-

55. A. Constantine Barry, "Wisconsin—Its Condition, Prospects, Etc.: Annual Address Delivered at the State Agricultural Fair," *Transactions of the Wisconsin State Agricultural Society, 4* (1856), pp. 266, 268.

56. Columbus *Ohio State Journal* (1827) as quoted in Roscoe Carlyle Buley, *The Old Northwest Pioneer Period, 1815–1840* (2 vols. Indianapolis, 1950), 2, 45; *Laws of Indiana* (1824–25) in Buley, 2, 46; Dr. S. P. Hildreth, "Early Emigration," *American Pioneer, 2* (1843), 134.

57. Andrew Jackson, "Second Annual Message," *A Compilation of the Messages and Papers of the Presidents,* ed. J. D. Richardson (10 vols. Washington, D.C., 1896–99), 2, 521. On the doctrine of progress and its incompatibility with appreciation of wilderness see Arthur A. Ekirch, Jr., *The Idea of Progress in America, 1815–1860* (New York, 1944); Moore, *Frontier Mind,* pp. 139–58; Weinberg, *Manifest Destiny;* and Alan Trachtenberg, *Brooklyn Bridge: Fact and Symbol* (New York, 1965), pp. 7–21.

men never forgot that one of their chief aims was the "extension of pure Christianity": they viewed with satisfaction the replacement of the "savage yell" with the "songs of Zion." Settlement and religion went together. Charles D. Kirk summarized in an 1860 novel the frontier view of the westward march as "the tramp, tramp, steady and slow, but sure, of the advancing hosts of Civilization and Christianity."[58]

Understandably, subjugation of wilderness was the chief source of pioneer pride. Indeed the whole nation considered the settlement of the West its outstanding accomplishment. Timothy Dwight even felt it worthy of comparison with the cultural magnificence of Europe. *"The conversion of a wilderness into a desirable residence for man,"* he declared early in the century, "at least . . . may compensate the want of ancient castles, ruined abbeys, and fine pictures."[59] For a young country, self-conscious about its achievements and anxious to justify independence with success, the conquest of wilderness bolstered the national ego.[60] "What a people we are! What a country is this of ours," chortled Josiah Grinnell in 1845, "which but as yesterday was a wilderness." On a humbler level the individual pioneer felt a glow of pride in clearing the land or breaking the virgin sod. One guidebook for settlers advertised: "you look around and whisper, 'I vanquished this wilderness and made the chaos pregnant with order and civilization, alone I did it.' " The same note often sounds in the rhetoric of a President who takes great pride in the way his family made the "barren" and "forbidding" country in the valley of Texas' Pedernales River "abundant with fruit, cattle, goats and sheep"[61]

Of course, many pioneers deliberately chose to live in the wilderness. Many moved westward to a new homestead, legend has it, when they could see a neighbor's smoke. Love of the wilds, however, did not prompt this behavior but rather a hunger for their

58. Gilpin, *Mission of the North American People: Geographical, Social and Political* (Philadelphia, 1873), p. 99; John Reynolds, *The Pioneer History of Illinois* (Belleville, Ill., 1852), p. 228; Hildreth, "Early Emigration," 134; Kirk, *Wooing and Warring in the Wilderness* (New York, 1860), p. 38.

59. Dwight, *Travels, 1,* 18.

60. For evidence that the *possession* of wilderness also served this purpose see Chapter 4.

61. Grinnell, *Sketches of the West* (Milwaukee, 1847), pp. 40–41; Sidney Smith, *The Settlers' New Home: or the Emigrant's Location* (London, 1849), p. 19; Lyndon B. Johnson, "State of the Union: The Great Society," *Vital Speeches, 31* (1965), 197.

destruction. Pioneers welcomed wild country as a challenge. They conceived of themselves as agents in the regenerating process that turned the ungodly and useless into a beneficent civilization. To perform this function wilderness was necessary, hence the westward urge. Only a handful of mountain men and voyageurs were literally absorbed by the forest and ignored the regenerative mission. Reverting to the primitive, in some cases even joining Indian tribes, these exceptions regarded civilization with the antipathy most pioneers reserved for wilderness.[62]

Tocqueville, on the whole, was correct in his analysis that "living in the wilds" produced a bias against them. Constant exposure to wilderness gave rise to fear and hatred on the part of those who had to fight it for survival and success. Although there were a few exceptions, American frontiersmen rarely judged wilderness with criteria other than the utilitarian or spoke of their relation to it in other than a military metaphor. It was their children and grandchildren, removed from a wilderness condition, who began to sense its ethical and aesthetic values. Yet even city dwellers found it difficult to ignore the older attitudes completely. Prejudice against wilderness had the strength of centuries behind it and continued to influence American opinion long after pioneering conditions disappeared. Against this darker background of repugnance more favorable responses haltingly took shape.

62. Almost by definition, written accounts of men who completely broke the ties with civilization are practically nonexistent. Moore, *Frontier Mind*, Billington, *American Frontiersman*, Stanley Vestal, *Mountain Men* (Boston, 1937), Sydney Greenbie, *Furs to Furrows: An Epic of Rugged Individualism* (Caldwell, Idaho, 1939), especially Chapter 19, Hiram Chittenden, *The American Fur Trade of the Far West* (3 vols. New York, 1902), *1*, 65 ff., and Grace Lee Nute, *The Voyageur* (New York, 1931) provide illuminating insights. Lewis Mumford, *The Golden Day: A Study in American Experience and Culture* (New York, 1926), pp. 55–56, argues against my interpretation.

CHAPTER 3

The Romantic Wilderness

> How great are the advantages of solitude!—How sublime is the silence of nature's ever-active energies! There is something in the very name of wilderness, which charms the ear, and soothes the spirit of man. There is religion in it.
>
> Estwick Evans, 1818

APPRECIATION of wilderness began in the cities. The literary gentleman wielding a pen, not the pioneer with his axe, made the first gestures of resistance against the strong currents of antipathy. The ideas of these literati determined their experience, because in large part they saw in wilderness what they wanted to see. In the sixteenth and seventeenth centuries Europeans laid the intellectual foundations for a favorable attitude. The concept of the sublime and picturesque led the way by enlisting aesthetics in wild country's behalf while deism associated nature and religion. Combined with the primitivistic idealization of a life closer to nature, these ideas fed the Romantic movement which had far-reaching implications for wilderness.

With the flowering of Romanticism in the eighteenth and early nineteenth centuries, wild country lost much of its repulsiveness. It was not that wilderness was any less solitary, mysterious, and chaotic, but rather in the new intellectual context these qualities were coveted. European Romantics responded to the New World wilderness, and gradually a few Americans, in urban situations and with literary interests, began to adopt favorable attitudes. To be sure, indifference and hostility toward wilderness remained generally dominant. Even the enthusiasts of the wild found it difficult to discount the pioneer point of view completely. Yet by mid-nineteenth century a few Americans had vigorously stated the case for appreciation.

While people conceived of wild country as cursed and ungodly land, hostility followed as a matter of course; appreciation arose with the association of God and wilderness. The change in attitude began with the breakthroughs of European astronomy and physics that marked the beginning of the Enlightenment.[1] As scientists revealed a universe that was at once vast, complex, and harmonious, they strengthened the belief that this majestic and marvelous creation had a divine source. In time the awe that increasing knowledge about the solar system engendered extended to the great physical features of the earth such as deserts and oceans. The upshot was a striking change in the concept of wild nature. Mountains, for example, had generally been regarded in the early seventeenth century as warts, pimples, blisters, and other ugly deformities on the earth's surface. Names of individual peaks such as the "Divels-Arse" in England, suggested the prevailing opinion.[2] But by the end of the century a contrary attitude appeared. Books with theses in their titles, as Thomas Burnet's *The Sacred Theory of the Earth* (1684) and John Ray's *The Wisdom of God Manifested in the Works of the Creation* (1691), used elaborate theological and geographical arguments to raise the possibility that mountains might be the handiwork of God if not His very image. From the feeling that uncivilized regions bespoke God's influence rather than Satan's, it was just a step to perceiving a beauty and grandeur in wild scenery comparable to that of God.

To signify this new feeling about wild places the concept of sublimity gained widespread usage in the eighteenth century. As an aesthetic category the sublime dispelled the notion that beauty in nature was seen only in the comfortable, fruitful, and well-ordered. Vast, chaotic scenery could also please. According to the criteria of sublimity even the fear that wilderness inspired was not a liability. In his *Philosophical Enquiry into the Origin of Our Ideas of the Sublime and Beautiful* of 1757, Edmund Burke formally expressed the idea that terror and horror in regard to nature stemmed from exultation, awe, and delight rather than from dread and loathing. Six years later Immanuel Kant's *Observations on the Feeling of*

1. In the following analysis I have followed closely the pathbreaking study of Marjorie Hope Nicolson: *Mountain Gloom and Mountain Glory: The Development of the Aesthetics of the Infinite* (Ithaca, N.Y., 1959).

2. For the use of this term and a description of the repulsiveness of the mountain in a 1613 account see Michael Drayton, *Poly-Olbion,* ed. J. William Hebel, Michael Drayton Tercentenary Edition (5 vols. Oxford, 1961), *4,* 531. Konrad Gessner's 1543 essay, *On the Admiration of Mountains,* trans. H. B. D. Soulé (San Francisco, 1937), is a notable exception.

the Beautiful and the Sublime distinguished between the two sensations in such a way as to make it possible to regard the wilder features of the natural world—mountains, deserts, and storms, in particular—as aesthetically agreeable. Kant pursued these ideas further in his *Critique of Judgment* (1790), while William Gilpin, an English aesthetician, pioneered in defining the "picturesque" as the pleasing quality of nature's roughness, irregularity, and intricacy. Such ideas greatly broadened the Classical conception of ordered, proportioned beauty. In 1792 Gilpin's *Remarks on Forest Scenery and Other Woodland Views* inspired a rhetorical style for articulating appreciation of uncivilized nature. The wilderness remained the same, but a change in taste was altering attitudes toward it.[3]

Sublimity suggested the association of God and wild nature; deism, with its emphasis on the Creator or First Cause of the universe, used the relationship as the basis for religion. Of course, since the beginnings of thought men believed that natural objects and processes had spiritual significance, but "natural" evidence was usually secondary and supplemental to revelation. And wilderness, somewhat illogically, was excluded from the category of nature. The deists, however, based their entire faith in the existence of God on the application of reason to nature. Moreover, they accorded wilderness, as pure nature, special importance as the clearest medium through which God showed His power and excellency. Spiritual truths emerged most forcefully from the uninhabited landscape, whereas in cities or rural countryside man's works were superimposed on those of God. Along with the sense of the sublime, deism helped lay the foundation for a striking intellectual about-face. By the mid-eighteenth century wilderness was associated with the beauty and godliness that previously had defined it by their absence. Men found it increasingly possible to praise, even to worship, what they had formerly detested.

3. J. T. Boulton's extended introduction to Burke's *Enquiry* (London, 1958) is a useful interpretation. Other secondary references include Nicolson, *Mountain Gloom;* Walter John Hipple, Jr., *The Beautiful, the Sublime, and the Picturesque in Eighteenth Century British Aesthetics* (Carbondale, Ill., 1957); Christopher Hussey, *The Picturesque: Studies in a Point of View* (London, 1927); Samuel H. Monk, *The Sublime: A Study of Critical Theories in Eighteenth-Century England* (New York, 1935); and Hans Huth, *Nature and the American: Three Centuries of Changing Attitude* (Berkeley, Cal., 1957), pp. 11–12. David D. Zink, "The Beauty of the Alps: A Study of the Victorian Mountain Aesthetic" (unpublished Ph.D. dissertation, University of Colorado, 1962) concerns a later period.

Although deism and the sublime sprang in large part from the Enlightenment, they contributed to a quite different conception of nature. "Romanticism" resists definition, but in general it implies an enthusiasm for the strange, remote, solitary, and mysterious.[4] Consequently in regard to nature Romantics preferred the wild. Rejecting the meticulously ordered gardens at Versailles, so attractive to the Enlightenment mind, they turned to the unkempt forest. Wilderness appealed to those bored or disgusted with man and his works. It not only offered an escape from society but also was an ideal stage for the Romantic individual to exercise the cult that he frequently made of his own soul. The solitude and total freedom of the wilderness created a perfect setting for either melancholy or exultation.

Primitivism was one of the more important ideas in the Romantic complex. Primitivists believed that man's happiness and well-being decreased in direct proportion to his degree of civilization. They idealized either contemporary cultures nearer to savagery or a previous age in which they believed all men led a simpler and better existence.[5] Precedents for primitivistic and Romantic attraction to wildness exist well back into Western thought, and by the late Middle Ages there were a number of popular traditions about the noble savage.[6] One concerned the mythical Wild Man whom medieval culture represented as having redeeming as well as repulsive characteristics (see Chapter 1). Captured in his wilderness retreats and brought back to civilization, the Wild Man supposedly made a better knight than ordinary persons. Contact with the wilds was believed to give him exceptional strength, ferocity, and hardi-

4. On the Romantic movement as a whole see Arthur O. Lovejoy, "On the Discrimination of Romanticisms" in *Essays in the History of Ideas* (New York, 1955), pp. 228–53; Lovejoy's "The Meaning of Romanticism for the Historian of Ideas," *Journal of the History of Ideas,* 2 (1941), 257–78; Hoxie Neale Fairchild, *The Romantic Quest* (New York, 1931); and Merle Curti, *The Growth of American Thought* (2nd ed. New York, 1951), pp. 238–42.

5. The best general treatments are Arthur O. Lovejoy and George Boas, *Primitivism and Related Ideas in Antiquity* (Baltimore, 1935), pp. ix, 1–22; George Boas, *Essays on Primitivism and Related Ideas in the Middle Ages* (Baltimore, 1948), pp. 1–14; and Lois Whitney, *Primitivism and the Idea of Progress in English Popular Literature of the Eighteenth Century* (Baltimore, 1934), pp. 7–68, along with Arthur O. Lovejoy's foreword to the last. Frank Buckley's "Trends in American Primitivism" (unpublished Ph.D. dissertation, University of Minnesota, 1939) is also valuable.

6. Lovejoy and Boas, *Primitivism in Antiquity,* pp. 287–367; Boas, *Primitivism in the Middle Ages,* pp. 129–53; Hoxie Neale Fairchild, *The Noble Savage: A Study in Romantic Naturalism* (New York, 1928), pp. 1–56.

ness combined with innocence and an innate nobility. Moreover, the Wild Man's erotic prowess allegedly made civilized man's pale in comparison.[7]

The Wild-Man-as-superman tradition led to the idea of a beneficial retreat to the wilderness. German writers of the fifteenth century suggested that instead of taming the Wild Man, the inhabitants of cities would do well to seek his environment. An idyllic life presumably awaited those who entered the woods. Peace, love, and harmony, it was thought, would replace the immorality, conflict, and materialism of the towns. Another theme implied that the reversion to the primitive would release man from the social restraints that thwarted the full expression of his sensuality.[8] Hans Sachs' *Lament of the Wild Men about the Unfaithful World* of 1530, for example, began with a catalog of the vices of the towns and went on to relate how, in protest, malcontents left civilization to dwell in caves in the wilderness. According to Sachs, they lived there in utmost simplicity, found tranquility, and waited for their civilized brethren to change their erring ways.

From Hans Sachs it was only a half century to Montaigne's essay *Of Cannibals,* marking the beginning of the flowering of European primitivism. After this seminal statement, enthusiasm for noble savages and for the wild in nature became increasingly popular literary conventions.[9] By the early eighteenth century, they were widely used as tools for criticizing civilization. In England poets like the Wartons, Shaftesbury, and Pope attacked the "smoky cities" with their "luxury and pomp" while yearning for the uncorrupted "pathless wilds."[10] More revealing of the general attitude was Daniel Defoe's *The Life and Surprising Adventures of Robinson Crusoe.* Published in 1719 and immediately an immense success, the story was inspired by the actual experiences of a mari-

7. Bernheimer, *Wild Men in the Middle Ages,* pp. 16–19, 121 ff.

8. Ibid., pp. 20, 112–17, 147 ff.

9. The definitive work on pre-Romantic primitivism is Paul Van Tieghem, *Le sentiment de la Nature Préromantisme Européen* (Paris, 1960).

10. Whitney, *Primitivism;* Margaret M. Fitzgerald, *First Follow Nature: Primitivism in English Poetry, 1725–50* (New York, 1947); Cecil A. Moore, "The Return to Nature in English Poetry of the 18th Century" in his *Backgrounds of English Literature, 1700–1760* (Minneapolis, 1953), pp. 53–103; Myra Reynolds, *The Treatment of Nature in English Poetry between Pope and Wordsworth* (Chicago, 1896). The quotations are from Joseph Warton's "The Enthusiast or the Lover of Nature" of 1740: *The Three Wartons: A Choice of Their Verse,* ed. Eric Partridge (London, 1927), pp. 72, 75, 77.

ner who some years previously had found himself stranded on a deserted island off the Chilean coast. While Defoe left no doubt that the wilderness condition had some disadvantages, his book invested Crusoe's island life with a charm that implied the shortcomings of eighteenth-century England.[11]

On the Continent the leading primitivist was Jean-Jacques Rousseau. While he did not idealize a completely wild condition and expressed no personal desire to revert to the woods, Rousseau argued in *Emile* (1762) that modern man should incorporate primitive qualities into his presently distorted civilized life. And his *Julie ou La Nouvelle Héloise* (1761) heaped such praise on the sublimity of wilderness scenes in the Alps that it stimulated a generation of artists and writers to adopt the Romantic mode.[12]

The New World, with its abundance of pathless forests and savages, intrigued the Romantic imagination.[13] Some Europeans even made the journey across the ocean to indulge their enthusiasm for the primitive. Among the first of these visitors was François-René de Chateaubriand, who spent five months of the winter of 1791–92 in the United States. Traveling in the wilderness of northern New York, he reported that "a sort of delirium" seized him when, to his delight, he found an absence of roads, towns, laws, and kings. Chateaubriand concluded: "in vain does the imagination try to roam at large midst [Europe's] cultivated plains . . . but in this deserted region the soul delights to bury and lose itself amidst boundless forests . . . to mix and confound . . . with the wild sublimities of Nature." When he returned to France, he wrote two

11. James Sutherland, *Defoe* (Philadelphia, 1938), pp. 227–36; Maximillian E. Novak, *Defoe and the Nature of Man* (Oxford, 1963), pp. 25 ff.

12. Van Tieghem, *Sentiment de la Nature,* passim; Fairchild, *Noble Savage,* pp. 120–39; William Henry Hudson, *Rousseau and Naturalism in Life and Thought* (Edinburgh, 1903); Richard Ashley Rice, *Rousseau and the Poetry of Nature in Eighteenth Century France,* Smith College Studies in Modern Languages, 6 (Menasha, Wis., 1925); Arthur O. Lovejoy, "The Supposed Primitivism of Rousseau's *Discourse on Inequality,*" in *Essays,* pp. 14–37. Geoffroy Atkinson, *Le Sentiment de la Nature et le Retour a la Vie Simple, 1690–1740,* Société de Publications Romanes et Françaises, 66 (Paris, 1960) and René Gonnard, *Le Legende du Bon Sauvage,* Collection D'Histoire Economique, 4 (Paris, 1946) discuss the background and influence of some of Rousseau's ideas.

13. Gilbert Chinard, *L'Amérique et le Rêve Exotique dans la Litterature Française au XVII et au XVIII Siècle* (Paris, 1913); George R. Healy, "The French Jesuits and the Idea of the Noble Savage," *William and Mary Quarterly, 15* (1958), 143–67; Durand Echeverria, *Mirage in the West: A History of the French Image of American Society to 1815* (Princeton, N.J., 1957), pp. 12, 32–33.

popular novelettes, *Atala* and *René,* which spread a Romantic glow over Indian life in "the magnificent wilds of Kentucky." The protagonist of these tales, an archetype Romantic hero searching for "something to fill the vast emptiness of my existence," found the freedom, excitement and novelty of the wilderness highly appealing.[14]

Following Chateaubriand, a succession of Europeans with Romantic tastes, including Alexis de Tocqueville (see Chapter 2), visited or wrote about the American wilderness. George Gordon, better known as Lord Byron, was one of the most outspoken and influential advocates of the wild. "From my youth upwards," one of his characters declares, "my spirit walk'd not with the souls of men . . . my griefs, my passions, and my powers, made me a stranger . . . my joy was in the Wilderness." As his heroes in other works Byron chose melancholy cynics whose disenchantment with civilization led them to value the solitude of wild places. His fascination with the theme of escape from society drew his attention to the wilderness of the New World and the men whom it absorbed. In a portion of *Don Juan* Byron celebrated Daniel Boone—as a Romantic hero, not a conquering pioneer. Byron's 1816 confession, taken by his generation to be a manifesto, read: "there is a pleasure in the pathless woods, / There is a rapture on the lonely shore. / There is society where none intrudes . . . / I love not man the less, but nature more."[15] The kind of nature Byron had in mind was wilderness, and his work climaxed European Romanticism's century-long achievement of creating an intellectual framework in which it could be favorably portrayed. The first Americans who appreciated wild country relied heavily on this tradition and vocabulary in articulating their ideas.

14. Chateaubriand, *Recollections of Italy, England and America* (Philadelphia, 1816), pp. 138–39, 144; Chateaubriand, *"Atala" and "René,"* trans. Irving Putter (Berkeley, Cal., 1952), pp. 21, 96.

15. Lord Byron, *Manfred: A Dramatic Poem* (London, 1817), pp. 33–34; *Childe Harold's Pilgrimage,* IV, clxxvii, as quoted in Joseph Warren Beach, *The Concept of Nature in Nineteenth Century English Poetry* (New York, 1936), p. 35. Byron's variety of Romantic attraction to wilderness is discussed in Andrew Rutherford, *Byron: A Critical Study* (Edinburgh, 1962), pp. 26 ff., and Ernest J. Lovell, Jr., *Byron, the Record of a Quest: Studies in a Poet's Concept and Treatment of Nature* (Austin, Texas, 1949), while his influence on American thought is the subject of William Ellery Leonard, *Byron and Byronism in America* (Boston, 1905).

Enthusiasm for wilderness based on Romanticism, deism, and the sense of the sublime developed among sophisticated Europeans surrounded by cities and books. So too in America the beginnings of appreciation are found among writers, artists, scientists, vacationers, gentlemen—people, in short, who did not face wilderness from the pioneer's perspective. William Byrd II is one of the earliest cases in point. A Virginian by birth, Byrd's formative years were spent in London, where he acquired the education and tastes of the English gentry. He returned to the colonies in 1705 to inherit Westover, the family's vast plantation, and to enter politics. But Byrd remained highly interested in English social and literary fashions, including the nascent Romantic delight in wildness.

In 1728 Byrd began work as Virginia's commissioner in a surveying operation to establish the boundary between his colony and North Carolina. The job took him well back into the southern Appalachian uplands and his description of the region in the *History of the Dividing Line* is the first extensive American commentary on wilderness that reveals a feeling other than hostility. Byrd portrayed the expedition into "this great Wilderness" as a delightful adventure. He reported that even when his party could have stayed in a planter's house, they preferred to sleep outdoors because "we took so much pleasure in that natural kind of Lodging." In the primitivistic manner he generalized that "Mankind are the great Losers by the Luxury of Feather-Beds and warm apartments."[16]

As the surveyors worked their way further west and out of the inhabited region, Byrd's excitement grew. On October 11, 1728, they caught sight for the first time of the Appalachian Mountains. Byrd described them as "Ranges of Blue Clouds rising one above another." Four days later the party camped in a "Charming Situation" from which the view was so spectacular "that we were perpetually climbing up to a Neighbouring eminence, that we might enjoy it in more Perfection." Once, when fog prevented a clear

16. *The Writings of 'Colonel William Byrd of Westover in Virginia Esqr'*, ed. John Spencer Bassett (New York, 1901), pp. 48–49, 192. Biographical accounts are Bassett's "Introduction," Ibid., pp. ix-lxxxviii; Richard Croom Beatty, *William Byrd of Westover* (Boston, 1932); and Louis B. Wright, "The Life of William Byrd of Virginia, 1674–1744" in Byrd, *The London Diary (1717–1721) and Other Writings*, ed. Wright and Marion Tinling (New York, 1958), pp. 1–46.

view of the scenery, Byrd lamented "the loss of this wild Prospect." But in a short while the "smoak" lifted and "open'd this Romantick Scene to us all at once." Leaving the mountains after the survey, Byrd noted how he frequently turned in his saddle to observe them "as if unwilling to part with a Prospect, which at the same time, like some Rake's, was very wild and very Agreeable."[17]

Although his lack of a strong religious orientation helped, William Byrd enjoyed wilderness primarily because of his gentlemanly leanings. In the first place, he was familiar with the aesthetic and literary conventions regarding wild nature of which most of his colonial contemporaries were unaware. And Byrd was determined to demonstrate his sophistication by publicly subscribing to the latest fashion in taste and so resist the stigma of cultural provincialism. He deliberately contrived the *History of the Dividing Line* to reflect on its author's polish and refinement.[18] In fact, the original journal, the so-called "Secret History," did not contain the passages celebrating the wild mountains. Byrd added them as embellishments a decade later when he prepared the manuscript for publication.[19] Given the current state of European taste, such enthusiasm for wilderness made Byrd appear *au courant*. Another factor shaping Byrd's attitude toward wild country was the fact that he did not confront it as a pioneer but from an opulent plantation situation. For the squire of Westover, there was much less compulsion to attack and conquer wilderness than for the frontiersman. Moreover, as a well-lettered gentleman Byrd could afford to take delight in wilderness without feeling himself a barbarian or in danger of reverting to one. He was not, to be sure, oblivious to this possibility—in the backwoods he saw and deplored people who had absorbed the wildness of their surroundings. But he carefully distinguished his own relation to wilderness from theirs.

Byrd's experience also reveals that American appreciation of wilderness was seldom pure. The older pioneer antipathy did not yield easily; to some extent the Romantic enthusiasm was a cover

17. *Writings of Byrd*, pp. 135, 146, 163, 172, 186.

18. Support for this interpretation may be found in Kenneth S. Lynn, *Mark Twain and Southwestern Humor* (Boston, 1959), pp. 3–22; and Louis B. Wright, *The First Gentlemen of Virginia* (San Marino, Cal., 1940), pp. 312–47.

19. The history of Byrd's *History* is told in the extensive introduction of *William Byrd's Histories of the Dividing Line Betwixt Virginia and North Carolina*, ed. William K. Boyd (Raleigh, 1929). This edition contains a useful juxtaposition of the finished account and earlier versions.

over contrary attitudes. It wore thin in Byrd's account when he referred to the "dolefull Wilderness" and when, at the end of his journey, he expressed gratitude that "we had, day by day, been fed by the Bountiful hand of Providence in the desolate Wilderness." And, in the frontiersman's manner, he idealized the useful, pastoral nature. At one point Byrd contemplated a wild valley and observed that it "wanted nothing but Cattle grazing in the Meadow, and Sheep and Goats feeding on the Hill, to make it a Compleat Rural LANDSCAPE."[20]

The scientists who pushed into the colonial backcountry anxious to make discoveries also occupied a vantage point from which wilderness could be regarded with something other than hostility. At first the students of "natural history" shared the dominant point of view. John Josselyn, the foremost botanist of the seventeenth century, climbed Mt. Washington in 1663 and described the view of "rocky Hills . . . cloathed with infinite thick Woods" as "daunting terrible."[21] Along with John Lawson, whose investigations took him into western North Carolina early in the eighteenth century, Josselyn often mixed fancy with fact and supplied the fuel with which the folk imagination built a conception of wilderness as the environment of weird and horrible monsters. But by mid-century a new note had sounded in descriptive, scientific writing. John Clayton, Peter Kalm, Andre Michoux, and the native, self-taught botanist, John Bartram, revealed considerable excitement about the American wilderness as a natural laboratory, not just as the raw material of civilization. Conquest was not their primary concern, and sometimes the naturalists even paused in their labors to admire the scenery.[22] Building on the European conception of the natural

20. Boyd, ed., *Histories*, p. 245; Bassett, ed., *Writings of Byrd*, pp. 233, 242.

21. Josselyn, *New England's Rarities* (1672), ed. Edward Tuckerman (Boston, 1865), p. 36.

22. For example, John Bartram, *Observations on the Inhabitants, Climate, Soil, Rivers, Productions, Animals . . . from Pennsylvania to Onondago, Oswego and the Lake Ontario* (London, 1751), p. 16. Also relevant are Edmund Berkeley and Dorothy Smith Berkeley, *The Reverend John Clayton, A Parson with a Scientific Mind: His Scientific Writings and Other Related Papers* (Charlottesville, Va., 1965) and their biography: *John Clayton: Pioneer of American Botany* (Chapel Hill, N.C., 1963); Peter Kalm, *The America of 1750*, ed. Adolph B. Benson (2 vols. New York, 1937); Donald Culross Peattie, *Green Laurels: The Lives and Achievements of the Great Naturalists* (New York, 1936), pp. 197 ff.; Philip Marshall Hicks, *The Development of the Natural History Essay in American Literature* (Philadelphia, 1924), pp. 7–38; and William Martin Smallwood, *Natural History and the American Mind* (New York, 1941), pp. 3–41.

world that gave rise to deism and the sense of the sublime, they assumed, as Mark Catesby put it, that in the wilderness they studied the "Glorious Works of the Creator."[23] From such a perspective the sinister motifs generally associated with wild country became increasingly untenable.

The second-generation botanist, William Bartram, articulated his impressions of wilderness to an exceptional degree. Born to a family which prized the life of the mind, Bartram was well versed in the Romantic outlook when, in 1773, he began extensive explorations in the unsettled regions of the Southeast. During the next four years he traveled some five thousand miles and kept a detailed journal. Previously botanists in the New World had been too engrossed in their studies to pay more than cursory attention to wilderness; Bartram frequently reversed this order. On one occasion in 1775 he climbed a mountain in northern Georgia "from whence I enjoyed a view inexpressibly magnificent and comprehensive . . . [of] the mountain wilderness through which I had lately traversed." Then he added: "my imagination thus wholly engaged in the contemplation of this magnificent landscape . . . I was almost insensible . . . of . . . a new species of Rhododendron."[24]

What made William Bartram forget the rhododendron and rejoice in wilderness was its sublimity. His descriptions mark the first extensive use of that term in American letters. Instances appear on almost every page of his *Travels*. Camping beside Florida's Lake George, Bartram admitted being "seduced by these sublime enchanting scenes of primitive nature," and in the Carolina wilderness he "beheld with rapture and astonishment, a sublimely awful scene of power and magnificence, a world of mountains piled upon mountains." For him, as for the European aesthetes, the sublime in nature was linked with God's grandeur, and Bartram frequently praised "the supreme author of nature" whose "wisdom and power" were manifested in wilderness.[25]

23. Catesby, *The Natural History of Carolina, Florida and the Bahama Islands* (2 vols. London, 1754), *1*, iii. See also George Frederick Frick and Raymond Phineas Stearns, *Mark Catesby: The Colonial Audubon* (Urbana, Ill., 1961).

24. *The Travels of William Bartram: Naturalist's Edition*, ed. Francis Harper (New Haven, 1958), pp. 212–13. Secondary treatments are Ernest Earnest, *John and William Bartram: Botanists and Explorers* (Philadelphia, 1940), pp. 84 ff.; and N. Bryllion Fagin, *William Bartram: Interpreter of the American Landscape* (Baltimore, 1933).

25. William Bartram, *Travels*, pp. 69, 229; Ibid., pp. 120–21.

Like William Byrd, William Bartram subscribed to the essentials of Romantic primitivism. "Our situation," he reported of one campsite in Florida, "was like that of the primitive state of man, peaceable, contented, and sociable." But, again like Byrd, Bartram's attitude toward wilderness was more complex. His most revealing comments came during a trip into the southern Appalachians. He planned to cross a sizeable stretch of wild, mountainous country and felt fortunate to find a traveling companion for the first fifteen miles. Then Bartram was alone and his solitary condition filled him with mixed emotions. The mountains seemed "dreary," even threatening. Bartram took the opportunity to observe that perhaps men were gregarious beings whose delight was in civilization. Recalling his recent pleasant stay in Charleston, he compared himself unhappily with Nebuchadnezzar who had been expelled from society "and constrained to roam in the mountains and wilderness, there to herd and feed with the wild beasts of the forest." While absorbed in these depressing thoughts, Bartram came to a cliff from which he could see the sweep of wilderness to the west. At once he put aside his fears and rapturously exclaimed at "this amazing prospect of grandeur."[26] Fears and doubts could not eclipse for long Bartram's love of the wild.

There were, to be sure, few Byrds and Bartrams in the colonies. Most of their contemporaries shared the pioneer aversion to wilderness, and even with them appreciation floated uneasily on an ocean of uncertainty. The new attitude coexisted with, rather than replaced, the old. Similarly, in the early national period the Romantic viewpoint was only a part, albeit a growing one, of the American estimation of wilderness.

Before the end of the eighteenth century a few Americans had discovered primitivism.[27] In 1781 and 1782 Philip Freneau published a series of essays under the running title "The Philosopher of the Forest" in which a hermit served as a mouthpiece for expressing the author's criticism of civilized society. Repeatedly the Phi-

26. Ibid., pp. 71, 227–29.

27. It would be inaccurate, however, to agree with Mary E. Woolley ["The Development of the Love of Romantic Scenery in America," *American Historical Review, 3* (1897), 56–66] that a "new spirit of admiration for wild and romantic scenery became fully established" between 1780 and 1785. This was a time of uncertain beginnings rather than climaxes.

losopher contrasted his simple, moral life in the woods of Pennsylvania with the distorted existences of city-dwellers. A decade later Freneau turned to the same theme in the "Tomo-Cheeki Essays." Here he assumed the guise of an Indian who visited civilization and contrasted "the wild genius of the forest" with the "tawdry productions of art." In 1800 Benjamin Rush, the Philadelphia physician, explicitly connected primitivism and wilderness by observing that "man is naturally a wild animal, and . . . taken from the woods, he is never happy . . . 'till he returns to them again."[28]

While both Freneau and Rush expounded their primitivism in Philadelphia drawing rooms, a remarkable New Hampshire lawyer named Estwick Evans actually put his philosophy into practice. In the winter of 1818, Evans donned a buffalo robe trimmed with bearskin and moccasins and, in the company of two dogs, set forth on a four-thousand-mile "pedestrious tour" into the West. "I wished to acquire," he declared, "the simplicity, native feelings, and virtues of savage life; to divest myself of the factitious habits, prejudices and imperfections of civilization . . . and to find amidst the solitude and grandeur of the western wilds, more correct views of human nature and of the true interest of man." This was the essence of primitivism, and Evans followed it with a succession of tributes to the wilderness. While skirting the southern shore of Lake Erie, his feelings welled into a Romantic paean: "how great are the advantages of solitude!—How sublime is the silence of nature's ever-active energies! There is something in the very name of wilderness, which charms the ear, and soothes the spirit of man. There is religion in it."[29] In the sweep of Western thought, this was a relatively young idea, and one with revolutionary implications. If religion was identified with wilderness rather than opposed to it, as had traditionally been the case, the basis for appreciation, rather than hatred, was created.

When Estwick Evans declared that he deliberately made his tour in the winter months so that he "might experience the *pleasure* of suffering, and the *novelty* of danger," he suggested another

28. *The Prose of Philip Freneau*, ed. Philip M. Marsh (New Brunswick, N.J., 1955), pp. 196–202, 338; *The Autobiography of Benjamin Rush*, ed., George W. Corner (Princeton, N.J., 1948), p. 72.

29. Evans, *A Pedestrious Tour of Four Thousand Miles through the Western States and Territories during the Winter and Spring of 1818* (Concord, N.H., 1819), pp. 6, 102.

reason why Americans of his generation could begin to look favorably at wilderness.[30] In the early nineteenth century, for the first time in American history, it was possible to live and even to travel widely without coming into contact with wild country. Increasingly people lived on established farms or in cities where they did not experience the hardships and fears of the wilderness. From the vantage point of comfortable farms, libraries, and city streets, wilderness assumed a far different character than from a pioneer's clearing. For Estwick Evans and other gentlemen of leisure and learning, wilderness had actually become a novelty which posed an exciting, temporary alternative to civilization.

While few emulated Evans, a number of his contemporaries with Romantic tastes began to take pleasure in wild country. As early as 1792 Jeremy Belknap, a Harvard graduate and Congregational minister at Dover, New Hampshire, published a descriptive tribute to the White Mountains. He noted that the region was a "thick wilderness," but was well worth the attention of "a contemplative mind." Explaining that "a poetic fancy may find full gratification amidst these wild and rugged scenes," Belknap singled out "aged mountains, stupendous elevations, rolling clouds, impending rocks, verdant woods . . . and the roaring torrent" as likely "to amaze, to soothe and to enrapture." He concluded that "almost everything in nature, which can be supposed capable of inspiring ideas of the sublime and beautiful, is here realized." Yet when Belknap revealed his conception of the ideal setting for the "happy society," wilderness had no place. The land in this utopia would be "well fenced and cultivated" and yeoman farmers would have created a thriving rural hamlet.[31]

Thaddeus Mason Harris also revealed an ambivalence toward wilderness in the journal of his 1803 tour into the upper Ohio Valley. Like Belknap, Harris was a Harvard man and a minister. He was described as sensitive, timid, and frail; recovery of his

30. Evans, *Pedestrious Tour,* p. 6. Italics supplied.

31. Belknap, *The History of New-Hampshire* (3 vols. Boston, 1792), *3,* 40, 51, 73, 333–34. Belknap's journal account of an earlier trip on which the *History's* description was based has been published as *Journal of a Tour to the White Mountains in 1784,* ed. Charles Deane (Boston, 1876). The secondary literature includes Sidney Kaplan, "The History of New Hampshire: Jeremy Belknap as Literary Craftsman," *William and Mary Quarterly, 31* (1964), 18–39. Timothy Dwight's *Travels in New-England and New-York* (4 vols. New Haven, 1821–22), 2, 142, 297–300, reveals an identical ambivalence in regard to the same region and at the same time.

health, in fact, was an object of the western trip. Starting from Philadelphia, Harris was, on the one hand, impressed by the "romantic wildness" of the Alleghenies. He especially liked the vastness of the mountain scenes which thrilled him "with awe as well as admiration." Attempting to understand his feelings, Harris declared: "there is something which impresses the mind with awe in the shade and silence of these vast forests. In the deep solitude, alone with nature, we converse with GOD."[32] As with the English originators of the idea of sublimity a century before, the immensity and grandeur of wild nature suggested similar qualities of the Creator.

Yet while Reverend Harris often delighted in the "romantic prospects" he encountered in the wilderness, his account also contained a quite different opinion. At times the "lonesome woods" were depressing and forbidding. "There is something very animating to the feelings," he declared, "when a traveller, after traversing a region without culture, emerges from the depths of solitude, and comes upon an open, pleasant, and cultivated country." Indeed the sight of wilderness becoming civilization excited Harris as much as wilderness itself. On the Ohio River near Wheeling he celebrated the peopling of a "solitary waste" and the erection of buildings "amidst the former retreats of wild beasts." The sight of settlements rising in the "desolate wilds" suggested Biblical rhetoric: man's efforts "can change the desert into a fruitful field." In conclusion, Harris reflected that "when we behold competence and plenty springing from the bosom of dreary forests—what a lesson is afforded of the benevolent intentions of Providence!"[33] In this attitude Harris was at one with the pioneer.

In spite of these reservations, Thaddeus Harris ultimately preferred the wild. On June 17, 1803, on a shoulder of North Mountain, farmland surrounded him but in the distance he could see uncut forest. This juxtaposition caused him to speculate on the comparative merits of the two kinds of landscape. Speaking first for the pastoral, he pointed out that pastures, ripening fields, and gar-

32. Harris, *The Journal of a Tour into the Territory Northwest of the Allegheny Mountains* (Boston, 1805), pp. 14, 21, 60. A biographical sketch of Harris appears in the *Dictionary of American Biography* which may be supplemented with Nathaniel L. Frothingham's "Memoir of Rev. Thaddeus Mason Harris, D.D.," *Collections of the Massachusetts Historical Society*, 2 (1854), pp. 130–55.

33. Harris, *Journal of a Tour*, pp. 27, 51–52.

dens full of flowers could provide "pleasant recreation." But "the majestic features of the uncultivated wilderness" produced "an expansion of fancy and an elevation of thought more dignified and noble." According to Harris, as the eye takes in the immensity of wilderness, the mind expands to comprehend its own dignity and power. "THE SUBLIME IN NATURE," he wrote in summary, "captivates while it awes, and charms while it elevates and expands the soul."[34]

The double-mindedness of Harris in regard to wilderness also appeared in many other early nineteenth-century reports. There is James Hall, for example. Like most of those who first expressed appreciation of the wilds, Hall's background was genteel.[35] He came from an upper-class Philadelphia family, and his mother, Sarah Ewing Hall, wrote for the elegant *Port Folio*. Young Hall developed a Romantic temperament, and when he moved in 1820 to Illinois he was prepared to regard wilderness favorably. The frontier situation and pioneer values, however, partially offset Hall's Romantic enthusiasm. As a result inconsistencies on the subject of wilderness abound in his writing. It was possible for Hall, as spokesman of the pioneer, to compose tributes to an advancing civilization. "From this land, so lately a wilderness," he wrote in 1828, "the savage has been expelled; towns and colleges have arisen; farms have been made; the mechanic arts cherished; the necessaries of life abound, and many of its luxuries are enjoyed." This transformation seemed to him to be the "beautiful consumation of that promise, 'thou shalt have dominion over all the earth.'" Yet Hall also saw wilderness in another light. A few pages before celebrating the conversion of the Ohio Valley "from a desert to a paradise," he declared: "I know of nothing more splendid than a forest of the west, standing in its original integrity, adorned with the exuberant beauties of a powerful vegetation, and crowned with the honors of a venerable age." Hall, the Romantic, was glad that the West was wild because "the forest is seen in its majesty; the pomp and pride of the wilderness is here. Here is nature unspoiled, and silence undisturbed."[36]

34. Ibid., pp. 71–72.

35. For the details of Hall's life see John T. Flanagan, *James Hall: Literary Pioneer of the Ohio Valley* (Minneapolis, 1941) and Randolph C. Randall, *James Hall: Spokesman of the New West* (Columbus, Ohio, 1964).

36. Hall, *Letters from the West* (London, 1828), p. 165; Hall, "Chase's Statutes of Ohio," *Western Monthly Magazine*, 5 (1836), 631–32; Hall, *Notes on the Western States* (Philadelphia, 1838), pp. 55, 54.

With the spread of the Romantic mood, the appreciation of wilderness became a literary genre. By the 1840s it was commonplace for literati of the major Eastern cities to make periodic excursions into the wilds, collect "impressions," and return to their desks to write descriptive essays which dripped love of scenery and solitude in the grand Romantic manner. The capacity to appreciate wilderness was, in fact, deemed one of the qualities of a gentleman. Invariably the essayists associated enjoyment of wild nature with refinement and good breeding. One author, who identified himself only as "a gentleman of Boston," remarked in the course of describing an 1833 excursion to New Hampshire that if parents desired to cultivate their children's taste, "let them look at, and become familiar with the woods, the wilds, and the mountains." He further declared that anyone aspiring to connoisseurship must first steep himself in nature "by living in the midst of her magnificence, by frequenting her romantic wildernesses; by surveying her picturesque and animated scenery."[37] Romantic writers like this represented themselves as a particular social type whose "sensibilities" were superior to those who brought only economic criteria to wild country. Enjoyment of wilderness, for them, was a function of gentility.

In spite of the premium Romanticism placed on the individual, Romantic celebration of wilderness in the early nineteenth century followed a predictable pattern in both style and language. Typical was an anonymous contribution to the fashionable *American Monthly Magazine* in 1833 tnat was concerned with "the tender feelings, which are almost invariably called forth by a lonely ramble in some sequestered glade." Sprinkling quotations from Byron and others into his prose, the writer declared "that even in our present state of refinement, there is still a hankering after the wild sports and wilder perils of the wilderness." There were references to the advantages of nature, which "speaks directly to the heart," over the "artificial" cities. Wilderness was a sanctuary both from "the turmoil, the anxieties, and the hollowness of society" and from "the busy haunts of sordid, money-making business."[38] Such ideas, the stock in trade of Romantic devotees of wilderness,

37. [Nathan Hale], *Notes made During an Excursion to the Highlands of New Hampshire and Lake Winnipiseogee* (Andover, Mass., 1833), p. 54.

38. Anonymous, "Rural Enjoyment," *American Monthly Magazine, 6* (1833), 397, 399.

appeared regularly in periodicals, "scenery" albums, literary "annuals," and other elegant, parlor literature of the time. The adjectives "sublime" and "picturesque" were applied so indiscriminately as to lose meaning.[39]

Charles Fenno Hoffman, a New York writer and editor, represented the gentlemen who contributed to the growing interest in wilderness. Seeking literary raw material, he embarked in 1833 on a trip to the Mississippi Valley. The letters he sent back to the New York *American*, later collected into a book, reveal a man enthralled with the "perfect wilderness" he encountered. While admitting with an "Alas!" that most people lacked a sense of "beauty and majesty," Hoffman pointed out that for him there was a "singular joyousness in a wilderness." His travels had taken him to places that required neither cultivation nor companionship to make them appealing. "I have felt," he reported, "among some scenes a kind of selfish pleasure, a wild delight, that the spot so lovely and so lonely . . . bloomed alone for me."[40] After his excursion into the West, Hoffman assumed the editorship of the *American Monthly* in New York City, but he continued to seek the wilderness on his vacations. He was, in fact, one of the first to extol the Adirondack Mountains as a mecca for lovers of wild scenery. For New Yorkers who could not get so far afield, Hoffman included in his magazine such articles as "Wild Scenes Near Home; or Hints for a Summer Tourist."[41]

After Charles Fenno Hoffman had "discovered" the Adirondacks, they gained popularity as a resort for wilderness enthusiasts. Joel T. Headley's *The Adirondack: or Life in the Woods* of 1849 described the pleasures a cultivated vacationer might find in the region. A prolific author and reporter for the New York *Tribune*, Headley employed all the standard conventions in praise of wilderness. The mountains manifested "vagueness, terror, sublimity, strength, and beauty" and were, in the deistic sense, God's

39. For the growing vogue of wild nature in literature see Huth, *Nature*, pp. 30 ff.; Frank Luther Mott, *A History of American Magazines, 1741–1850* (New York, 1930), pp. 119 ff.; Ralph Thompson, *American Literary Annuals and Gift Books* (New York, 1936); Ola Elizabeth Winslow, "Books for the Lady Reader," in *Romanticism in America*, ed. George Boas (New York, 1961), pp. 89 ff.

40. Hoffman, *A Winter in the West* (2 vols. New York, 1835), 2, 225, 316, 317. Homer F. Barnes, *Charles Fenno Hoffman* (New York, 1930) is the best biographical source.

41. *American Monthly Magazine, 8* (1836), 469–78.

creation and "a symbol of His omnipotence." For a "man of sensibility," Headley asserted, there was "enchantment" in finding in the wilderness escape from "the strifes of men and the discords of life." As for himself: "I love the freedom of the wilderness and the absence of conventional forms there. I love the long stretch through the forest on foot, and the thrilling, glorious prospect from some hoary mountain top. I love it, and I know it is better for me than the thronged city, aye, better for soul and body both." Headley concluded his book with "Directions to the Traveler." Equipped with strong legs, a stout heart, and "a love for the wild, and free" anyone could enjoy an Adirondack vacation "and come back to civilized life a healthier and a better man."[42]

While Hoffman and Headley drowned most of their doubts about wilderness in a deluge of Romantic euphoria, Charles Lanman demonstrated that even the literati were not immune to the darker wind of the pioneer past. An editor, librarian, and landscape painter, Lanman began a series of summertime trips in the 1830s to places as widespread as northern Maine and northern Minnesota. Returning with bulging notebooks, he produced volumes of elegant essays, bearing such titles as *A Summer in the Wilderness* and *Letters from the Allegheny Mountains,* that described the joys of forests primeval. The woods became "those glorious forests, the homes of solitude and silence, where I was wont to be so happy alone with my God." In 1846 Lanman described the "wild and silent wilderness" near Lake Superior as "beautiful beyond any thing I had imagined to exist in any country on the globe." On the other hand, he subscribed to older attitudes. An Indian medicine dance at Leech Lake, Minnesota reminded him that wilderness was the fearsome environment of evil and unearthly creatures. In writing about the Michigan wilderness Lanman's ambivalence appeared on a single page. First he praised "nature in her primitive beauty and strength"; immediately following was an expression of delight that "instead of the howl of the wolf, the songs of husbandmen now echo through . . . vales, where may be found many comfortable dwellings."[43]

42. Headley, *The Adirondack: or Life in the Woods* (New York, 1849), pp. 45–46, 63, 167, 217, 288.

43. Lanman, *Letters from a Landscape Painter* (Boston, 1845), p. 264; Lanman, *A Summer in the Wilderness: Embracing a Canoe Voyage up the Mississippi and Around Lake Superior* (New York, 1847), pp. 105, 126, 171.

Those whose business it was to explore, trap, farm and otherwise conquer the wilderness were less susceptible than urban sophisticates and vacationers to the Romantic posture. Yet its occasional appearance in frontiersmen's reports testified to the potency of this opinion. As early as 1784 Daniel Boone's alleged "autobiography" (it was mostly the work of a fellow Kentuckian, John Filson[44]) revealed a new motif alongside the usual condemnation of wild country. It began with the standard references to a "howling wilderness" suitable only for conversion into a "fruitful field." But the account also revealed Boone's "astonishing delight" in wild scenery. The view from one ridge turned pioneer into primitivistic philosopher. "No populous city," Boone declared, "with all the varieties of commerce and stately structures, could afford so much pleasure to my mind, as the beauties of nature I found here." Even when Boone concluded his narrative with a reference to himself as "an instrument ordained to settle the wilderness," he left the impression that he performed this role somewhat reluctantly.[45] Regardless of whether these were Boone's actual sentiments, it was significant that they could be attributed to the archetypical pioneer.

A growing number of frontiersmen after Boone subscribed at times to the idea that wilderness had aesthetic values. To be sure, most of the response of ordinary Americans to wilderness went unrecorded (any pioneer who wrote down his impressions was, by that fact, exceptional) but a few traces suggest probabilities.[46] For instance, James Ohio Pattie, the son of a frontier family and himself a trapper in the trans-Missouri West, noted in his journal that "I have seen much that is beautiful, interesting, and commanding in the wild scenery of nature."[47] Osbourne Russell, another trapper, was more specific. On August 20, 1836, he camped in the

44. Apparently Filson wrote the "autobiography" after receiving oral information from Boone and other Kentucky pioneers: John Walton, *John Filson of Kentucke* (Lexington, Ky., 1956), pp. 50 ff.; Reuben T. Durrett, *John Filson, the First Historian of Kentucky,* Filson Club Publications, 1 (Cincinnati, 1884).

45. *The Discovery, Settlement and present State of Kentucky by John Filson,* ed. William H. Masterson (New York, 1962), pp. 49, 50, 54–56, 81.

46. Lucy L. Hazard, *The Frontier in American Literature* (New York, 1927), p. 113, rightly points out the difficulty of assessing "campfire" opinion.

47. *The Personal Narrative of James O. Pattie,* ed. Timothy Flint (Cincinnati, 1831), p. 14. Flint assured the reader that in editing Pattie's account he had not interjected his own opinions but merely punctuated and clarified.

Lamar Valley of northwestern Wyoming, a region later included in Yellowstone National Park, and wrote:

> There is something in the wild romantic scenery of this valley which I cannot . . . describe but the impression made upon my mind while gazing from a high eminence on the surrounding landscape one evening as the sun was gently gliding behind the western mountain and casting its gigantic shadows accross [sic] the vale were such as time can never efface from my memory but as I am neither Poet Painter or Romance writer I must content myself to be what I am a humble journalist and leave this beautiful Vale in Obscurity until visited by some more skillful admirer of the beauties of nature.[48]

Russell's struggle to express his feelings resulted in turgid prose, but it testified to the presence, even in an unaffected backwoodsman, of the capacity to recognize aesthetic qualities in wilderness.

Romanticism softened the opinions of those for whom the necessity of battling wild country might otherwise have produced unmitigated hostility. Slogging through the Everglades in pursuit of Seminole Indians in the late 1830s, an army surgeon temporarily set aside his discomfort and "gazed with a mingled emotion of delight and awe" at "the wild romance of nature." John C. Fremont's journal of an 1842 trip to Wyoming's Wind River Mountains is replete with references to "grand," "magnificent," and "romantic" scenery. Even when the Fremont party upset in a rapids on the Platte River and lost their equipment, he could report that "the scenery was extremely picturesque, and notwithstanding our forlorn condition, we were frequently obliged to stop and admire it."[49]

For some pioneers the opportunity wilderness afforded for freedom and adventure made it appealing. At the conclusion of a series

48. Russell, *Journal of a Trapper*, ed. Aubrey L. Haines (Portland, Ore., 1955), p. 46. This edition was published from the original manuscript in the William Robertson Coe collection at Yale University. Haines has written a biographical sketch of Russell in *The Mountain Men and the Fur Trade of the Far West*, ed. LeRoy R. Hafen (2 vols. Glendale, Cal., 1965), 2, 305–16.

49. Jacob Rhett Motte, *Journey into Wilderness: An Army Surgeon's Account of Life in Camp and Field during the Creek and Seminole Wars*, 1836–1838, ed. James F. Sunderland (Gainesville, Fla., 1953), p. 192; Fremont, *Narrative of the Exploring Expedition to the Rocky Mountains in the Year 1842* (New York, 1846), pp. 40, 42, 50.

of explorations in the Rocky Mountains in the 1830s, Benjamin L. E. Bonneville observed that returning to civilization displeased "those of us whose whole lives had been spent in the stirring excitement and perpetual watchfulness of adventures in the wilderness." He concluded that he would gladly turn from "the splendors and gayeties of the metropolis, and plunge again amidst the hardships and perils of the wilderness."[50] Josiah Gregg agreed. One of the first of the Santa Fe traders, Gregg made his final trip in 1839 and settled down. But he could not tolerate "the even tenor of civilized life" after his "high excitements" in the wilderness. Explaining his attachment to the prairies, Gregg dwelt on the "perfect freedom" of this environment. After such liberty, he found it difficult to live where his "physical and moral freedom are invaded at every turn by the complicated machinery of social institutions." The only solution, Gregg decided, was to return to the wilds.[51]

In spite of such sentiments Romantic enthusiasm for wilderness never seriously challenged the aversion in the pioneer mind. Appreciation, rather, resulted from a momentary relaxation of the dominant antipathy. A surprising number of fur traders, for instance, were acquainted with the noble savage convention and occasionally used Indian virtues as a foil for society's shortcomings, but they did not accept the idea as literal truth. Contact with the red man served to undermine their Romantic hopes.[52] Pioneer response to wild country was also complicated. Edwin Bryant, emigrating to California in 1846, employed the rhetoric of appreciation and repulsion with equal facility. On crossing the Rocky Mountains he declared "it is scarcely possible to imagine a landscape blending more variety, beauty, and sublimity, than is here presented," and later he confessed to having never seen anything in nature "more wild, more rugged, more grand, more romantic, and

50. *The Adventures of Captain Bonneville USA in the Rocky Mountains and the Far West, digested from his Journal by Washington Irving*, ed. Edgeley W. Todd (Norman, Okla., 1961), p. 371. In this instance Irving was quoting directly from Bonneville's manuscript version of his travels.

51. Gregg, *Commerce of the Prairies or the Journal of a Santa Fe Trader* (2 vols. New York, 1845), 2, 156, 158. But for an indication that wilderness adventure sometimes became terrifying, see Gregg's impression of Indians: Chapter 2, p. 28.

52. Lewis O. Saum, *The Fur Trader and the Indian* (Seattle, 1965), pp. 91 ff., 280 ff., and his "The Fur Trader and the Noble Savage," *American Quarterly, 15* (1963), 554–71. Fred A. Crane, "The Noble Savage in America, 1815–1860" (unpublished Ph.D. dissertation, Yale University, 1952) agrees that enthusiasm for noble savages was largely restricted to Eastern literati.

more enchantingly picturesque and beautiful" than the uncivilized West. But Bryant was also deeply distressed at leaving "civilization" behind and trepidatious about the prospect of "a weary journey through a desolate wilderness." When he finally reached California settlements, he gave thanks to God for being able "to sleep once more within the boundaries of civilization."[53]

To Bryant's ambivalence could be added that of many other early nineteenth-century Americans. Opinion was in a state of transition. While appreciation of wild country existed, it was seldom unqualified. Romanticism, including deism and the aesthetics of the wild, had cleared away enough of the old assumptions to permit a favorable attitude toward wilderness without entirely eliminating the instinctive fear and hostility a wilderness condition had produced.

53. Edwin Bryant, *What I Saw in California . . . in the Years 1846, 1847* (New York, 1848), pp. 155–56, 228, 48, 247. A similar ambivalence appears in Samuel Parker, *Journal of an Exploring Tour beyond the Rocky Mountains . . . in the Years 1835, 1836, and 1837* (Ithaca, N.Y., 1838): compare pages 47–48 with page 87 and, in the third edition of 1842, page 146.

CHAPTER 4

The *American* Wilderness

> Though American scenery is destitute of many of those circumstances that give value to the European, still it has features, and glorious ones, unknown to Europe . . . the most distinctive, and perhaps the most impressive, characteristic of American scenery is its wildness.
>
> Thomas Cole, 1836

WHILE Romanticism was creating a climate of opinion in the new American nation in which wilderness could be appreciated, the fact of independence gave rise to a second major source of enthusiasm. It was widely assumed that America's primary task was the justification of its newly won freedom. This entailed more than building a flourishing economy or even a stable government. Creation of a distinctive culture was thought to be the mark of true nationhood. Americans sought something uniquely "American," yet valuable enough to transform embarrassed provincials into proud and confident citizens. Difficulties appeared at once. The nation's short history, weak traditions, and minor literary and artistic achievements seemed negligible compared to those of Europe. But in at least one respect Americans sensed that their country was different: wilderness had no counterpart in the Old World.

Seizing on this distinction and adding to it deistic and Romantic assumptions about the value of wild country, nationalists argued that far from being a liability, wilderness was actually an American asset. Of course, pride continued to stem from the *conquest* of wild country (see Chapter 2), but by the middle decades of the nineteenth century wilderness was recognized as a cultural and moral resource and a basis for national self-esteem.

Immediately after independence nationalists began investigating the significances of nature. At first they ignored wild scenery in preference for specific natural objects of unusual size or character. Thus Philip Freneau, searching in the early 1780s for ways to praise his country, referred to the Mississippi as "this prince of rivers in comparison of whom the *Nile* is but a small rivulet, and the *Danube* a ditch."[1] Thomas Jefferson was most proud of Virginia's Natural Bridge, and of places such as the gorge that the Potomac River cut as it passed through the Allegheny Mountains near the present site of Harper's Ferry, West Virginia. Of the latter he declared in 1784: "this scene is worth a voyage across the Atlantic."[2] America's nature, if not her culture, would command the world's admiration.

Realizing that natural environment was one of the few bases on which a favorable comparison could be made with other nations, Americans were quick to defend nature in their country against the aspersions of Europeans. Jefferson's *Notes on Virginia* was in part a vindication of the New World from charges of French scientists that its natural products were inferior, even runty. He insisted that his country was second to none where nature was concerned and pointed for evidence to the recently exhumed skeleton of a mammoth, contending that its descendants possibly still roamed the interior of the continent.[3] Samuel Williams, a minister with an interest in natural history, argued similarly in his 1794 history of Vermont. "Instead of finding nature but weak and feeble in America," he concluded, "her animals appear to be marked with an energy and a magnitude superior to what is found in Europe."[4]

Americans traveling in the Old World resorted to similar tactics to vindicate their country. In the summer of 1784 Abigail Adams joined her husband, who was serving as his country's representative in Paris. The following year the Adamses moved to London. In spite of her patriotism, the glamor and sophistication of Europe awed Mrs. Adams. Almost desperately she sought ways to reconfirm her faith in America. Nature offered a possibility, which she explored in a letter dated November 21, 1786, to a friend in Massachusetts. "I will not dispute," she remarked, "what every person must assent to; that [in Europe] the fine arts, manufactures, and agriculture have arrived at a greater degree of maturity and perfec-

1. *Prose of Freneau,* ed. Marsh, p. 228.

2. Jefferson, *Notes on the State of Virginia* (New York, 1964), p. 17.

3. Ibid., pp. 37ff.

4. Williams, *The Natural and Civil History of Vermont* (2d rev. ed. 2 vols. Burlington, Vt., 1809), *1*, 159. For a secondary discussion of this international scientific debate see Ralph N. Miller, "American Nationalism as a Theory of Nature," *William and Mary Quarterly, 12* (1955), 74–95.

tion." But in some respects she felt the New World had the edge: "do you know that European birds have not half the melody of ours? Nor is their fruit half so sweet, nor their flowers half so fragrant, nor their manners half so pure, nor their people half so virtuous." Still Abigail Adams was only half convinced, and she warned her correspondent to "keep this to yourself, or I shall be thought more than half deficient in understanding and taste."[5]

Such lack of confidence in nature as the ground for nationalism stemmed in part from the realization of Americans that, after all, other countries had impressive birds, fruit, and flowers too. In spite of Freneau, the Danube was not a ditch, nor was there anything wrong with the size or vigor of European animals. And, impressive scenery existed in the Old World to match the views Jefferson extolled. Clearly "nature" was not enough; an attribute unique to nature in the New World had to be found. The search led to the wilderness. In the early nineteenth century American nationalists began to understand that it was in the *wildness* of its nature that their country was unmatched. While other nations might have an occasional wild peak or patch of heath, there was no equivalent of a wild continent. And if, as many suspected, wilderness was the medium through which God spoke most clearly, then America had a distinct moral advantage over Europe, where centuries of civilization had deposited a layer of artificiality over His works. The same logic worked to convince Americans that because of the aesthetic and inspirational qualities of wilderness they were destined for artistic and literary excellence.[6]

After Alexander Wilson's 1804 poem "The Foresters," American letters and oratory contained numerous predictions, sometimes confident, sometimes anxious, that wilderness would inspire a great

5. Philip Rahv, ed., *Discovery of Europe: The Story of American Experience in the Old World* (Garden City, N.Y., 1960), p. 52. The same point is brought out by a Kentuckian in a letter to England: Gilbert Imlay, *A Topographical Description of the Western Territory of North America* (London, 1792), pp. 39–40.

6. In this analysis and that which follows I have drawn on Merle Curti, *The Roots of American Loyalty* (New York, 1946), pp. 30–64; Perry Miller, "Nature and the National Ego" in *Errand into the Wilderness* (Cambridge, Mass., 1956), pp. 204–16; Sanford, *Quest for Paradise*, especially pp. 135–54; and Sanford's "The Concept of the Sublime in the Works of Cole and Bryant," *American Literature, 28* (1957), 434–48. Especially important for understanding the American conception of the moral influence of nature is Neil Harris, *The Artist in American Society: The Formative Years, 1790–1860* (New York, 1966), Chs. 7 and 8.

culture.[7] Wilson, a Scottish-born ornithologist, pointed out that if "bare bleak heathes and brooks of half a mile can rouse the thousand bards of Britain's Isle," then America's "boundless woods" should stimulate even more distinguished verse. However, Wilson lamented, the "wild grandeur" of the New World was yet unsung.[8] Many felt that this was only a matter of time. After all, declaimed Daniel Bryan, one need only stand on "the wildest cliffs of Allegany" in order to begin "warbling . . . the sweetest raptures of Inspiration."[9]

De Witt Clinton agreed that his country could be optimistic about its cultural prospects. After reviewing the artistic achievements of other nations in an address before the American Academy of Art, he asked rhetorically: "and can there be a country in the world better calculated than ours to exercise and to exhalt the imagination—to call into activity the creative powers of the mind, and to afford just views of the beautiful, the wonderful, and the sublime?" Clinton went on, blending Romanticism and nationalism, to argue that "here Nature has conducted her operations on a magnificent scale." America had mountains, lakes, rivers, waterfalls, and "boundless forests" unequalled in all the world. "The wild, romantic, and awful scenery," he concluded, "is calculated to produce a correspondent impression in the imagination—to elevate all the faculties of the mind, and to exhalt all the feelings of the heart." Similar statements were legion. Anyone venturing to suggest that "a man will not necessarily be a great poet because he lives near a great mountain" was shouted down as disloyal to his country.[10]

7. On the pressure Americans felt to find a distinctive national character and culture and the role of nature in this process, see Benjamin T. Spencer, *The Quest for Nationality: An American Literary Campaign* (Syracuse, N.Y., 1957), pp. 25 ff.; Hans Kohn, *American Nationalism* (New York, 1957), pp. 41 ff.; Wilson O. Clough, *The Necessary Earth: Nature and Solitude in American Literature* (Austin, Texas, 1964), pp. 58–74; and John C. McCloskey, "The Campaign of Periodicals After the War of 1812 for a National American Literature," *Publications of the Modern Language Association of America*, 50 (1935), 262–73.

8. Wilson, "The Foresters" (West Chester, Pa., 1838), p. 6. Robert Cantwell's *Alexander Wilson: Naturalist and Pioneer* (Philadelphia, 1961), pp. 127–31, discusses the circumstances of the poem.

9. Bryan, *The Mountain Muse* (Harrisonburg, Va., 1813), [p. 9].

10. Clinton in Thomas S. Cummings, *Historic Annals of the National Academy of Design* (Philadelphia, 1865), p. 12; as quoted from Henry Wadsworth Longfellow's *Kavanagh* in Jones, *O Strange New World*, p. 347. Jones, pp. 346–89, contains many insights into the use of nature as a basis for American nationalism.

One of the manifestations of the emphasis on America's wild landscape was a series of illustrated "scenery" albums reflecting the nationalism of nature. In 1820 plans were made for a volume entitled *Picturesque Views of the American Scene* that would show "our lofty mountains . . . the unexampled magnitude of our cataracts, the wild grandeur of our western forests . . . unsurpassed by any of the boasted scenery of other countries."[11] Three issues appeared, and as Romantic interest in nature increased in the subsequent decades, there were numerous similar ventures. Nathaniel P. Willis' text for *American Scenery* characteristically asserted that "Nature has wrought with a bolder hand in America." According to Willis, the American wilderness presented "a lavish and large-featured sublimity . . . quite dissimilar to the picturesque of all other countries."[12] A few years later came *The Home Book of the Picturesque* with a lead essay "Scenery and Mind." Its author, Elias Lyman Magoon, relied heavily on the assumption that nature was a source of revelation: in his final paragraphs he thanked God "that there are yet wild spots and wildernesses left . . . whence thought may take the wildest range." Such places, Magoon believed, "have ever developed the strongest patriotism, intensest energy, and most valuable letters of the world."[13] Another instance of this variety of publishing endeavor was *The Scenery of the United States Illustrated.* As usual there was an introductory essay defending the American landscape as being "as wild, romantic, and lovely as can be seen in any other part of the world. And, certainly, our forests," exulted its author, "fresh as it were, from the hands of the Creator, are, beyond dispute, incomparable."[14]

Confident trumpeting obscured the anxiety many Americans felt about the relation of their country to Europe.[15] In spite of their hopes and official pronouncements, nationalists could but covertly regard the Old World as the mecca of all that was tasteful, refined, and creative. Theirs was the dilemma of provincials who desired

11. As quoted in Frank Weitenkampf, "Early American Landscape Prints," *Art Quarterly, 8* (1945), 61.

12. Willis, *American Scenery* (2 vols. London, 1840), *1*, v. William Bartlett did the lavish engravings for the book, popularly known as "Bartlett's Views."

13. Magoon, *The Home Book of the Picturesque* (New York, 1852), pp. 37–38.

14. Anonymous, *The Scenery of the United States Illustrated* (New York, 1855), p. 1.

15. Cushing Strout, *The American Image of the Old World* (New York, 1963), especially pp. 62–85, has explored this tension in detail.

cultural independence and yet were unable to tear their eyes from the European sun or to resist going abroad for training and inspiration. It was especially difficult to ignore the Old World's long history and rich accumulation of custom and tradition which stood in such sharp contrast to America's comparative rawness. No one could deny that Europe was enjoying a brilliant artistic renaissance based on two thousand years of cultural development at the same time that the New World was discovered.

Washington Irving gave this provincial dilemma classic expression. He was already a well-known literary figure and the subject of considerable American pride when in 1815 he sailed to the Old World. In England Irving felt the pull of conflicting emotions, and he expressed them in one portion of his *Sketch Book* (1819–20). On the credit side of "my own country," Irving itemized the "charms of nature" including "her valleys, teeming with wild fertility . . . her boundless plains . . . [and] her trackless forests." He concluded: "no, never, need an American look beyond his own country for the sublime and beautiful of natural scenery." But Europe had much to recommend it, in Irving's estimation: qualities that depended on the absence of the same wildness that glorified America. He was especially impressed with "the accumulated treasures of age"; the chronicle of man's past achievements that the landscape reflected. "I longed to wander," Irving declared, "over the scenes of renowned achievement—to tread, as it were, in the footsteps of antiquity—to loiter about the ruined castle—to meditate on the falling tower—to escape, in short, from the commonplace reality of the present, and lose myself among the shadowy grandeurs of the past."[16] The Romantic temperament that attracted him to wilderness also made Europe's history appealing.

For seventeen years Irving remained overseas, and his countrymen could not suppress the idea that he had turned his back on America. In fact, however, Irving's patriotism persisted and, in a corner of his mind, an urge for wilderness remained. In 1832, just before sailing for the United States, he wrote to his brother of his desire to see the American West "while still in a state of pristine

16. *The Sketch-Book,* Irving's Works, Geoffrey Crayon edition (27 vols. New York, 1880), 2, 16–17. Irving's biography and further analysis of his relationship to Europe can be found in William L. Hedges, *Washington Irving: An American Study, 1802–1832* (Baltimore, 1965) and George S. Hellman, *Washington Irving Esquire: Ambassador at Large from the New World to the Old* (New York, 1925).

wildness, and behold herds of buffaloes scouring the native prairies." After landing in New York, Irving joined a party of commissioners to Indians in the Kansas and Oklahoma territories. This contact with the wilderness had special meaning for a man recently returned from Europe. Several weeks of camping convinced him that nothing could be more beneficial to young men than the "wild wood life . . . of a magnificent wilderness." He added: "we send our youth abroad to grow luxurious and effeminate in Europe; it appears to me, that a previous tour on the prairies would be more likely to produce that manliness, simplicity, and self-dependence most in unison with our political institutions."[17] If Irving's purpose in such a statement was to vindicate himself from the stigma of a long, voluntary stay in Europe, as critics at the time alleged, the contrast of Old World and New on the basis of wildness was effective. Still, Irving disdained his own advice and in 1842 recrossed the ocean for four more years. Ambivalence rather than hypocrisy explains his conduct. Like many of his contemporaries, Irving's loyalties were divided. The civilized refinement of the Old World and the wildness of the New were both magnetic.

The antiquity of Europe that attracted Washington Irving was, of course, unanswerable, yet it occurred to other writers that its implication might be reversed. By the 1830s some intellectual patriots were seizing on America's very lack of history—its wilderness condition—as an answer to Europe's claims and their own doubts. On his tour of the West in 1833, for instance, Charles Fenno Hoffman paused to confess that he venerated "a hoary oak" more than "a mouldering column." These symbols of New World and Old suggested a more emotional contrast:

> What are the temples which Roman robbers have reared,—what are the towers in which feudal oppression has fortified itself,—what are the blood-stained associations of the one, or the despotic superstitions of the other, to the deep forests which the eye of God has alone pervaded, and where Nature, in her unviolated sanctuary, has for ages laid her fruits and flowers on His altar! What is the echo of roofs that a few centuries since rung with barbaric revels, or of aisles that pealed the anthems of painted pomp, to the silence that has reigned

17. Irving, *A Tour of the Prairies*, ed. John Francis McDermott (Norman, Okla., 1956), p. xvii, 55. The original edition was 1835.

in these dim groves since the first fiat of Creation was spoken.[18]

Employing wilderness, Hoffman invested America with a history. Moreover, in comparing robbers, blood, despotism, and barbarity with sanctuaries and altars, he left no doubt about his conviction that the American heritage was more innocent and moral. Unable to duplicate Europe's castles and cathedrals, Hoffman dispensed with them by substituting wilderness.

After Irving and Hoffman, travelers with Romantic tastes frequently expressed the idea that America's wilderness constituted an advantage over other countries. A few individuals like Joel T. Headley had actually seen the Alps and were willing to pronounce the Adirondacks superior. Others less well informed were still satisfied that "the Alps, so celebrated in history and by all travellers and admirers of mountain landscape, cannot . . . present a scenery more wild, more rugged, more grand, more romantic, and more enchantingly picturesque and beautiful, than that which surrounds [Lake Tahoe]." Sometimes American defense became impassioned: "a fig for your Italian scenery!" shouted one patriot, "this is the country where nature reigns in her virgin beauty . . . this is the land to study nature in all her luxuriant charms . . . to feel your soul expand under the mighty influences of nature in her primitive beauty and strength!"[19] Again wilderness was the nationalists' trump.

So much effort in the early nineteenth century went into calling for and worrying about a national style that there was little actual progress toward achieving one. Gradually, however, American letters and art acquired some distinction and distinctiveness. New-World themes were essential, and wilderness fulfilled this requirement. Romantics invested it with value while nationalists proclaimed its uniqueness. Creative minds soon found uses for wilderness in poetry, fiction, and painting.

William Cullen Bryant was one of the first major American writers to turn to wilderness. In his precocious poem, "Thana-

18. Hoffman, *Winter in the West,* pp. 193–94. For an indication of the way such ideas permeated popular culture see Ruth Miller Elsen, *Guardians of Tradition: American Schoolbooks of the Nineteenth Century* (Lincoln, Neb., 1964), pp. 35–40.

19. Headley, *Adirondack,* pp. iv, 146; Edwin Bryant, *What I Saw in California,* p. 228; Lanman, *Summer in the Wilderness,* p. 171.

topsis" (1811), he referred to "the continuous woods where rolls the Oregon." Four years later Bryant revealed his full acceptance of the Romantic mood when he advised anyone who had seen enough of "sorrows, crimes, and cares" of civilized life to "enter this wild wood and view the haunts of Nature." He also grasped the moral and religious significance of wild country: "A Forest Hymn" (1825) began with the idea that "the groves were God's first temples" and Bryant professed his own intention of retiring to "the woody wilderness" for reassurance and worship. Proud that his country had such places, Bryant declared in a poem celebrating Monument Mountain in the Berkshires that "thou who wouldst see the lovely and the wild mingled in harmony on Nature's face, ascend our rocky mountains." In 1833 "The Prairies" sounded a paean to the isolation and vastness of the Great Plains. Bryant concluded with an expression of the delight that he felt in being "in the wilderness alone."[20] Forty years later he was no less enthusiastic. In 1872 he edited and wrote the introduction for *Picturesque America,* a scenery album, and took the opportunity to declare that "we have some of the wildest and most beautiful scenery in the world." Why travel to Switzerland, Bryant wondered, when there was an abundance of wild mountains in the American West.[21]

Novelists also responded. In James Kirke Paulding's *The Backwoodsman* of 1818, the protagonist, a "hardy swain," left the Hudson Valley to roam "in western wilds." The story deliberately alerted American writers to the literary potential of the frontier. Looking west, rather than to Europe, Pauling thought, would be "the means of attaining to novelty of subject."[22] Initially James Fenimore Cooper disregarded this advice. His first novel, *Precaution,* (1820) was a patent imitation of the English manners-and-mores genre. *The Spy,* of the following year, used the American Revolution as a setting and was well received. But with *The Pio-*

20. The quotations are from *The Poetical Works of William Cullen Bryant,* ed. Parke Godwin (2 vols. New York, 1883), *1,* 19, 23, 102, 133, 228–32. In the light of the debate on the quality of nature in the New World compared to Europe's see Ralph N. Miller, "Nationalism in Bryant's 'The Prairies,'" *American Literature, 21* (1949), 227–32.

21. Bryant, ed., *Picturesque America* (2 vols. New York, 1872), *1,* iii. Bryant's relation to nature is elaborated upon in Norman Foerster, *Nature in American Literature* (New York, 1923), pp. 1–19, and Donald A. Ringe, "Kindred Spirits: Bryant and Cole," *American Quarterly, 6* (1954), 233–44. The most recent biography is Albert F. McLean, Jr., *William Cullen Bryant* (New York, 1964), see especially pp. 39–64.

22. Paulding, *The Backwoodsman* (Philadelphia, 1818), pp. 3, 7.

neers (1823) Cooper became a national literary hero. In this first native best-seller and the four other highly popular Leatherstocking tales that followed in the next eighteen years,[23] he discovered the literary possibilities of wilderness. Wild forests and plains, as Cooper both knew and imagined them, dominate the action and determine the plots of these novels. The Leatherstocking stories and the other early "backwoods" novels of Robert Montgomery Byrd, Timothy Flint, and William Gilmore Simms were preeminently American fiction because they bore the stamp of the unique in the American environment.

From the standpoint of the nascent American appreciation of wilderness, it was significant that although Cooper was concerned with the advance of civilization into the west, he did not portray wild country as a loathsome obstacle to be conquered and destroyed. Instead Cooper took great pains to show that wilderness had value as a moral influence, a source of beauty, and a place of exciting adventure. Natty Bumppo, or Leatherstocking, became the mouthpiece for the standard Romantic conventions regarding the sublimity and holiness of wild nature. Indeed Natty is his own best evidence, since lifelong exposure to the woods has given him an innate goodness and moral sense. His nobility and that of many of Cooper's savages caused them to cringe before the evils of settlers and settlements. In *The Pioneers* Natty flees from the town to the solitude of the forest and reports that no city dweller can "know how often the hand of God is seen in the wilderness." He also slaps at Europe, contending in *The Prairie* (1827) that in contrast to the virgin New World the Old should really be called "a *worn* out, and an *abused,* and a *sacrilegious* world." Both Natty and Cooper believed in "the honesty of the woods!"[24]

Cooper indirectly dignified wilderness by deprecating those insensitive to its ethical and aesthetic values. Although set on the frontier, his Leatherstocking novels held no brief for exploitation. Pioneers who wastefully slash the forest and its creatures, such as Billy Kirby in *The Pioneers,* the family of Ishmael Bush in *The Prairie,* and Hurry Harry in *The Deerslayer* (1841) occupied the

23. James D. Hart, *The Popular Book: A History of America's Literary Taste* (Berkeley, Cal., 1961), pp. 80–82.

24. Cooper, *The Pioneers,* Mohawk edition (New York, c. 1912), p. 302; Cooper, *The Prairies,* Rinehart edition (New York, 1950), pp. 246, 275. Cooper's idea of noble savagery is discussed in Fred A. Crane, "The Noble Savage in America, 1815–60" (unpublished Ph.D. dissertation, Yale University, 1952), Ch. 5.

lowest positions in Cooper's elaborate social scale. Leatherstocking, on the other hand, was the ideal pioneer because he honored the wilderness and used it respectfully. Cooper put his condemnation of the exploiter into Leatherstocking's mouth: "they scourge the very 'arth with their axes. Such hills and hunting grounds as I have seen stripped of the gifts of the Lord, without remorse or shame!" Natty was near the end of his trail at this point. He had retreated beyond the Mississippi, but the tide of settlement was not far behind. On his deathbed he summarized his reaction: "how much has the beauty of the wilderness been deformed in two short lives![25]

While Cooper could appreciate the strength of Natty's position, his own attitude was more complex. Attraction to wilderness and sadness at its disappearance was only a part of his thinking. Cooper knew that civilization also had its claims and that ultimately they must prevail. The elimination of wilderness was tragic, but it was a necessary tragedy; civilization was the greater good. To be sure, in its crude, frontier stage civilized society might contain persons of much less worth than Leatherstocking and even many Indians, but to Cooper this was only semi-civilization. In time he knew that refined gentlemen and ladies would evolve, people such as Captain Middleton and Inez de Certavallos of *The Prairie,* Judge Marmaduke Temple and Oliver Effingham of *The Pioneers,* and, one suspects, Cooper himself. This was the elite whose sense of law and beauty lifted man above the beast. Even Natty Bumppo, for all his virtues, lacked the social status to fraternize on such levels. To have them, Cooper made clear, was worth the price of losing wilderness.[26] He had reached the pioneers' conclusion without using the pioneers' rationale, without condemning wilderness. For Cooper it was not a case of good versus evil, light fighting darkness, but of two kinds of good with the greater prevailing. The Leatherstocking novels gave Cooper's countrymen reason to feel both proud and ashamed at conquering wilderness.

25. Cooper, *Prairie,* pp. 80, 290.

26. The outlines of this interpretation as it concerns the Indian and the frontiersman have been drawn in Pearce, *Savages of America,* pp. 200–12; Smith, *Virgin Land,* pp. 59–70, 220–24; Moore, *Frontier Mind,* pp. 159 ff.; and Donald A. Ringe, *James Fenimore Cooper* (New York, 1962). Two excellent shorter pieces are Roy Harvey Pearce, "The Leatherstocking Tales Re-examined," *South Atlantic Quarterly, 46* (1947), 524–36, and Henry Nash Smith's "Introduction" to Cooper's *The Prairie,* Rinehart edition (New York, 1950), pp. v–xx. Lillian Fischer, "Social Criticism in Cooper's Leatherstocking Tales: The Meaning of the Forest" (unpublished Ph.D. dissertation, Yale University, 1957) is less useful.

In 1823, the year of Cooper's *Pioneers,* a young man gave up a shaky career as a portrait painter in frontier Ohio and turned his considerable talents to depicting, as he put it, "the wild and great features of nature: mountainous forests that know not man."[27] Over the next several decades, Thomas Cole attracted wide attention as a celebrant of the American wilderness. His landscapes added art to poetry and fiction as a medium through which his countrymen could be instructed in the glories of the native landscape. But as with Cooper, Cole's love of wilderness was at times clouded over with doubts and offset by an antipodal attraction to civilization. Cole the Romantic enthusiast, pantheist, and inspirer of the Hudson River School was not the whole man. Fortunately, he wrote as well as painted, and his letters, journals, and essays reveal a mind engaged in a dialogue with itself about the advantages and limitations of America's wilderness.

Cole immigrated to the United States from England in 1818 as a youth of seventeen and settled with his family in the upper Ohio Valley. The beauty he perceived in the wild forests of that region moved him deeply and determined his choice of career. With hopes of translating his feelings into pictures, Cole went to New York in 1825 and quickly discovered the Catskill Mountains. Three scenes, hesitatingly exhibited in a gallery, excited the artistic community and encouraged Cole to pursue his art. In the next four years he ranged, note and sketch books in hand, through the wildest regions he could find. Wilderness had a religious as well as an aesthetic significance for him, and he exulted with Romantic abandon in what he saw. The outcome of this Catskill period were paintings such as "Mountain Sunrise," "Landscape with Tree Trunks," and "View Near Ticonderoga," dramatic compositions filled with precipitous cliffs, dark gorges, and surging storm clouds.[28] These and "North-

27. As quoted in James Thomas Flexner, *That Wilder Image: The Painting of America's Native School from Thomas Cole to Winslow Homer* (Boston, 1962), p. 39. Compare Cole's statement in Louis Legrand Noble, *The Life and Works of Thomas Cole,* ed. Elliott S. Vesell (Cambridge, Mass., 1964), p. 62. Noble's account, originally published in 1853, is the best biographical notice.

28. These pictures are reproduced and Cole's work discussed in Frederick A. Sweet, *The Hudson River School and the Early American Landscape Tradition* (New York, 1945), pp. 55–69. Also pertinent are Wolfgang Born, *American Landscape Painting* (New Haven, 1948), pp. 24 ff.; Walter L. Nathan, "Thomas Cole and the Romantic Landscape" in *Romanticism in America,* ed. George Boas (New York, 1961), pp. 24–62; and Oliver W. Larkin, *Art and Life in America* (rev. ed. New York, 1960), pp. 200 ff. Two dissertations supplement the published material: Kenneth James

West Bay, Lake Winnepesaukee, N.H." broke with landscape painting tradition by either omitting any sign of man and his works or reducing the human figures to ant-like proportions. Wilderness dominated the canvas, and Cooper and Bryant joined in the applause of Cole as a contributor to the rising vogue of wild nature and to American nationalism. According to a fellow artist, Cole "studied to embody whatever was characteristic of the singular grandeur and wildness of mountain, lake, and forest, in the American wilderness."[29]

Although Cole wrote in the late 1820s that "pleasures spring like flowers within the bosom of the wilderness" and declared that he always returned from the mountains to the city "with a presentiment of evil," at times he dreaded the wilds. The line between the sublime's delightful horror and genuine terror was thin. Once in the Catskills, Cole experienced a violent thunderstorm. At first, according to his journal, he gave himself up to the wildness of the elements and he pronounced the situation "romantic." But as the fury increased, ecstasy changed to apprehension. When the storm departed, Cole was relieved to see "in a neighbouring dell, the blue smoke curling up quietly from a cottage chimney."[30] In the fall of 1828 the artist journeyed to the White Mountains and recognized conflicting emotions in the presence of wilderness. In his journal he generalized: "man may seek such scenes and find pleasure in the discovery, but there is a mysterious fear [that] comes over him and hurries him away. The sublime features of nature are too severe for a lone man to look upon and be happy."[31] A later, unpublished poem, "The Spirits of the Wilderness," reiterated the point that wilderness alone could not cheer and revive; love and friendship were necessary too.[32] The impulse to solitude and wildness and

---

LaBudde, "The Mind of Thomas Cole" (University of Minnesota, 1954), and Barbara H. Deutsch, "Cole and Durand: Criticism and Patronage, A Study of American Taste in Landscape, 1825–1865" (Harvard University, 1957).

29. Daniel Huntington as quoted in Noble, *Cole,* pp. 56–57. Compare the similar tribute from William Cullen Bryant: *A Funeral Oration Occasioned by the Death of Thomas Cole* (New York, 1848), p. 14. On the similarities of the two men, which included a love of wilderness, see Ringe, "Kindred Spirits," 233–44. James A. Beard, "Cooper and His Artistic Contemporaries," *New York History, 35* (1954), 480–495, discusses the friendship and mutual artistic debt of Cole and Cooper.

30. Noble, pp. 40, 43–45.

31. As quoted in Flexner, *That Wilder Image,* p. 40. Compare Noble, p. 67.

32. Thomas Cole Collection, New York State Library, Albany, N.Y. Box 6, Folder 2.

the attractiveness of society and civilization pulled Cole and his art in different directions.

The same disturbing conflicts that Cole had felt in the Catskills and White Mountains reappeared on a large scale in his relation to Europe. By 1829 he had acquired the patronage to finance a trip abroad, but his American admirers, and probably Cole himself, had doubts. Would not exposure to the Old World lure him away from the American wilderness as a subject for art? His friend, Bryant, certainly recognized the danger, and in 1829 wrote "To Cole, the Painter, Departing for Europe." Its import was that throughout his travels Cole must strive to "keep that earlier, wilder image bright."[33]

Cole remained overseas, principally in London, Paris, and Florence, three years, and, as Bryant suspected, the grandeur of Europe was not lost upon him. Although he did not hesitate to comment critically on contemporary painters, the Old Masters were above reproach. Like Washington Irving, Cole was especially sensitive to the thick crust that history and tradition had deposited on European scenery. "Although American scenery is often so fine," he asserted, "we feel the want of associations such as cling to scenes in the old world. Simple nature is not quite sufficient. We want human interest, incident and action to render the effect of landscape complete." Yet Cole struggled, almost desperately, to resist this train of thought. In 1832 he wrote from Florence that the canvas he was sending home would cause its viewers to "give me credit for not having forgotten those sublime scenes of the wilderness . . . scenes whose peculiar grandeur has no counterpart in this section of Europe."[34] At the same time, however, he was also painting castles, and aqueducts, and ruined temples.

Back in America, Cole continued to explore these tensions. He organized his thoughts in an "Essay on American Scenery" read on May 16, 1835, before the National Academy of Design. Drawing on his observations abroad, Cole reported that "in civilized Europe the primitive features of scenery have long since been destroyed or modified . . . crags that could not be removed have been crowned with towers, and the rudest valley tamed by the plough." Everywhere the landscape bespoke man's imprint and his "heroic deeds." "Time and genius," said Cole, "have suspended an imperishable halo" over Old World scenes. This was "glorious," but Cole quickly

33. *Works of Bryant, 1,* 219.

34. Noble, p. 219; Cole to J. L. Morton, Jan. 31, 1832 in Noble, pp. 99–100.

added that Americans need not feel inferior. While lacking a storied past, "American scenery . . . has features, and glorious ones, unknown to Europe. The most distinctive, and perhaps the most impressive, characteristic of American scenery is its wildness." For one thing, this meant that in the native landscape the associations were not of man but of "God the creator." The wilderness exhibited His "undefiled works, and the mind is cast into the contemplation of eternal things."[35] Moreover, Cole wrote a few weeks later, in America "all nature . . . is new to art [not] . . . worn by the daily pencils of hundreds; but primeval forests, virgin lakes and water falls."[36]

As a nationalist Cole vindicated wilderness, but as the awed provincial he had another opinion. In the same address in which he had rejoiced in his country's lack of ploughed fields and mountain castles, he proudly predicted a future strikingly similar to Europe's: "where the wolf roams, the plough shall glisten; on the gray crag shall rise the temple and tower—mighty deeds shall be done in the new pathless wilderness." In a similar vein Cole anticipated the time when the wild shores of the Hudson River would be covered with "temple, and tower, and dome, in every variety of picturesqueness and magnificence."[37] After renouncing the Rhine, Cole recreated it on the Hudson.

Cole, as Cooper, could not completely affirm the American wilderness. As Bryant anticipated, Europe *had* dimmed "that earlier, wilder image." More precisely, the European experience led Cole to idealize a combination of the wild and the civilized. "The Oxbow," a view of the Connecticut River valley from Mt. Holyoke painted in 1836, serves as an example. The left half of the picture is a rugged cliff with the shattered tree trunks and dark, violent clouds that Cole used to represent wilderness. On the right, along the far side of the river, is a vista of rural bliss. Manicured fields and neat groves separate well-kept homes while a warm sun bathes the countryside in a pleasant light. Cole's divided canvas implied the idea Henry David Thoreau accepted as axiomatic: man's optimum environment is a blend of wildness and civilization. In his five-panel "The Course of Empire," painted in 1836, Cole made his

35. Cole, "Essay on American Scenery," *American Monthly Magazine, 1* (1836), 4–5.

36. Noble, p. 148.

37. Cole, "Essay on American Scenery," 9, 12.

point another way. Here, in sequence, we see a wilderness giving way to a pastoral society and then to a glorious civilization. But in the fourth painting new savages sack the great city, and in the fifth wilderness conditions are gradually returning as the cycle is completed. Vitality, Cole implied, was sapped in proportion to the distance a society departed from its wild roots. The intent was clear: Cole hoped to instruct his countrymen in the importance of appreciating their wilderness heritage.

Thomas Cole died prematurely in 1848, but by then American landscape painting was fully prepared to embrace the American wilderness. In 1855 Ashur B. Durand, a pioneer with Cole in the Hudson River School, called forthrightly for a wilderness art. "Go not abroad then in search of material for the exercise of your pencil," he wrote in the *Crayon,* "while the virgin charms of our native land have claims on your deepest affections." America's "untrodden wilds," Durand continued, "yet spared from the pollutions of civilization, afford a guarantee for a reputation of originality that you may elsewhere long seek and find not."[38] As his contribution Durand had already painted "Kindred Spirits" as a memorial to Cole. It showed the painter and William Cullen Bryant discussing the beauties of a wild mountain gorge.

In the art of Frederic E. Church, a student of Cole, the American wilderness received triumphant portrayal. The turning point in Church's development as an artist was an 1856 camping trip of eight days into the Mt. Katahdin region of northern Maine. The immediate result was "Sunset," a portrayal of a Maine lake and surrounding mountains. In the foreground a crude road and a few sheep are the only reminders of civilization. Four years later Church painted the magnificent "Twilight in the Wilderness" which in many ways was a realization of the promise of the American setting as an inspiration to art. All traces of the pastoral have vanished as the viewer looks from a spruce-covered cliff, over a river, to Katahdin-like mountains in the distance. The scene is suffused with the light of a brilliant sunset suggestive of the apocalyptical expectations a virgin continent aroused.[39]

38. Durand, "Letters on Landscape Painting: Letter II," *Crayon, 1* (1855), 34–35. On Durand see Barbara H. Deutsch, "Cole and Durand: Criticism and Patronage, A Study of American Taste in Landscape, 1825–1865" (unpublished Ph.D. dissertation, Harvard University, 1957) and Frederick A. Sweet, "Ashur B. Durand, Pioneer American Landscape Painter," *Art Quarterly, 8* (1945), 141–60.

39. David C. Huntington's *The Landscapes of Frederic Edwin Church* (New York, 1966), pp. 71–83, discusses his wilderness art and reproduces the paintings in question.

In the latter half of the nineteenth century a second generation of landscapists took their palettes and their national pride across the Mississippi; in the wilderness of the Far West they found subjects for both. Within a few years of his first visit to the Rocky Mountains in 1858, Albert Bierstadt was depicting the peaks and canyons of that region on colossal canvases. Responding to public acclaim, Bierstadt in time painted all the famous early showplaces: Yosemite, Yellowstone, and the Grand Canyon. His exaggerated, dramatic style provoked some criticism, but represented a sincere attempt to communicate his intense excitement in the western landscape.

Thomas Moran rivaled Bierstadt as a painter of the wilderness. He too used huge canvases and dazzling colors in an effort to express his emotions. A genuine explorer, Moran participated in the 1871 Yellowstone expedition of Ferdinand V. Hayden (see Chapter 7), and his art assisted the campaign for the establishment of the national park. Subsequently, Moran ranged throughout the West, painting Wyoming's Teton Range (Mt. Moran bears his name), California's Sierra, and the Mountain of the Holy Cross in Colorado. When Congress in 1874 appropriated $10,000 for one of Moran's paintings of the Grand Canyon to hang in the Senate Lobby, the American wilderness received official endorsement as a subject for national pride. On some of his western trips Moran's companion was William H. Jackson, a pioneer landscape photographer, whose artistic medium soon became a potent new force in directing American attention to wilderness as a source of nationalism.[40]

40. Sweet, *Hudson River School,* pp. 96–112; Flexner, *That Wilder Image,* pp. 293–302; John C. Ewers, *Artists of the Old West* (New York, 1965), pp. 174–94. For Moran, Thurman Wilkins' *Thomas Moran: Artist of the Mountains* (Norman, Okla., 1966) is definitive. The William Henry Jackson Papers, State Historical Society of Colorado, Denver, and his autobiography *Time Exposure* (New York, 1940), shed light on the early history of wilderness photography while Ansel Adams' "The Artist and the Ideals of Wilderness" in *Wilderness: America's Living Heritage,* ed. David Brower (San Francisco, 1961), pp. 49–59, is a recent interpretation of the camera's role by a photographer whose work has helped create a new genre.

CHAPTER 5

Henry David Thoreau: Philosopher

From the forest and wilderness come the tonics and barks which brace mankind.

Henry David Thoreau, 1851

ON APRIL 23, 1851 Henry David Thoreau, slight and stooped, ascended the lecture platform before the Concord Lyceum. "I wish," he began, "to speak a word for Nature, for absolute freedom and wildness." Thoreau promised his statement would be extreme in an effort to answer the numerous champions of civilization. "Let me live where I will," he declared, "on this side is the city, on that the wilderness, and ever I am leaving the city more and more, and withdrawing into the wilderness." Near the end of the address, he concentrated his message in eight words: "in Wildness is the preservation of the World."[1]

Americans had not heard the like before. Previous discussion of wilderness had been mostly in terms of Romantic or nationalistic cliches. Thoreau tossed these aside in an effort to approach the significance of the wild more closely. In so doing he came to grips with issues which others had only faintly discerned. At the same time he cut the channels in which a large portion of thought about wilderness subsequently flowed.

The complex of attitudes toward man, nature, and God known as Transcendentalism was one of the major factors conditioning Thoreau's ideas regarding wilderness. In the tradition of Idealists such as Plato and Kant, the American Transcendentalists postu-

1. Thoreau, "Walking" in *Excursions, The Writings of Henry David Thoreau,* Riverside edition (11 vols. Boston, 1893) *9,* 251, 267, 275. For the circumstances of the lecture see Walter Harding, *The Days of Henry Thoreau* (New York, 1935), p. 286, and Harding, "A Check List of Thoreau's Lectures," *Bulletin of the New York Public Library, 52* (1948), 82. This was the first occasion Thoreau delivered the paper in question, and since he revised it shortly before his death, the quoted portions may not have been the exact words spoken at the Lyceum. For evidence that they are very close, however, see the fragment of lecture text quoted in Harding, p. 315.

lated the existence of a reality higher than the physical. The core of Transcendentalism was the belief that a correspondence or parallelism existed between the higher realm of spiritual truth and the lower one of material objects. For this reason natural objects assumed importance because, if rightly seen, they reflected universal spiritual truths. It was this belief that led Ralph Waldo Emerson to declare in his manifesto of 1836 that "nature is the symbol of the spirit . . . the world is emblematic."[2] Six years later Thoreau offered another interpretation: "let us not underrate the value of a fact; it will one day flower in a truth." Nature mirrored the currents of higher law emanating from God. Indeed, the natural world might be more than a reflector, as Thoreau implied when he asked: "is not Nature, rightly read, that of which she is commonly taken to be the symbol merely?"[3]

Transcendentalists had a definite conception of man's place in a universe divided between object and essence. His physical existence rooted him to the material portion, like all natural objects, but his soul gave him the potential to *transcend* this condition. Using intuition or imagination (as distinct from rational understanding), man might penetrate to spiritual truths. In the same manner he could discover his own correspondence with the divine being and appreciate his capacity for moral improvement. Every individual, the Transcendentalists emphasized, possessed this ability, but the process of insight was so difficult and delicate that it was seldom exercised. The great majority was indifferent, yet even those who sought higher truths intuitively found them in frustratingly brief flashes. Nonetheless, Thoreau pointed out, "man cannot afford to be a naturalist to look at Nature directly. . . . He must look through and beyond her."[4]

As a way of thinking about man and nature, Transcendentalism

2. Emerson, "Nature" in *Nature, Addresses and Lectures, The Works of Ralph Waldo Emerson,* Standard Library edition (14 vols. Boston, 1883) *1,* 31, 38. The best secondary studies of Transcendentalism concern Emerson: Sherman Paul, *Emerson's Angle of Vision: Man and Nature in the American Experience* (Cambridge, Mass., 1952); Stephen E. Whicher, *Freedom and Fate: An Inner Life of Ralph Waldo Emerson* (Philadelphia, 1953); Vivian C. Hopkins, *Spires of Form: A Study of Emerson's Esthetic Theory* (Cambridge, Mass., 1951); and Philip L. Nicoloff, *Emerson on Race and History* (New York, 1961).

3. Thoreau, "The Natural History of Massachusetts" in *Writings, 9,* 160; Thoreau, *A Week on the Concord and Merrimack Rivers, Writings, 1,* 504.

4. *The Journal of Henry David Thoreau,* eds. Bradford Torrey and Francis H. Allen (14 vols. Boston, 1906) *5,* 45.

had important implications for the meaning of the American wilderness. The doctrine climaxed and gave forceful expression to older ideas about the presence of divinity in the natural world. While rejecting the deists' assumption of the power of reason, Transcendentalists agreed with them that nature was the proper source of religion. They were even more in accord with English Romantic poets such as William Wordsworth who believed in moral "impulses" emanating from fields and woods. In theory, at least, Transcendentalists left little room for the earlier ideas about the amorality of wild country. Instead, the wilderness, in contrast to the city, was regarded as the environment where spiritual truths were least blunted. Making the point explicit, Emerson wrote: "in the wilderness, I find something more dear and connate than in the streets or villages . . . in the woods we return to reason and faith."[5]

The Transcendental conception of man added indirectly to the attractiveness of wilderness. Instead of the residue of evil in every heart, which Calvinism postulated, Emerson, Thoreau, and their colleagues discerned a spark of divinity. Under the prod of Calvin, Puritans feared the innate sinfulness of human nature would run rampant if left to itself in the moral vacuum of wilderness. Men might degenerate to beasts or worse on stepping into the woods. Transcendentalists, on the contrary, saw no such danger in wild country because they believed in man's basic goodness. Reversing Puritan assumptions, they argued that one's chances of attaining moral perfection and knowing God were *maximized* by entering wilderness. The fears which the first New Englanders experienced in contact with the primeval forest gave way in their Concord descendants to confidence—in wilderness and in man.

A second factor shaping Thoreau's attitude toward wilderness was his opinion of civilization. By mid-century American life had acquired a bustling tempo and materialistic tone that left Thoreau and many of his contemporaries vaguely disturbed and insecure. To be sure, the official faith in progress ran strong. Yet the idea that a technological civilization and the pursuit of progress was disrupting older, better patterns of living could not be entirely set aside. A mechanized way of life seemed on the verge of overwhelming innocence, simplicity, and good taste.[6] "Things are in the saddle,"

5. Emerson, "Nature" in *Works, 1,* 15, 16.

6. Marx, *Machine in the Garden;* Marvin Meyers, *The Jacksonian Persuasion: Politics and Belief* (Stanford, Cal., 1957); and William R. Taylor, *Cavalier and*

quipped Emerson, "and ride mankind."[7] Thoreau lamented his inability to buy a blank notebook for recording thoughts; the only ones the merchants in Concord offered were ledgers ruled for dollars and cents. At the Harvard commencement of 1837 he spoke about "the commercial spirit" as a virus infecting his age.[8] The development of Thoreau's wilderness philosophy is most meaningful when juxtaposed to this sense of discontent with his society.

Thoreau began to formulate his conception of the value of the wild from self-examination. In his twenty-third year, 1841, he wrote to a friend: "I grow savager and savager every day, as if fed on raw meat, and my tameness is only the repose of untamableness." A few months later he confessed in his journal that "it does seem as if mine were a peculiarly wild nature, which so yearns toward all wildness." Wandering through the Concord countryside, he delighted in discovering Indian arrowheads, wild apple trees, and animals of the deep woods such as the lynx. They were evidence "that all is not garden and cultivated field crops, that there are square rods in Middlesex County as purely primitive as they were a thousand years ago . . . little oases of wildness in the desert of our civilization." For Thoreau the presence of this wild country was of utmost importance. "Our lives," he pointed out in 1849 in his first book, "need the relief of [the wilderness] where the pine flourishes and the jay still screams."[9] When Thoreau could not find enough wildness near Concord, he journeyed to Maine and Canada. Just being "on the verge of the uninhabited, and, for the most part, unexplored wilderness stretching toward Hudson's Bay" braced Thoreau; the very names "Great Slave Lake" and "Esquimaux" cheered and encouraged him. While admitting his love for Concord, Thoreau made clear how glad he was "when I discover, in oceans and wilderness far away, the materials out of which a million Concords can be made—indeed unless I discover them, I am lost myself."[10]

Yankee: The Old South and American National Character (New York, 1961) base their conclusions on similar estimations of American anxiety at this time.

7. Emerson, "Ode, Inscribed to W. H. Channing," *Poems* (4th ed. Boston, 1847), p. 119.

8. Reginald L. Cook, *Passage to Walden* (Boston, 1949), pp. 99–100.

9. Thoreau, *Familiar Letters, Writings, 6,* 36; Torrey and Allen, eds., *Journal, 1,* 296; *9,* 44; Thoreau, *Week, Writings, 1,* 223.

10. Thoreau, "A Yankee in Canada" in *Writings, 9,* 52; Thoreau, "Natural History" in *Writings, 9,* 129–30; Torrey and Allen, eds., *Journal, 2,* 46.

Unlike many Romantic contemporaries, Thoreau was not satisfied merely to announce his passion for wilderness. He wanted to understand its value. The 1851 talk to the Concord Lyceum offered an opportunity to defend the proposition that "the forest and wilderness" furnish "the tonics and barks which brace mankind." Thoreau grounded his argument on the idea that wildness was the source of vigor, inspiration, and strength. It was, in fact, the essential "raw-material of life."[11] Human greatness of any kind depended on tapping this primordial vitality. Thoreau believed that to the extent a culture, or an individual, lost contact with wildness it became weak and dull.

This was difficult to explain to the Lyceum that April afternoon. Seeking illustration in the history of creative writing, Thoreau maintained that "in literature it is only the wild that attracts us." What appealed about Hamlet, the Iliad, and the Scripture was "the uncivilized free and wild thinking." These books were "as wildly natural and primitive, mysterious and marvellous, ambrosial and fertile, as a fungus or a lichen."[12] Contemporary poets and philosophers, Thoreau added, would likewise profit by maintaining contact with a wild base. As an inexhaustible fertilizer of the intellect, it had no peer.

Thoreau also appealed to his audience's knowledge of ancient history. Empires had risen and declined according to the firmness of their wild roots. For Thoreau it was not a "meaningless fable" that Rome's founders had been suckled by a wolf, but a metaphorical illustration of a fundamental truth. "It was because the children of the Empire were not suckled by the wolf," he reasoned, "that they were conquered and displaced by the children of the northern forests who were." "In short," he told the Lyceum in conclusion, "all good things are wild, and free."[13]

For Thoreau wilderness was a reservoir of wildness vitally important for keeping the spark of the wild alive in man. He prized it,

11. Thoreau, "Walking" in *Writings, 9*, 275, 277.

12. I am citing the more dramatic statement of these ideas in Torrey and Allen, eds., *Journal, 2*, 97, on which the similar passage in "Walking" (*Writings, 9*, 283) was based.

13. Thoreau, "Walking" in *Writings, 9*, 275, 287. Thomas Cole's 1836 series "The Course of Empire" (see Chapter 4) and James Fenimore Cooper's *The Crater* (1847) express the same idea in the media of art and fiction. Cooper, in fact, clearly drew on Cole for his conception: Donald A. Ringe, "James Fenimore Cooper and Thomas Cole: An Analogous Technique," *American Literature, 30* (1958), 26–36.

as he wrote in an 1856 letter, "chiefly for its intellectual value."[14] More than once he referred to the "tonic" effect of wild country on his spirit.[15] "There at last," he remarked in 1857, "my nerves are steadied, my senses and my mind do their office." Thoreau, the Transcendentalist, believed that in the wilderness he found "some grand, serene, immortal, infinitely encouraging, though invisible, companion, and walked with him." As an author Thoreau also knew the forest's value. Using his trips to the Maine woods as a case in point, he contended that "not only for strength, but for beauty, the poet must, from time to time, travel the logger's path and the Indian's trail, to drink at some new and more bracing fountain of the Muses, far in the recesses of the wilderness."[16] The crucial environment was within. Wilderness was ultimately significant to Thoreau for its beneficial effect on thought.

Much of Thoreau's writing was only superficially about the natural world. Following Emerson's dictum that "the whole of nature is a metaphor of the human mind," he turned to it repeatedly as a figurative tool.[17] Wilderness symbolized the unexplored qualities and untapped capacities of every individual. The burden of his message was to penetrate the "wildness . . . in our brain and bowels, the primitive vigor of Nature in us." In *Walden* (1854) he exhorted his reader to "be . . . the Lewis and Clark and Frobisher of your own streams and oceans; explore your own higher latitudes." The essential frontier, in Thoreau's estimation, had no geographic location but was found "wherever a man *fronts* a fact."[18] But going to the outward, physical wilderness was highly conducive to an inward journey. Wild country offered the necessary freedom and solitude. Moreover, it offered life stripped down to essentials. Because of

14. As quoted from an unpublished letter of Oct. 20, 1856 in Sherman Paul, *The Shores of America: Thoreau's Inward Exploration* (Urbana, Ill., 1958), p. 415.

15. Thoreau, *Walden, Writings, 2,* 489, is one instance.

16. Torrey and Allen, eds., *Journal, 9,* 209; Thoreau, *The Maine Woods, Writings, 3,* 212.

17. Emerson, "Nature" in *Works, 1,* 38. For guidelines in the following analysis I have used Fussell, *Frontier,* pp. 175–231; Foerster, *Nature,* pp. 69–142; Clough, *Necessary Earth,* pp. 78 ff.; R. W. B. Lewis, *The American Adam: Innocence, Tragedy, and Tradition in the Nineteenth Century* (Chicago, 1955), pp. 20–27; F. O. Matthiesson, *American Renaissance: Art and Expression in the Age of Emerson and Whitman* (New York, 1941), pp. 153 ff.; and Lawrence Willson, "The Transcendentalist View of the West," *Western Humanities Review, 14* (1960), 183–91. The best general treatment of Thoreau's mind is Paul, *Shores of America.*

18. Torrey and Allen, eds., *Journal, 9,* 43; Thoreau, *Walden, Writings, 2,* 495; Thoreau, *Week, Writings, 1,* 401.

this rawness, wilderness was the best environment in which to "settle ourselves, and work and wedge our feet downward through the mud and slush of opinion, and prejudice, and tradition, and delusion . . . through Paris and London, through New York and Boston . . . till we come to a hard bottom and rocks in place, which we call *reality*." With this in mind Thoreau sought Walden Pond. "I went to the woods," he declared, "because I wished to live deliberately." A decade after the Walden interlude Thoreau still felt the necessity from time to time to "go off to some wilderness where I can have a better opportunity to play life."[19] And "playing" life in Thoreau's terms meant living it with the utmost seriousness.

Given his ideas about the value of wilderness, it was inevitable that Thoreau should take up the nationalists' defense of American scenery. Some of his statements were trite ("our understanding more comprehensive and broader, like our plains") but occasionally he penetrated to new levels of meaning. Having linked Rome's initial greatness with the fact that Romulus and Remus were suckled by a wolf, Thoreau reasoned that "America is the she wolf to-day."[20] The immigrants who left a tame, civilized Europe partook of the vigor of a wild New World and held the future in their hands. England, for instance, was effete, sterile, and moribund because "the wild man in her became extinct." America, on the other hand, had wilderness in abundance and, as a consequence, an unequaled cultural and moral potential. "I believe," Thoreau wrote, "that Adam in paradise was not so favorably situated on the whole as is the backwoodsman in America." Yet with typical caution he added that it "remains to be seen how the western Adam in the wilderness will turn out."[21]

While Thoreau was unprecedented in his praise of the American wilderness, his enthusiasm was not undiluted; some of the old antipathy and fear lingered even in *his* thought. Encountering the Maine woods underscored it. Thoreau left Concord in 1846 for the first of three trips to northern Maine. His expectations were high because he hoped to find genuine, primeval America. But contact

19. Thoreau, *Walden*, *Writings*, *2*, 143, 154; Torrey and Allen, eds., *Journal*, *7*, 519.

20. Thoreau, "Walking" in *Writings*, *9*, 273, 275.

21. Torrey and Allen, eds., *Journal*, *2*, 144, 152–53. On the Adamic theme in American letters, which was in part inspired by the virgin continent, see Lewis, *American Adam*.

with real wilderness in Maine affected him far differently than had the idea of wilderness in Concord. Instead of coming out of the woods with a deepened appreciation of the wilds, Thoreau felt a greater respect for civilization and realized the necessity of balance.

The wilderness of Maine shocked Thoreau. He reported it as "even more grim and wild than you had anticipated, a deep and intricate wilderness." Climbing Mt. Katahdin, he was struck by its contrast to the kind of scenery he knew around Concord. The wild landscape was "savage and dreary" and instead of his usual exultation in the presence of nature, he felt "more lone than you can imagine." It seemed as if he were robbed of his capacity for thought and transcendence. Speaking of man's situation in wilderness, he observed: "vast, Titanic, inhuman Nature has got him at disadvantage, caught him alone, and pilfers him of some of his divine faculty. She does not smile on him as in the plains." To Thoreau, clinging to the bare rocks of Katahdin's summit, wilderness seemed "a place for heathenism and superstitious rites—to be inhabited by men nearer of kin to the rocks and wild animals than we." On the mountain, Transcendental confidence in the symbolic significance of natural objects faltered. Wilderness seemed a more fitting environment for pagan idols than for God. "What is this Titan that has possession of me?", a near-hysterical Thoreau asked on Katahdin. "*Who* are we? *where* are we?"[22] Identity itself had vanished. It was a rude awakening for a man who in another mood had wondered "what shall we do with a man who is afraid of the woods, their solitude and darkness? What salvation is there for him?"[23]

The Maine experience also sharpened Thoreau's thinking about the savage and civilized conditions of man. In his youth he saw the good as being almost entirely on the side of the former. A college essay, "Barbarism and Civilization," argued for the Indian's superiority since he maintained constant contact with nature's educational and moral influence. In his journal a few years later Thoreau praised the savage because he stood "free and unconstrained in Nature, is her inhabitant and not her guest, and wears her easily and

22. Thoreau, *Maine Woods, Writings, 3,* 82, 85–86, 94–95, 107. Secondary comment on Thoreau in Maine may be found in Fannie Hardy Ekstrom, "Thoreau's 'Maine Woods,'" *Atlantic Monthly, 102* (1908), 242–50; Ethel Seybold, *Thoreau: The Quest and the Classics* (New Haven, Conn., 1951), p. 65; John G. Blair and Augustus Trowbridge, "Thoreau on Katahdin," *American Quarterly, 12* (1960), 508–17; and Paul, *Shores of America*, pp. 359 ff.

23. Torrey and Allen, eds., *Journal, 2,* 100.

gracefully."[24] But what he saw in Maine raised questions about the validity of these primitivistic assumptions. The Indians appeared to be "sinister and slouching fellows" who made but a "coarse and imperfect use . . . of Nature." The savage was hardly the "child of nature" he once supposed.[25] In an entry in his journal for July 1, 1852, Thoreau condensed his critique in the idea that roses "bloomed in vain while only wild men roamed." It was, rather, the philosopher or poet (Thoreau thought himself his own best example) who appreciated the higher values and experienced the greatest benefits of wilderness. Yet for the most part, civilized men ignored these things. In the outdoors their eyes were fixed on material gain or trivial sport. "For one that comes with a pencil to sketch or sing, a thousand come with an axe or rifle," Thoreau lamented. The lesson he drew was that "savages have their high and low estates and so have civilized nations."[26]

The problem now was clear: was it possible "to combine the hardiness of these savages with the intellectualness of the civilized man?" Put another way, could men live so as "to secure all the advantage [of civilization] without suffering any of the disadvantage?" The answer for Thoreau lay in a combination of the good inherent in wildness with the benefits of cultural refinement. An excess of either condition must be avoided. The vitality, heroism, and toughness that came with a wilderness condition had to be balanced by the delicacy, sensitivity, and "intellectual and moral growth" characteristic of civilization. "The natural remedy," he continued, "is to be found in the proportion which the night bears to the day, the winter to the summer, thought to experience."[27]

The ideal man occupied such a middling position, drawing on both the wild and the refined.[28] Thoreau used his own life as a case

24. F. B. Sanborn, *The Life of Henry David Thoreau* (Boston, 1917), pp. 180–83; Torrey and Allen, eds., *Journal, 1*, 253.

25. Thoreau, *Maine Woods, Writings, 3*, 105. Pearce, *Savages of America*, pp. 148–50, contends that Thoreau was a primitivist. On the other hand, John Aldrich Christie, *Thoreau as World Traveler*, American Geographical Society Special Publication, 37 (New York, 1965), pp. 211–30, supports the present position that Thoreau saw little to be admired in the purely savage state.

26. Torrey and Allen, eds., *Journal, 4*, 166; Thoreau, *Maine Woods, Writings, 3*, 162; Torrey and Allen, eds., *Journal, 3*, 301.

27. Thoreau, *Walden, Writings, 2*, 23; Torrey and Allen, eds., *Journal, 3*, 301; Thoreau, "Walking" in *Writings, 9*, 258.

28. John W. Ward, *Andrew Jackson: Symbol for an Age* (New York, 1955), pp. 30–45, discussed this point with reference to Jackson, a man regarded as occupying

in point. In *Walden* he reported recognizing in himself "an instinct toward a higher, or, as it is named, spiritual life . . . and another toward a primitive, rank and savage one." Rejoicing in both, Thoreau strove to make himself, as his bean field at the Pond, "half-cultivated." "I would not," he explained, "have . . . every part of a man cultivated, any more than I would have every acre of earth." Some of each, of course, should be controlled and tilled, but along with the tame must be blended some wildness or wilderness as a strength-giving fertilizer. As long as its potency was partially diluted, superb crops could grow. Emerson aided his Concord neighbor in expressing the idea: "in history the great moment is when the savage is just ceasing to be a savage. . . . Everything good in nature and the world is in that moment of transition, when the swarthy juices still flow plentifully from nature, but their astringency or acridity is got out by ethics or humanity." Thoreau extended the metaphor to the question of American nationalism. In terms of culture, the Old World was an exhausted field; the New a wild peat bog. Yet this was no reason for smugness. America needed "some of the sand of the Old World to be carted on to her rich but as yet unassimilated meadows" as a precondition for cultural greatness.[29] Again the answer lay in balancing the wild and the cultivated.

For his own part in regard to wilderness Thoreau felt he lived "a sort of border life." Occasionally he sought the wilds for nourishment and the opportunity to exercise his savage instinct, but at the same time he knew he could not remain permanently. "A civilized man . . . must at length pine there, like a cultivated plant, which clasps its fibres about a crude and undissolved mass of peat." For an optimum existence Thoreau believed, one should alternate between wilderness and civilization, or, if necessary, choose for a permanent residence "partially cultivated country."[30] The essential requirement was to maintain contact with both ends of the spectrum.

---

the optimum midpoint between the Britisher and the Indian and consequently able to defeat both in battle. Charles L. Sanford has made a similar analysis of ideal American character: *Quest for Paradise*, pp. viii, 28 ff., 135ff.

29. Thoreau, *Walden, Writings, 2*, 246, 327; Thoreau, "Walking" in *Writings, 9*, 292; Emerson, "Power" in *Essays: Second Series, Works, 3*, 71; Torrey and Allen, eds., *Journal, 2*, 147.

30. Thoreau, "Walking" in *Writings, 9*, 296–97; Thoreau, *Maine Woods, Writings, 3*, 210–11.

Thoreau knew wildness (the "animal in us") as man's most valuable quality, but only when checked and utilized by his "higher nature."[31] Since he idealized a balance, it always distressed him to have someone ask after a lecture: " 'would you have us return to the savage state? etc. etc.' "[32] But others in his generation understood what Thoreau meant by proportioning. A fellow Transcendentalist, Charles Lane, advocated in the *Dial* an "amalgamation" of life in the wilderness and in civilization. "To unite the advantages of the two modes," he felt, "has doubtless been the aim of many." Orestes Brownson's perfected society strove to make possible "all the individual freedom of the savage state with all the order and social harmony of the highest degree of civilization." Cooper's Leatherstocking inspired the same idea in Francis Parkman. For the Boston historian there was "something admirably felicitous in the conception of this hybrid offspring of civilization and barbarism." In Parkman's opinion Natty Bumppo joined "uprightness, kindliness, innate philosophy, and the truest moral perceptions" with "the wandering instincts and hatred of restraint which stamp the Indian." In 1850 Cooper himself discussed his famous protagonist as inclined to tread the middle way between "civilization" and "savage life." Leatherstocking represented "the better qualities of both conditions, without pushing either to extremes."[33]

In providing a philosophic defense of the half-savage, Thoreau gave the American idealization of the pastoral a new foundation. Previously most Americans had revered the rural, agrarian condition as a release both from wilderness and from high civilization. They stood, so to speak, with both feet in the center of the spectrum of environments.[34] Thoreau, on the other hand, arrived at the middle by straddling. He rejoiced in the extremes and, by keeping a foot in each, believed he could extract the best of both worlds.

31. Thoreau, *Walden, Writings, 2,* 341.

32. As quoted in Walter Harding, "Thoreau on the Lecture Platform," *New England Quarterly, 34* (1951), 369.

33. Lane, "Life in the Woods," *Dial, 4* (1844), 422; *The Works of Orestes A. Brownson,* ed. Henry F. Brownson (20 vols. Detroit, 1882–1907) *15,* 60; Parkman, "The Works of James Fenimore Cooper," *North American Review, 74* (1852), 151; *James Fenimore Cooper: Representative Selections,* ed. Robert Spiller (New York, 1936), pp. 306–07.

34. Marx, *Machine in the Garden;* Richard Hofstadter, *The Age of Reform* (New York, 1960), pp. 23–59; and Smith, *Virgin Land,* pp. 123 ff. examine the American attraction to the pastoral or what Marx calls "the middle landscape" (p. 113).

The rural was the point of equilibrium between the poles. According to Thoreau, wildness and refinement were not fatal extremes but equally beneficent influences Americans would do well to blend. With this concept Thoreau led the intellectual revolution that was beginning to invest wilderness with attractive rather than repulsive qualities.

CHAPTER 6

Preserve the Wilderness!

> Friends at home! I charge you to spare, preserve and cherish some portion of your primitive forests; for when these are cut away I apprehend they will not easily be replaced.
>
> Horace Greeley, 1851

APPRECIATION of wilderness led easily to sadness at its disappearance from the American scene. What to do beyond regretting, however, was a problem, especially in view of the strength of rationales for conquering wild country. But as the Romantic and nationalistic vindications of wilderness developed, a few Americans conceived of the possibility of its deliberate preservation. Perhaps society could legally protect selected areas, exempting them from the transforming energies of civilization. Such a policy, of course, completely countered dominant American purposes. For the pioneer, wilderness preservation was absurd, and even those who recognized the advantages of reservoirs of wildness had to admit the force of civilization's claims. This ambivalence, moreover, was no idle matter. Preservation entailed action. The dilemmas which had previously been chiefly philosophical now figured in the very practical matter of land allocation. In confronting them Americans began to deepen their understanding of wilderness. In fact, since the middle of the nineteenth century the preservation issue has been the major vehicle for national discussion of wilderness.

Concern over the loss of wilderness necessarily preceded the first calls for its protection. The protest originated in the same social class that led the way in appreciating wild country: Easterners of literary and artistic bents. John James Audubon is a case in point. His *Birds of America* (*1827–38*) marked him as a leader in calling attention to natural beauty. As he traveled through the Ohio Valley in the 1820s in search of specimens, Audubon had many occasions to observe "the destruction of the forest." Even though he sensed that this meant the end of what he loved, he hesitated about condemning the westward march. "Whether these changes are for the better or worse," he wrote, "I shall not pretend to say." But as he heard "the din of hammers and machinery" and saw "the woods . . . fast disappearing under the axe," Audubon put restraint aside. "The greedy mills," he concluded, "told the sad tale, that in a century the noble forests . . . should exist no more."[1]

The writers responsible for the Romantic interpretation of the American wilderness joined Audubon in his lament. Cooper expressed similar sentiments in *The Prairie,* while with Thomas Cole the denunciation of an all-consuming civilization attained the proportions of a tirade. Indifference to wilderness, Cole declared in 1836, was symptomatic of the "meagre utilitarianism" of the age. The landscape already revealed the "ravages of the axe," and no end appeared in sight. Drawing on a favorite image of wilderness advocates, Cole pleaded with his countrymen to remember "we are still in Eden; the wall that shuts us out of the garden is our own ignorance and folly."[2] Five years later he attempted to be the mouthpiece of the virgin continent in a poem entitled "Lament of the Forest." Speaking through Cole, the forest grieved at the way man, "the destroyer," invaded its New World sanctuary. "Our doom is near: behold from east to west the skies are darkened by ascending smoke; each hill and every valley is become an altar unto Mammon." In only "a few short years" the wilderness would vanish.[3] William Cullen Bryant was equally pessimistic. After touring the Great Lakes region in 1846 he sadly anticipated a future in which even its "wild and lonely woods" would be "filled with cottages and boarding-houses." In view of the poet's earlier concern for maintaining his country's "wilder image," this was cause for alarm.[4] And Charles Lanman, the Romantic traveler and essayist, minced few words in recounting the fate of places "despoiled by the hand of civilization of almost everything which gives charm to the wilderness."[5]

1. Audubon, *Delineations of American Scenery and Character,* ed. Francis Hobart Herrick (New York, 1926), pp. 4, 9–10. These descriptive essays, written from 1818 to 1834, supplemented Audubon's *Birds of America:* Alice Ford, *John James Audubon* (Norman, Okla., 1964), pp. 41 ff.

2. Cole, "Essay on American Scenery," *American Monthly Magazine, 1* (1836), 3, 12. See also Cole to Luman Reed, March 26, 1836 in Noble, *Cole,* pp. 160–61.

3. Cole, "Lament of the Forest," *Knickerbocker Magazine, 17* (1841), 518–19.

4. Bryant, *Letters of a Traveller; or Notes of Things seen in Europe and America* (New York, 1850), 302.

5. Lanman, *Letters from the Allegheny Mountains* (New York, 1849), p. 171.

Washington Irving also deplored the elimination of wildness from the American landscape. He assisted in 1837 in preparing for publication Captain Benjamin L. E. Bonneville's journal of western exploration because of a desire to preserve something of "the romance of savage life." Weaving his own impressions into Bonneville's account, Irving observed that geography had provided wild country with one remaining hope. The Rocky Mountains constituted a "belt" of uninhabited land "where there is nothing to tempt the cupidity of the white man." While civilization sprang up around it, this region would remain "irreclaimable wilderness" and a refuge for Indian, trapper, and explorer. In Irving's estimation the advantages of having such a primeval resource far outweighed the loss to civilization in lumber and other raw materials.[6]

For the Bostonian Francis Parkman, Jr. sadness at the disappearance of wilderness stemmed from personal tastes combined with a keen sense of the historical process. As long as he could remember, Parkman was, by his own admission, "enamored of the woods."[7] Wildness tantalized his imagination, possibly because it contrasted so sharply with his ultra-sophisticated Brahmin milieu. As a Harvard student he indulged his passion with a series of summer camping trips into northern New England and Canada. In a journal account of an 1841 excursion in the White Mountains, Parkman explained that "my chief object in coming so far was merely to have a taste of the half-savage kind of life . . . and to see the wilderness where it was as yet uninvaded by the hand of man."[8] During his college years Parkman also decided on a career, history, and a subject for research, the conflict between France and Great Britain for the North American continent. He hoped to write a book that would be distinctively American because of its central concern with wilderness. "My theme fascinated me," Parkman remarked, "and I was haunted with wilderness images day and night." The French

6. Irving, *The Adventures of Captain Bonneville USA in the Rocky Mountains and the Far West, digested from his journal by Washington Irving*, ed. Edgeley W. Todd (Norman, Okla., 1961), p. 372.

7. Parkman to George E. Ellis, c. 1864 in *Letters of Francis Parkman*, ed. Wilbur R. Jacobs (2 vols. Norman, Okla., 1960) *1*, 176. For Parkman's life see Mason Wade, *Francis Parkman: Heroic Historian* (New York, 1942), especially pp. 23–75; Howard Doughty, *Francis Parkman* (New York, 1962); Lewis, *American Adam*, pp. 165–73; and David Levin, *History as Romantic Art* (Palo Alto, Calif., 1959), passim.

8. *The Journals of Francis Parkman*, ed. Mason Wade (2 vols. New York, 1947) *1*, 31.

and Indian Wars only gave him an excuse to pursue his real interest, "the history of the American forest."[9] But before settling into a career, Parkman used the summer of 1846 to make an arduous but memorable journey across the Oregon Trail. Although it broke his health, the trip readied him intellectually to give wilderness the Romantic interpretation in history that Bryant had given it in poetry, Cooper in fiction, and Cole in art.

As an historian Parkman was especially sensitive to change; as a lover of wilderness he deplored the effects of civilization in North America. In an oration delivered at his Harvard graduation in 1844, Parkman revealed his emotions. He began with an ecstatic celebration of the New World on the eve of discovery: "when Columbus first saw land, America was the sublimest object in the world. Here was the domain of Nature." But, he sadly concluded, "the charm is broken now. The stern and solemn poetry that breathed from her endless wilderness is gone; and the dullest plainest prose has fixed its home in America."[10] In 1851, in the preface to his first volumes, Parkman stated his aim as the portrayal of the American forest and Indian "at the period when both received their final doom." A year later, in a review of Cooper's novels, he found an opportunity for forthright criticism of the civilizing process. "Civilization," in Parkman's opinion, had "a destroying as well as a creating power." Among its casualties were the Indian, the buffalo, and the frontiersman, "a class of men . . . so remarkable both in their virtues and their faults, that few will see their extinction without regret."[11] Parkman illustrated his point with Cooper's protagonist, Leatherstocking.

In 1849, after serialization in *Knickerbocker Magazine,* Parkman's *The California and Oregon Trail* appeared in book form. Its light and breezy tone reflected the buoyancy of the author's spirit in contact with wilderness. In the 1840s it hardly seemed possible that the Far West would be anything but wild. Time, however, altered Parkman's opinion, and the need to write new prefaces for

9. Parkman, "Autobiography of Francis Parkman," *Proceedings of the Massachusetts Historical Society, 8* (1894), 351–52.

10. As quoted in Wilbur R. Jacobs, "Francis Parkman's Oration 'Romance in America,'" *American Historical Review, 68* (1963), 696.

11. Parkman, *History of the Conspiracy of Pontiac and the War of the North American Tribes against the English Colonies after the Conquest of Canada* (Boston, 1851), p. viii; Parkman, "The Works of James Fenimore Cooper," *North American Review, 74* (1852), 151.

subsequent editions of his book provided a chance to express it. In the 1873 edition of *The Oregon Trail* he added a lengthy paragraph to the preface concerning the vanishing wilderness. Although he had omitted it from the initial account, he now recalled a conversation with his traveling companion while riding near Pike's Peak. The wilderness, they agreed, was doomed. Cattle would soon replace the buffalo and farms transform the range of the wolf, bear, and Indian. While pioneers might celebrate such events, the young gentlemen from Boston felt nothing but regret at the prospect. Returning to 1873 Parkman added that his earlier premonitions had not suggested the extent of the changes. Not only farms but "cities . . . hotels and gambling-houses" had invaded the Rockies as men sought gold in "those untrodden mountains." Moreover, "polygamous hordes of Mormon" had arrived. Capping it all was the "disenchanting screech of the locomotive" which broke "the spell of weird mysterious mountains." Parkman sadly concluded that "the mountain trapper is no more, and the grim romance of his wild, hard life is a memory of the past."[12]

In 1892 just before his death, Parkman again revised the preface of *Oregon Trail*. There was no longer any doubt: "the Wild West is tamed, and its savage charms have withered."[13] This frame of mind produced the first expressions of the idea of preserving some of the remaining American wilderness.

George Catlin, an early student and painter of the American Indian, was the first to move beyond regret to the preservation concept. In 1829 he began a series of summer excursions in the West; during the winters he completed his sketches and journal in an Eastern studio. The spring of 1832 found Catlin impatient to leave once more for the frontier where his brush and pen could capture "the grace and beauty of Nature" before the advance of civilization obliterated it.[14] Setting out from St. Louis on board the *Yellowstone* for the headwaters of the Missouri River, Catlin arrived at

12. Parkman, *The Oregon Trail: Sketches of Prairie and Rocky-Mountain Life* (Boston, 1873), pp. vii–viii. Marx, *Machine in the Garden,* alerted me to the significance of the railroad-disrupting-nature theme in American letters. But in Parkman's case it was wilderness, not a pastoral paradise, that was invaded. More exactly, in his mind wilderness had reversed its traditional role and become a sort of paradise.

13. Parkman, *The Oregon Trail* (Boston, 1892), p. ix.

14. George Catlin, *North American Indians: Being Letters and Notes on their Manners, Customs, and Conditions, written during Eight Years' Travel amongst the*

Fort Pierre, South Dakota, in May. A large number of Sioux were camped near the Fort, and when Catlin observed them slaughtering buffalo to trade for whisky, it confirmed his suspicion that the extinction of both Indian and buffalo was imminent. Saddened at this thought he climbed a bluff, spread a pocket map of the United States before him, and considered the effects of an expanding civilization. "Many are the rudenesses and wilds in Nature's works," he reflected, "which are destined to fall before the deadly axe and desolating hands of cultivating man." Yet Catlin was convinced that the primitive was "worthy of our preservation and protection." Keeping it mattered because "the further we become separated from that pristine wildness and beauty, the more pleasure does the mind of enlightened man feel in recurring to those scenes."[15]

Others had said as much, but Catlin's 1832 reflections went beyond to the idea that Indians, buffaloes, and the wilderness in which they existed might not have to yield completely to civilization if the government would protect them in "a *magnificent park.*" Fascinated with this conception, Catlin continued: "what a beautiful and thrilling specimen for America to preserve and hold up to the view of her refined citizens and the world, in future ages! A *nation's Park,* containing man and beast, in all the wild[ness] and freshness of their nature's beauty!"[16]

Similar recognition of the value of the American wilderness led to other calls for its preservation. In the late 1840s Thomas Cole, whose European travels dramatized the fate of unprotected wilderness in a populous civilization, proposed to write a book concerning, in part, "the wilderness passing away, and the necessity of saving and perpetuating its features." Contact with the Old World in 1851 also prompted Horace Greeley to charge Americans "to spare, preserve and cherish some portion of your primitive forests." If

---

Wildest Tribes of Indians in North America (2 vols. Philadelphia, 1913) *1*, 2–3. These volumes were published originally in London in 1841 as a collection of articles which Catlin had written in the 1830s.

For Catlin's life see Marion Annette Evans, "Indian-Loving Catlin," *Proceedings and Collections of the Wyoming Historical and Geological Society, 21* (1930), 68–82; Loyd Haberly, *Pursuit of the Horizon: A Life of George Catlin* (New York, 1948); and Harold McCracken, *George Catlin and the Old Frontier* (New York, 1959). Catlin's art is treated in Flexner, *That Wilder Image,* pp. 77–102.

15. Catlin, *North American Indians, 1,* 289, 292–93.

16. Ibid., *1,* 294–95.

these disappeared, he warned, they could not be replaced easily. Seeing Europe carried Greeley's thoughts back to the "glorious . . . still unscathed forests" of his country which he had "never before prized so highly."[17]

Henry David Thoreau, with his refined philosophy of the importance of wildness, made the classic early call for wilderness preservation. Like the others, the disappearance of wild country made him uneasy. Of course primitive places might still be found in Maine and the West, but every year brought more lumbermen and settlers into the forests. Maine was tending toward Massachusetts and Massachusetts toward England. "This winter," Thoreau commented in his journal for 1852, "they are cutting down our woods more seriously than ever. . . . It is a thorough process, this war with the wilderness." Faced with the prospect of a totally civilized America, Thoreau concluded that the nation must formally preserve "a certain sample of wild nature, a certain primitiveness." His thoughts came to a head in 1858, in an *Atlantic Monthly* article describing his second trip to Maine five years previously. Near the end of the essay Thoreau defended wilderness as a reservoir of intellectual nourishment for civilized men. Next he asked: "why should not we . . . have our national preserves . . . in which the bear and panther, and some even of the hunter race, may still exist, and not be 'civilized off the face of the earth'—our forests . . . not for idle sport or food, but for inspiration and our own true recreation?"[18] Along with Catlin, Thoreau desired to prevent the extinction of Indians and wild animals, but he went beyond this to the position that protecting wilderness was ultimately important for the preservation of civilization.

In 1859 Thoreau again advocated reserving wild areas, this time with reference to the Massachusetts townships in which he lived. Each of them, he contended, "should have a park, or rather a primitive forest, of five hundred or a thousand acres." The public should own such places and make them sacrosanct. Thoreau's defense for this proposal climaxed several decades of American nationalism: "let us keep the New World *new*, preserve all the advantages of liv-

17. Noble, *Cole*, p. 299. Noble does not make clear if these were Cole's actual words or a paraphrase. The book in question was never written. See also Greeley, *Glances at Europe* (New York, 1851), p. 39.

18. Thoreau, *Maine Woods, Writings, 3*, 208; Torrey and Allen, eds., *Journal, 14*, 306; *3*, 125, 212–13, 269; Thoreau, *Maine Woods, Writings, 3*, 212–13.

ing in the country." As a parting thought Thoreau urged that a few wild places be kept wild "for modesty and reverence's sake, or if only to suggest that earth has higher uses than we put her to."[19]

Even those who desired to protect wilderness were not exempt from divided loyalties. In the work of Samuel H. Hammond, an Albany lawyer, preservation sentiments conflicted with a pride in the material aspects of American civilization. Starting in the 1840s Hammond made annual summer camping trips into the Adirondack Mountains with friends who, like himself, "loved the old woods, the wilderness, and all the wild things pertaining to them." Amidst wildness he found relief from the anxieties of civilized existence. "I have generally gone into the woods," he declared, "weakened in body and depressed in mind. I have always come out of them with renewed health and strength, a perfect digestion, and a buoyant and cheerful spirit." On these trips he found the chance "to lay around loose for a season, vagabondizing among the wild and savage things of the wilderness." This was a necessity for health and happiness, Hammond reasoned, because it permitted the indulgence of the "streak of the savage" which all men possessed.[20]

As a device for ridiculing the utilitarian credo that considered wilderness valueless, Hammond created an imaginary conversation which took place on an Adirondack lake at sundown. His boating companion, the materialist, asked:

> What inspiration can there be . . . in a desolate wilderness. . . . Can you grow corn on these hills, or make pastures of these rocky lowlands? . . . Can you convert these old forests into lumber and cordwood? Can you quarry these rocks, lay them up with mortar into houses, mills, churches, public edifices? Can you make what you call these "old primeval things" utilitarian? Can you make them minister to the progress of civilization, or coin them into dollars?

Hammond replied in the name of beauty and non-utility: "Pshaw! You have spoiled, with your worldliness, your greed for progress, your thirst for gain a pleasant fancy, a glorious dream, as if every-

19. Torrey and Allen, eds., *Journal, 12,* 387; *14,* 305.

20. Hammond, *Wild Northern Scenes; or Sporting Adventures with the Rifle and Rod* (New York, 1857), pp. x, 23, 90–91. Occasionally Hammond put his discussion of wilderness in the form of a dialogue between members of his camping party, but for purposes of simplification I have attributed all remarks to him.

thing were to be measured by the dollar and cent standard." Yet on other occasions Hammond embraced the very values he apparently rejected. In campfire discussions he and his friends applauded the retreat of the forest in pioneer terms: "the march of civilization has crossed a continent . . . making the old wilderness blossom as a rose." The result of this "progressive influence" was not only miracles like locomotives, telegraphs, and photography but "moral prestige" as well.[21]

Given his simultaneous attraction toward wilderness and civilization, Hammond understandably desired conditions under which both could flourish. Preservation of limited wild areas resolved his dilemma. Describing his plan, Hammond declared he would "mark out a circle of a hundred miles in diameter, and throw around it the protecting aegis of the constitution." This land would be "a forest forever" in which "the old woods should stand . . . always as God made them." Lumbering or settling would be prohibited.[22] Wilderness was to be maintained, but immediately Hammond made clear that he had no intention for civilization to suffer. The "circles" of primitive forest, while insuring the continued existence of some wild country, at the same time served to keep wilderness out of the path of progress. Civilization could expand unimpeded "in regions better fitted for it. . . . Let it go where labor will garner a richer harvest, and industry reap a better reward for its toil. It will be of stunted growth at best here."[23] In this roundabout way Hammond justified wilderness preservation without gainsaying the values of civilization.

While Hammond and Thoreau talked of compromising between the conflicting interests of wilderness and civilization, George Perkins Marsh contended that in the case of forests wildness served utility. He expounded his influential thesis in *Man and Nature: or, Physical Geography as Modified by Human Action* (1864). In a varied career[24] Marsh observed how man had abused his power to alter nature. The disruptive effects of civilization on natural harmonies appeared everywhere. Endeavoring to present an alternative to the pioneer interpretation of Genesis 1:28, Marsh declared: "man has too long forgotten that the earth was given to him for

21. Ibid., pp. 33–34, 158, 216, 309–11.

22. Ibid., p. 83. Hammond came close to this idea in an earlier statement in his *Hunting Adventures in the Northern Wilds* (New York, 1856), p. v.

23. Hammond, *Wild Northern Scenes*, pp. 83–84.

24. David Lowenthal's *George Perkins Marsh: Versatile Vermonter* (New York, 1958) is excellent.

usufruct alone, not for consumption, still less for profligate waste." This was not an academic or even an ethical question to Marsh, but involved the earth's ability to support mankind.

As his principal illustration Marsh chose the effects of indiscriminate lumbering. Clean cutting of the forests on the watersheds of rivers resulted in drought, flood, erosion, and unfavorable climatic changes. Such disasters, Marsh believed, were responsible for the decline of Mediterranean empires in power and influence. The New World must school itself in history. "Let us be wise in time," Marsh pleaded, "and profit by the errors of our older brethren." In Marsh's opinion, the sponge-like qualities of a primeval forest made it the best possible regulator of stream flow. Wilderness preservation, consequently, had "economical" as well as "poetical" justifications. With the Adirondacks in mind, Marsh applauded the idea of keeping a large portion of "American soil . . . as far as possible, in its primitive condition." Such a preserve could serve as "a garden for the recreation of the lover of nature" and an "asylum" for wildlife along with its utilitarian functions.[25]

Primarily because it made protecting wilderness compatible with progress and economic welfare, Marsh's arguments became a staple for preservationists.[26] Even Romantics recognized their force. The year after *Man and Nature* appeared, William Cullen Bryant wrote: "thus it is that forests protect a country against drought, and keep its streams constantly flowing and its wells constantly full."[27]

Along with sentiment for saving wilderness, the idea of governmental responsibility was necessary to set the stage for actual preservation. As early as 1832 a natural object, the Arkansas Hot Springs, was set aside as a national reservation.[28] Far more important from the standpoint of the subsequent history of wilderness,

25. Marsh, *Man and Nature; or, Physical Geography as Modified by Human Action* (New York, 1864), pp. 35, 228, 235. For further analysis of Marsh's ideas see Stewart L. Udall, *The Quiet Crisis* (New York, 1963), pp. 69–82, and Arthur Ekirch, Jr., *Man and Nature in America* (New York, 1963), pp. 70–80.

26. For example, see Chapter 7, pp. 118–19; I. A. Lapham, et al., *Report of the Disastrous Effects of the Destruction of Forest Trees* (Madison, Wis., 1867); "Forest Preservation," New York *Times*, May 30, 1872; "Spare the Trees," *Appleton's Journal, 1* (1876), 470–73; and Felix L. Oswald, "The Preservation of Forests," *North American Review, 128* (1879), 35–46.

27. "The Utility of Trees," *Prose Writings of William Cullen Bryant*, ed. Parke Godwin (2 vols. New York, 1884) 2, 405.

28. John Ise, *Our National Park Policy: A Critical History* (Baltimore, 1961), p. 13.

however, was the 1864 federal grant of Yosemite Valley to the State of California as a park "for public use, resort and recreation."[29] The reserved area was only about ten square miles, and a flourishing tourist-catering business soon altered its wild character, but the legal preservation of part of the public domain for scenic and recreational values created a significant precedent in American history.

Frederick Law Olmsted, in the process of becoming the leading American landscape architect of his time, recognized the importance of the Yosemite reservation. He went to California in 1863, became familiar with the Valley, and received an appointment as one of the first commissioners entrusted with its care.[30] In 1865 Olmsted completed an advisory report on the park for the California Legislature. It opened with a commendation of the preservation idea which precluded "natural scenes of an impressive character" from becoming "private property." Olmsted next launched a philosophical defense of scenic beauty: it had a favorable influence on "the health and vigor of men" and especially on their "intellect." Of course, Olmsted agreed with previous exponents of wilderness that "the power of scenery to affect men is, in a large way, proportionate to the degree of their civilization and the degree in which their taste has been cultivated." Still, almost everyone derived some benefit from the contemplation of places like Yosemite. Capping his argument, Olmsted declared: "the enjoyment of scenery employs the mind without fatigue and yet exercises it; tranquilizes it and yet enlivens it; and thus, through the influence of the mind over the body, gives the effect of refreshing rest and reinvigoration to the whole system." If areas were not provided where people could find the glories of nature, he added, serious mental disorders might well result. There was a need to slough off the tensions

29. U.S., *Statutes at Large, 15,* p. 325. The present-day Yosemite National Park composed of some two million acres of wilderness in the high Sierra was not created until 1890 (see Chapter 8). In 1906 California receded Yosemite Valley to the federal government, and it became part of the national park.

For the full story of the 1864 grant see Hans Huth, "Yosemite: The Story of an Idea," *Sierra Club Bulletin, 33* (1948), 47–78; Ise, *National Park Policy,* pp. 52–55; and especially Holway R. Jones, *John Muir and the Sierra Club: The Battle for Yosemite* (San Francisco, 1965), pp. 25 ff.

30. Frederick Law Olmsted Papers, Library of Congress, Washington, D.C., Box 32; Diane Kostial McGuire, "Frederick Law Olmsted in California: An Analysis of his Contributions to Landscape Architecture and City Planning" (unpublished M.A. thesis, University of California, Berkeley, 1956).

and cares of civilization. California and the Yosemite Commissioners, Olmsted concluded, had a "duty of preservation."[31]

At least one early visitor to Yosemite recognized that it might be a model for a nationwide system of reservations. Samuel Bowles, editor of the Springfield, Massachusetts, *Republican,* toured the Valley in August 1865 and hoped the park would stimulate concern for other scenic places. Niagara Falls occurred to him as an obvious candidate. But Bowles went on to state the need of preserving from "destruction by settlement" a "fifty miles square of the Adirondacks in New York, and a similar area of Maine lake and forest."[32] With the idea of saving wild country gaining momentum and the precedent of Yosemite State Park established, actual wilderness preservation, such as Bowles envisaged, was not far off.

31. Olmsted Papers, Box 32. Olmsted's report has been published as "The Yosemite Valley and the Mariposa Big Tree Grove," *Landscape Architecture, 43* (1952), 12–25.

32. Bowles, *Our New West* (Hartford, Conn., 1869), p. 385.

CHAPTER 7

Wilderness Preserved

> [The Yellowstone region] is hereby reserved and withdrawn from settlement, occupancy, or sale . . . and set apart as a public park or pleasuring ground for the benefit and enjoyment of the people. . . . [The Secretary of the Interior] shall provide for the preservation . . . of all timber, mineral deposits, natural curiosities, or wonders within said park . . . in their natural condition.
>
> United States Statutes at Large, 1872

THE world's first instance of large-scale wilderness preservation in the public interest occurred on March 1, 1872, when President Ulysses S. Grant signed an act designating over two million acres of northwestern Wyoming as Yellowstone National Park.[1] Thirteen years later the State of New York established a 715,000-acre "Forest Preserve" in the Adirondacks with the stipulation that it "shall be kept forever as wild forest lands."[2] With these milestones in the early history of American wilderness preservation, the ideas of Catlin, Thoreau, Hammond and Marsh bore fruit. Yet in neither case did the rationale for action take account of the aesthetic, spiritual, or cultural values of wilderness which had previously stimulated appreciation. Yellowstone's initial advocates were not concerned with wilderness; they acted to prevent private acquisition and exploitation of geysers, hot springs, waterfalls, and similar curiosities. In New York the decisive argument concerned the necessity of forested land for an adequate water supply. In both places wilderness was preserved unintentionally. Only later did a few persons begin to realize that one of the most significant results of the establishment of the first national and state park had been the preservation of *wilderness*.

1. For Yellowstone's seminal importance in the history of world preservation see Ise, *National Park Policy*, pp. 658–69; C. Frank Brockman, *Recreational Use of Wild Lands* (New York, 1959), pp. 259–311; Carl P. Russell, "Wilderness Preservation," *National Parks Magazine, 71* (1944), 3–6, 26–28; Lee Merriman Talbot, "Wilderness Overseas" in *Wildlands in Our Civilization*, ed. David Brower (San Francisco, 1964), pp. 75–80; and Charles E. Doell and Gerald B. Fitzgerald, *A Brief History of Parks and Recreation in the United States* (Chicago, 1954), pp. 12–22.

2. *New York Laws*, 1885, Chap. 238, p. 482.

Only a few white men had visited the Yellowstone region during the first six decades of the nineteenth century, but enough information filtered back from a handful of trappers and prospectors to excite the interest of several residents of Montana Territory.[3] Fear of Indian attack discouraged the first projected expeditions, but in the summer of 1869 David E. Folsom, Charles W. Cook, and William Peterson explored the fabled area. Their reports of the waterfalls and canyons along the Yellowstone River as well as the spectacular eruptions of geysers stimulated several acquaintances to plan a major exploration the following summer.[4] Of those who participated in the 1870 expedition, Nathaniel P. Langford and Cornelius Hedges were later to spearhead the movement to establish Yellowstone National Park. Both were Easterners who went to Montana in the early 1860s and rose to positions of some political importance. Langford received an appointment as territorial governor but differences between the Senate and President Andrew Johnson denied him the actual office.[5] Hedges graduated from Yale in 1853 and also held a degree from the Harvard Law School. He served as United States District Attorney in Montana and presided over the state's historical society.[6]

In August 1870 Langford and Hedges joined a nineteen-man Yellowstone party under the leadership of Henry D. Washburn and Gustavus C. Doane.[7] For over a month the group wandered

3. Merril J. Mattes, "Behind the Legend of Colter's Hell: The Early Exploration of Yellowstone National Park," *Mississippi Valley Historical Review, 36* (1949), 251–82; Hiram M. Chittenden, *The Yellowstone National Park* (Cincinnati, 1915), pp. 1–73; Merrill D. Beal, *The Story of Man in Yellowstone* (Caldwell, Idaho, 1946).

4. C. W. Cook [i.e., David E. Folsom], "The Valley of the Upper Yellowstone," *Western Monthly, 4* (1870), 60–67; David E. Folsom, "The Folsom-Cook Exploration of the Upper Yellowstone in the Year 1869," *Contributions to the Historical Society of Montana, 5* (1904), 349–69. An excellent recent edition of the accounts stemming from the 1869 exploration is Aubrey L. Haines, ed., *The Valley of the Upper Yellowstone . . . As Recorded by Charles W. Cook, David E. Folsom, and William Peterson,* American Exploration and Travel Series, 47 (Norman, Okla., 1965). A secondary study is W. Turrentine Jackson, "The Cook-Folsom Exploration of the Upper Yellowstone, 1869," *Pacific Northwest Quarterly, 32* (1941), 307–22.

5. Olin D. Wheeler, "Nathaniel Pitt Langford," *Collections of the Minnesota Historical Society, 15* (1915), 631–68; Chittenden, *Yellowstone,* p. 339.

6. Wyllys A. Hedges, "Cornelius Hedges," *Contributions to the Historical Society of Montana,* 7 (1910), 181–96; Louis C. Cramton, *Early History of Yellowstone National Park and its Relation to National Park Policies* (Washington D.C., 1932), p. 13.

7. W. Turrentine Jackson, "The Washburn-Doane Expedition into the Upper Yellowstone, 1870," *Pacific Historical Review, 10* (1941), 189–208.

through the wilderness marveling at what they termed "curiosities" and "wonders"—the geysers, hot springs, and canyons.[8] On September 19, as they were leaving for home, the explorers participated in a campfire discussion of Yellowstone's future. Most said they intended to file claims on the land around the geysers and waterfalls in anticipation of the demands which tourists would make to see them. But Hedges dissented. According to Langford, he proposed that instead of being divided among private speculators, Yellowstone "ought to be set apart as a great National Park."[9] Langford added that he lay awake most of the night thinking about the idea. He felt a reservation was possible if Congress could be persuaded of the uniqueness of Yellowstone's natural attractions. The "park" Hedges and Langford envisaged consisted of a few acres around each of the geysers and along the rims of the canyons. In this manner the right of the public to see these sights would be safeguarded and the scenery itself saved from defacement. *Wilderness* preservation did not figure in the 1870 plans.[10]

During the winter following his trip, Nathaniel P. Langford lectured several times in the East in an effort to arouse enthusiasm for the park proposal.[11] In addition, he published two articles on Yellowstone in *Scribner's Monthly,* complete with engraved illustrations of its canyons and geysers.[12] The public was interested, but some of the things Langford reported as fact seemed beyond cre-

8. The following accounts of participants substantiate the *lack* of interest in wilderness: Nathaniel P. Langford, "The Wonders of the Yellowstone," *Scribner's Monthly,* 2 (1871), 1–17, 113–28; Langford, *The Discovery of Yellowstone Park, 1870: Diary of the Washburn Expedition to the Yellowstone and Firehole Rivers in the Year 1870* (St. Paul, Minn., 1905); Walter Trumbull, "The Washburn Yellowstone Expedition," *Overland Monthly, 6* (1871), 431–37, 489–96; Gustavus C. Doane, *The Report of Lieutenant Gustavus C. Doane upon the so-called Yellowstone Expedition of 1870,* 41st Cong., 3d Sess., Senate Ex. Doc. 51 (March 3, 1871); and "Journal of Judge Cornelius Hedges," *Contributions to the Historical Society of Montana, 5* (1904), 370–94.

9. Langford, *Discovery of Yellowstone,* pp. 117–18.

10. Aubrey L. Haines, Park Historian, Yellowstone National Park, sustained this analysis in a letter to the author, March 24, 1964. Neither was preserving the wilderness a factor in the previous suggestions by Acting Territorial Governor Thomas E. Meagher (1865) and David E. Folsom (1869) that a park be established: Francis X. Kuppens, "On the Origin of the Yellowstone National Park," *Jesuit Bulletin, 41* (1962), 6–7, 14; Aubrey L. Haines, "History of Yellowstone National Park," (mimeographed Ranger Naturalist Training Manual, Yellowstone National Park, n.d.), pp. 110–18; Cramton, *Early History,* p. 11; W. Turrentine Jackson, "The Creation of Yellowstone National Park," *Mississippi Valley Historical Review, 29* (1942), 188–89.

11. Washington, D.C. *Daily Morning Chronicle,* Jan. 20, 1871; New York *Times,* Jan. 22, 1871.

12. Langford, "The Wonders of the Yellowstone," 1–17, 113–28.

dence. One of those who heard Langford lecture and was in a position to test their validity was Ferdinand Vandiveer Hayden, director of the Geological and Geographical Survey of the Territories. Hayden was leading annual scientific expeditions in the West, and determined to include Yellowstone on his 1871 trip. He persuaded Thomas Moran, the landscape artist, and William Henry Jackson, a pioneer photographer of outdoor scenes, to accompany him and gather a pictorial record.[13]

Hayden's expedition generated considerable interest in the East. In an editorial in the issue of September 18, 1871, the New York *Times* seemed vaguely aware of the wilderness qualities of the Yellowstone country. "There is something romantic in the thought," it declared, "that, in spite of the restless activity of our people, and the almost fabulous rapidity of their increase, vast tracts of national domain yet remain unexplored." But more typical of the general reaction was the *Times*' subsequent description of the "New Wonder Land" as a place whose attractions were limited to unusual natural phenomena such as geysers.[14]

The firm of Jay Cooke and Company, financeers of the Northern Pacific Railroad through Montana, also evinced an interest in a Yellowstone park. In October a Cooke representative wrote to Hayden with the proposition that he lead a campaign for an act that would reserve "the Great Geyser Basin as a public park forever—just as it has reserved that far inferior wonder the Yosemite Valley and the big trees." The railroad interests hoped that Yellowstone would become a popular national vacation mecca like Niagara Falls or Saratoga Springs with resulting profit to the only transportation line serving it.[15] A wilderness was the last thing they wanted.

13. Richard A. Bartlett, *Great Surveys of the American West* (Norman, Okla., 1962), pp. 4 ff.; Wallace Stegner, *Beyond the Hundredth Meridian: John Wesley Powell and the Second Opening of the West* (Boston, 1954), pp. 174 ff.; Wilkins, *Moran*, pp. 57–71; William Henry Jackson Papers, State Historical Society of Colorado, Denver, Colorado; Clarence S. Jackson, *Picture Maker of the Old West: William H. Jackson* (New York, 1947), pp. 81 ff.; William Henry Jackson, *Time Exposure: The Autobiography of William Henry Jackson* (New York, 1940), pp. 196 ff.

14. New York *Times*, Oct. 23, 1871.

15. As quoted in Bartlett, *Great Surveys*, p. 57. The Northern Pacific Railroad was interested in Yellowstone from the time of the first expeditions. Jay Cooke helped finance the lectures that Langford gave early in 1871 and quite probably paid the expenses necessary to insure a speedy passage of the park bill through Congress: Ellis P. Oberholtzer, *Jay Cooke: Financier of the Civil War* (2 vols. Philadelphia, 1907) 2, 226–36, 316; Henrietta M. Larson, *Jay Cooke: Private Banker* (Cambridge, Mass., 1936), pp. 254 ff.

The suggestion that he father a national park movement appealed to the publicity-hungry Hayden. Along with Nathaniel P. Langford (whose initials and enthusiasm inevitably earned him the sobriquet "National Park") and Montana's Congressional delegate William H. Clagett, he began to build pressure for a reservation. Wilderness preservation did not figure in the appeal the park proponents made before Congress. They argued that speculators and squatters who were allegedly ready to move into the Yellowstone region endangered what Hayden called "the beautiful decorations." When the question of park boundaries arose, legislators called on Hayden as the man most familiar with the region. His reason for including over three thousand square miles had no relation to wilderness preservation, but rather stemmed from the feeling that there might be other "decorations," as yet undiscovered, in the vicinity of the known ones.[16]

On December 18, 1871, Congress began consideration of a park bill. The brief debate that followed focused on the need for protecting "remarkable curiosities" and "rare wonders" from private claims.[17] Supporters of the bill assured their colleagues that the Yellowstone country was too high and cold to be cultivated; consequently its reservation would do "no harm to the material interests of the people."[18] The strategy was not to justify the park positively as wilderness, but to demonstrate its uselessness to civilization. Before voting, the legislators received copies of Langford's articles in *Scribner's* and William H. Jackson's photographs.[19] Since neither these documents, nor the Congressional debate, nor the text of the bill itself made mention of wilderness, it is clear that no *intentional* preservation of wild country occurred on March 1, 1872, when President Grant signed an act creating "a public park

16. F. V. Hayden, "The Hot Springs and Geysers of the Yellowstone and Firehole Rivers," *American Journal of Science and Art, 3* (1872), 176. In his other published writings Hayden failed to demonstrate the slightest awareness of the wilderness attributes of Yellowstone: see "The Wonders of the West II: More About the Yellowstone," *Scribner's Monthly, 3* (1872), 388–96; *Preliminary Report of the United States Geological Survey on Montana and Portions of Adjacent Territories; being a Fifth Annual Report of Progress* (Washington, D.C., 1872); and *The Great West* (Bloomington, Ill., 1880), pp. 1–88.

17. As quoted from the report on the Yellowstone bill by the House Committee on the Public Lands in Hayden, *Preliminary Report*, p. 163.

18. *Congressional Globe*, 42d Cong., 2d Sess., *1* (January 30, 1872), p. 697.

19. Jackson, "The Creation of Yellowstone National Park," 187 ff.; Cramton, *Early History*, pp. 24–28; Jackson, *Picture Maker of the Old West*, pp. 145–58.

or pleasuring ground." Yet the stipulation that "all timber, mineral deposits, natural curiosities, or wonders" within the park be retained "in their natural condition" left the way open for later observers to construe its purposes as preserving wild country.[20]

The initial public reaction to the creation of Yellowstone National Park also ignored wilderness. It was praised as a "museum" and "marvellous valley," an area where people could see the "freaks and phenomena of Nature" along with "wonderful natural curiosities." Far from recognizing the park as a wilderness preserve, *Scribner's* anticipated the time when "Yankee enterprise will dot the new Park with hostelries and furrow it with lines of travel."[21] And a Montana newspaper went so far as to *regret* the park because it tended to keep the Yellowstone country wild and undeveloped.[22] A few joined Hayden in regarding the act as "a tribute from our legislators to science," and one writer in the *American Naturalist* felt its value lay in the provision of a habitat where bison might be saved from extinction. Others pointed out that the forests within the park were situated on the watershed of both the Missouri and the Snake Rivers and served to regulate their flow.[23]

Gradually later Congresses realized that Yellowstone National Park was not just a collection of natural curiosities but, in fact, a wilderness preserve. Yet indifference and hostility persisted. In 1883, for example, Senator John J. Ingalls of Kansas attacked Yellowstone as an expensive irrelevancy. Speaking in opposition to an appropriation for its upkeep, he declared there was no need for the government to enter into the "show business." "The best thing the Government could do with the Yellowstone National Park," Ingalls contended, "is to survey it and sell it as other public lands are sold." George G. Vest of Missouri arose to reply. He referred to the park as a "mountain wilderness" and defended it in the Romantic manner as esthetically important in counteracting America's ma-

20. U.S., *Statutes at Large, 17,* p. 32.

21. *Ohio State Journal* as quoted in Jackson, "The Creation of Yellowstone National Park," 199; New York *Herald,* Feb. 28, 1872; Edwin J. Stanley, *Rambles in Wonderland* (New York, 1880), p. 63; New York *Times,* Feb. 29, 1872; "The Yellowstone National Park," *Scribner's Monthly, 4* (1872), 121.

22. Helena, Mont., *Rocky Mountain Gazette,* March 6, 1872.

23. Hayden, *Preliminary Report,* p. 162; Theodore B. Comstock, "The Yellowstone National Park," *American Naturalist, 8* (1874), 65–79, 155–66; George Bird Grinnell to the editor of the New York *Times,* New York *Times,* Jan. 29, 1885; Arnold Hague, "The Yellowstone Park as a Forest Reservation," *Nation, 46* (1888), 9–10.

terialistic tendency. After touching this raw nerve of the national conscience, Vest argued that a nation whose population was expected to exceed 150,000,000 needed Yellowstone "as a great breathing-place for the national lungs."[24] Ingalls had no rejoinder, and the Senate passed an appropriation of $40,000 for the park.

In the mid-1880s, debate in Congress concerning Yellowstone centered on the attempt of the Cinnabar and Clark's Fork Railroad Company to assist several mining ventures by securing a right-of-way across park land. Representative Lewis E. Payson of Illinois, who approved the railroad's plans, pointed out on December 11, 1886, that no harm could come to the geysers and hot springs. In his opinion the question was whether or not a mine "whose output . . . will be measured by millions upon millions of dollars, shall be permitted to have access to the markets of the world." A spokesman for the railroad appeared before the House to express his astonishment that anyone would question hallowed American values. "Is it true," he demanded, "that the rights and privileges of citizenship, the vast accumulation of property, and the demands of commerce . . . are to yield to . . . a few sportsmen bent only on the protection of a few buffalo."[25] Previously wilderness had always succumbed to arguments such as these.

Samuel S. Cox of New York replied to the demand for a right-of-way. "This is a measure," he declared, "which is inspired by corporate greed and natural selfishness against national pride and beauty." In Cox's opinion utilitarian criteria were irrelevant in evaluating Yellowstone. In the tradition of the Transcendentalists and Frederick Law Olmsted, he saw support of the park as a matter of keeping inviolate "all that gives elevation and grace to human nature, by the observation of the works of physical nature." Posterity had a stake in the park's "marvelous scenery," he concluded. The House burst into applause.

Representative Payson leaped back to his feet to assure the House that, except for Mammoth Hot Springs, which was four miles away, there was not "another object of natural curiosity within 40 miles" of the proposed railroad. Along with most of the early commenta-

24. *Congressional Record*, 47th Cong., 2d Sess., *14* (March 1, 1883), p. 3488. For a discussion of the administrative history of the park see Haines, "History of Yellowstone National Park," pp. 119–37 and his "Yellowstone's Role in Conversation," *Yellowstone Interpreter, 1* (1963), 3–9, along with Ise, *National Park Policy*, pp. 20 ff.

25. *Congressional Record*, 49th Cong., 2d Sess., *18* (Dec. 11, 1886), p. 94, (Dec. 14), p. 150.

tors, Payson understood the park's function as the protection of curiosities. "I can not understand the sentiment," he admitted, "which favors the retention of a few buffaloes to the development of mining interests amounting to millions of dollars."

But to Representative William McAdoo of New Jersey, Yellowstone performed a larger function. Answering Payson, he pointed out that the park also preserved wilderness which the railroad would destroy even if it did not harm the hot springs. He added that the park had been created for people who might care to seek "in the great West the inspiring sights and mysteries of nature that elevate mankind and bring it closer communion with omniscience" and that it "should be preserved on this, if for no other ground." McAdoo continued with a vindication of the principle of wilderness preservation: "the glory of this territory is its sublime solitude. Civilization is so universal that man can only see nature in her majesty and primal glory, as it were, in these as yet virgin regions." In conclusion he put the issue in terms that previous advocates of wilderness had long used, pleading with his colleagues to "prefer the beautiful and sublime . . . to heartless mammon and the greed of capital."[26]

A vote followed in which the railroad's application for a right-of-way was turned down 107 to 65. Never before had wilderness values withstood such a direct confrontation with civilization.

Recognition of the wilderness attributes of Yellowstone National Park also appeared in the 1886 report of Secretary of the Interior Lucius Q. C. Lamar. In a manner reminiscent of George Catlin and Francis Parkman, he interpreted the intention of Congress in establishing the park as "the preservation of wilderness of forests, geysers, mountains . . . and the game common to that region in as nearly the condition of nature as possible, with a view to holding for the benefit of those who shall come after us something of the original 'wild West' that shall stand while the rest of the world moves, affording the student of nature and the pleasure tourist a restful contrast to . . . busy and progressive scenes." In fact, Lamar was wrong in his interpretation of Congress' purposes. With the exception of the geysers and game this had not been the reason for action in 1872, but from Lamar's vantage point almost fifteen years later, it seemed increasingly credible that the Park was a wilderness

26. Ibid. (Dec. 14), pp. 152, 153, 154.

preserve and should be defended as such. And in 1892, twenty years after the Yellowstone Act, Senator William B. Bate of Tennessee explained its purpose as protecting a region for Americans who desired to see "primeval nature, simple and pure."[27] Certainly not all Americans at the time agreed, or even cared about Yellowstone, but Bate's opinion was a harbinger.

Westward expansion left a large island of heavily forested, mountainous country in northern New York generally uninhabited. By the 1880s more had been written about the Adirondack country than any other wilderness area in the United States. Charles Fenno Hoffman, Joel T. Headley, and Samuel H. Hammond (see Chapters 3, 4 and 6) were among the first to describe the pleasures of vacations in the area. As the population of the East increased and more people lived in urban situations, the Adirondacks received still more attention. The upland was said to be an "enchanted island" where men in quest of health and refreshment could find relief from "the busy world, away from its noise and tumult, its cares and perplexities."[28] No single statement did more to publicize the region than William H. H. Murray's *Adventures in the Wilderness: or, Camp-Life in the Adirondacks* of 1869. A Yale graduate and pastor of Boston's fashionable Park Street Congregational Church, "Adirondack" Murray's book not only described the hunting and fishing of the area in a manner that sent hundreds of eager sportsmen into it the following summer, but attempted to give his personal reasons for seeking wilderness. For clergymen like himself, Murray declared, "the wilderness provides that perfect relaxation which all jaded minds require." After seeing the works of God in wild nature, the preacher would return "swarth and tough as an Indian, elasticity in his step, fire in his eye, depth and clearness in his reinvigorated voice, [and] wouldn't there be some preaching!"[29]

27. United States Department of the Interior, *Annual Report for 1886* (Washington, D.C., 1886), p. 77; *Congressional Record*, 52d Cong., 1st Sess., *23* (May 10, 1892), p. 4124.

28. New York *Times*, June 10, 1871; "The Wilds of Northern New York," *Putnam's*, *4* (1854), 269.

29. William H. H. Murray, *Adventures in the Wilderness; or, Camp-Life in the Adirondacks* (Boston, 1869), pp. 22, 24. On Murray and the impact of his book see Alfred L. Donaldson, *A History of the Adirondacks* (2 vols. New York, 1921) *1*, 190–201.

The popularity of the Adirondacks focused attention on the disappearance of their wilderness qualities.[30] One anonymous writer, describing the region's charm, sadly concluded that "in a few years, the railroad with its iron web will bind the free forest, the lakes will lose their solitude, the deer and moose will flee to a safer resort . . . and men with axe and spade will work out a revolution."[31] The idea of preservation followed. Samuel H. Hammond's plea for a one-hundred-mile "circle" of wilderness (Chapter 6) came in 1857; two years later the Northwoods Walton Club called for laws protecting "our Northern Wilderness." The result would be a "vast and noble preserve" where fish and game could flourish and where "no screeching locomotive [would] ever startle . . . Fauns and Water Sprites."[32] In 1864 the New York *Times* seconded the idea with an editorial urging the state to acquire this land before it was "despoiled." Lumber mills and iron foundries could operate in places not reserved, the *Times* believed, thus ensuring the balance "which should always exist between utility and enjoyment."[33]

As the editorial in the *Times* suggested, even those who favored wilderness preservation avoided placing themselves in opposition to progress and industry; the argument that eventually secured protection for the Adirondacks had the same characteristic of supporting civilization. The technique appeared in the first report of the New York State Park Commission, created in 1872 to investigate the possibilities of establishing a public park in the Adirondacks.[34] "We do not favor the creation of an expensive and exclu-

30. For a general discussion see William C. White, *Adirondack Country* (New York, 1954), pp. 85–139.

31. "The Wilds," *Putnam's,* 269–70. A similar statement appeared in *The Forest Arcadia of Northern New York* (Boston, 1864), pp. 193–97.

32. Quoted in Harold C. Anderson, "The Unknown Genesis of the Wilderness Idea," *Living Wilderness, 5* (1940), 15.

33. New York *Times,* August 9, 1864. The editorial is reprinted and the question of its purpose and author discussed in Donaldson, *History of the Adirondacks, 1,* 350; *2,* 280–82. White, *Adirondack Country,* p. 111, offers another interpretation.

34. For the work of the Commission and the political history of forest preservation in New York for the next several decades there is a large secondary literature: Charles Z. Lincoln, *The Constitutional History of New York* (5 vols. Rochester, N.Y., 1906) *3,* 391 ff.; Marvin W. Kranz, "Pioneering in Conservation: A History of the Conservation Movement in New York State, 1816–1903" (unpublished Ph.D. dissertation, Syracuse University, 1961), pp. 57 ff.; James P. Gilligan, "The Development of Policy and Administration of Forest Service Primitive and Wilderness Areas in the Western United States" (unpublished Ph.D. dissertation, University of

sive park for mere purposes of recreation," the commissioners began, "but, condemning such suggestions, recommend the simple preservation of the timber as a measure of political economy." Specifically, the wilderness ensured a regulated water supply for New York's rivers and canals. "Without a *steady, constant* supply of water from these streams of the wilderness," the report continued, "our canals would be dry, and a great portion of the grain and other produce of the western part of the State would be unable to find cheap transportation to the markets of the Hudson river valley."[35] In this manner wilderness preservation and commercial prosperity were tied together.

In 1873 a new periodical for sportsmen, *Forest and Stream,* declared that the watershed argument held the key to success in the matter of an Adirondack wilderness preserve. The most effective way to propose the idea to the state legislature, it added, "is to have them look at the preservation of the Adirondacks as a question of self-interest."[36] However much they might desire the wilderness for non-utilitarian purposes, sportsmen and Romantics realized that arguments on those grounds alone would not suffice. Consequently they were willing to give full support to the watershed rationale.

By the 1880s, evidence of declining water levels in the Erie Canal and Hudson River generated widespread concern. An intensive campaign began in the fall of 1883 with the New York *Tribune* contending that the wilderness to the north must be preserved "seeing that it contains the fountainheads of the noble streams that conserve our physical and commercial prosperity." Other news-

---

Michigan, 1953), pp. 25–35; and Roger C. Thompson, "The Doctrine of Wilderness: A Study of the Policy and Politics of the Adirondack Preserve-Park" (unpublished Ph.D. dissertation, Syracuse University, State University College of Forestry, 1962), passim. Some of Thompson's findings have been published in article form: "Politics in the Wilderness: New York's Adirondack Forest Preserve," *Forest History, 6* (1963), 14–23.

35. Commissioners of State Parks of the State of New York, *First Annual Report,* New York Senate Doc. 102 (May 15, 1873), pp. 3, 10. Verplank Colvin of Albany was largely responsible for the report. Toward its conclusion, and in later reports as state surveyor, he interspersed pleas for the Adirondack wilderness on aesthetic and recreational grounds with the watershed argument.

36. "The Adirondack Park," *Forest and Stream, 1* (1873), 73. A similar statement appeared as "The State Park," *Forest and Stream, 1* (1873), 136–37. See also Nathaniel B. Sylvester, *Historical Sketches of Northern New York and the Adirondack Wilderness* (Troy, N.Y., 1877), pp. 41–43.

papers added to the campaign, and preservation became the local issue of the day. Residents of New York City who were previously indifferent about wilderness, suddenly became incensed at the lumber and mining companies alleged to be stripping the Adirondack forests. It was predicted that without protection of the woodlands municipal water supplies could run dry and periodic droughts render the state waterways useless. At other times disastrous floods might inundate the lowlands. Obviously the effect on commerce would be catastrophic. As the *Tribune* succinctly expressed it, to cut the wild forests in the Adirondacks was equivalent to "tampering with the goose that lays the golden egg."[37]

The New York Chamber of Commerce, led by Morris K. Jesup, joined the fight for preservation and brought the politically powerful business interests of New York City into play.[38] Jesup petitioned the legislature that it was necessary to save the forests because "their destruction will seriously injure the internal commerce of the State."[39] Moreover, the merchants believed that if drought eliminated the Erie-Hudson route as a means of shipping goods, railroads would have a monopoly and be able to raise rates at will. It did not require a love of wilderness to come to the defense of the Adirondacks on these grounds. With business interests applying the necessary pressure, on May 15, 1885, Governor David B. Hill approved a bill establishing a "Forest Preserve" of 715,000 acres that was to remain permanently "as wild forest lands."[40] The aim of the law was the preservation of wilderness, but for commercial ends.

Although indisputably effective, the watershed argument took no account of other values of wild country that many were coming to feel had at least equal importance. For one commentator who felt the Adirondacks should be made a national park instead of a state reserve, the wilderness was "of higher importance to man than that of a mere industrial and commercial utility."[41] And a person who lived near the reserve declared of one location in his neighborhood: "it is the most wild and beautiful spot in the whole wilder-

37. New York *Tribune,* Sept. 2, 1883.

38. Kranz, "Pioneering in Conservation," pp. 152 ff.; William Adams Brown, *Morris Ketchum Jesup: A Character Sketch* (New York, 1910), pp. 40, 60–64, 165.

39. As quoted in Brown, *Jesup,* p. 61.

40. *New York Laws,* 1885, Chap. 238, p. 482.

41. William Hosea Ballou, "An Adirondack National Park," *American Naturalist, 19* (1885), 579.

ness and its beauty should be enough to save it. But," he added, "that sentiment has little chance with our lawmakers."[42] On the contrary, New York's legislators were taking increasing notice of the nonutilitarian values of wilderness. In 1891 the New York Forest Commission suggested that the state consider redesignating the forest preserve as a park. Among its reasons, to be sure, was the standard one about forested watersheds, but the Commission also observed that a park would provide "a place where rest, recuperation and vigor may be gained by our highly nervous and overworked people."[43] A year later the legislature established a state park embracing over three million acres. The wording of the act indicated a change in motivation: Adirondack State Park was to be "ground open for the free use of all the people for their health and pleasure, and as forest land necessary to the preservation of the headwaters of the chief rivers of the state, and as a future supply of timber."[44] The recreational rationale for wilderness preservation had finally achieved equal legal recognition with more practical arguments.

Many New Yorkers were dissatisfied with the protection the Adirondacks received under the park act and desired to have the principle of wilderness preservation written into the state constitution. The constitutional convention of 1894 presented an opportunity. Commercial interests in New York City, that continued to be the mainstay of political support for preservation, sent David McClure, a New York attorney, to the convention as their personal representative on the Adirondack question. McClure headed the committee responsible for Article 7, Section 7, guaranteeing permanent preservation for the Adirondack wilderness. On September 8 he rose to defend this provision. He reiterated all the old points about the importance of the Adirondacks in maintaining the capacity of rivers to carry trade, in providing adequate supplies of drinking water, and in guaranteeing enough water for fire protection in the large cities. But he also gave consideration to "the higher uses of the great wilderness." In fact McClure declared that the "first" reason for preserving it was "as a great resort for the people of this State. When tired of the trials, tribulations and annoy-

42. New York *Times*, July 12, 1889.

43. *Special Report of the New York Forest Commission on the Establishment of an Adirondack State Park*, New York Senate Doc. 19 (Jan. 28, 1891), p. 29.

44. *New York Laws*, 1892, Chap. 709, p. 1459.

ances of business and every-day life in the man-made towns, [the Adirondacks] offer to man a place of retirement. There . . . he may find some consolation in communing with that great Father of all. . . . For man and for woman thoroughly tired out, desiring peace and quiet, these woods are inestimable in value."[45]

Others came to McClure's support, and Article 7, Section 7 received the unanimous consent of the 1894 convention. When New York's voters approved it in November, wilderness values were given preeminence in an area the size of Connecticut. Unquestionably the watershed argument had been the preservationists' mainstay, but by the 1890s those justifying the Adirondack wilderness, like Yellowstone's supporters, began to turn to non-utilitarian arguments. The rationale for wilderness preservation was gradually catching up with the ideology of appreciation.

45. *Revised Record of the Constitutional Convention of the State of New York,* ed. William H. Steele (5 vols. Albany, N.Y., 1900), *4*, 132–33.

CHAPTER 8

John Muir: Publicizer

> You know that I have not lagged behind in the work of exploring our grand wildernesses, and in calling everybody to come and enjoy the thousand blessings they have to offer.
>
> John Muir, 1895

ALTHOUGH the creation of Yellowstone National Park and the Adirondack Forest Preserve marked a weakening of traditional American assumptions about uninhabited land, in each case *wilderness* preservation was almost accidental and certainly not the result of a national movement. Wild country needed a champion, and in a self-styled "poetico-trampo-geologist-bot. and ornith-natural, etc!—!—!—!"[1] named John Muir it found one. Starting in the 1870s, Muir made exploring wilderness and extoling its values a way of life. Many of his ideas merely echoed the thoughts of earlier deists and Romantics, especially Thoreau, but he articulated them with an intensity and enthusiasm that commanded widespread attention. Muir's books were minor best-sellers, and the nation's foremost periodicals competed for his essays. The best universities tried to persuade him to join their faculties and, when unsuccessful, settled for his acceptance of honorary degrees. As a publicizer of the American wilderness Muir had no equal. At his death in 1914 he had earned a reputation as "the most magnificent enthusiast about nature in the United States, the most rapt of all prophets of our out-of-door gospel."[2]

"When I was a boy in Scotland," John Muir recalled, "I was fond of everything that was wild, and all my life I've been growing fonder and fonder of wild places and wild creatures."[3] He did

1. Muir to Robert Underwood Johnson, Sept. 13, 1889, as quoted in "The Creation of Yosemite National Park," *Sierra Club Bulletin, 39* (1944), 50.
2. "About the Yosemite," *American Review of Reviews, 45* (1912), 766–67.
3. Muir, *The Story of My Boyhood and Youth* (Boston, 1913), p. 1.

not do so, however, without overcoming several formidable obstacles. One was a father whose Calvinistic conception of Christianity brooked no religion of nature. Scripture, postulated Daniel Muir, was the only source of God's truth, and young John was obliged to commit the entire New Testament and most of the Old to memory. The Muir children were also schooled in the ethics of hard work. Only slackers or sinners approached nature without axe or plough.[4]

In 1849, during John's eleventh year, his family left Scotland for a homestead on the central Wisconsin frontier. Indians lingered in the region, and the conquest of the forest was an economic necessity. As the eldest son, John bore many of the burdens of pioneering. Back-breaking days of toil gave him ample reason to hate the wilderness, but Muir was not the typical frontiersman. The thrill of being in what he later called "that glorious Wisconsin wilderness"[5] never abated. And instead of lauding civilization, Muir expressed displeasure at its cruel, repressive, and utilitarian tendencies. Wild nature, in contrast, appeared to have a liberating influence conducive to human happiness.

Inevitably, John Muir left his father's Wisconsin farm. His skill as an inventor provided a passport south to Madison. At the State Agricultural Fair of 1860, Muir's mechanical devices won acclaim as the work of a genius. Job opportunities opened at once, but Muir took more interest in the world of ideas he glimpsed at the University of Wisconsin. Here he found scientists and theologians who supported his revulsion from his father's attitudes toward nature and religion. In Professor Ezra Slocum Carr's geology class Muir learned to look at the land with a new awareness of order and pattern. Botanical studies provided similar lessons and helped him understand the argument that natural science com-

4. Linnie Marsh Wolfe, *Son of the Wilderness: The Life of John Muir* (New York, 1945), pp. 3–57. Another important biographical source is William F. Badè, *The Life and Letters of John Muir* (2 vols. Boston, 1923). Norman Foerster, *Nature in American Literature* (New York, 1923), pp. 238–63, Edith Jane Hadley, "John Muir's Views of Nature and their Consequences" (unpublished Ph.D. dissertation, University of Wisconsin, 1956), and Daniel Barr Weber, "John Muir: The Function of Wilderness in an Industrial Society" (unpublished Ph.D. dissertation, University of Minnesota, 1964) analyze various aspects of Muir's thought. A bibliography, largely complete except for some posthumous collections, compiled by Jennie Elliot Doran and Cornelius Beach Bradley may be found in the *Sierra Club Bulletin, 10* (1916), 41–59.

5. Muir, *Boyhood and Youth*, p. 63.

plemented rather than conflicted with worship. Eagerly Muir turned to the writing of Asa Gray for amplifications of this doctrine of design. Under the guidance of Mrs. Jeanne C. Carr and Dr. James Davie Butler, a professor of classics, he also discovered Wordsworth, Emerson, Thoreau, and a lesser-known Transcendental minister, Walter Rollins Brooks. Transcendentalism removed the last of Muir's doubts concerning the conflict of religion and the study of the natural world. Early in 1866 he wrote triumphantly to Mrs. Carr that the Bible and "Nature" were "two books [which] harmonize beautifully." Indeed, he continued, "I will confess that I take more intense delight from reading the power and goodness of God from 'the things which are made' than from the Bible."[6]

Muir's two and a half years in Madison were insufficient for a degree, but he left with the thought that "I was only leaving one University for another, the Wisconsin University for the University of the Wilderness." Yet it required a near-disaster to convince him that his true calling lay in the woods and mountains rather than the machine shop where his talents as an inventor might well have earned him a fortune. The pivotal event occurred in March 1867, while Muir was working in an Indianapolis carriage factory. Late one evening a sharp file slipped in Muir's usually sure hands and pierced the cornea of his right eye. As he stood silently by a window, the aqueous humor fell out into his cupped hand. Within hours his other eye had also become blind from sympathetic nervous shock. Reduced to an invalid's bed in a darkened room, Muir contemplated a life without sight. After a month, however, he recovered his vision, and vowed to waste no more time getting to the wilderness. "God has to nearly kill us sometimes, to teach us lessons," he concluded.[7]

As his first project Muir elected to wander "just anywhere in the wilderness southward" and ended by hiking a thousand miles from Indiana to the Gulf of Mexico. The journal of his trip contains the seeds of most of his basic ideas. Wild nature was replete with "Divine beauty" and "harmony." Especially to "lovers of the wild," its "spiritual power" emanated from the landscape. If civi-

6. Badè, *Life and Letters, 1,* 147. A comprehensive discussion of the early influences on Muir's attitude toward nature appears in Hadley, pp. 78 ff. Weber's account, pp. 178 ff., is shallow in comparison.

7. Muir, *Boyhood and Youth,* p. 286; Wolfe, *Muir,* p. 105.

lized man would only seek the wilderness, he could purge himself of the "sediments of society" and become a "new creature."[8] Muir's own appetite for wildness knew no bounds. Only a serious bout with malaria persuaded him to give up plans to track the Amazon to its source. Instead, he sailed for the colder climate of northern California. Arriving in San Francisco in March 1868, Muir allegedly inquired of the first passer-by the way out of town. Asked to specify his destination, he simply replied "any place that is wild."[9] The trail led across the Bay, into the San Joaquin Valley, and, finally, into the Sierra. There it ended amidst mountains capable of satisfying Muir's enthusiasm, developing his wilderness philosophy, and inspiring his most powerful writing.

For John Muir Transcendentalism was always the essential philosophy for interpreting the value of wilderness. Mrs. Carr's personal friendship with Emerson and admiration for Thoreau encouraged Muir to steep himself in their works during his first long winters in Yosemite Valley. When the high-country trails opened again, a tattered volume of Emerson's essays, heavily glossed in Muir's hand, went along in his pack.[10] Understandably, most of Muir's ideas were variations on the Transcendentalists' staple theme: natural objects were "the terrestrial manifestations of God."[11] At one point he described nature as a "window opening into heaven, a mirror reflecting the Creator." Leaves, rocks, and bodies of water became "sparks of the Divine Soul."[12]

It followed that *wild* nature provided the best "conductor of divinity" because it was least associated with man's artificial constructs. Making the point another way, Muir remarked that while God's glory was written over all His works, in the wilderness the letters were capitalized. In this frame of mind, primitive forests became "temples," while trees were "psalm-singing." Of the Sierra

8. Muir, *A Thousand-Mile Walk to the Gulf*, ed. William F. Badè (Boston, 1916), pp. 11–12, 71, 211–12.

9. Muir, *The Yosemite* (New York, 1912), p. 4.

10. This first volume of the 1870 edition of *The Prose Works of Ralph Waldo Emerson* now resides in the rare books collection of the Yale University Library. I consulted a microfilm reproduction in the University of Wisconsin Library, Madison.

11. Muir, *Our National Parks* (Boston, 1901), p. 74; Muir, *The Mountains of California* (New York, 1894), p. 56.

12. Muir, *My First Summer in the Sierra* (Boston, 1911), p. 211; *John of the Mountains: The Unpublished Journals of John Muir*, ed. Linnie Marsh Wolfe (Boston, 1938), p. 138.

wilderness as a whole Muir exulted: "everything in it seems equally divine—one smooth, pure, wild glow of Heaven's love."[13]

Wilderness glowed, to be sure, only for those who approached it on a higher, spiritual plane. Intuition was essential. Describing the process of insight, Muir drew his rhetoric directly from Emerson's *Nature:* "you bathe in these spirit-beams, turning round and round, as if warming at a camp-fire. Presently you lose consciousness of your separate existence: you blend with the landscape, and become part and parcel of nature." In this condition he believed life's inner harmonies, fundamental truths of existence, stood out in bold relief. "The clearest way into the Universe," Muir wrote, "is through a forest wilderness."[14]

In May of 1871 Muir learned from Mrs. Carr that Emerson himself would shortly arrive in Yosemite. Greatly excited, he anticipated meeting the man best equipped to interpret the wilderness. A letter from Mrs. Carr prepared Emerson to find in the mountains someone who excelled in putting Transcendentalism into practice. Muir lived up to his advance billing, and Emerson was drawn to him immediately. Muir hoped he could persuade his mentor to join him "in a month's worship with Nature in the high temples of the great Sierra Crown beyond our holy Yosemite," but the elderly sage's traveling companions demurred on his behalf and found lodging in a hotel. Lamenting Emerson's "sadly civilized" friends, Muir declared the incident a "sad commentary on culture and the glorious transcendentalism."[15]

In spite of this disappointment Muir continued to regard Transcendentalism as glorious and to correspond with Emerson. But in regard to wilderness the men differed fundamentally. On February 5, 1872, Emerson urged Muir "to bring to an early close your absolute contracts with any yet unvisited glaciers or volcanoes" and come to Massachusetts as his permanent guest. The solitude of the wilderness, he warned, "is a sublime mistress, but an intolerable wife."[16] Muir, however, did not share such reservations, and politely refused the invitation. Indeed his unadulterated joy in wild country frequently conveyed the impression that man might dispense with civilization entirely and, roaming the mountains in

13. Wolfe, ed., *Journals*, p. 47, 118; Muir, *Yosemite*, p. 255; Muir, *Travels in Alaska* (Boston, 1915), p. 24; Muir, *First Summer*, p. 90.

14. Badè, ed., *Thousand-Mile Walk*, p. 212; Wolfe, ed., *Journals*, p. 313.

15. Muir to Emerson, May 8, 1871, in *The Letters of Ralph Waldo Emerson*, ed. Ralph L. Rusk (6 vols. New York, 1939), *6*, 154–55; Muir, *National Parks*, pp. 134–35.

16. Badè, *Life and Letters*, *1*, 259–60.

close contact with God, be none the worse for the loss. Muir's enthusiasm for wilderness was seldom qualified. Compared to Thoreau, who cringed at an excess of wildness and idealized the half-cultivated,[17] Muir was wild indeed. "I am often asked," he wrote in his Alaskan journal in the 1890s, "if I am not lonesome on my solitary excursions. It seems so self-evident that one cannot be lonesome where everything is wild and beautiful and busy and steeped with God that the question is hard to answer—seems silly." Elsewhere he derisively remarked that "some have strange, morbid fears as soon as they find themselves with Nature, even in the kindest and wildest of her solitudes, like very sick children afraid of their mother."[18] Much as he admired Thoreau's philosophy, Muir could not suppress a chuckle at a man who could "see forests in orchards and patches of huckleberry brush" or whose outpost at Walden was a "mere saunter" from Concord.[19]

Yet Muir's intellectual debt to Thoreau and to primitivism appeared throughout his writing. In 1874, at the beginning of his literary career, he noted a great difference between domestic sheep and those living wild in the mountains. The former, he contended, were timid, dirty, and "only half alive" while the sheep of the Sierra were bold, elegant, and glowing with life. Muir returned to the theme the following year, this time choosing a comparison of wild and domestic wool as his metaphoric vehicle. As an answer to those who felt nothing wild could equal the civilized product, Muir presented evidence that the fleece of mountain sheep was superior in quality to that of commercial flocks. "Well done for wildness," he exclaimed, "wild wool is finer than tame!" From this point Muir jumped to his conclusion: "all wildness is finer than tameness." After a reference to wild and cultivated apples, which Thoreau had used as *his* metaphor in a similar discussion, Muir declared that "a little pure wildness is the one great present want, both of men and sheep."[20]

Muir's ideas developed as a result of observing the stifling effect

17. See Chapter 5. For an elaboration of the point see Edwin Way Teale, "John Muir Was the Wildest," *Living Wilderness, 19* (1954–55), 1–6, and Teale's introduction to *The Wilderness World of John Muir,* ed. Teale (Boston, 1954).

18. Wolfe, ed., *Journals,* p. 319; Muir, *Steep Trails,* ed. William F. Badè (New York, 1918), p. 82.

19. Badè, *Life and Letters, 2,* 268; Muir, "The Wild Parks and Forest Reservations of the West," *Atlantic Monthly, 81* (1898), 16.

20. Muir, "The Wild Sheep of California," *Overland Monthly, 12* (1874), 359; Muir, "Wild Wool," *Overland Monthly, 14* (1875), 361, 366.

on man's spirit of "the galling harness of civilization." "Civilized man chokes his soul," he noted in 1871, "as the heathen Chinese their feet." Muir believed that centuries of existence as primitive beings had implanted in modern men yearnings for adventure, freedom, and contact with nature that city life could not satisfy. Recognizing in himself "a constant tendency to return to primitive wildness," Muir generalized for his race: "going to the woods is going home; for I suppose we came from the woods originally." Consequently, "there is a love of wild Nature in everybody, an ancient mother-love showing itself whether recognized or no, and however covered by cares and duties."[21] Deny this love, and the thwarted longings produced tension and despair; indulge it periodically in the wilderness, and mental and physical reinvigoration resulted.

Wild country, according to Muir, had a mystical ability to inspire and refresh. "Climb the mountains and get their good tidings," he advised. "Nature's peace will flow into you as the sunshine into the trees. The winds will blow their freshness into you, and the storms their energy, while cares will drop off like autumn leaves." Wilderness was medicinal to lives "bound by clocks, almanacs . . . and dust and din" and limited to places where "Nature is covered and her voice smothered." Furthermore, following Thoreau, Muir argued that great poetry and philosophy depended on contact with mountains and forests. For these reasons he concluded, in a near-plagiarism of Thoreau: "in God's wildness lies the hope of the world—the great fresh, unblighted, unredeemed wilderness."[22]

Muir also valued wilderness as an environment in which the totality of creation existed in undisturbed harmony. Civilization, he felt, had distorted man's sense of his relationship to other living things. Modern man asks " 'what are rattlesnakes good for?' " with the implication that for their existence to be justified they had to benefit human beings. For Muir, snakes were "good for themselves, and we need not begrudge them their share of life." Elsewhere he declared that "the universe would be incomplete without man; but it would also be incomplete without the smallest transmicroscopic

21. Wolfe, ed., *Journals*, pp. 82, 90, 315, 317; Muir, *National Parks*, p. 98.

22. Teale, ed., *Wilderness World*, p. 311; Muir, *First Summer*, p. 250; Wolfe, ed., *Journals*, pp. 315–16, 317. Thoreau said "in wildness is the preservation of the World" (see Chapter 5).

creature that dwells beyond our conceitful eyes and knowledge." In the wilderness this truth was readily apparent, and men could feel themselves "part of wild Nature, kin to everything." From such knowledge came respect for "the rights of all the rest of creation."[23] In these ideas—his most original—Muir anticipated the insights of the ecologists, especially Aldo Leopold.

John Muir took as his life's mission the education of his countrymen in the advantages of wild country. Indeed, he conceived himself similar to John the Baptist in attempting to immerse "in the beauty of God's mountains" the "sinners" imprisoned in civilization. "I care to live," he wrote in 1874, "only to entice people to look at Nature's loveliness." His many later writings had a unifying message: buried in the cities, Americans defrauded themselves of the joy that could be theirs if they would but turn to "the freedom and glory of God's wilderness."[24]

The prime of John Muir's life coincided with the advent of national concern over conservation. At first, and superficially, the problem seemed simple: "exploiters" of natural resources had to be checked by those determined to "protect" them. Initially, anxiety over the rapid depletion of raw materials, particularly forests, was broad enough to embrace many points of view. A common enemy united the early conservationists. But they soon realized that as wide differences existed within their own house as between it and the exploiters. Men who thought they were colleagues found themselves opponents. The schism ran between those who defined conservation as the wise use or planned development of resources and those who have been termed preservationists, with their rejection of utilitarianism and advocacy of nature unaltered by man. Juxtaposing the needs of civilization with the spiritual and aesthetic value of wilderness, the conservation issue extended the old dialogue between pioneers and Romantics.

At the outset John Muir and his followers tried to keep a foot in both camps, recognizing the claims of both wilderness and civilization to the American landscape. In theory this was possible. But

23. Muir, *National Parks*, pp. 57–58; Badè, ed., *Thousand-Mile Walk*, p. 139; Muir, *First Summer*, p. 326; Badè, ed., *Thousand-Mile Walk*, p. 98. For amplification see Hadley, "John Muir," pp. 137 ff.

24. Wolfe, ed., *Journals*, p. 86; Badè, *Life and Letters*, 2, 29; Muir, *First Summer*, p. 250.

the pressure of making decisions about specific tracts of undeveloped land forced ambivalence into dogmatism. After a period of vacillation and confusion, Muir ended, inevitably, by opting for the preservationist interpretation of conservation, while others followed Gifford Pinchot and the professional foresters into the "wise use" school. The resulting conflict in the American conservation movement, still prevalent today, had profound implications for wilderness.

The Muir farm in Wisconsin included a forty-acre bog adjoining Fountain Lake. As a young man John Muir coveted it for the touch of "pure wildness" it lent to the landscape.[25] In the mid-1860s, about the time he left home, it occurred to him that unless the swamp was protected it would soon become a well-trampled stockyard. Muir repeatedly offered to purchase the land from his brother-in-law with the idea of keeping it wild, but was rebuffed as a foolish sentimentalist. Yet his interest in preserving parts of the American wilderness continued to grow.

During his first years in California, Muir noticed with regret how sheep (he called them "hoofed locusts"[26]) were moving into the high Sierra wilderness. "As sheep advance," he declared, "flowers, vegetation, grass, soil, plenty, and poetry vanish."[27] At the same time Muir also encountered Henry George's ideas about the evils of private ownership of land. Equipped with a passion for wilderness and the concept of public ownership, Muir began to write and lecture in favor of preservation through state action. "God's First Temples: How Shall We Preserve Our Forests?" appeared in the Sacramento *Record-Union* for February 5, 1876, with the suggestion that the answer lay in government control. Five years later Muir endeavored to persuade Congress to create a national park, on the model of Yellowstone, in the Kings River region of the southern Sierra, but the bill he helped draft died in the Senate's Public Lands Committee. Mt. Shasta in northern California also attracted his attention. In 1888 he urged that its "fresh unspoiled wilderness" be protected as a public park.[28]

In June of 1889 Robert Underwood Johnson, the associate edi-

25. "Proceedings of the Meeting of the Sierra Club held Nov. 23, 1895," *Sierra Club Bulletin, 1* (1896), 276; Badè, *Life and Letters, 1,* 158–60; 2, 393.

26. In Muir, *First Summer,* p. 113, for one example.

27. Wolfe, ed., *Journals,* p. 351.

28. Wolfe, *Muir,* pp. 227–28; Muir, *Picturesque California* (2 vols. San Francisco, 1888) *1,* 173–74.

tor of the nation's leading literary monthly, *Century*, arrived in San Francisco looking for copy. He contacted Muir, already well known as a writer, and the two planned a trip into the wilderness above Yosemite Valley. One evening around the campfire Johnson asked what had become of the luxuriant meadows and wildflowers he supposed existed in the mountains. Muir sadly replied that overgrazing had destroyed them throughout the Sierra, prompting his companion to remark: "obviously the thing to do is to make Yosemite National Park around the Valley on the plan of Yellowstone."[29] Muir heartily agreed and eventually committed himself to write two articles for *Century* as part of the plan to publicize Yosemite and the park idea.[30]

Muir's articles, complete with elaborate illustrations, appeared in the fall of 1890. He believed they would have over a million readers, but a more realistic figure was probably closer to the 200,000 copies of each issue *Century* actually circulated.[31] At any rate, this was far more publicity than preservation had ever received before. The greater part of the two essays was descriptive, and in contrast to the original proponents of Yellowstone National Park and the Adirondack reservation, Muir made it clear that wilderness was the object to be protected. He declared the Sierra around Yosemite Valley to be "a noble mark for the . . . lover of wilderness pure and simple." Drawing on the ideas of George Perkins Marsh (Chapter 6), Muir emphasized the importance of safeguarding the Sierra's soil and forests as watershed cover. But his final sentence left no doubt that his primary concern was to prevent "the destruction of the fineness of wildness."[32]

While Muir was preparing his articles, Robert Underwood

29. Robert Underwood Johnson, *Remembered Yesterdays* (Boston, 1923), p. 287. To understand Johnson's suggestion, it is necessary to recall that in 1864 the federal government had granted Yosemite Valley to California as a state park (see Chapter 6). What Johnson had in mind was a much larger, doughnut-shaped national park around the Valley.

30. John Muir Papers, Bancroft Library, University of California, Berkeley, Box 1; John Muir Papers, American Academy of Arts and Letters, New York, N.Y.; Robert Underwood Johnson Papers, Bancroft Library, University of California, Berkeley, Box 7. Some of the correspondence between Muir and Johnson has been printed in "The Creation of Yosemite National Park," *Sierra Club Bulletin, 29* (1944), 49–60.

31. Muir to John Bidwell, June 18, 1889, Bidwell Papers, Bancroft Library, University of California, Berkeley, Box 2; Frank Luther Mott, *A History of American Magazines, 1865–1885* (Cambridge, Mass., 1938), p. 475.

32. Muir, "The Treasures of the Yosemite," *Century, 40* (1890), 483; Muir, "Features of the Proposed Yosemite National Park," *Century, 41* (1890), 666–67.

Johnson lobbied for a Yosemite park before the House of Representatives Committee on Public Lands. He also editorialized in *Century* for the preservation of "the beauty of nature in its wildest aspects."[33] One of Johnson's first tasks was to convince the legislators that Muir's proposal for a 1500-square-mile park was preferable to Representative William Vandever's idea of a reserve approximately one-fifth that size. In all probability Johnson received assistance from the powerful Southern Pacific Railroad, which had its eye on the profitable tourist trade Yosemite would generate.[34] On September 30, 1890, a park bill following John Muir's specifications passed both houses of Congress with little discussion. The following day Benjamin Harrison's signature gave the nation its first preserve consciously designed to protect wilderness.

The Yosemite Act marked a great triumph, but Muir knew from experience that without close watching, even legally protected wilderness was not safe from the utilitarian instinct. Consequently he welcomed Johnson's 1891 idea for "a Yosemite and Yellowstone defense association."[35] At the same time a group of professors at the University of California in Berkeley and at Stanford were discussing plans for an alpine club. Muir saw the connection at once and took the lead in planning an organization which would "be able to do something for wildness and make the mountains glad."[36] On June 4, 1892, in the offices of San Francisco lawyer Warren Olney, twenty-seven men formed the Sierra Club and dedicated it to "exploring, enjoying and rendering accessible the mountain regions of the Pacific Coast." They also proposed "to enlist the support of the people and the government in preserving

33. Johnson, "The Care of Yosemite Valley," *Century, 39* (1890), 478.

34. Holway R. Jones, *John Muir and the Sierra Club: The Battle for Yosemite* (San Francisco, 1965), pp. 37–47; Ise, *National Park Policy,* pp. 55 ff. The Southern Pacific appears to have also been highly interested in the Sequoia National Park, created on September 25, 1890, and tripled in size six days later in the act establishing the Yosemite reservation: Oscar Berland, "Giant Forest's Reservation: The Legend and the Mystery," *Sierra Club Bulletin, 47* (1962), 68–82; Douglas Hillman Strong, "A History of Sequoia National Park" (unpublished Ph.D. dissertation, Syracuse University, 1964), pp. 111 ff.

35. George Bird Grinnell to Johnson, Jan. 19, 1891, Johnson Papers, Berkeley, Box 4. Grinnell was responding to Johnson's idea for an association.

36. Muir to J. Henry Senger, May 22, 1892, Muir Papers, Berkeley, Box 1. For details see Jones, *John Muir and the Sierra Club,* pp. 3–23, and Joseph N. Le Conte, "The Sierra Club," *Sierra Club Bulletin, 10* (1917), 135–45.

the forests and other features of the Sierra Nevada Mountains."[37] Muir was the unanimous choice for president (an office he held for twenty-two years until his death) and the Sierra Club grew rapidly as a mecca for those interested in wilderness and its preservation.

Although Yosemite National Park and the Sierra Club commanded most of Muir's attention in the early 1890s, he also followed with interest the beginnings of federal forest protection. On March 3, 1891, an amendment to an act revising the general land laws passed Congress almost unnoticed. Under its terms the President was empowered to create "forest reserves" (later renamed "National Forests") by withdrawing land from the public domain, and Benjamin Harrison promptly proclaimed fifteen reserves totaling more than 13,000,000 acres.[38] Since the Forest Reserve Act did not specify the function of the reserved areas, John Muir had reason to believe it was intended to preserve undeveloped forests. To him the act seemed indistinguishable from legislation establishing national parks. Indeed, a renewed plea from Muir for a park around Kings Canyon stimulated Secretary of the Interior John W. Noble's determination to push the reserve bill through Congress. After listening to Muir and Robert Underwood Johnson, Noble decided that if the legislators refused to establish a park around Kings Canyon, the region might be protected as a forest reserva-

37. *Articles of Association, Articles of Incorporation, By-Laws, and a List of Charter Members of the Sierra Club*, Publications of the Sierra Club, 1 (San Francisco, 1892), p. 4.

38. For the political history of forest conservation in the 1890s see John Ise, *The United States Forest Policy* (New Haven, Conn., 1920), pp. 109 ff.; Jenks Cameron, *The Development of Governmental Forest Control in the United States*, Institute for Government Research Studies in Administration, 19 (Baltimore, 1928), pp. 202 ff.; Roy M. Robbins, *Our Landed Heritage: The Public Domain, 1776–1936* (Princeton, N.J., 1942), pp. 303 ff.; and James P. Gilligan, "The Development of Policy and Administration of Forest Service Primitive and Wilderness Areas in the Western United States" (unpublished Ph.D. dissertation, University of Michigan, 1953), pp. 37 ff.

Important background studies are Gilbert Chinard, "The Early History of Forestry in America," *Proceedings of the American Philosophical Society, 89* (1945), 444–88; Herbert A. Smith, "The Early Forestry Movement in the United States," *Agricultural History, 12* (1938), 326–46; Ralph M. Van Brocklin, "The Movement for the Conservation of Natural Resources in the United States Before 1901" (unpublished Ph.D. dissertation, University of Michigan, 1952), pp. 4–82; and Lawrence Rakestraw, "A History of Forest Conservation in the Pacific Northwest" (unpublished Ph.D. dissertation, University of Washington, 1955), pp. 1–34.

tion. Shortly thereafter he and Assistant Land Commissioner Edward A. Bowers drafted the seminal act in National Forest history.[39]

The new forest reserves received only paper protection. In practice, exploitation was not even checked. Also disconcerting to conservationists was the lack of any clear definition of the purpose of the reserves. Muir was content simply to protect the forests in their undeveloped condition. But Bowers, Bernhard E. Fernow of the federal Division of Forestry, and a young Yale graduate named Gifford Pinchot had other ideas. Pinchot ultimately became the leading spokesman for the foresters' position.[40] He had received graduate training in Europe where timberland was managed as a crop for maximum sustained yield. On returning late in 1890, Pinchot attempted to arouse interest in applying these forestry principles to America's timberland. He pointed out that while the lumberman was concerned with squeezing the last penny from the woods without regard to consequences, the forester managed them scientifically so as to obtain a steady and continuing supply of valuable products.[41] In theory this was a compelling argument—the nation could have its forests and use them too. At first even John Muir agreed. Forestry seemed so much of an improvement on unregulated lumbering practices that he did not immediately see its incompatibility with wilderness preservation. Moreover, Muir recognized the material needs of a growing nation. In 1895 he contributed along with Pinchot, Fernow, and others to a symposium on forest management conducted by *Century*. "It is impossible, in the nature of things, to stop at preservation," Muir declared. "The forests must be, and will be, not only preserved, but used; and . . . like perennial fountains . . . be made to yield a sure harvest

39. Wolfe, *Muir,* p. 252. Suggestive of the sort of argument Muir was making for Kings Canyon in the early 1890s is his "A Rival of the Yosemite: The Cañon of the South Fork of King's River, California," *Century, 43* (1891), 77–97.

40. Harold T. Pinkett, "Gifford Pinchot and the Early Conservation Movement in the United States" (unpublished Ph.D. dissertation, American University, 1953) is the best treatment of Pinchot's interest in forestry. M. Nelson McGeary, *Gifford Pinchot: Forester-Politician* (Princeton, N.J., 1960) and Martin L. Fausold, *Gifford Pinchot: Bull Moose Progressive* (Syracuse, 1961) are recent biographies. Andrew D. Rodgers, *Bernhard Eduard Fernow: A Story of North American Forestry* (Princeton, N.J., 1951) is also valuable in understanding the foresters' position.

41. Pinchot, "Forester and Lumberman in the North Woods" (c. 1894), Gifford Pinchot Papers, Library of Congress, Box 62.

of timber, while at the same time all their far-reaching [aesthetic and spiritual] uses may be maintained unimpaired."[42]

This assumption, however, proved short-lived. In 1896 a chain of events began that awakened Muir's antipathy to forestry and permanently split the ranks of American conservationists. Early in the year the agitation of Robert Underwood Johnson, Harvard botanist Charles Sprague Sargent, and the American Forestry Association succeeded in convincing Secretary of the Interior Hoke Smith of the advisability of formulating explicit policy for the management of the reserves. Smith, in turn, asked the National Academy of Science to appoint an advisory commission. Along with Sargent, who headed the group, its membership consisted of William Brewer and Alexander Agassiz of Yale and Harvard respectively, General H. L. Abbott, an engineer, Arnold Hague of the United States Geological Survey, and Gifford Pinchot. A $25,000 appropriation from Congress in June, 1896 enabled the Forestry Commission to tour the Western woodlands that summer.

When Pinchot joined the Commission in Montana in July, he discovered, to his "great delight," that John Muir had agreed to assist in the survey in an ex-officio capacity. Describing Muir as "in his late fifties, tall, thin, cordial, and a most fascinating talker," he "took to him at once." "It amazed me to learn," Pinchot, an ardent fisherman, added, "that he never carried even a fishhook with him on his solitary explorations. He said fishing wasted too much time." There was a hint of different temperaments here, but initially Muir and Pinchot became close friends. They found much in common, since, by his own admission, Pinchot "loved the woods and everything about them." He had, in fact, selected forestry as a career because it involved contact with the outdoors, and during the summer of 1896 he cherished those times that he and Muir left the others to talk around campfires alone in the forest.[43] Yet their common interests had definite limits. For all his love of the woods, Pinchot's ultimate loyalty was to civilization and forestry; Muir's to wilderness and preservation.

These differences emerged in the fall of 1896 as the Forestry Commission prepared to make its final report. The commissioners could not agree about the purpose of their work. Muir and Sargent

42. Muir, "A Plan to Save the Forests," *Century, 49* (1895), 631.
43. Pinchot, *Breaking New Ground* (New York, 1947), pp. 2, 100, 103.

assumed their task was to determine which areas of undeveloped forest needed preservation. They hoped the government could be persuaded to reserve more forests without provision for commercial use, in the manner of the 1891 Forest Reserve Act. Pinchot and Hague, on the other hand, felt the whole object of the Commission was to "get ready for practical forestry" and favored opening all the reserves to carefully managed economic development.[44] They accused the preservationists of wanting to lock up valuable natural resources.

The Sargent-Muir faction won a temporary victory on February 22, 1897, when President Grover Cleveland, in the closing days of his administration, established over 21,000,000 acres of forest reserves with no mention of utilitarian objectives. A recommendation from Sargent, made without the consent of his fellow commissioners, had precipitated the unexpected action. At once the foresters, seconded by lumber, grazing, and mining interests, howled in protest. Within a week bills appeared in both Houses to repeal Cleveland's order. When President William McKinley and the new Congress took office in March, the whole reserve idea seemed in jeopardy. Walter Hines Page, the editor of the *Atlantic Monthly,* asked Sargent to recommend someone to write in the forests' behalf. "There is but one man in the United States who can do it justice," he replied, "and his name is John Muir!"[45]

The article Muir wrote for Page in the late spring of 1897 did indeed strike furiously at the opponents of the reserves. At the same time it revealed Muir's continuing ambivalence on the forestry-or-preservation issue. He began with a diatribe against the pioneer who found the American forest "rejoicing in wildness" and, regarding "God's trees as only a large kind of pernicious weeds," waged "interminable forest wars." But Muir tried hard not to block progress. "Wild trees," he admitted, "had to make way for orchards and cornfields." A similar inconsistency marked his discussion of conservation. At one point he treated the campaign to save the forests as pure preservation: "clearing has surely gone far enough; soon . . . not a grove will be left to rest in or pray in." Yet he also advocated the foresters' concept of sustained yield, explicitly lauding Pinchot for his ideas about "wise management." Taking the experience of European countries as a model for

44. Ibid., p. 94.
45. As quoted in Wolfe, *Muir,* p. 273.

America, Muir declared that optimum conditions prevail when "the state woodlands are not allowed to lie idle [but] . . . are made to produce as much timber as is possible without spoiling them." In conclusion, Muir stated that selective cutting of mature trees would keep forests "a never failing fountain of wealth and beauty."[46]

The Achilles heel of this compromise attempt was the fact that even the wisest lumbering methods necessarily involved killing trees and clearing land. The existence of wilderness was simply not compatible with productive forest management. Muir's willingness to overlook this difficulty in the spring of 1897, and to join hands with Pinchot, stemmed largely from the fact that the great opposition to *any* form of forest reserve temporarily unified all supporters of the reservation principle. But even before Muir's *Atlantic Monthly* essay appeared in print in August, cracks developed in the conservation front. On June 4, 1897, Congress passed the Forest Management Act, which left no doubt that the reserves would not be wilderness. In response to the demands of foresters and most Western legislators, the Act made clear that one of the primary purposes of the reserves was "to furnish a continuous supply of timber for the use and necessities of citizens of the United States."[47] It also opened the forests to mining and grazing. Muir could no longer hope that the reserves would remain wild. It was now impossible to ignore or misinterpret foresters' statements such as that of Fernow: "the main service, the principal object of the forest has nothing to do with beauty or pleasure. It is not, except incidentally, an object of esthetics, but an object of economics."[48] From this viewpoint forest protection meant something quite different than it did from Muir's.

The decisive blow to Muir's confidence in forestry came late in the summer of 1897 when he and Pinchot met in Seattle. They had not seen each other since the Forestry Commission trip of the previous summer, but this time there was no camaraderie. Pinchot, acting on his philosophy that natural resources should be *used,* albeit wisely, had released a statement to the Seattle newspapers approv-

46. "The American Forests," *Atlantic Monthly, 80* (1897), 146, 147, 155, 156. Another expression of Muir's willingness to support forestry appeared in his "The National Parks and Forest Reservations," *Harper's Weekly, 41* (1897), 563–67.

47. U.S., *Statutes at Large, 30,* p. 35.

48. Fernow, "Letter to the Editor," *The Forester, 2* (1896), 45.

ing of the grazing of sheep in the forest reserves. For Muir this compromise with the "hoofed locusts" was intolerable. Confronting Pinchot in a hotel lobby, he demanded an explanation. When Pinchot admitted he had been correctly quoted, Muir shot back: "then . . . I don't want anything more to do with you. When we were in the Cascades last summer, you yourself stated that the sheep did a great deal of harm."[49] This personal break symbolized the conflict of values that was destroying the cohesiveness of the conservation movement.

Muir's new attitude was apparent in January 1898 in his second *Atlantic Monthly* essay. In sharp contrast to the article of the previous August, the new one made no mention of forestry and wise use. Instead it raised a paean to wilderness. Muir described the reserves as "virgin forests" and elaborated on the "thousands of God's wild blessings" they contained. Withdrawing all support from the Pinchot school, he labored to make his readers understand the importance of wilderness and the necessity of its preservation.[50]

While John Muir did not discourage the creation of forest reserves after the critical summer of 1897, he realized that under the foresters' control they held little promise for the preservation of wilderness. Consequently, he took every opportunity to promote and defend the national parks. With this purpose in mind he postponed a 1903 world tour with Charles Sargent for the chance to "do some forest good in freely talking around the campfire" with Theodore Roosevelt. The President had personally requested Muir's companionship in the Yosemite region, and returned from the trip, which included sleeping out during a four-inch snowfall, shouting ecstatically about "the grandest day of my life!"[51] This was in spite of Muir's disarming frankness about the

49. As quoted in Wolfe, *Muir*, pp. 275–76. Amplification of the grazing controversy appears in Lawrence Rakestraw, "Sheep Grazing in the Cascade Range: John Minto *vs.* John Muir," *Pacific Historical Review, 27* (1958), 371–82. For further discussion of the schism in the conservation movement between developers and preservationists see Samuel P. Hays, *Conservation and the Gospel of Efficiency: The Progressive Conservation Movement, 1890–1920* (Cambridge, Mass., 1959), pp. 122 ff., 189–98; Gilligan, "Policy and Administration," pp. 37 ff.; and Hadley, "Muir's Views of Nature," pp. 607 ff.

50. Muir, "The Wild Parks and Forest Reservations of the West," *Atlantic Monthly, 81* (1898), 21, 24.

51. As quoted in Wolfe, *Muir*, p. 293.

President's affection for hunting: "Mr. Roosevelt," he asked at one point, "when are you going to get beyond the boyishness of killing things . . . are you not getting far enough along to leave that off?" Taken aback, the President replied, "Muir, I guess you are right."[52] One of the results of the excursion into the Sierra was Roosevelt's receptivity to Muir's proposal that California recede Yosemite Valley to the federal government for inclusion in the adjacent national park.[53] Congress acted to this effect in 1906, and two years later Muir's many efforts on behalf of the Grand Canyon met with success when Roosevelt designated this region a national monument.[54] Muir poured his last energies into resisting plans to dam Yosemite National Park's wild Hetch Hetchy Valley (Chapter 10).

After 1905, crusading for wilderness also entailed countering the influence that Gifford Pinchot exerted as Chief Forester in the United States Forest Service and custodian of the reserves. A highly effective publicizer in his own right, Pinchot, and his colleagues like W J McGee and Frederick H. Newell, soon succeeded in appropriating the term "conservation" for the wise-use viewpoint.[55] The frustrated advocates of wilderness preservation had no choice but to call Pinchot a "de-conservationist."[56] The dramatic Governors' Conference on the Conservation of Natural Resources held at the White House in 1908 championed utilitarianism and wise resource development. As the primary organizer of the conference, Pinchot carefully kept Muir, Johnson, and most other preservationists off the invitation list.[57] But Pinchot could not suppress the groundswell of popular enthusiasm for wilderness that by the early

52. Johnson, *Remembered Yesterdays*, p. 388.

53. William E. Colby, "Yosemite and the Sierra Club," *Sierra Club Bulletin*, *23* (1938), 11–19; Jones, *John Muir and the Sierra Club*, pp. 55–80.

54. Muir had called for national park status for the "cañon wilderness" in 1898: see "Wild Parks," 27. He also wrote "Grand Canyon of the Colorado," *Century*, *65* (1902), 107–60. Ise, *National Park Policy*, pp. 230 ff. provides the political history.

55. Pinchot claimed he originated the term "conservation": *Breaking New Ground*, 322–26, but for evidence of much earlier usage see Hays, *Conservation*, 5–6. Relevant also is Whitney R. Cross, "W J McGee and the Idea of Conservation," *Historian*, *15* (1953), 148–62.

56. Robert Underwood Johnson to Senator [Hoke] Smith, Dec. 1, 1913, Johnson Papers, Berkeley, Box 1.

57. For an indication of the bitterness this caused in the preservationist camp see Johnson, *Remembered Yesterdays*, pp. 300–307, and an open letter: Johnson to "Dear Sir," June 5, 1911, Johnson Papers, Berkeley Box 1.

twentieth century had attained the dimensions of a national cult. As Muir put it: "thousands of tired, nerve-shaken, over-civilized people are beginning to find out that going to the mountains is going home; that wildness is a necessity; and that mountain parks and reservations are useful not only as fountains of timber and irrigating rivers, but as fountains of life."[58] Muir could take some pride in this phenomenon, because his life work had been devoted to bringing it about. But there were deeper reasons, rooted in the mood of the early twentieth century, for the unprecedented popularity of wilderness and, indeed, for the American public's favorable reception of Muir himself.

58. Muir, "Wild Parks," 15.

CHAPTER 9

The Wilderness Cult

> Whenever the light of civilization falls upon you with a blighting power . . . go to the wilderness. . . . Dull business routine, the fierce passions of the market place, the perils of envious cities become but a memory. . . . The wilderness will take hold of you. It will give you good red blood; it will turn you from a weakling into a man. . . . You will soon behold all with a peaceful soul.
>
> George S. Evans, 1904

ON the morning of August 10, 1913, the Boston *Post* headlined its lead story: NAKED HE PLUNGES INTO MAINE WOODS TO LIVE ALONE TWO MONTHS. The following article told how six days previously a husky, part-time illustrator in his mid-forties named Joseph Knowles had disrobed in a cold drizzle at the edge of a lake in northeastern Maine, smoked a final cigarette, shaken hands around a group of sportsmen and reporters, and trudged off into the wilderness. There was even a photograph of an unclothed Knowles, discreetly shielded by underbrush, waving farewell to civilization. The *Post* explained that Joe Knowles had gone into the woods to be a primitive man for sixty days. He took no equipment of any kind and promised to remain completely isolated, living off the land "as Adam lived."[1]

For the next two months Knowles was the talk of Boston. He provided information about his experiment with periodic dispatches written with charcoal on birchbark. These reports, printed in the *Post,* revealed to an astonished and delighted public that Knowles was succeeding in his planned reversion to the primitive. Using heat from the friction of two sticks, he obtained fire. Clothing came from woven strips of bark. Knowles' first few meals consisted of berries, but he soon varied his diet with trout, partridge, and even venison. On August 24 a front-page banner in the *Post* announced that Knowles had lured a bear into a pit, killed it with a club, and fashioned a coat from its skin. By this time newspapers throughout the East and as far away as Kansas City were featuring the story.

1. Boston *Post,* Aug. 17, 1913.

When on October 4, 1913, a disheveled but healthy Knowles finally emerged from the Maine woods extolling the values of a primitive way of life, he was swept up in a wave of public enthusiasm. His triumphant return to Boston included stops at Augusta, Lewiston, and Portland, with speeches before throngs of eight to ten thousand people. The cheers persisted in spite of the fine of $205 which an unyielding Maine Fish and Game Commission imposed on Knowles for killing a bear out of season! But Maine's welcome paled next to that of Boston. The city had not had a hero like "the modern primitive man"[2] in a generation. On October 9 a huge crowd jammed North Station to meet Knowles' train and shouted itself hoarse when he appeared. Thousands more lined the streets through which his motorcade passed. Still clad in the bear skin, Knowles went to Boston Common where an estimated twenty thousand persons waited. His speech was disappointingly brief, but the gathering thrilled to the way he leaped onto the podium with "the quick, graceful movements of a tiger."[3]

In the next few days news of Knowles even upstaged an exciting World Series. At Harvard physicians reported on the excellence of his physical condition, and there were numerous banquets and interviews, including one with the governor of Massachusetts. Publishers besieged Knowles for the rights to a book version of his experience, which, as *Alone in the Wilderness,* sold 300,000 copies, and he toured the vaudeville circuit with top billing. The *Post* published full-page color reproductions of his paintings of wild animals, pointing out that they were suitable for framing and "just the thing to hang in your den."[4] Even when the *Post*'s rival newspaper presented substantial evidence that Knowles was a fraud whose saga had actually taken place in a secret, snug cabin,[5] a vociferous denial arose in reply: quite a few Americans in 1913 apparently wanted to believe in the authenticity of the "Nature Man." In fact, the Joe Knowles fad was just a single and rather grotesque manifestation of popular interest in wildness.[6] It added

2. Ibid., Oct. 10, 1913.

3. Boston *Evening Transcript,* Oct. 9, 1913.

4. Boston *Post,* Sept. 28, Oct. 5, 12, 19, 1913.

5. Boston *American,* Dec. 2, 1913.

6. After his venture in Maine, Knowles tried to repeat his stunt in California and, with a "primitive" female companion, in New York, but without success. Nor did his plan materialize for a wilderness colony where Americans could live close to nature. Ultimately, Knowles retired to an isolated shack on the coast of Washington; he died

to the evidence suggesting that by the early twentieth century appreciation of wilderness had spread from a relatively small group of Romantic and patriotic literati to become a national cult.

By the 1890s sufficient change had occurred in American life and thought to make possible a widespread reaction against the previous condemnation of wilderness. Civilization had largely subdued the continent. Labor-saving agricultural machinery and a burgeoning industry, coupled with a surge in population, turned the American focus from country to city. The census of 1890 only gave statistical confirmation to what most Americans knew first hand: the frontier was moribund, wilderness no longer dominant. From the perspective of city streets and comfortable homes, wild country inspired quite different attitudes than it had when observed from a frontiersman's clearing. No longer did the forest and Indian have to be battled in hand-to-hand combat. The average citizen could approach wilderness with the viewpoint of the vacationer rather than the conquerer. Specifically, the qualities of solitude and hardship that had intimidated many pioneers were likely to be magnetically attractive to their city-dwelling grandchildren.

Indicative of the change was the way in which many of the repugnant connotations of wilderness were transferred to the new urban environment. At the end of the nineteenth century, cities were regarded with a hostility once reserved for wild forests. In 1898 Robert A. Woods entitled a collection of exposures of Boston's slum conditions *The City Wilderness.* A few years later, Upton Sinclair's *The Jungle* employed a similar metaphor in describing the horrors of the Chicago stockyards. Too much civilization, not too little, seemed at the root of the nation's difficulties. The bugaboos of the time—"Wall Street," "trusts," "invisible government"—were phenomena of the urban, industrialized East. In regard to primitive man, American opinion was also tending to reverse the flow of two and a half centuries. Increasing numbers

October 21, 1942: Fred Lockley, "Interesting People: A Modern Cave Man," *American Magazine, 91* (1921), 48; Boston *Post,* July 16, 1933; Stewart H. Holbrook, "The Original Nature Man," *American Mercury, 39* (1936), 417–25, reprinted in Holbrook's *Little Annie Oakley and Other Rugged People* (New York, 1948), pp. 8–18; Richard O. Boyer, "Where Are They Now? The Nature Man," *New Yorker, 14* (June 18, 1938), 21–25.

joined Helen Hunt Jackson in sympathizing with the Indian and identifying the disease, whiskey, and deception of civilization, not his savageness, as the crux of his problem.[7]

Along with the physical change in American life went a closely related intellectual change in temper or mood.[8] The general optimism and hope of the antebellum years partially yielded toward the end of the century to more sober assessments, doubts, and uncertainties. Many considered the defects of their society evidence that an earlier age's bland confidence in progress was unfounded. Reasons for pessimism appeared on every hand. A flood of immigrants seemed to many to be diluting the American strain and weakening American traditions. Business values and urban living were felt to be undermining character, taste, and morality. The vast size and highly organized nature of the economy and government posed seeming obstacles to the effectiveness of the individual. Instead of the millennium, American civilization appeared to have brought confusion, corruption, and a debilitating overabundance. There existed, to be sure, a countercurrent in American thought of pride and hope, but the belief persisted that the United States, if not the entire Western world, had seen its greatest moments and was in an incipient state of decline.

7. H[elen] H. Jackson, *A Century of Dishonor: A Sketch of the United States Government's Dealings with Some of the Indian Tribes* (New York, 1881). In the succeeding decades the crimes of the white man against the Indian received extensive treatment in books and popular periodicals, while organizations like the National Indian Association and the Indian Defense Association were established to translate sentiment into action. Pearce, *Savages of America,* stops short of this period, but William T. Hagan, *American Indians* (Chicago, 1961), pp. 123 ff. is a useful discussion.

8. John Higham, "The Reorientation of American Culture in the 1890's," *The Origins of Modern Consciousness,* ed. John Weiss (Detroit, 1965) has commented perceptively on this phenomenon. I have also relied on Higham's *Strangers in the Land: Patterns of American Nativism,* 1860–1925 (New York, 1963), pp. 35 ff., 158 ff.; Leo Marx, *The Machine in the Garden;* Morton and Lucia White, *The Intellectual Versus the City* (Cambridge, Mass., 1962), pp. 83 ff.; Mark Sullivan, *Our Times, 1900–1925* (6 vols. New York, 1935) *1,* 137–50; Richard Hofstadter, *The Age of Reform* (New York, 1960), pp. 7–59; George E. Mowry, *The Era of Theodore Roosevelt and the Birth of Modern America, 1900–1912* (New York, 1962), pp. 85–105; Henry Steele Commager, *The American Mind: An Interpretation of American Thought and Character Since the 1880's* (New Haven, 1950), pp. 41–54, 297; Samuel P. Hays, *The Response to Industrialism, 1885–1915* (Chicago, 1957), pp. 1–47; and David Noble, "The Paradox of Progressive Thought," *American Quarterly, 5* (1953), 201–12.

Henry F. May's *The End of American Innocence: A Study of the First Years of Our Own Time, 1912–1917* (New York, 1959) dates the breakdown in optimism and the belief in progress somewhat later.

As a result of this sense of discontent with civilization, which was no less uncomfortable because of its vagueness, *fin-de-siècle* America was ripe for the widespread appeal of the uncivilized. The cult had several facets. In the first place, there was a growing tendency to associate wilderness with America's frontier and pioneer past that was believed responsible for many unique and desirable national characteristics. Wilderness also acquired importance as a source of virility, toughness, and savagery—qualities that defined fitness in Darwinian terms. Finally, an increasing number of Americans invested wild places with aesthetic and ethical values, emphasizing the opportunity they afforded for contemplation and worship.

With a considerable sense of shock, Americans of the late nineteenth century realized that many of the forces which had shaped their national character were disappearing. Primary among these were the frontier and the frontier way of life. Long a hero of his culture, the pioneer acquired added luster at a time when the pace and complexity of American life seemed on the verge of overwhelming the independent individual. It was tempting to venerate his existence as one in which men confronted tangible obstacles and, so the myth usually ran, overcame them on the strength of ability alone. Before the 1890s it was generally assumed that because the frontiersman was good, the wilderness, as his primary adversary, was bad—the villain of the national drama. But the growing perception that the frontier era was over prompted a re-evaluation of the role of primitive conditions. Many Americans came to understand that wilderness was essential to pioneering: without wild country the concepts of frontier and pioneer were meaningless. The villain, it appeared, was as vital to the play as the hero, and, in view of the admirable qualities that contact with wilderness were thought to have produced, perhaps not so villainous as had been supposed. Toward the end of the nineteenth century, esteem for the frontiersman extended to include his environment. Pioneering, in short, came to be regarded as important not only for spearheading the advance of civilization but also for bringing Americans into contact with the primitive.

The connection between living in the wilderness and the development of desirable American traits received dramatic statement after 1893 in the historical essays of Frederick Jackson Turner. His nominal subject, of course, was the "frontier," but he made clear that the wildness of the country was its most basic ingredient and the essential formative influence on the national character. "The frontier," he declared, "is . . . determined by the reactions between wilderness and the edge of expanding settlement."[9] Consequently, when Turner came to summarize the central theme of his collected essays, it was to "the transforming influence of the American wilderness" that he turned. The idea had been present in his first major address, when he spoke of the way "the wilderness masters the colonist." Gradually, to be sure, the pioneer "transforms the wilderness, but the outcome is not the old Europe. . . . The fact is, that here is a new product that is American."[10] The bulk of Turner's subsequent effort was devoted to assessing the effect on American ideals and institutions of contact with a primitive environment.

Turner's most widely discussed article appeared in the *Atlantic Monthly* for September, 1896. It argued that the frontier not only made the American different from the European but better. "Out of his wilderness experience," Turner wrote, "out of the freedom of his opportunities, he fashioned a formula for social regeneration —the freedom of the individual to seek his own." Turner believed, in short, that democracy was a forest product. Living in the wilderness, "the return to primitive conditions," fostered individualism, independence, and confidence in the common man that encouraged self-government. While Turner occasionally admitted that frontier democracy had its liabilities, his attempts at impartiality only thinly masked a conviction that government by the people was far superior to Old World despotism. Indeed by virtue of being wild, the New World was a clean slate to which idealists could bring their dreams for a better life. Triumphantly, Turner concluded: "the very fact of the wilderness appealed to men as a fair, blank page on which to write a new chapter in the story of man's struggle for a higher type of society."[11] Associated in this way with democracy and messianic idealism, wild country acquired new value. Turner recast its role from that of an enemy which civilization had to conquer to a beneficent influence on men and institutions. His greatest service to wilderness consisted of linking it in the minds of his countrymen with sacred American virtues.

9. Turner, *The Significance of Sections in American History* (New York, 1932), p. 183.

10. Turner, *The Frontier in American History* (New York, 1920), pp. 1, 4.

11. Ibid., pp. 2, 213, 311.

In 1903 Turner noted that the 1890s marked a watershed in American history: it was the first decade without a frontier. "The . . . rough conquest of the wilderness is accomplished," he pointed out, "and . . . the great supply of free lands which year after year has served to reinforce the democratic influences in the United States is exhausted." Inevitably, he wondered if American ideals "have acquired sufficient momentum to sustain themselves under conditions so radically unlike those in the days of their origin?"[12]

Turner never explicitly answered this question in his published work,[13] but his tone suggested pessimism and contributed to a general sense of nostalgic regret over the disappearance of wilderness conditions. Articles in the nation's leading periodicals voiced concern over the "drift to the cities" and the consequent loss of pioneer qualities. Authors celebrating the "pathfinders" wondered how post-frontier Americans could comprehend their achievement.[14] In 1902 Frank Norris took time from his novels to contribute "The Frontier Gone At Last" to *World's Work.* "Suddenly," it begins, "we have found that there is no longer any Frontier." The remainder of the article speculates on the meaning of this fact. Norris felt that since "there is no longer a wilderness to conquer," the "overplus" of American energy might drive the country to attempt the conquest of the world.[15]

The ending of the frontier prompted many Americans to seek ways of retaining the influence of wilderness in modern civilization. The Boy Scout movement was one answer. Although the English hero of the Boer War, Sir Robert S. S. Baden-Powell, was its official founder in 1907, his efforts were anticipated in this country. In 1902 the popular nature writer Ernest Thompson Seton revealed in a series of articles in the *Ladies Home Journal* his ideas for an organization of boys called Woodcraft Indians. And Seton's meeting with Baden-Powell two years later was important in arousing the Englishman's interest in scouting. Baden-Powell also had the example of organizations such as the Sons of Daniel

12. Ibid., pp. 244–45, 260–61.

13. However, as a student of Turner's at Harvard during the First World War, Merle Curti remembers the concern he expressed in conversation about the future of the American character now that an urban-industrial civilization had replaced frontier conditions: interview with Merle Curti, Jan. 9, 1963.

14. G. S. Dickerson, "The Drift to the Cities," *Atlantic Monthly, 112* (1913), 349–53; George Bird Grinnell, *Trails of the Pathfinders* (New York, 1911), pp. 11–12.

15. Norris, "The Frontier Gone At Last," *World's Work, 3* (1902), 1728, 1729.

Boone and the Boy Pioneers which Daniel C. Beard launched in 1905. But soon after the Boy Scout concept came to America, it absorbed these forerunners, and both Seton and Beard transferred their allegiances.[16]

Seton set forth the methods and goals of the Boy Scouts of America in 1910 in a way that revealed the new importance Americans were according wilderness. A century ago, the Scouts' first *Handbook* begins, every American boy lived close to nature. But since then the country had undergone an "unfortunate change" marked by industrialization and the "growth of immense cities." According to Seton, the result was "degeneracy" and people who were "strained and broken by the grind of the over-busy world." As a remedy for this condition, the *Handbook* proposes that the boys of America lead the nation back to an emphasis of "Outdoor Life." This would include the realization that long and happy lives were most common among "those . . . who live nearest to the ground, that is, who live the simple life of primitive times."[17] Seton then went on to give instruction in woodlore and campcraft, in the hope that boys would spend at least a month of every year away from civilization, keeping in contact with frontier skills and values.

The Boy Scouts' striking success (it quickly became the largest youth organization in the country) is a significant commentary on American thinking in the early twentieth century. In thirty years the *Handbook* sold an alleged seven million copies in the United States, second only to the Bible.[18] The Scouting movement caught the public eye by offering a solution to the disturbing phenomenon of a civilization that seemed to be tearing itself away from the frontier roots that many felt to be the source of its greatness. It implemented the boast of Joe Knowles that "simply because we are

16. William Hillcourt, *Baden-Powell: The Two Lives of a Hero* (New York, 1964), pp. 247 ff.; Howard Fast, *Lord Baden-Powell of the Boy Scouts* (New York, 1941), pp. 171 ff.; Seton, *Trail of an Artist-Naturalist: The Autobiography of Ernest Thompson Seton* (New York, 1940), pp. 374–85; Beard, *Hardly a Man is Now Alive: The Autobiography of Dan Beard* (New York, 1939), pp. 351–61; Harold P. Levy, *Building a Popular Movement: A Case Study of the Public Relations of the Boy Scouts of America* (New York, 1944).

17. Seton, *Boy Scouts of America: A Handbook of Woodcraft, Scouting, and Lifecraft* (New York, 1910), pp. xi, xii, 1, 2.

18. Fast, *Baden-Powell*, p. 192; Boy Scouts of America, *Handbook for Boys* (New York, 1938), p. 6. For a history of the movement see William D. Murray, *The History of the Boy Scouts of America* (New York, 1937).

a civilized people does not mean that the days of wilderness colonization are over."[19]

Another response to the vanishing frontier was the rise of popular interest in preserving portions of the American wilderness. While wild country still existed to the West, the preservation concept had found favor with only a few farsighted individuals. Yellowstone National Park (1872) and the Adirondack Forest Preserve (1885) were not established to protect wilderness. After 1890, however, the disappearance of the frontier environment became more obvious. The resulting sense of nostalgia prompted, for one thing, belated recognition of the wilderness values of the first national and state reservations in Wyoming and northern New York (Chapter 7). The 1890s were also the years in which John Muir found numerous countrymen ready to join the preservationist wing of the conservation movement. Americans of this generation also responded to the ideas of another important wilderness publicizer: Theodore Roosevelt.

On February 10, 1894, Roosevelt wrote to Frederick Jackson Turner thanking him for a copy of his 1893 address on the significance of the American frontier. "I think you have struck some first class ideas," Roosevelt asserted, "and have put into definite shape a good deal of thought which has been floating around rather loosely."[20] Indeed, Roosevelt himself anticipated many of Turner's ideas, and even his rhetoric, in his 1889 *The Winning of the West.* "Under the hard conditions of life in the wilderness," Roosevelt wrote, those who migrated to the New World "lost all remembrance of Europe" and became new men "in dress, in customs, and in mode of life."[21] He too realized that by the 1890s "the frontier had come to an end; it had vanished."[22] This alarmed Roosevelt chiefly because of its anticipated effect on national virility and greatness.

19. Joseph Knowles, *Alone in the Wilderness* (Boston, 1913), p. 286. As might be expected, Knowles enthusiastically supported Scouting: *Alone*, pp. 239–53.

20. *Letters of Theodore Roosevelt,* ed. Elting Morison (8 vols. Cambridge, Mass., 1951–54) 1, 363.

21. Roosevelt, *The Winning of the West, The Works of Theodore Roosevelt,* Memorial edition (23 vols. New York, 1924–26) *10,* 101–102. For an indication of the extent of Turner's debt to Roosevelt see Wilbur R. Jacobs, *Frederick Jackson Turner's Legacy* (San Marino, Cal., 1965), p. 153. The present quotation (1889) is too similar in both conception and wording to Turner's "transformation" passage (1893) in *Frontier,* p. 4, to be purely coincidental.

22. Roosevelt, *The Wilderness Hunter, Works, 2,* 13.

The study of American history and personal experience combined to convince Roosevelt that living in wilderness promoted "that vigorous manliness for the lack of which in a nation, as in an individual, the possession of no other qualities can possibly atone." Conversely, he felt, the modern American was in real danger of becoming an "overcivilized man, who has lost the great fighting, masterful virtues." To counter this trend toward "flabbiness" and "slothful ease" Roosevelt in 1899 called upon his countrymen to lead a "life of strenuous endeavor." This included keeping in contact with wilderness: pioneering was an important antidote to dull mediocrity. "As our civilization grows older and more complex," Roosevelt explained, "we need a greater and not a less development of the fundamental frontier virtues."[23]

Roosevelt led the way personally. Immediately after graduating from Harvard, he spent considerable time in the 1880s on his ranch in the Dakota Territories, exulting in the frontiersman's life. He even had himself photographed posing proudly in a buckskin suit.[24] Later, when official duties demanded attention, he still found time for hunting and camping trips in wild country. Once, in a preface to a collection of hunting stories, Roosevelt attempted to articulate his feelings. "There are no words," he began, "that can tell of the hidden spirit of the wilderness, that can reveal its mystery, its melancholy, and its charm. There is delight in the hardy life of the open, in long rides rifle in hand, in the thrill of the fight with dangerous game." In addition he confessed a strong aesthetic attraction to "the silent places . . . the wide waste places of the earth, unworn of man, and changed only by the slow change of the ages through time everlasting."[25]

Understandably, Roosevelt was delighted that his country had taken the lead in establishing wilderness preserves and urged "every believer in manliness . . . every lover of nature, every man who appreciates the majesty and beauty of the wilderness and of wild life" to give them full support. In 1903, as President, he toured Yellowstone and Yosemite National Parks and came away delighted that these "bits of the old wilderness scenery and the old

23. Ibid., xxxi; Roosevelt, "The Strenuous Life" in *Works, 15,* 267, 271, 281; Roosevelt, "The Pioneer Spirit and American Problems" in *Works, 18,* 23.

24. Herman Hagedorn, *Roosevelt in the Bad Lands* (Boston, 1921). Photographs appear as a frontispiece and on p. 236.

25. Roosevelt, *African Game Trails, Works, 5,* xxvii.

wilderness life are to be kept unspoiled for the benefit of our children's children." In Roosevelt's opinion, America needed these remnants of the pioneer environment, because "no nation facing the unhealthy softening and relaxation of fibre that tends to accompany civilization can afford to neglect anything that will develop hardihood, resolution, and the scorn of discomfort and danger."[26] The wilderness preserves would serve this purpose by providing a perpetual frontier and keeping Americans in contact with primitive conditions. The rapid growth of the preservation movement, which reached a climax after 1910 in the Hetch Hetchy controversy (Chapter 10), suggests that a sizeable number of Americans joined with their President in detecting a national malaise and shared his faith in a wilderness cure.

"The friendly and flowing savage, who is he? Is he waiting for civilization, or past it and mastering it?" So asked Walt Whitman in a poem given final form in 1881. His question was not idle for the growing portion of his generation that entertained doubts about the happiness and vigor of modern man. Evidence of American decadence spurred primitivism. Wilderness and savages seemed to have advantages over civilized nature and man. Whitman himself sought wildness in 1876 when, broken in health and depressed from the experience of civil war, he retreated to Timber Creek, New Jersey. Along its "primitive windings" he found relief from "the whole cast-iron civilized life" and the chance to return to "the naked source-life of us all—to the breast of the great silent savage all-acceptive Mother."[27] Gradually Whitman recovered his physical strength and creative powers. Combined with his constant literary apotheosis of the unrepressed and wild, the Timber Creek interlude made Whitman's initial question seem rhetorical.

Whitman was a precursor of the American celebration of savagery. In full stride by the second decade of the twentieth century, it contributed to the rising popularity of wilderness. While related to the attraction of the frontier and pioneer, this aspect of the cult had more to do with racism, Darwinism, and a tradition of idealiz-

26. Roosevelt, "Wilderness Reserves: The Yellowstone Park" in *Works, 3,* 267, 288, 311–12.

27. Whitman, "Song of Myself" in *Leaves of Grass* (Garden City, N.Y., 1917), p. 88; Whitman, *Specimen Days* (Philadelphia, 1882–83), pp. 83–84. Secondary commentary appears in Fussell, *Frontier,* pp. 397–441.

ing the noble savage in his wilderness setting that ran back several thousand years (see Chapter 3). Ancient cultures, when inclined to self-criticism, began the practice of regarding those less civilized than themselves as superior. The spectacle of barbaric hordes sweeping down on a moribund and effete Roman Empire permanently impressed Western thought with the idea that virile manliness and wildness were closely linked. Early American experimenters with primitivistic themes, notably Thoreau, Melville, and Whitman, provided the immediate literary background for the growth of interest in savagery.[28] But it owed much more to a general feeling that the American male was suffering from over-civilization.

Theodore Roosevelt again took the lead in applauding savage virtues. Without advocating a return to cave-dwelling on a permanent basis, he still hoped that the opportunity for modern Americans to experience wilderness and lead for a time the savage way of life would not be totally eliminated. In 1888, with a view to implementing his ideas, Roosevelt organized the Boone and Crockett Club. Its stated purpose was the encouragement of big-game hunting, but the character of the hunter was the real object of concern. To qualify for membership it was necessary to have collected three trophy heads, and along with Roosevelt (who had eight) the founding nucleus included Elihu Root, Madison Grant, and Henry Cabot Lodge.[29] Of course Americans had always shot game, but this group of wealthy hunters coupled their sport with an unprecedented primitivistic philosophy. As Roosevelt and co-author George Bird Grinnell expressed it in a Boone and Crockett publication of 1893, "hunting big game in the wilderness is . . . a sport for a vigorous and masterful people." To succeed in a primitive environment, they continued, the hunter "must be sound of body and firm of mind, and must possess energy, resolution, manliness, self-reliance, and a capacity for self-help." The statement ended with the thought that these were characteristics "without which

28. See Chapter 5 for Thoreau and, for Melville, Fussell, pp. 232 ff. along with James Baird, *Ishmael* (Baltimore, 1956) and Charles Roberts Anderson, *Melville in the South Seas* (New York, 1939).

29. Paul Russell Cutright, *Theodore Roosevelt: The Naturalist* (New York, 1956), pp. 68–79; James B. Trefethen, *Crusade for Wildlife: Highlights in Conservation Progress* (New York, 1961), pp. 24 ff.; George Bird Grinnell, ed., *Brief History of the Boone and Crockett Club* (New York, 1910).

no race can do its life work well; and . . . the very qualities which it is the purpose of this Club . . . to develop and foster."[30]

Testimony from individual sportsmen supported this point of view. William Kent, a California congressman and conservationist (see Chapter 10), regretted that "since the days of the cave men our race has gone . . . degenerate." As a corrective measure, he rejoiced in the savagery of hunting. After a kill, Kent declared, "you are a barbarian, and you're glad of it. It's good to be a barbarian . . . and you know that if you are a barbarian, you are at any rate a man." In conclusion Kent called on his contemporaries to "go out into the wilderness and learn the endurance of nature which endures."[31] Hunting, once strictly a utilitarian activity, had been given a new rationale.

The surge of interest among Americans in primitive environments for purposes of recreation indicated that the ideology of the Boone and Crockett Club and William Kent was not esoteric. Wilderness camping and mountain climbing became an important part of the widespread "outdoor movement."[32] These pursuits had a special appeal to city people, who found in them temporary relief from artificiality and confinement. As one enthusiast put it in 1904, "whenever the light of civilization falls upon you with a blighting power . . . go to the wilderness." There, he continued, it was possible "to return to the primitive, the elemental" and escape "the perils of envious cities." Temporarily one partook of "the ruggedness of the mountains, the sturdiness of the oaks, the relentless savagery of the wind." The end result was to "give you good red blood; [to] turn you from a weakling into a man."[33] A tribute to Joe Knowles at a banquet in his honor took up the same theme: "there is too much refinement. It leads to degeneration. My friend Knowles has taught us how to live on nothing. It is better than living on too much. We should all get down to nature."[34]

30. Grinnell, "The Boone and Crockett Club" in *American Big Game Hunting: The Book of the Boone and Crockett Club,* ed. Roosevelt and Grinnell (Edinburgh, 1893), pp. 14–15.

31. William Kent, "Out Doors," Kent Family Papers, Historical Manuscripts Room, Yale University Library, New Haven, Conn., Box 100.

32. Foster Rhea Dulles, *America Learns to Play: A History of Popular Recreation* (New York, 1940), pp. 202 ff.

33. George S. Evans, "The Wilderness," *Overland Monthly, 43* (1904), 33.

34. James B. Connolly as quoted in the Boston *Post,* Oct. 12, 1913.

Americans with similar sentiments formed the core of the numerous outdoor clubs that appeared in the late nineteenth century. The Appalachian Mountain Club (1876) in the East, and the Sierra Club (1892) in the West organized wilderness enthusiasts and became stalwarts in the campaign for its preservation. The Mazamas of Portland, Oregon began in 1894 with a meeting of 155 hardy climbers on top of Mount Hood. Three years later the Campfire Club of America was founded.[35] For the members of these and other groups, part of the value of a wilderness trip was masochistic in that it provided a chance to play the savage, accept punishment, struggle, and, hopefully, triumph over the forces of raw nature. "The man in the woods," declared Stewart Edward White in 1903, "matches himself against the forces of nature." Confronting wilderness "is a test, a measuring of strength, a proving of his essential pluck and resourcefulness and manhood, an assurance of man's highest potency, the ability to endure and to take care of himself."[36] Meeting such a challenge assuaged fears that Americans were not what they used to be.

Carried to the extent of Joe Knowles' alleged exploit, the successful struggle against the primitive had a tonic effect on national pride and confidence. Knowles himself was aware of this implication and declared that his purpose in spending two months in the wilderness without equipment was "to demonstrate the self-sustaining power of modern man; to prove that man, though handicapped with the habits of civilization, is the physical equal of his early ancestors, and has not altogether lost . . . [their] resourcefulness."[37] Reacting to the reported success of the experiment, many felt Knowles' greatest significance was to put the human element back into the spotlight; to show that even without machines man still deserved his place atop the Darwinian tree of life. As one

35. See Chapter 8, and Allen H. Bent, "The Mountaineering Clubs of America," *Appalachia, 14* (1916), 5–18. For the Appalachian Mountain Club, in particular, the records at the Clubs' Headquarters, Boston, are most useful.

It is interesting that the German *Wandervogel,* under the leadership of Karl Fischer and Hermann Hoffmann, took to Europe's woodlands and mountains as a protest against the emptiness of civilization at precisely the same time that the American wilderness cult flourished. See Gerhard Masur, *Prophets of Yesterday: Studies in European Culture, 1890–1914* (New York, 1961), pp. 356–68, and Walter Z. Laqueur, *Young Germany: A History of the German Youth Movement* (London, 1962), pp. 3–38.

36. White, *The Forest* (New York, 1903), p. 5.

37. Boston *Post,* Aug. 17, 1913.

journal commented editorially, what Knowles accomplished in Maine "is a good deal more comforting to our proper human pride than the erection of a Woolworth building."[38]

Realizing the growing attractiveness of the wild for recreation, advertisers took account in their publicity of the thirst for the primitive. In 1911, for example, the Bangor and Aroostook Railroad Company, anxious to have vacationers ride its cars into Maine, began issuing a yearly publication, *In the Maine Woods.* A typical passage began with the observation that "there's a good deal of the primitive in most of us" and concluded that consequently "we feel the magic beckoning of old Mother Nature to rise up from the thralldom of business . . . and to betake ourselves to the woods." Maine, of course, was the suggested destination as a region "still rich in primeval charms."[39] For those who could not travel this far, landscape architects such as Frederick Law Olmsted and Charles Eliot proposed that in addition to city parks patches of "wild forest" be preserved close to metropolitan areas.[40] In them, Eliot contended in 1891, men could find relief from the "poisonous struggling . . . of city life" and the resulting feeling of exhaustion and depression.[41] Olmsted felt the current surge of interest in natural landscapes was the result of many Americans' perceiving that "we grow more and more artificial day by day." A "self-preserving instinct of civilization," he thought, led it to parks and preserves as a means of resisting " 'vital exhaustion,' " " 'nervous irritation,' " and " 'constitutional depression.' "[42]

The reading as well as the recreational tastes of many Americans of the early twentieth century were inclined toward the wild and savage. "Natural history" became a major literary genre. John Burroughs was only the best known of several score writers who kept

38. Anonymous, "Naked Man," *Hearst's Magazine, 24* (1913), 954.

39. Bangor and Aroostook Railroad Company, *In the Maine Woods* (Bangor, 1911), p. 7.

40. Charles Eliot to Charles Francis Adams, Oct. 6, 1892, Charles Eliot Manuscript Letters, 1892–97, Eliot Papers, Library of the Graduate School of Design, Harvard University.

41. Eliot, "The Need of Parks," *Souvenir of the Banquet of the Advance Club,* Publications of the Advance Club, 6 (Providence, R.I., 1891), p. 63.

42. Olmsted, *A Consideration of the Justifying Value of a Public Park* (Boston, 1881), p. 19. For Olmsted's earlier arguments in favor of the protection of Yosemite Valley see Chapter 6. John William Ward's "The Politics of Design," *Massachusetts Review, 6* (1965), 660–88, analyzes the motives of Olmsted as well as earlier designers of the American landscape.

the public's appetite satiated with a deluge of articles and books ranging from robins to grizzlies.[43] Among works of fiction, one of the best sellers of the early twentieth century was Jack London's *The Call of the Wild.* Published in 1903, it told the story of a huge dog, Buck, who was stolen from his master's ranch in California and sold into the Klondike to haul sleds. Exposed to primitive conditions, Buck gradually threw off his domesticated habits and became "the dominant primordial beast." At the close of the novel he had reverted all the way to the wolf, and London pictured him "running at the head of the pack through the pale moonlight or glimmering borealis, leaping gigantic above his fellows, his great throat a-bellow as he sings a song of the younger world." London left no doubt that it was also the song of a more vital, stronger and generally superior world, and his readers had little difficulty seeing the moral for their own lives in Buck's reversion to the primitive. Significantly, London's *White Fang* (1906), in which a wolf became a family dog, never enjoyed the popularity of *The Call of the Wild.*

Savagery, of course, received its most triumphant literary expression at this time in Edgar Rice Burroughs' stories about an English infant reared in the jungle by apes. Burroughs began experimenting with the theme in 1912, and two years later published one of America's most widely read books, *Tarzan of the Apes.* Like Buck, Tarzan benefitted from his contact with the wilderness to the extent of becoming a superman.[44]

The third major component of the wilderness cult lacked the hairy-chestedness of the previous ideas and instead accorded wild country value as a source of beauty and spiritual truth. This outlook, of course, depended on an intellectual revolution occurring over the previous several centuries, and echoed the familiar Romantic rhetoric (see Chapter 3). But several circumstances of late-

43. Hans Huth, *Nature and the American: Three Centuries of Changing Attitudes* (Berkeley, Cal., 1957), p. 87 ff.; Philip Marshall Hicks, *The Development of the Natural History Essay in American Literature* (Philadelphia, 1924), pp. 100–158; Norman Foerster, *Nature in American Literature* (New York, 1923), pp. 264–305; Francis C. Halsey, "The Rise of the Nature Writers," *American Monthly Review of Reviews, 26* (1902), 567–71; Anonymous, "Back to Nature," *Outlook, 74* (1903), 305–07.

44. London, *The Call of the Wild* (New York, 1903), pp. 99, 231. The popularity of London and Burroughs is discussed in Alice Payne Hackett, *60 Years of Best Sellers, 1895–1955* (New York, 1956) and Frank Luther Mott, *Golden Multitudes: The Story of Best Sellers in the United States* (New York, 1947).

nineteenth century America combined to give it new urgency and unprecedented public appeal. As the antipode of civilization, of cities, and of machines, wilderness could be associated with the virtues these entities lacked. In the primitive, specifically, many Americans detected the qualities of innocence, purity, cleanliness, and morality which seemed on the verge of succumbing to utilitarianism and the surge of progress. And at a time when the force of religion seemed vitiated by the new scientism on the one hand and social conflict on the other,[45] wilderness acquired special significance as a resuscitator of faith. Joe Knowles, for one, knew the value of his trip was partly spiritual. "My God is in the wilderness," he wrote, "the great open book of nature is my religion. My church is the church of the forest."[46]

Wild scenery enthralled Americans of this mind. They provided the market for elaborate albums such as James W. Buel's 1893 prodigy, *America's Wonderlands: Pictorial and Descriptive History of Our Country's Scenic Marvels as Delineated by Pen and Camera,* and for their vacations thronged the White and Adirondack Mountains, and later the Rockies and Sierra.[47] These people also looked favorably on wilderness preservation: protection of wild country seemed part of the defense of the finer things of life. Frederick Law Olmsted expressed the idea when he defended "the contemplation of beauty in natural scenery" for its effect in countering "excessive materialism, . . . loss of faith and lowness of spirit."[48] In the United States Senate, George G. Vest of Missouri made a similar analysis. Speaking in defense of Yellowstone National Park, he declared that "the great curse of this age and of the American people is its materialistic tendency. Money, money, l'argent, l'argent is the cry everywhere, until our people are held up . . . to the world as noted for nothing except the acquisition of money at the expense of all esthetic taste and of all love of nature."[49] In 1890, Olmsted generalized that any time a wilderness preserve was endangered the public

45. Arthur Schlesinger, "A Critical Period in American Religion, 1875–1900," *Proceedings of the Massachusetts Historical Society, 64* (1932), 523–47.

46. Knowles, *Alone,* pp. 224–25.

47. Huth, *Nature,* pp. 54–86, 105–47. The White Mountain Collection, Baker Library, Dartmouth College, Hanover, N.H. and the Frederick W. Kilborne White Mountain Collection, Appalachian Mountain Club, Boston, reveal the varied forms of popular enthusiasm for wilderness vacationing.

48. Olmsted, *Consideration,* pp. 19–20.

49. *Congressional Record,* 47th Cong., 2d Sess., *14* (March 1, 1883), p. 3488.

should respond as they would "to any crisis threatening a national treasure of art."[50]

It was precisely this sentiment that John Muir and Robert Underwood Johnson endeavored to arouse in the following decades. Muir continually lamented "these mad, God-forgetting progressive days,"[51] and his rhetoric, steeped in Transcendentalism, created a style for appreciating wilderness. Echoing their president, Sierra Club members like Marion Randall returned from mountain trips with the feeling that "for a little while you have dwealt close to the heart of things . . . [and] drawn near Him." She declared herself ready at once "to turn to the hills again, whence comes, not only your help, but your strength, your inspiration, and some of the brightest hours you have ever lived." In 1894, the *Sierra Club Bulletin* carried a reproof of anyone "blessed" with a view of wilderness "yet who feels no exaltation of soul, no supreme delight in the conscious exercise or stirring of that something within us we call the aesthetic." Muir himself went still further in labeling as "selfish seekers of immediate Mammon" those who could bring only utilitarian criteria to wild places.[52]

As a self-styled upholder of his country's "standards"[53] and one of the pillars of its "genteel tradition,"[54] Robert Underwood Johnson represented the social type that furnished a large proportion of wilderness enthusiasts. The bookish, dapper Johnson had little desire for actual contact with the primitive and, by his own admission, was an inept outdoorsman. His interest, rather, lay in the *idea* of wilderness as something pure, beautiful, and delicate, embattled against what he conceived to be ruthless exploitation. Indeed, he referred to his many efforts before Congress on behalf of preserva-

50. Olmsted, "Governmental Preservation of Natural Scenery," *Sierra Club Bulletin, 29* (1944), 62.

51. Muir to George Plimpton, Dec. 9, 1913, Johnson Papers, Berkeley, Box 7.

52. Randall, "Some Aspects of a Sierra Club Outing," *Sierra Club Bulletin, 5* (1905), 227–28; P. B. Van Trump, "Mt. Tahoma," *Sierra Club Bulletin, 1* (1894), 115; Muir to Robert Underwood Johnson, March 14, 1894, Johnson Papers, Berkeley, Box 7.

53. U.S. Congress, Senate, Committee on the Public Lands, Hearings, *Hetch Hetchy Reservoir Site*, 63rd Cong., 1st Sess. (Sept. 24, 1913), p. 46.

54. George Santayana, *The Genteel Tradition in American Philosophy* (Berkeley, Cal., 1911); John Tomsich, "The Genteel Tradition in America, 1850–1910" (unpublished Ph.D. dissertation, University of Wisconsin, 1963); Richard Cary, *The Genteel Circle: Bayard Taylor and his New York Friends,* Cornell Studies in American History, Literature, and Folklore, 5 (Ithaca, N.Y., 1952), pp. 1–21.

tion as " 'spiritual lobbying.' "[55] Johnson hoped they might contribute to advancing Americans to the point where they could "throw off the two shackles that retard our progress as an artistic nation—philistinism and commercialism—and advance with freedom toward the Love of Beauty as a Principle."[56] Appreciating the value of wilderness was a step in the right direction, and it was especially significant to Johnson that this recognition had spread by the early twentieth century far beyond a coterie of Romantic writers. The successes John Muir and Johnson himself enjoyed with the wilderness theme in prominent magazines such as *Century, Harper's,* and *Atlantic* testified to the nation's receptivity. So, in part, did the growth of the preservation movement: lovers of wild scenery became a major force within conservation.[57] Even at the utilitarian-minded Governors' Conference on Conservation in 1908, the Romantic viewpoint had its exponents. J. Horace McFarland, president of the American Civic Association, spoke of God's refuge "in the very bosom of nature, to which we may flee from the noise and strain of the market-place for that renewing of spirit and strength which can not be had elsewhere." The representative of the American Scenic and Historic Preservation Society, George F. Kunz, added that it was not "empty sentimentalism" which led many in his generation to covet the aesthetic and spiritual qualities of wilderness, but rather the realization that happiness and "the highest development of our people" depended on them.[58] The widespread public acceptance of ideas such as these made it possible for Johnson, Muir, and other preservationists to arouse a national protest in 1913 against the construction of a dam in Yosemite National Park's wild Hetch Hetchy Valley (Chapter 10).

A comparison of the reputations of John Muir and Henry David Thoreau among their contemporaries dramatizes the appearance of

55. Johnson, *Remembered Yesterdays,* pp. 239 ff. The Robert Underwood Johnson Papers at the New York Public Library substantiate his wideranging interest in art, culture, creativity, and refinement.

56. Johnson, "John Muir as I Knew Him," (typescript c. 1915) John Muir Papers, American Academy of Arts and Letters, New York.

57. Hays, *Conservation,* pp. 141 ff.; Charles D. Smith, "The Movement for Eastern National Forests, 1890–1911" (unpublished Ph.D. dissertation, Harvard University, 1956), esp. pp. 1–17 and 357 ff.

58. *Proceedings of a Conference of Governors in the White House . . . May 13–15, 1908,* ed. Newton C. Blanchard et al., U.S. House of Representatives Doc. 1425, 60th Cong., 2d Sess., pp. 140, 156, 419.

a wilderness cult. Both men made wildness their dominant concern, yet the extent to which they were successful and influential figures in their lifetimes differed markedly. In 1853 Thoreau was obliged to find storage space for the seven hundred unsold volumes of a thousand-copy printing of his first book, *A Week on the Concord and Merrimack Rivers*.[59] Just over forty years later, Muir happily wrote Johnson that bookstores could not supply the demand for *his* initial book-length work, *The Mountains of California*.[60] The authors' comments were symbolic. While he lived, Thoreau's supporters consisted of a handful of personal friends. His writings went unsold and his lectures were sparsely attended. The general public regarded the Walden Pond episode as incomprehensible at best.[61] Muir, on the contrary, was highly successful and nationally acclaimed in spite of the fact that most of his thoughts were simply restatements of the Transcendentalists' case for wilderness. The context rather than the content of the respective philosophies determined their popularity. Like Joe Knowles, it was Muir's good fortune to live at a time when he could reap the honors that belatedly came to Thoreau's ideas.

The American cult of the wilderness that lifted Muir, and for that matter, Thoreau, into prominence was not, to be sure, overwhelming, nor was the popularity of primitivism the only manifestation of discontent and frustration at the end of the nineteenth century. In a complex age, it was but a single current of thought. Even in the minds of those who championed wilderness, pride in the accomplishments of American civilization and a belief in the virtues of further development of natural resources persisted. Yet by the twentieth century's second decade something of a divide had been passed. Sufficient misgivings about the effects of civilization had arisen to encourage a favorable opinion of wilderness that contrasted sharply with earlier American attitudes.

59. Torrey and Allen, eds, *Journal*, *5*, 459.

60. Muir to Johnson, Jan. 10, 1895, Johnson Papers, Berkeley, Box 7.

61. On Thoreau's unpopularity in his own time see Carl Bode, *The Anatomy of American Popular Culture* (Berkeley, 1959), p. x, and Walter Harding, "Thoreau on the Lecture Platform," *New England Quarterly*, *24* (1951), 365–67.

CHAPTER 10

Hetch Hetchy

As to my attitude regarding the proposed use of Hetch Hetchy by the city of San Francisco . . . I am fully persuaded that . . . the injury . . . by substituting a lake for the present swampy floor of the valley . . . is altogether unimportant compared with the benefits to be derived from its use as a reservoir.

Gifford Pinchot, 1913

These temple destroyers, devotees of ravaging commercialism, seem to have a perfect contempt for Nature, and instead of lifting their eyes to the God of the Mountains, lift them to the Almighty Dollar.

John Muir, 1912

SITUATED on a dry, sandy peninsula, the city of San Francisco faced a chronic fresh-water shortage. In the Sierra, about one hundred and fifty miles distant, the erosive action of glaciers and the Tuolumne River scooped the spectacular, high-walled Hetch Hetchy Valley. As early as 1882, city engineers pointed out the possibility of damming its narrow, lower end to make a reservoir. They also recognized the opportunity of using the fall of the impounded water for the generation of hydroelectric power. In 1890, however, the act creating Yosemite National Park designated Hetch Hetchy and its environs a wilderness preserve. Undaunted, San Francisco's mayor James D. Phelan applied for the valley as a reservoir site shortly after the turn of the century. Secretary of the Interior Ethan A. Hitchcock's refusal to violate the sanctity of a national park was only a temporary setback, because on April 18, 1906, an earthquake and fire devastated San Francisco and added urgency and public sympathy to the search for an adequate water supply. The city immediately reapplied for Hetch Hetchy, and on May 11, 1908, Secretary James R. Garfield approved the new application. "Domestic use," he wrote, "is the highest use to which water and available storage basins . . . can be put."[1]

1. *Decisions of the Department of the Interior . . . June 1, 1907–June 30, 1908,* ed. George J. Hesselman (Washington, D.C., 1908), p. 411.

The best political histories of the Hetch Hetchy controversy are Jones, *John Muir*

John Muir, Robert Underwood Johnson, and those whom they had won to the cause of wilderness preservation disagreed. Secretary Garfield's approval stimulated them to launch a national protest campaign. Given the flourishing cult of wilderness on the one hand and the strength of traditional assumptions about the desirability of putting undeveloped natural resources to use on the other, the battle over Hetch Hetchy was bound to be bitter. Before Congress and President Woodrow Wilson made a final decision in 1913, the valley became a *cause célèbre.* The principle of preserving wilderness was put to the test. For the first time in the American experience the competing claims of wilderness and civilization to a specific area received a thorough hearing before a national audience.

When the preservationists first learned of San Francisco's plans for Hetch Hetchy, Theodore Roosevelt occupied the White House, and the choice of reservoir or wilderness placed him in an awkward position. There were few Americans so committed to a belief in the value of wild country (see Chapter 9). Yet Roosevelt appreciated the importance of water, lumber, and similar commodities to national welfare and as President felt responsible for providing them. The result of this ambivalence was inconsistency in Roosevelt's early policy statements. In 1901 he declared in his first annual message that "the fundamental idea of forestry is the perpetuation of forests by use. Forest protection is not an end in itself; it is a means to increase and sustain the resources of our country and the industries which depend on them." But later in the message, he revealed his hope that some of the forest reserves could be made

---

and the Sierra Club, pp. 83–169; Elmo R. Richardson, "The Struggle for the Valley: California's Hetch Hetchy Controversy, 1905–1913," *California Historical Society Quarterly, 38* (1959), 249–58; and Ise, *National Park Policy*, pp. 85–96. Richardson's *The Politics of Conservation: Crusades and Controversies, 1897–1913*, University of California Publications in History, 70 (Berkeley, 1962) discusses the context of the dispute. Unpublished studies include Suzette Dornberger, "The Struggle for Hetch Hetchy, 1900–1913" (unpublished M.A. thesis, University of California, Berkeley, 1935) and Florence Riley Monroy, "Water and Power in San Francisco Since 1900: A Study in Municipal Government" (unpublished M.A. thesis, University of California, Berkeley, 1944). There are several accounts of the engineering aspects, principally Ray W. Taylor, *Hetch Hetchy: The Story of San Francisco's Struggle to Provide a Water Supply for Future Needs* (San Francisco, 1926) and M. M. O'Shaughnessy, *Hetch Hetchy: Its Origin and History* (San Francisco, 1934).

"preserves for the wild forest creatures."[2] The same uncertainty appeared two years later in an address on the goal of forestry: "primarily the object is not to preserve forests because they are beautiful—though that is good in itself—not to preserve them because they are refuges for the wild creatures of the wilderness—though that too is good in itself—but the primary object of forest policy . . . is the making of prosperous nomes, is part of the traditional policy of homemaking in our country."[3]

In this seesaw manner Roosevelt hoped to hold the two wings of the conservation movement together on a united front. The task was formidable: Muir already had found his position incompatible with Gifford Pinchot's. But after 1905 Pinchot was Chief Forester and the principal spokesman of the utilitarian conception of conservation. Moreover, he enjoyed a close friendship with Roosevelt. According to Johnson, the President went so far as to declare that " 'in all forestry matters I have put my conscience in the keeping of Gifford Pinchot.' "[4] And Pinchot favored converting Hetch Hetchy into a reservoir. Yet Roosevelt had camped in Yosemite with Muir and appreciated the growing political strength of the preservationist position. Early in September 1907, he received a letter from Muir that brought the issue to a head. Reminding the President of their 1903 trip into the Sierra wilderness, Muir expressed his desire that the region "be saved from all sorts of commercialism and marks of man's works." While acknowledging the need for an adequate municipal water supply, he maintained that it could be secured outside "our wild mountain parks." Concluding the letter, Muir expressed his belief that over ninety per cent of the American people would oppose San Francisco's plans if they were apprised of their consequences.[5]

Roosevelt's initial reaction, made even before Muir's communication, was to seek advice from engineers about alternative reservoir sites.[6] The report, however, was that Hetch Hetchy offered the only practical solution to San Francisco's problem. Reluctantly

2. Roosevelt, "First Annual Message" in *Works, 17,* 118–19, 120.

3. Roosevelt, "The Forest Problem" in *Works, 18,* 127.

4. Johnson, *Remembered Yesterdays,* p. 307.

5. Muir to Roosevelt, Sept. 9, 1907, in "Water Supply for San Francisco," Record Group 95 [United States Forest Service], National Archives, Washington, D.C.

6. Roosevelt to James R. Garfield, Aug. 6, 1907, and Garfield to Roosevelt, Aug. 8, 1907, ibid.

Roosevelt made up his mind. While assuring Muir that he would do everything possible to protect the national parks, the President reminded him that if these reservations "interfere with the permanent material development of the State instead of helping . . . the result will be bad." Roosevelt ended with an expression of doubt that the great majority would take the side of wilderness in a showdown with the material needs of an expanding civilization.[7] Pinchot seconded the judgment in favor of San Francisco. Writing to the President in October 1907 that "I fully sympathize with the desire of Mr. Johnson and Mr. Muir to protect the Yosemite National Park, but I believe that the highest possible use which could be made of it would be to supply pure water to a great center of population."[8] Still Roosevelt was not comfortable in his decision against wilderness, and confessed to Johnson that Hetch Hetchy was "one of those cases where I was extremely doubtful."[9]

In spite of his doubts Roosevelt had made a choice, and in the spring of 1908 the Garfield permit opened the way for the development of the valley. Muir was discouraged but not defeated. He believed it still was possible to arouse a national protest and demonstrate to federal authorities that Roosevelt was mistaken in his judgment about the lack of public sentiment for keeping Hetch Hetchy wild. But Muir fully realized that "public opinion is not yet awakened."[10] The first task of the preservationists was to capitalize on the wilderness cult and replace ignorance with anger. Telling arguments against the reservoir were needed. As the basis for their protest, the friends of wilderness turned to the old Romantic case against "Mammon." They made Hetch Hetchy into a symbol of ethical and aesthetic qualities, while disparaging San Francisco's proposal as tragically typical of American indifference toward them. This line of defense took advantage of national sensitivity to charges of being a culture devoted entirely to the frantic pursuit of the main chance. It criticized the commercialism and sordidness of American civilization, while defending wilderness.

John Muir opened the argument for the Valley on aesthetic grounds with an article in *Outlook*. After describing its beauties,

7. Roosevelt to Muir, Sept. 16, 1907, in Morison, ed., *Letters of Theodore Roosevelt*, 5, 793.

8. Pinchot to Roosevelt, Oct. 11, 1907, "Water Supply," National Archives.

9. Roosevelt to Johnson, Dec. 17, 1908, Johnson Papers, Berkeley, Box 6.

10. Muir, "The Tuolumne Yosemite in Danger," *Outlook*, 87 (1907), 489.

he declared that its maintainence as a wilderness was essential, "for everybody needs beauty as well as bread, places to play in and pray in where Nature may heal and cheer and give strength to body and soul alike."[11] Others took up the same theme in the national press. Writing in *Century,* which he now edited, Robert Underwood Johnson charged that only those who had not advanced beyond the "pseudo-'practical' stage" could favor San Francisco. The presence of these individuals in the nation, he added, "is one of the retarding influences of American civilization and brings us back to the materialistic declaration that 'Good is only good to eat.' "[12] As a self-appointed spokesman for culture and refinement, Johnson took it upon himself to defend intangibles. In a brief submitted at the first Congressional hearing on the Hetch Hetchy question in December, 1908, he made his protest "in the name of all lovers of beauty . . . against the materialistic idea that there must be something wrong about a man who finds one of the highest uses of nature in the fact that it is made to be looked at."[13]

As president of the American Civic Association, J. Horace McFarland took every opportunity to preach the desirability, indeed the necessity, of maintaining some element of beauty in man's environment. He believed the aesthetic should have a place in the conservation movement, and in 1909 expressed his displeasure at its concentration on utilitarian aims. In the same year he told Pinchot that "the conservation movement is now weak, because it has failed to join hands with the preservation of scenery."[14] For McFarland, Hetch Hetchy was a test case, and he spoke and wrote widely in its defense. If even national parks were to be given over to utilitarian purposes, there was no guarantee that ultimately all the beauty of unspoiled nature would be destroyed. Speaking before the Secretary of the Interior on the Hetch Hetchy question, McFarland contended that such undeveloped places would become increasingly valuable for recreation as more and more Americans

11. Ibid., 488. Large portions of the article were borrowed from Muir's earlier essay: "Hetch Hetchy Valley: The Lower Tuolumne Yosemite," *Overland Monthly, 11* (1873), 42–50.

12. Robert Underwood Johnson, "A High Price to Pay for Water," *Century, 86* (1908), 633.

13. U.S. Congress, House, Committee on the Public Lands, Hearings, *San Francisco and the Hetch Hetchy Reservoir,* 60th Cong., 1st Sess. (Dec. 16, 1908), pp. 37–38.

14. McFarland to Johnson, Feb. 4, 1909, Johnson Papers, Berkeley, Box 5; McFarland to Pinchot, Nov. 26, 1909, Pinchot Papers, Box 1809.

lived in cities. Yet when the preservation of wilderness conflicted with "material interests," those financially affected cried: " 'that is sentimentalism; that is aestheticism; that is pleasure-loving; that is unnecessary; that is not practical.' " Usually such resistance carried the day and wildness was sacrificed. McFarland objected because "it is not sentimentalism, Mr. Secretary; it is living."[15] Elsewhere he elaborated on his ideas: "the primary function of the national forests is to supply lumber. The primary function of the national parks is to maintain in healthful efficiency the lives of the people who must use that lumber. . . . The true ideal of their maintenance does not run parallel to the making of the most timber, or the most pasturage, or the most water power."[16]

Lyman Abbott, the editor of *Outlook,* also felt it was a mistake "to turn every tree and waterfall into dollars and cents." His magazine found most of its readers among a class of people concerned over what they thought was the eclipse of morality, refinement, and idealism by urbanization, industrialization, and an emphasis on business values. The defense of wilderness attracted them because it permitted making a positive case—they could be for something (wilderness) rather than merely against amorphous forces. Protecting the wild from an exploitative civilization, in short, represented the broader struggle to maintain intangibles against the pressure of utilitarian demands. Sensing this, Abbott made *Outlook* one of the chief organs of the Hetch Hetchy campaign. He explained his stand in an editorial in 1909: "if this country were in danger of habitually ignoring utilitarian practice for the sake of running after sentimental dreams and aesthetic visions we should advise it . . . to dam the Tuolumne River in order to instruct its citizens in the use of the bathtub. But the danger is all the other way. The national habit is to waste the beauty of Nature and save the dollars of business."[17]

The same disparaging reference to American tastes and values appeared in the statements of preservationists in early 1909 at the House and Senate hearings in regard to Hetch Hetchy. One man, who had camped in the valley, pointedly asked: "is it never ceas-

15. *Proceedings Before the Secretary of the Interior in re Use of Hetch Hetchy Reservoir by the City of San Francisco* (Washington, D.C., 1910), pp. 18–19.

16. McFarland, "Are National Parks Worthwhile?" *Sierra Club Bulletin, 8* (1912), 237.

17. Abbott, "The Hetch-Hetchy Valley Again," *Outlook, 91* (1909), 330–31; Abbott, "Saving the Yosemite Park," *Outlook, 91* (1909), 235–36.

ing; is there nothing to be held sacred by this nation; is it to be dollars only; are we to be cramped in soul and mind by the lust after filthy lucre only; shall we be left some of the more glorious places?" Others joined him in pleading that "loftier motives" than saving money for San Francisco be taken into consideration. "May we live down our national reputation for commercialism," one letter concluded.[18]

In the Senate hearings, Henry E. Gregory of the American Scenic and Historic Preservation Society appeared in person and spoke of the need to counteract "business and utilitarian motives" that seemed to him to dominate the age. He pointed out that wildernesses such as Hetch Hetchy had value beyond computation in monetary terms "as an educator of the people and as a restorer and liberator of the spirit enslaved by Mammon."[19] Arguments along these lines struck home, especially at a time when many Americans squirmed uncomfortably at charges that their nation's aesthetic sense was stunted and deformed.

Another tactic of the preservationists emphasized the spiritual significance of wild places and the tendency of money-minded America to ignore religion. Hetch Hetchy became a sanctuary or temple in the eyes of the defenders. John Muir, for one, believed so strongly in the divinity of wild nature that he was convinced he was doing the Lord's battle in resisting the reservoir. The preservationists' innumerable puns about "damning" Hetch Hetchy were only partly in jest. John Muir and his colleagues believed they were preaching "the Tuolumne gospel." San Francisco became "the Prince of the powers of Darkness" and "Satan and Co." Muir wrote: "we may lose this particular fight but truth and right must prevail at last. Anyhow we must be true to ourselves and the Lord."[20] This conviction that they were engaged in a battle between right and wrong prompted the preservationists to vituperative outbursts against their opponents. In a popular book of 1912, Muir labeled his foes "temple destroyers" who scorned the "God of

18. U.S. Congress, House, Committee on the Public Lands, Hearings, *San Francisco and the Hetch Hetchy Reservoir*, 60th Cong., 2d Sess. (Jan. 9, 12, 20, 21, 1909), pp. 179, 323.

19. U.S. Congress, Senate, Committee on the Public Lands, Hearings, *Hetch Hetchy Reservoir Site*, 60th Cong., 2d Sess. (Feb. 10, 12, 1909), p. 14.

20. Muir to Johnson, Feb. 7, 1909, Muir Papers, New York; Muir to Johnson, March 23, 1913, ibid; Muir to "Kelloggs Three," Dec. 27, 1913, Muir Papers, Berkeley, Box 1; Muir to William E. Colby, Dec. 31, 1908, ibid.

the Mountains" in pursuit of the "Almighty Dollar." A ringing and widely quoted denunciation followed: "Dam Hetch Hetchy! As well dam for water-tanks the people's cathedrals and churches, for no holier temple has ever been consecrated by the heart of man."[21]

Using these arguments, and the especially effective one (unrelated to wilderness) that the valley as part of Yosemite National Park was a "public playground" which should not be turned over to any special interest,[22] the preservationists were able to arouse considerable opposition to San Francisco's plans. Members of the Sierra and Appalachian Mountain Clubs took the lead in preparing pamphlet literature for mass distribution. *Let All the People Speak and Prevent the Destruction of the Yosemite Park* of 1909, for example, contained a history of the issue, reprints of articles and statements opposing the dam, a discussion of alternative sources of water, and photographs of the valley. Preservationists also obtained the sympathies of numerous newspaper and magazine editors in all parts of the nation. Even Theodore Roosevelt retreated from his earlier endorsement of the reservoir and declared in his eighth annual message of December 8, 1908, that Yellowstone and Yosemite "should be kept as a great national playground. In both, all wild things should be protected and the scenery kept wholly unmarred."[23]

Evidence of the effectiveness of the protest appeared in the action of the House after its 1909 hearings. Although the Committee on the Public Lands had approved the grant in a close vote, a strong minority report dissented on the grounds that such action would deny the public's right to the valley for recreational purposes. Testifying to the amount of popular opposition, the report observed that "there has been an exceedingly widespread, earnest, and vigorous protest voiced by scientists, naturalists, mountain climbers,

21. John Muir, *The Yosemite* (New York, 1912), pp. 261–62. Muir used a similar statement as early as 1908: "The Hetch-Hetchy Valley," *Sierra Club Bulletin, 6* (1908), 220. For another defense on religious grounds, see Cora C. Foy, "Save the Hetch-Hetchy," *Out West, 1* (1910), 11.

22. For example, Portland *Oregonian,* Dec. 30, 1908; French Strother, "San Francisco Against the Nation for the Yosemite," *World's Work, 17* (1909), 11441–445; Edward T. Parsons, "Proposed Destruction of Hetch Hetchy," *Out West, 31* (1909), 607–27; "Hetch-Hetchy," *Independent, 73* (1912), 1203–1204; and I. R. Branson, *Yosemite Against Corporation Greed* (Aurora, Neb., c. 1909).

23. Roosevelt, *Works, 17,* 618.

travelers, and others in person, by letters, and telegrams, and in newspaper and magazine articles."[24] In the face of this expression of public opinion, the House pigeonholed and killed San Francisco's application in the Sixtieth Congress.

San Francisco was bewildered and incensed at the public unwillingness that it should have Hetch Hetchy as a reservoir. Was not supplying water to a large city a worthy cause, one that certainly took priority over preserving wilderness? The San Francisco *Chronicle* referred to the preservationists as "hoggish and mushy esthetes,"[25] while the city's engineer, Marsden Manson, wrote in 1910 that the opposition was largely composed of "short-haired women and long-haired men."[26] San Francisco argued that the beauties of wilderness were admirable, but in this case human health, comfort, and even human life were the alternatives. Phrased in these terms, even some of the members of the Appalachian Mountain Club and the Sierra Club felt compelled to place the needs of civilization ahead of protecting wild country. In the Sierra Club, Warren Olney, one of the founders, led a faction which supported the city.[27] In 1910 the Club held a referendum in which preservation won 589 to 161, but in order to prosecute the defense of Hetch Hetchy, the preservationists were obliged to act in a separate organization: the California Branch of the Society for the Preservation of National Parks. The wilderness enthusiasts in the Appalachian group formed an Eastern Branch of the Society.[28]

At every opportunity the proponents of the dam expressed their belief that a lake in Hetch Hetchy would not spoil its beauty but, rather, enhance it. A prominent engineer reported on the City's behalf that roads and walks could be built which would open the

24. U.S. Congress, House, Committee on the Public Lands, *Granting Use of Hetch Hetchy to City of San Francisco,* 60th Cong., 2d Sess., House Rpt. 2085 (Feb. 8, 1909), pp. 11–12.

Several hundred of the communications addressed to the President, Secretary of the Interior, and various Congressmen have been preserved in chronological files in "Water Supply," National Archives.

25. As quoted in House, Committee on the Public Lands, *Granting Hetch Hetchy,* p. 16.

26. Marsden Manson to G. W. Woodruff, April 6, 1910, Marsden Manson Correspondence and Papers, Bancroft Library, University of California, Berkeley.

27. Olney, "Water Supply for the Cities about the Bay of San Francisco," *Out West, 31* (1909), 599–605.

28. Jones, *John Muir and the Sierra Club,* pp. 83–117; Johnson Papers, Berkeley, Box 13.

region for public recreation in the manner of European mountain-lake resorts.[29] Since the preservationists frequently based their opposition on the need to maintain a "scenic wonder" or "beauty spot,"[30] and on the desirability of maintaining a public playground, the claims of San Francisco were difficult to dismiss. If, instead, more attention had been paid specifically to the wilderness qualities of Hetch Hetchy—which *any* man-made construction would have eliminated—San Francisco's point about the scenic attraction of an artificial lake could have been more easily answered. As it was, this tactical error cost the preservationists considerable support.

The Hetch Hetchy controversy entered its climactic stage on March 4, 1913, when the Woodrow Wilson administration took office. San Francisco's hopes soared, because the new Secretary of the Interior, Franklin K. Lane, was a native, a former attorney for the city, and a proponent of the reservoir. But Lane upheld the policy of previous Secretaries that in cases involving national parks Congress must make the final decision. On behalf of San Francisco, Representative John E. Raker immediately introduced a bill to the Sixty-third Congress approving the grant. The preservationists prepared to send protest literature to 1418 newspapers and to make known their views before Congress.[31] Robert Underwood Johnson distributed an *Open Letter to the American People* in which he declared Hetch Hetchy to be "a veritable temple of the living God" and warned that "again the money-changers are in the temple."[32] The stage was set for a showdown.

On June 25 the House Committee on the Public Lands opened hearings on the Hetch Hetchy issue, with Gifford Pinchot as the star witness. Pinchot simplified the question into "whether the advantage of leaving this valley in a state of nature is greater than

29. John R. Freeman, *On the Proposed Use of a Portion of the Hetch Hetchy* (San Francisco, 1912), pp. 6 ff.

30. House, *Hearings* (1909), pp. 129 ff., 138 ff., 172 ff. provides numerous examples.

31. Johnson Papers, Berkeley, Boxes 7, 12. The Society for the Preservation of National Parks-Eastern Branch's *The Truth about the Hetch Hetchy and the Application to Congress by San Francisco to Flood this Valley in the Yosemite National Park* (Boston, 1913) is representative of the tracts the preservationists circulated.

32. Robert Underwood Johnson, *The Hetch Hetchy Scheme: Why It Should Not Be Rushed Through the Extra Session: An Open Letter to the American People* (New York, 1913).

. . . using it for the benefit of the city of San Francisco." He admitted that the idea of preserving wilderness appealed to him "if nothing else were at stake," but in this case the need of the city seemed "overwhelming." Explaining his reasoning, Pinchot declared that "the fundamental principle of the whole conservation policy is that of use, to take every part of the land and its resources and put it to that use in which it will serve the most people." Former San Francisco mayor James D. Phelan told the Committee that the criteria for a decision should be the needs of the "little children, men and women . . . who swarm the shore of San Francisco Bay" rather than the few who liked "solitary loneliness" and "the mere scenic value of the mountains."

Since the House hearings were called on short notice, Edmund D. Whitman of the Appalachian Mountain Club was the only preservationist to testify. He attempted to show that the reservoir would substantially reduce the value of Yosemite National Park as a public recreation ground and beauty spot. But Whitman did not bring out the fact that wilderness was at stake in Hetch Hetchy. As a result Phelan's rejoinder that San Francisco would cover the dam with moss, vines, and trees and would build picnic spots and trails around the reservoir seemed to answer his objections. Whitman concluded his testimony more effectively with a quotation from a Robert Underwood Johnson letter on the danger that without unspoiled nature to provide a "touch of idealism," life degenerated into "a race for the trough."[33]

On the basis of the June hearings, the Committee submitted a report unanimously endorsing the reservoir plans.[34] When the bill reached the floor of the House on August 29, 1913, strong support immediately developed for its passage. Applying the time-honored utilitarian yardstick to the problem, Representative Raker of California asserted that the "old barren rocks" of the valley have a "cash value" of less than $300,000 whereas a reservoir would be worth millions. But most proponents of the dam were not so positive. They prefaced their support of the dam with a declaration of their love of wilderness and reluctance to have it destroyed. Finly

33. U.S. Congress, House, Committee on the Public Lands, Hearings, *Hetch Hetchy Dam Site,* 63rd Cong., 1st Sess. (June 25–28, July 7, 1913), pp. 25–26, 166, 170, 237.

34. U.S. Congress, House, Committee on the Public Lands, *Hetch Hetchy Grant to San Francisco,* 63rd Cong., 1st Sess., House Rpt. 41 (Aug. 5, 1913).

H. Gray of Indiana, for example, explained: "Mr. Chairman, much as I admire the beauties of nature and deplore the desecration of God's Creation, yet when these two considerations come in conflict the conservation of nature should yield to the conservation of human welfare, health, and life."[35]

The choice Representative Gray made between wilderness and the needs of civilization was especially difficult for William Kent, a Representative from California. Independently wealthy, he had chosen a career as a reformer in politics, first in Chicago and after 1906 in Marin County, north of San Francisco, where he had lived as a boy. Kent's devotion to wild country had the same characteristics as Theodore Roosevelt's. "My life," he declared in an autobiographical fragment, "has been largely spent outdoors . . . I have ridden the prairies, the mountains and the desert."[36] A skilled hunter who deprecated the softness of his contemporaries, Kent called for a revitalization of the savage virtues. Understandably, he believed in the wisdom of preserving wilderness, and in 1903 bought several hundred acres of virgin redwood forest on the shoulder of Marin County's Mt. Tamalpais. In December 1907 Kent informed the Secretary of the Interior of his desire to give this land to the federal government as a national monument under the provisions of the Antiquities Act. His purpose was to keep in a primitive condition "the most attractive bit of wilderness I have ever seen."[37] Kent requested the area be named in honor of John Muir, and on January 9, 1908, President Roosevelt issued a proclamation designating the Muir Woods National Monument.

In view of this record, preservationists believed they had found a champion in William Kent. The Sierra Club made him an honorary member while letters poured in from all parts of the country applauding him for upholding aesthetic and spiritual values in a

35. *Congressional Record,* 63rd Cong., 1st Sess., *50* (Aug. 29, 1913), p. 3904; (Aug. 30), p. 3991.

36. Kent Family Papers, Historical Manuscripts Room, Yale University Library, New Haven, Conn., Box 95. For Kent's life see Elizabeth T. Kent, *William Kent, Independent: A Biography* (privately published, 1951) and Gilson Gardner, "Life of William Kent" (unpublished typescript, c. 1933) in the Kent Family Papers, Box 152. The first professional biography is Robert Woodbury's "William Kent: Progressive Gadfly, 1864–1928" (unpublished Ph.D. dissertation, Yale University, 1967).

37. Kent to James A. Garfield, Dec. 23, 1907, Kent Family Papers, Box 6. Kent's account of his acquisition and disposition of the land in question may be found in Kent, "The Story of Muir Woods" (undated typescript), Kent Family Papers, Box 111.

materialistic age.[38] Deeply touched by Kent's tribute, John Muir wrote personally, calling Muir Woods "the finest forest and park thing done in California in many a day." A few weeks later he again thanked Kent for "the best tree-lover's monument that could be found in all the forests of the world." Protecting the redwoods, Muir thought, was "a much needed lesson to saint and sinner alike, and a credit and encouragement to God." It astonished Muir that "so fine divine a thing should have come out of money-mad Chicago" and he ended by wishing Kent "immortal Sequoia life." Kent replied at once, inviting Muir to speak in Marin County and proposing collaboration in "the general cause of nature preservation."[39]

A few weeks after arriving in Washington in 1911 to begin his first term as a California Congressman, William Kent received a letter from his friend John Muir about Hetch Hetchy. Assuming that Kent, the donor of Muir Woods, would champion the cause of wilderness preservation, Muir simply encouraged him to follow the Hetch Hetchy issue and "do lots of good work."[40] But for Kent the matter was not so simple. While he realized that Hetch Hetchy was valuable as wilderness and part of a national park, he also knew that the powerful Pacific Gas and Electric Company wanted the valley as a step toward consolidating its control over California hydroelectric resources. Municipal control of Hetch Hetchy's water by San Francisco would block this plan, be a significant victory for the ideal of public ownership, and, beyond that, assert the democratic principle. Moreover, Kent had decided with his political friend Gifford Pinchot that "real conservation meant proper use and not locking up of natural resources."[41] The sacrifice of Hetch Hetchy's wilderness qualities, Kent concluded, was regrettable but

38. Kent carefully preserved clippings and correspondence in regard to Muir Woods: Kent Family Papers, Boxes 6 and 162.

39. Muir to Kent, Jan. 14 and Feb. 6, 1908, Kent to Muir, Feb. 10, 1908, Kent Family Papers, Box 6.

40. Muir to Kent, March 31, 1911, Kent Family Papers, Box 26.

41. As quoted in Gardner, "Life of William Kent," pp. 347–48. See also Kent's testimony in U.S. Congress, Senate, Committee on the Public Lands, Hearings, *Hetch Hetchy Reservoir Site,* 63rd Cong., 1st Sess. (Sept. 24, 1913), p. 70, and his dispatch on the passage of the Hetch Hetchy bill, *San Francisco Bulletin,* Dec. 20, 1913. A discussion of Kent's efforts on behalf of public control of waterpower by Judson King, a fellow crusader, is included in Judson King Papers, Library of Congress, Washington, D.C., Box 77. See also King's *The Conservation Fight from Theodore Roosevelt to the Tennessee Valley Authority* (Washington, D.C., 1959), esp. pp. 40 ff. Compare footnote 56 below.

in this case necessary for a greater good. Answering Muir indirectly in a letter to Robert Underwood Johnson, Kent stated his conviction that conservation could best be served by granting the valley to San Francisco.[42]

In 1913, as a key member of the House Committee on the Public Lands, William Kent was in a position to exert considerable influence. He began by helping draft a bill permitting San Francisco to build its reservoir; then opened his home to the city's supporters as a campaign headquarters. The fact that Kent was widely known as the donor of Muir Woods lent extra weight to his opinions. Certainly *he* would not dismiss the claims of wilderness preservation lightly. Kent exploited this advantage fully. When the Hetch Hetchy bill came to the floor of the House, he stated simply: "I can lay claim to being a nature lover myself. I think that is a matter of record." The same technique appeared in a letter to President Woodrow Wilson in which Kent advocated San Francisco's claim and then added that in the cause of protecting nature he had personally "spent more time and effort . . . than any of the men who are opposing this bill."[43]

It remained for Kent, as an acknowledged admirer of Muir, to provide public explanation for their divergence over Hetch Hetchy. He did so in the summer of 1913 in a series of letters to his Congressional colleagues. To Representative Sydney Anderson of Minnesota he wrote: "I hope you will not take my friend, Muir, seriously, for he is a man entirely without social sense. With him, it is me and God and the rock where God put it, and that is the end of the story. I know him well and as far as this proposition is concerned, he is mistaken." Similarly, Kent wired Pinchot that the Hetch Hetchy protest was the work of private waterpower interests using "misinformed nature lovers" as their spokesmen. In October Kent told a meeting in California that because Muir had spent so much time in the wilderness he had not acquired the social instincts of the average man.[44]

42. Kent to Robert Underwood Johnson, April 6, 1911 (carbon), Kent Family Papers, Box 17.

43. *Congressional Record,* 63rd Cong., 1st Sess., *50* (Aug. 30, 1913), p. 3963; Kent to Woodrow Wilson, Oct. 1, 1913, Woodrow Wilson Papers, Library of Congress, Washington, D.C., File VI, Box 199, Folder 169.

44. Kent to Sydney Anderson, July 2, 1913, Kent Family Papers, Box 26; Kent to Gifford Pinchot, Oct. 8, 1913, Gifford Pinchot Papers, Box 1823; San Rafael *Independent,* Oct. 21, 1913, in Kent Family Papers, Box 171.

It was not the case that Kent changed his mind about the value of wilderness between 1908 and 1913. In fact, at the very time he was advocating development of Hetch Hetchy, he asked Gifford Pinchot for a statement in support of a state park on Mt. Tamalpais. Specifically, Kent wanted Pinchot to show "the advantage of such a wilderness, particularly near San Francisco."[45] And after Hetch Hetchy, Kent went on to help author the bill establishing the National Park Service, participate in the founding of the Save-the-Redwoods League, and add more land to Muir Woods National Monument. Kent's problem was that the necessity of deciding about Hetch Hetchy left no room for an expression of his ambivalence. The valley could not be a wilderness and a publicly owned reservoir simultaneously. And, ultimately, Kent and Muir gave wilderness preservation a different priority at the price of their earlier friendship.

As the consideration of the Hetch Hetchy question in the House continued into September, 1913, the sentiments of William Kent and other supporters of San Francisco encountered stiffer opposition. Halvor Steenerson of Minnesota declared it was nonsense to claim that an artificial lake would add to the beauty of the valley. "You may as well improve upon the lily of the field by handpainting it," he pointed out, and added that all the city offered was a power plant making a "devilish hissing noise" and a "dirty muddy pond." Concluding his remarks, Steenerson spoke in the agrarian tradition, deploring the tendency of Americans to live in cities, and in the Romantic manner, hoping that some day a poet would use the "pristine glory" of Hetch Hetchy "to produce something more valuable than money." Horace M. Towner of Iowa agreed, and pleaded with his colleagues to recognize that "dishwashing is not the only use for water, nor lumber for trees, nor pasture for grass." But Martin Dies of Texas rose to say the final word before the House vote. He felt that natural resources should serve civilization. "I want them to open the reservations in this country," Dies declared. "I am not for reservations and parks." Applause and cries of "Vote!" greeted the conclusion of Dies' remarks.[46]

On September 3 the House passed the Hetch Hetchy bill 183 to

45. Kent to Gifford Pinchot, March 5, 1913, Gifford Pinchot Papers, Box 164.

46. *Congressional Record*, 63rd Cong., 1st Sess., *50* (Aug. 30, 1913), pp. 3972–74; ibid. (Extension of Remarks made on Aug. 29, 1913), p. 461; ibid. (Aug. 30, 1913), p. 4003.

43, with 203 Representatives not voting. No Congressman from a Western state voted against it. Most of its support came from Southern and Middle Western Democrats. In fact, the bill was rumored to be an administration measure, connected, in some minds, with the votes California had given to Wilson in the recent election.[47]

The Senate still had to decide on San Francisco's application, and in preparation the preservationists worked frantically. Their plan was "to flood the Senate with letters from influential people."[48] In addition, the Society for the Preservation of National Parks and the newly organized National Committee for the Preservation of the Yosemite National Park published several pamphlets which called on Americans to write or wire their President and Congressmen and suggested arguments against the dam.[49] Thousands of copies circulated, and the public responded. Between the time of the House passage and early December when the Senate began its debate, the destruction of the wilderness qualities of Hetch Hetchy Valley became a major national issue. Hundreds of newspapers throughout the country, including such opinion leaders as the New York *Times,* published editorials on the question, most of which took the side of preservation.[50] Leading magazines, such as *Outlook, Nation, Independent,* and *Collier's,* carried articles protesting the reservoir. A mass meeting on behalf of the valley took place at the Museum of Natural History in New York City. Mail poured into the offices of key Senators: Reed Smoot of Utah estimated late in November that he had received five thousand letters in opposition to the bill, and other Senators were likewise besieged.[51] The protests came from women's groups, outing and sportsmen's clubs, scientific societies, and the faculties of colleges

47. Richardson, "The Struggle for the Valley," 255; New York *Times,* Dec. 4, 1913.

48. Robert Underwood Johnson to Bernhard E. Fernow, Oct. 17, 1913, Johnson Papers, Berkeley, Box 1.

49. National Committee for the Preservation of the Yosemite National Park, *Bulletin No. 1: The Hetch Hetchy 'Grab': Who Oppose It and Why* (New York, 1913) and *Bulletin No. 2* (New York, 1913); Society for the Preservation of National Parks, *Circular Number Seven* (San Francisco, 1913).

50. The Committee's *Bulletins* list and quote from several hundred papers.

51. *Congressional Record,* 63rd Cong., 1st Sess., *50* (Nov. 25, 1913), p. 6012. Additional indication of the scope of the protest may be found in the voluminous files which the United States Forest Service kept on the controversy: "Water Supply," National Archives.

and universities as well as from individuals. The American wilderness had never been so popular before.

The arguments the preservationists used against the dam followed the lines laid down in the earlier stages of the controversy. The issue was represented to be between the intangible values of wilderness and the insensitivity of utilitarianism. One widely circulated statement from an editorial in the Brooklyn [N.Y.] *Standard Union* maintained that keeping Hetch Hetchy wild was an opportunity to answer the taunts of detractors and demonstrate "that there are some things even in America which money cannot buy."[52] Frederick Law Olmsted, Jr., who had succeeded to his father's place as a leader in the field of landscape architecture, also published a defense of the valley. After distinguishing between the "beauty-value" and the "use-value" of nature, he observed that the previous century "has shown . . . an enormous increase in the appreciation of and resort to the wilder and less man-handled scenery as a means of recreation from the intensifying strain of civilization." As a consequence, Olmsted contended, wildernesses like Hetch Hetchy had great importance to modern society. They must be preserved and held inviolate "if beauty of scenery is not to be pushed to the wall at every point of conflict [with] the more obvious claims of utilitarian advantages."[53]

Robert Underwood Johnson worked for Hetch Hetchy at a fever pitch through the summer and fall of 1913 because he believed that "this is a fight between the sordid commercialism on the one hand and the higher interests of the whole people on the other." The difference between a wild Hetch Hetchy and an artificial reservoir, he asserted, was not "a tweedledee and tweedledum distinction between two equally good kinds of scenery" but rather involved "worship and sacrilege." In Johnson's eyes there could be no compromise with San Francisco. "I am so confident that we are right in this matter," he wrote young Franklin D. Roosevelt at the height of the controversy, that he would debate anyone anywhere on the subject.[54] Johnson and his colleagues constantly emphasized that

52. As quoted in Society for the Preservation of National Parks, *The Truth About the Hetch-Hetchy,* p. 1.

53. Frederick Law Olmsted, Jr., "Hetch Hetchy: The San Francisco Water-Supply Controversy," Boston *Evening Transcript,* Nov. 19, 1913.

54. Johnson to William R. Nelson, Oct. 27, 1913 (carbon); Johnson to William E. Borah, Nov. 6, 1913 (carbon); Johnson to Franklin D. Roosevelt, Nov. 11, 1913 (carbon), Johnson Papers, Berkeley, Box 1.

they had no desire of denying San Francisco an adequate water supply. Of course civilization must have its due, they conceded, but in this case other sources of water were available and keeping Hetch Hetchy wild was worth the extra cost of their development.

The wilderness advocates looked forward hopefully to the Senate debate and vote. They had succeeded in demonstrating that a large number of Americans resented the proposed alteration of Yosemite National Park. In mid-November 1913, Muir cheered the hard-working Johnson: "we're bound to win, enemy badly frightened, Up and smite em!"[55] But when the Senate began its consideration of the bill on December 1, it was apparent that San Francisco's representatives, who had not campaigned nationally but rather lobbied quietly in Washington, had done effective work. As was the case with many Representatives, most Senators first made clear that they too appreciated the values of unspoiled nature but went on to support the dam. "I appreciate the importance of preserving beautiful natural features of a landscape as much as anybody else," Frank B. Brandegee of Connecticut declared. Yet ultimately civilization won out because the "mere preservation of a beautiful, romantic, and picturesque spot . . . for esthetic purposes" could not conceivably take precedence over "the urgent needs of great masses of human beings for the necessities of life." Echoing Brandegee, Marcus A. Smith of Arizona said that his affection for natural beauty "leads me as nothing else could to sympathize with those thousands of people who have sent their protests against the destruction of . . . Yosemite National Park." However, Smith, too, was in favor of the reservoir, because while "we all love the sound of whispering winds amid the trees . . . the wail of a hungry baby will make us forget it . . . as we try to minister to its wants." Few Senators supported the dam because they opposed wilderness. Most either thought the benefits coming to San Francisco greater than the good that accrued from the wild park or, as with George D. Norris of Nebraska, conceived of the issue only in terms of publicly owned hydroelectric development.[56]

55. Muir to Johnson, Nov. 10, 1913, Muir Papers, New York.

56. *Congressional Record*, 63rd Cong., 2d Sess., *51* (Dec. 4, 1913), p. 198; ibid. (Dec. 5, 1913), p. 273; ibid. (Dec. 6, 1913), pp. 339 ff. In *Fighting Liberal* (New York, 1945), pp. 163 ff., Norris describes in retrospect his impressions of the Hetch Hetchy controversy and his part in it. For evidence that he hoped San Francisco's control of its water supply and the resulting hydroelectric power would be a step in the direction of intelligent national policy see Richard Lowitt, "A Neglected Aspect

The Senators opposing San Francisco stressed the availability of other reservoir sites and the need to respect the sanctity of a region that had been dedicated to providing the public with a sample of wilderness. Asle J. Gronna of North Dakota believed it was a mistake "to commercialize every bit of land" and to "destroy the handiwork of God's creation."[57] Exchanges were heated, and for several evenings the lights of the Senate burned late into the night.

A decision had been made to vote on December 6, and when the Senators entered their chamber that morning they found copies of a "Special Washington Edition" of the San Francisco *Examiner* on their desks. Skillful drawings showed how the valley might appear as a man-made lake with scenic drives for automobiles and boating facilities for happy family groups. The *Examiner* also published experts' testimony justifying the grant in a variety of ways.[58] In comparison, the preservationists' campaign literature was considerably less impressive.

At three minutes before midnight on December 6, the Senate voted. Forty-three favored the grant, twenty-five opposed it, and twenty-nine did not vote or were absent. Eighteen votes from Southern Democrats were the decisive factor, and suggested, as in the case of the House, that the Wilson administration was behind San Francisco. Only nine of the "yeas" came from Republicans.[59]

A Presidential veto was the last hope of the preservationists. After the Senate passage, Wilson received numerous letters calling upon him to defend Yosemite National Park. Robert Underwood Johnson wrote, characteristically, that "God invented courage for just such emergencies. The moral effect of a veto would be immense."[60] He even called in person on the President, but when he left the office, William Kent was waiting to enter![61] On December 19, 1913, Wilson approved the Hetch Hetchy grant. In signing he declared that "the bill was opposed by so many public-spirited men . . . that I have naturally sought to scrutinize it very closely. I take

of the Progressive Movement: George W. Norris and Public Control of Hydro-electric Power, 1913–1919," *Historian, 27* (1965), 350–65.

57. *Congressional Record,* 63rd Cong., 2d Sess., *51* (Dec. 4, 1913), p. 199.

58. San Francisco *Examiner,* Dec. 2, 1913.

59. For a detailed account of the final stages of the controversy and the political factors behind the decision see Jones, pp. 153–69.

60. Wilson Papers, File VI, Box 199; Johnson to Wilson, Dec. 9, 1913, Wilson Papers, File VI, Box 199, Folder 169.

61. Gardner, "Life of Kent," pp. 351–52.

the liberty of thinking that their fears and objections were not well founded."[62]

The preservationists had lost the fight for the valley, but they had gained much ground in the larger war for the existence of wilderness. A deeply disappointed John Muir took some consolation from the fact that "the conscience of the whole country has been aroused from sleep."[63] Scattered sentiment for wilderness preservation had, in truth, become a national movement in the course of the Hetch Hetchy controversy. Moreover, the defenders of wilderness discovered their political muscles and how to flex them by arousing an expression of public opinion, and in Hetch Hetchy they had a symbol which, like the *Maine,* would not easily be forgotten. In fact, immediately after the Hetch Hetchy defeat the fortunes of wilderness preservation took an abrupt turn for the better. Early in 1915 Stephen T. Mather, a highly successful businessman and wilderness enthusiast, became director of the national parks. Along with Horace M. Albright, Robert Sterling Yard, J. Horace McFarland, and the Sierra Club, Mather generated a campaign on the park's behalf that resulted in the enactment in 1916 of the National Park Service Act. The publicity that accompanied its passage did much to increase the national interest in preserving wilderness that the Hetch Hetchy fight had aroused.[64]

Near the close of the Senate debate on Hetch Hetchy, James A. Reed of Missouri arose to confess his incredulity at the entire controversy. How could it be, he wondered, that over the future of a piece of wilderness "the Senate goes into profound debate, the country is thrown into a condition of hysteria." Observing, accurately, that the intensity of resistance to the dam increased with the distance from Yosemite, he remarked that "when we get as far east as New England the opposition has become a frenzy." In Senator

62. *Congressional Record,* 63rd Cong., 2d Sess., *51* (Dec. 19, 1913), p. 1189.

63. Muir to Robert Underwood Johnson, Jan. 1, 1914, Johnson Papers, Berkeley, Box 7.

64. Donald C. Swain, "The Passage of the National Park Service Act of 1916," *Wisconsin Magazine of History, 50* (1966), 4–17; Robert Shankland, *Steve Mather of the National Parks* (New York, 1951). One indication of the extent of public interest was the number of articles on the national parks published in popular magazines. Between September 1916 and October of the following year over 300 appeared in 95 journals. The figures for the next two years were equally impressive: *Annual Report of the Director of the National Park Service* (1917) (1918) (1919), pp. 1017–30, 1051–63, and 1247–61.

Reed's opinion this was clearly "much ado about little."[65] He might have said the same about the enthusiasm for Joe Knowles, the Boy Scouts, or *Tarzan of the Apes* (see Chapter 9) that occurred simultaneously with the Hetch Hetchy battle. But the point, as Reed himself suggested, was that a great many of his contemporaries *did* regard wilderness as worth getting excited about.

Indeed the most significant thing about the controversy over the valley was that it occurred at all. One hundred or even fifty years earlier a similar proposal to dam a wilderness river would not have occasioned the slightest ripple of public protest. Traditional American assumptions about the use of undeveloped country did not include reserving it in national parks for its recreational, aesthetic, and inspirational values. The emphasis was all the other way—on civilizing it in the name of progress and prosperity. Older generations conceived of the thrust of civilization into the wilderness as the beneficent working out of divine intentions, but in the twentieth century a handful of preservationists generated widespread resistance against this very process. What had formerly been the subject of national celebration was made to appear a national tragedy.

Muir, Johnson, and their colleagues were able to create a protest because the American people were ready to be aroused. Appreciation of wild country and the desire for its preservation had spread in the closing decades of the nineteenth century from a small number of literati to a sizeable segment of the population. The extent and vigor of the resistance to San Francisco's plans for Hetch Hetchy constituted tangible evidence for the existence of a wilderness cult. Equally revealing was the fact that very few favored the dam *because* they opposed wilderness. Even the partisans of San Francisco phrased the issue as not between a good (civilization) and an evil (wilderness) but between two goods. While placing material needs first, they still proclaimed their love of unspoiled nature. Previously most Americans had not felt compelled to rationalize the conquest of wild country in this manner. For three centuries they had chosen civilization without any hesitation. By 1913 they were no longer so sure.

65. *Congressional Record,* 63rd Cong., 2d Sess., *51* (Dec. 6, 1913), p. 362.

CHAPTER 11

Aldo Leopold: Prophet

> Ability to see the cultural value of wilderness boils down, in the last analysis, to a question of intellectual humility. . . . It is only the scholar who understands why the raw wilderness gives definition and meaning to the human enterprise.
>
> Aldo Leopold, 1949

IN 1854 Henry David Thoreau remarked on the transformation that occasionally took place in a person's relation to the natural world. A young man commonly sought the woods as a hunter and fisherman, but "at last, if he has the seeds of a better life in him, he distinguishes his proper objects, as a poet or a naturalist it may be, and leaves the gun and fish-pole behind."[1] Aldo Leopold fitted this pattern closely, except that he found his proper object in ecology. With it he built a philosophy of the importance of wilderness comparable in acuteness and influence to that of Thoreau himself. Less than a decade after the Hetch Hetchy struggle, Leopold campaigned successfully for a policy of wilderness preservation in the National Forest system. A few years later his growing awareness of the interrelations of organisms and their environment led him to the realization that protecting wild country was a matter of scientific necessity as well as sentiment. This synthesis of the logic of a scientist with the ethical and aesthetic sensitivity of a Romantic was effective armament for the defense of wilderness. While Leopold's concepts of an "ecological conscience" and a "land ethic" remained ideals, preservationists recognized them as pointing the way to a new relationship between man and land as well as to a new significance for wilderness.

Leopold began his acquaintance with the outdoors among the bluffs and bottom lands of the Mississippi River. His parents, both enthusiastic sportsmen, lived in Burlington, Iowa, and encouraged their son's early interest in the identification of the birds around

1. Thoreau, *Walden*, *Writings*, 2, 331.

his home. Aldo continued his ornithological studies during his student years at Lawrenceville School in New Jersey and at Yale. Graduating in the Class of 1908 he decided, like Gifford Pinchot, to indulge his love of the outdoors with a career in forestry. There was no need to change campuses to obtain further training. The Yale Forest School, which the philanthropy of the Pinchot family had enabled to open in 1900, was the leading center of graduate work in the country and supplied most of the personnel for the United States Forest Service. In 1909 Leopold received a degree which qualified him for the position of "Forest Assistant" in the Southwest with the Service's District III.[2] At this time Arizona and New Mexico were still territories, and Aldo Leopold grew up with the country.

Concern for the protection of wildlife led Leopold to an understanding and appreciation of wilderness. His work in District III showed him the problem of rapidly diminishing supplies of big game, fish, and waterfowl. As a sportsman, Leopold was concerned about the situation, but in 1913 a near-fatal attack of Bright's disease incapacitated him for over a year. On returning to active duty he began to organize local hunters and fishermen around Albuquerque, New Mexico into game protective associations.[3] One group published a newspaper in which Leopold wrote in 1915: "the aim and purpose of this little paper is to promote the protection and enjoyment of wild things . . . may it scatter the seeds of wisdom and understanding among men, to the end that every citizen may learn to hold the lives of harmless wild creatures as a public trust for human good, against the abuse of which he stands personally responsible."[4] These ideas were also the seeds of Leopold's later philosophy.

District III Forester Arthur C. Ringland recognized his assistant's enthusiasm and ability for wildlife conservation by placing him in charge of game, fish, and recreation. Leopold responded eagerly, and soon had his fellow foresters enforcing game laws and

2. Henry S. Graves, et al., *The First Half Century of the Yale School of Forestry* (n.p., 1950), pp. 6 ff.; Overton Price to Leopold, June 18, 1909, Aldo Leopold Official Personnel Folder, Federal Records Center, St. Louis, Mo.

3. Aldo Leopold, "History of Game Protection in New Mexico" (unpublished typescript c. 1922), Aldo Leopold Papers, University Archives, University of Wisconsin, Madison, Box 8.

4. Leopold, "Our Aim," *Pine Cone* (Christmas, 1915), 1, in the Leopold Papers, Box 5.

exterminating predators as well as aiding in the stocking of streams and ranges. He wrote a game handbook for the District, and toyed with the idea of leaving the Forest Service to head the New Mexico State Game Department.[5] But Leopold did not change jobs, and in 1916 refused to accept an attractive public relations position at the Service's Washington office on the grounds that his illness had left him not knowing "whether I have twenty days or twenty years ahead of me," and anxious to accomplish something definite for the protection of wildlife in the Southwest.[6] In the same year the first of his published articles on game management appeared.[7] Soon Leopold's efforts were attracting national attention: he received a medal of recognition from the Permanent Wild Life Protection Fund, and no less a figure than Theodore Roosevelt commended his work as setting an example for the entire nation.[8]

At the beginning of 1918 the movement for the conservation of game in Arizona and New Mexico was flourishing, but the ranking officers of the Forest Service did not share Leopold's enthusiasm. Reluctantly he resigned on January 3 and accepted a job as secretary of the Albuquerque Chamber of Commerce, but with the intention of rejoining the Service "as soon as that organization was ready to proceed with the handling of national forest game."[9] He did not have long to wait. New ideas about the nonmaterial values of the National Forests were beginning to challenge the traditional utilitarian objectives of foresters. Moreover, the National Park Service, which had been led since its establishment in 1916 by the energetic Stephen T. Mather, was attracting considerable attention to the parks as recreation meccas for the newly motorized American traveler.[10] Loath to see a newcomer steal the public thunder, and possibly some of its land, the Forest Service countered by giving unprecedented publicity to scenery and outdoor recreation as ma-

5. Interview with Arthur C. Ringland, Washington, D.C., Dec. 20, 1963; Arthur C. Ringland to D. D. Bronson, Dec. 18, 1915, Official Folder.

6. Leopold to Arthur C. Ringland, Feb. 14, 1916, Official Folder.

7. A substantially complete bibliography for Leopold appeared in the *Wildlife Research News Letter, 35* (May 3, 1948), 4–19, published by the Department of Wildlife Management, University of Wisconsin.

8. Paul G. Redington to Henry S. Graves, July 30, 1917, Official Folder; Trefethen, *Crusade for Wildlife,* pp. 247 ff.

9. Leopold to John B. Burnham, Jan. 14, 1919 (carbon), Leopold Papers, Box 3.

10. Paul Herman Buck, "The Evolution of the National Park System in the United States" (unpublished M.A. thesis, Ohio State University, 1922); Shankland, *Steve Mather;* Swain, "The Passage of the National Park Service Act."

jor "products" of the National Forests. In this way it hoped to attract the support of the growing number of Americans interested in wilderness.[11] In 1917 the Service commissioned a landscape architect, Frank A. Waugh, to conduct a study of the recreational potential of the land under its administration. Waugh concluded that the "enticing wildness" and "notable beauty" of the forests had a "direct human value," and recommended that sightseeing, camping, and hiking be given equal consideration with economic criteria in determining the use of the forests.[12]

Sensing a more favorable attitude in Washington, Leopold rejoined the Forest Service in the summer of 1919. His interest in game conservation continued, but gradually he recognized that the maintenance and indeed the appeal of hunting and fishing was part of the larger problem of preserving the wilderness conditions in which these activities took place. Along with Ward Shepard, Frederic Winn, and others in the Southwest, Leopold had already discussed the possibilities of keeping part of the National Forests wild[13] when late in 1919 he went to Denver to confer with Service personnel in District II. On December 6, Arthur H. Carhart, a young landscape architect serving the District as "Recreation Engineer," told Leopold of his experience the previous summer on a survey project at Trappers Lake, Colorado. Carhart had been ordered to submit a design for the placement of vacation homes around the lake, but after making his study, he decided that its best possible use was for wilderness recreation. That same summer he had also toured the Quetico-Superior region between Minnesota and Ontario and recognized its potential as undeveloped canoe country. Following these trips, Carhart recommended that such areas of superlative wild scenery in the National Forests be man-

11. Donald F. Cate, "Recreation and the U.S. Forest Service: A Study of Organizational Response to Changing Demands" (unpublished Ph.D. dissertation, Stanford University, 1963), pp. 26–85, 99–103; Gilligan, "Forest Service Primitive and Wilderness Areas," pp. 62 ff., 81; Donald C. Swain, *Federal Conservation Policy*, University of California Publications in History, 76 (Berkeley, 1963), pp. 28, 123 ff.; Donald Nicholas Baldwin, "An Historical Study of the Western Origin, Application, and Development of the Wilderness Concept, 1919–1933" (unpublished Ph.D. dissertation, University of Denver, 1965), pp. 16–41, 62–86.

12. Frank A. Waugh, *Recreation Uses on the National Forests* (Washington, D.C., 1918), pp. 3, 10–11, 27–28.

13. Interview with Raymond E. Marsh and Arthur C. Ringland, Washington, D.C., Dec. 20, 1963; Harvey Broome, "Our Basis of Understanding," *Living Wilderness, 19* (1954–55), 47–49. Paul H. Roberts' *Them Were the Days* (San Antonio, 1965) is a historical reminiscense of this period of southwestern National Forest history.

aged for their value as wilderness.[14] It was a bold suggestion for a young employee of the traditionally utilitarian U.S. Forest Service but Carhart found a strong supporter in Leopold. In the course of their conversation the problem of resisting total development in the name of scenic and aesthetic values received thorough support.[15]

Encouraged at finding a kindred spirit in Denver, Leopold returned to Albuquerque determined to push his plans for a wilderness preservation. But it was Carhart and District II Forester Carl J. Stahl who made the first application of the preservation principle to the National Forests: early in 1920 Trappers Lake received designation as an area to be kept roadless and undeveloped.[16] Leopold's conception of a wilderness preserve, however, necessitated considerably more area than a single lake and valley. In 1921 he wrote an article for the *Journal of Forestry* with the object of giving "definite form to the issue of wilderness conservation." Leopold defined wilderness as "a continuous stretch of country preserved in its natural state, open to lawful hunting and fishing, big enough to absorb a two weeks' pack trip, and kept devoid of roads, artificial trails, cottages, or other works of man." While admitting that the majority probably favored mechanized access to recreation grounds, he contended that those of the minority who coveted primitive conditions of travel and life in a wilderness situation also deserved consideration. Wild country was essential to their happiness, and the opportunity of finding it was vanishing rapidly. Concluding the article, Leopold suggested that an undeveloped portion of

14. A thorough secondary treatment, which clearly establishes Carhart's seminal role in Forest Service wilderness policy, is Baldwin, "Historical Study of the . . . Wilderness Concept," pp. 42–53, 134–59. Carhart discussed his own ideas in the following writings: *Timber in Your Life* (Philadelphia, 1955), pp. 140–43; *The National Forests* (New York, 1959), pp. 119 ff.; "Recreation in the Forests," *American Forestry, 26* (1920), 268–72; "The Superior Forest," *Parks and Recreation, 6* (1923), 502–04; and *Preliminary Prospectus: An Outline Plan for the Recreational Development of the Superior National Forest* (n.p., c. 1921). Carhart to the author, April 24, 1964, supplemented these sources.

15. Arthur H. Carhart, "Memorandum for Mr. Leopold, District 3" (typescript dated Dec. 10, 1919), Arthur Carhart Papers, Conservation Library Center, Denver Public Library, Denver.

16. Arthur H. Carhart, "L Uses, White River: Memorandum, Feb. 1, 1920" and "L Recreation, White River: Memorandum, April 7, 1920" (typescripts), Carhart Papers; C. J. Stahl, "Where Forestry and Recreation Meet," *Journal of Forestry, 19* (1921), 526–29.

the Gila National Forest in New Mexico be made a permanent wilderness reserve.[17]

The *Journal of Forestry* article provided the stimulus for action. Early in 1922 Frank C. W. Pooler, the District III Forester, instructed Leopold to make a personal inspection of the Gila. Frederic Winn, the immediate supervisor of the forest, collaborated with Leopold in working out a policy for protecting wilderness.[18] Local sportsmen's associations put their weight behind the proposal, and on June 3, 1924, Pooler designated 574,000 acres as devoted primarily to wilderness recreation.[19]

Thus far in his campaign to inaugurate the preservation of wilderness in the Forest Service, Leopold had been acting with only a vague rationale. However, when he left District III in the summer of 1924 to assume the post of assistant director of the Service's Forest Products Laboratory in Madison, Wisconsin, he found more opportunity to mull over the significance of keeping portions of the Southwest wild. This led to the beginning of a lifelong concern with the meaning of wilderness. Leopold felt that what was at stake in keeping some wild land was the quality of American life—the welfare of the nation beyond its material needs. He had no desire to gainsay the achievements of civilization, but he insisted that they could go too far: "while the reduction of the wilderness has been a good thing, its extermination would be a very bad one."[20] Following Thoreau, he saw the solution in a balance between two desirables (Chapter 5). Groping for a comprehensible metaphor, Leopold declared: "what I am trying to make clear is that if in a

17. Leopold, "The Wilderness and its Place in Forest Recreational Policy," *Journal of Forestry, 19* (1921), 718–21.

18. Aldo Leopold, "General Inspection Report of the Gila National Forest" (typescript c. July 1922) and "Report on Proposed Wilderness Area" (Oct. 2, 1922), United States Forest Service Records, Region III Headquarters, Albuquerque, N.M. The reports were examined in Madison, Wis. through the courtesy of Fred H. Kennedy, Regional Forester.

19. Aldo Leopold, "Origin and Ideals of Wilderness Areas," *Living Wilderness, 5,* (1940), 7; Baldwin, "Historical Study of the . . . Wilderness Concept," pp. 228–48; Gilligan, "Forest Service Primitive and Wilderness Areas," pp. 82–85; Wildland Research Center, University of California, Berkeley, *Wilderness and Recreation—A Report on Resources, Values and Problems,* Outdoor Recreation Resources Review Commission Study Report, 3 (Washington, D.C., 1962), pp. 279 ff.

20. *National Conference on Outdoor Recreation Proceedings 1926,* 69th Cong., 1st Sess., Senate Doc. 117 (April 14, 1926), p. 63.

city we had six vacant lots available to the youngsters of a certain neighborhood for playing ball, it might be 'development' to build houses on the first, and the second, and the third, and the fourth, and even on the fifth, but when we build houses on the last one, we forget what houses are for. The sixth house would not be development at all, but rather . . . stupidity." He realized this was a difficult point to make to a people who "are so accustomed to a plentiful supply [of wilderness] that we are *unconscious* of what the disappearance of wild places would mean." The American measurement of progress "has been to conquer the wilderness and convert it to economic use." In other words, "a stump was our symbol of progress."[21] Needed was a new criterion which would redefine a progressive civilization as one that valued and preserved its remaining wilderness.

The problem was to convince Americans that the development of their last wildernesses would entail more sacrifice than gain. Using Frederick Jackson Turner's insights as a base, Leopold began his argument with the contention that "many of the attributes most distinctive of America and Americans are [due to] the impress of the wilderness and the life that accompanied it." He went on to clarify the point: "if we have such a thing as an American culture (and I think we have), its distinguishing marks are a certain vigorous individualism combined with ability to organize, a certain intellectual curiosity bent to practical ends, a lack of subservience to stiff social forms, and an intolerance of drones, all of which are distinctive characteristics of successful pioneers. These, if anything, are the indigenous part of our Americanism, the qualities that set it apart as a new rather than an imitative contribution to civilization." Finally, Leopold drew the conclusion that Turner only implied: "is it not a bit beside the point for us to be so solicitous about preserving [American] institutions without giving so much as a thought to preserving the environment which produced them and which may now be one of our effective means of keeping them alive?"[22] Wilderness preserves, then, were not just for fun. They maintained the opportunity for successive generations of Ameri-

21. Leopold, "A Plea for Wilderness Hunting Grounds" (typescript, c. 1924), Leopold Papers, Box 8; Leopold, "The Last Stand of the Wilderness," *American Forests and Forest Life, 31* (1925), 602; Leopold, "Wilderness as a Form of Land Use," *Journal of Land and Public Utility Economics, 1* (1925), 398; Leopold, "The Wilderness Fallacy" (typescript c. 1925), Leopold Papers, Box 8.

22. Leopold, "Wilderness as a Form of Land Use," 401.

cans to acquire the characteristics of pioneers and to acquaint themselves firsthand with the conditions that shaped their culture.[23] Speaking for himself, Leopold declared: "I am glad I shall never be young without wild country to be young in. Of what avail are forty freedoms without a blank spot on the map?"[24]

Commenting in the 1920s on the tendency of Americans to take wilderness for granted, Leopold pointed out that only "when the end of the supply is in sight [do] we 'discover' that the thing is valuable."[25] But even as he wrote, post-war opinion was according wilderness importance as a panacea for the nation's ills. Numerous voices joined Leopold's in extolling the virtues of outdoor recreation. "Without parks and outdoor life," asserted Enos Mills, a Colorado mountain guide and publicizer of the national parks, "all that is best in civilization will be smothered." He conceived of the "wilderness empires of our National Parks" as a means to "rebuild the past" and added that they would help "keep the nation young."[26] The popular nature writer and aesthetician, John C. Van Dyke, pointed out that the recent war had left the American West undisturbed and asked: "was there ever a time in human history when a return to Nature was so much needed as just now? How shall the nations be rebuilded, the lost faith and hope renewed, the race live again save through the Great Mother whom we have forsaken?"[27] Over two million Americans saw Emerson Hough's 1922 plea in the *Saturday Evening Post* for the preservation of Arizona's Kaibab Plateau as a "typical portion of the American wilderness" designed to show future citizens "what the old America once was, how beautiful, how splendid."[28]

Benton MacKaye, a pioneer regional planner, quoted from Leopold's articles and expressed his own concern for providing outdoor recreation space, "primeval areas" which would help to stem

23. Aldo Leopold, "Conserving the Covered Wagon," *Sunset, 54* (1925), 21, 56. For a later statement see Leopold, *A Sand County Almanac and Sketches Here and There* (New York, 1949), pp. 188 ff.

24. Leopold, "The Green Lagoons," *American Forests, 51* (1945), 414.

25. Leopold, "The Last Stand of the Wilderness," 599–600.

26. Enos Mills, *Your National Parks* (Boston, 1917), pp. x-xi, 379. The influence of Muir upon Mills and Mills' role in the creation of Rocky Mountain National Park in 1915 are the subject of much of the Enos Mills Collection, Western History Division, Denver Public Library, Denver.

27. Van Dyke, *The Grand Canyon of the Colorado: Recurrent Studies in Impressions and Appearances* (New York, 1920), p. vi.

28. Hough, "The President's Forest," *Saturday Evening Post, 196* (1922), 63.

"the metropolitan invasion and the spread of its mechanized environment." As an illustration, MacKaye began in 1921 his successful campaign for an Appalachian Trail running along the crest of the mountains from Maine to Georgia and providing many Americans with the chance to hike in wild country close to home.[29]

On April 14, 1924, President Calvin Coolidge gave organized form to the enthusiasm for regaining contact with the outdoors when he issued a call for a National Conference on Outdoor Recreation. Coolidge declared that "the physical vigor, moral strength, and clean simplicity of mind of the American people can be immeasurably furthered by the properly developed opportunities for life in the open. . . . From such life much of the American spirit of freedom springs."[30] Over a hundred organizations sent delegates to the May meeting. The tone of the proceedings was symbolized by a photograph in the program of a group camping in the wilderness. Under it appeared the caption, "It is the American Heritage."[31] In one of the many addresses Colonel Theodore Roosevelt, the son of the President and a leader in organizing the Conference, declared that pioneer virtues "form the bedrock of our national greatness."[32] But no one commented specifically on the need for wilderness, and Aldo Leopold regarded this as an extremely unfortunate omission.[33] At the Conference's next session in 1926 he appeared in person and pointed out that "wilderness is the fundamental recreational resource." Camping, hiking, fishing, and similar activities "are merely the salt and spices which give it savor and variety." Leopold argued for the need of careful planning, immediately undertaken, if America wished to preserve enough wild country to meet its needs and concluded with a plea for a national policy of preservation.[34]

Since early in the decade Leopold had labored to convince the nation, and the Forest Service in particular, of the importance of protecting wilderness. Indifference and open hostility to his "crazy"

29. MacKaye, *The New Exploration: A Philosophy of Regional Planning* (New York, 1928), p. 225; MacKaye, "An Appalachian Trail, A Project in Regional Planning," *Journal of the American Institute of Architects, 9* (1921), 325–30.

30. *National Conference on Outdoor Recreation Proceedings 1924,* 68th Cong., 1st Sess., Senate Doc. 151 (June 6, 1924), p. 2.

31. National Conference on Outdoor Recreation, *Organization and Program, 1924–1925* (Washington, D.C., 1925), frontispiece.

32. NCOR, *Proceedings* (1924), p. 14.

33. Leopold, "The Last Stand of the Wilderness," 604.

34. NCOR, *Proceedings* (1926), pp. 61–65.

ideas still existed in the Service,[35] but the groundswell of public opinion worked in Leopold's favor. Late in 1926 Chief Forester William B. Greeley indicated his approval of the Gila wilderness reservation and encouraged other Districts to undertake similar designations.[36] A year later, echoing Leopold, he asked: "how completely do we want to conquer the wilderness?" Greeley's answer was that the conquest had gone far enough. Wilderness had been too beneficent an influence in American history to sacrifice completely. He called for a new point of view: "the frontier has long ceased to be a barrier to civilization. The question is rather how much of it should be kept to preserve our civilization."[37] The wilderness movement gained strength in 1928 when the National Conference on Outdoor Recreation sponsored a study of the recreational resources of federal lands. For two pages the resulting report quoted from Leopold, after which it inventoried the remaining wildernesses in continental United States.[38] In 1929 the Service's recreation specialist, L. F. Kneipp, whom Leopold had also inspired, issued the "L-20" regulations establishing an official policy of preservation in the National Forests.[39]

At the end of the decade Frank A. Waugh reviewed the rapid spread of the wilderness movement and explained it as largely the result of the efforts of one man. "The first loud protest which I heard," he declared, "came from Aldo Leopold. . . . When Leopold's trumpet call rang through the forests, echos came back from every quarter. Thousands of Foresters and hundreds of common nature lovers felt the same way about it."[40]

Near the end of his life Aldo Leopold described how his interest in wilderness preservation gradually broadened and deepened into

35. Interview with Mrs. Aldo Leopold, Madison, Wis., July 18, 1961; interview with Donald C. Coleman, Chief of Research Publication and Information, U.S. Department of Agriculture, Forest Products Laboratory, Madison, Wis., July 14, 1961; Fred Winn to Aldo Leopold, May 2, 1924, Leopold Papers, Box 3.

36. Gilligan, "Forest Service Primitive and Wilderness Areas," pp. 101 ff.

37. Greeley, "What Shall We Do With Our Mountains?" *Sunset, 59* (1927), 14–15, 81–85.

38. National Conference on Outdoor Recreation, *Recreational Resources of Federal Lands* (Washington, D.C., 1928), pp. 86–103.

39. Gilligan, "Forest Service Primitive and Wilderness Areas," pp. 126 ff.; Cate, "Recreation and the U.S. Forest Service," pp. 86–99; Baldwin, "Historical Study of the . . . Wilderness Concept," pp. 249–93.

40. Waugh, "Wilderness to Keep," *Review of Reviews, 81* (1930), 146.

a philosophy of man's responsibility to the rest of life. He recalled returning to Iowa as a college student to find his favorite duck marsh drained and planted to corn. While the economic advantages were readily perceptible, Leopold could not suppress a feeling that thus breaking the land to man's will was somehow wrong. Later in the Southwest he participated in, indeed encouraged, a campaign to exterminate predatory animals but again sensed "a vague uneasiness about the ethics of this action." At the Forest Products Laboratory he instinctively recoiled at the preoccupation with utilitarianism. But it was not until early in the 1930s, about the time he accepted a position on the faculty of the University of Wisconsin as a specialist in game management, that these feelings acquired focus and clarity. The immediate cause was a series of hunting vacations to the wilderness of the Sierra Madre in northern Mexico. "It was here," Leopold remembered, "that I first clearly realized that land is an organism, that all my life I had seen only sick land, whereas here was a biota still in perfect aboriginal health."[41]

Equally important with the exposure to the Mexican wilderness in the maturation of Leopold's thought was the ecological insight he brought to it. Ecology taught him the interdependence of all living things which shared an environment. It gave meaning to the bits and pieces of evidence he had been collecting on the consequences of man's abuse of the natural world. Acquaintance with ecology also suggested the need for a new approach, based on ethics, that would make men aware that their environment was a community to which they belonged, not a commodity that they possessed. An "ecological conscience," as Leopold termed it, would produce a genuine respect for all forms of life. For conservation the result would be a broadening in rationale from the strictly economic to the ethical and aesthetic.

Leopold's ideas rested on an intellectual foundation of considerable extent. Ancient Eastern cultures were the sources of respect for and religious veneration of the natural world (see Chapter 1). As early as the eighth century B.C., the Indian philosophy of Jainism proposed that man not kill or harm any living creature. While

41. Aldo Leopold, "Foreword" (typescript dated July 31, 1947), Leopold Papers, Box 8. The essay was written for *Sand County Almanac* but not included in the published book. Additional information on the evolution of Leopold's thought was obtained in an interview with Mrs. Aldo Leopold, Madison, Wis., July 18, 1961.

the Jains were largely intent on maintaining absolute detachment from the world, early Buddhists and Hindus professed a feeling of compassion and a code of ethical conduct for all that was alive. Likewise, China and Tibet produced philosophies which honored life other than man's and promulgated elaborate dietary rules in this interest. In the West, on the other hand, the Judeo-Christian tradition, with its concept of man as superior to other living things by virtue of being made in the image of the Creator, discouraged similar thinking. The commandment (Genesis 1:28) which gave man dominion over his environment encouraged arrogance rather than respect. Scholastic logic held that as man was made to serve God, so the world was made for the benefit of man. Moreover, the early Christian belief in the imminency of the end of the world made efforts to protect nature seem futile.[42]

Within Western thought since the Greeks, however, was the concept of a "great chain of being."[43] It held that the Creator had produced an unlimited quantity of life-forms and arranged them along a scale or chain from lowest to highest. Man occupied a position midway between the simplest creatures and divine beings. The chain-of-being idea implied that any given species existed for the sake of the completeness of the whole and the fulfillment of God's intent rather than for its utility to any other species. It followed that all living things had an equal claim to existence. The notion that nature was subservient to man was made to seem synthetic and absurd, but few, to be sure, had drawn these conclusions before the nineteenth century.

"The two great cultural advances of the past century," Aldo Leopold believed, "were the Darwinian theory and the development of geology."[44] Both helped tear down the wall Christian thought had so carefully erected between man and other forms of life. The concept of evolution from a common origin over eons of time vividly dramatized man's membership in rather than lordship

42. Albert Schweitzer, *Indian Thought and Its Development,* trans. Mrs. Charles E. B. Russell (New York, 1936), passim; *The Animal World of Albert Schweitzer,* trans. and ed. Charles R. Joy (Boston, 1951), pp. 143–92; A. L. Basham, *The Wonder that Was India* (New York, 1954), pp. 276 ff. For another discussion see footnotes 29, 31–33 and the relevant text in Chapter 1.

43. Arthur O. Lovejoy, *The Great Chain of Being: A Study in the History of an Idea* (Cambridge, Mass., 1936), especially pp. 183–207.

44. Leopold, "Wilderness" (undated typescript), Leopold Papers, Box 8; Paul B. Sears, *Charles Darwin: The Naturalist as a Cultural Force* (New York, 1950), pp. 85 ff. offers interesting commentary on this point.

over the community of living things. On this axiom Leopold built his philosophy.

Before Leopold and the ecologists the source of American respect for nature had been more sentimental and spiritual than scientific. Nineteenth-century Romantics and Transcendentalists sensed the unity of the natural world and related it to the presence or reflection of divinity. In calling attention to the higher uses of the environment than the service of man's material needs, they manifested a belief in the sanctity of all life. Thoreau, for instance, declared that his contemporaries were ignorant of "how much might be done to improve our relation to animated nature" and wistfully thought "what kindness and refined courtesy there might be."[45] John Muir also protested man's indifference to other living things. "Why should man value himself as more than a small part of the one great unit of creation?" he asked in 1867. Several years later he stated that he had "never yet happened upon a trace of evidence to show that any one animal was ever made for another as much as it was made for itself." Consequently Muir believed the opinion "that the world was made especially for the uses of man" was an "enormous conceit."[46] George Perkins Marsh joined the attack on man's disruption of nature's harmonies and stood practically alone among his contemporaries in bringing a rudimentary scientific analysis to man-land relations. It was clear to Marsh that wilderness was characterized by the balance that developed land usually lacked.

Aldo Leopold's most direct intellectual debt was to Liberty Hyde Bailey and Albert Schweitzer. From his position on the faculty of Cornell University, Bailey began in the opening years of the twentieth century to call for recognition of the beneficial effects of contact with nature. In 1915, he published *The Holy Earth,* which suggested that the natural world was divine because it was God's handiwork. From this basis Bailey reasoned that man's abuse of the earth was not only economically unsound but morally wrong. It was necessary, he wrote, to overcome "cosmic selfishness" and de-

45. Thoreau, "Paradise (To Be) Regained" in *Writings, 5,* 43. Katherine Whitford's "Thoreau and the Woodlots of Concord," *New England Quarterly, 23* (1950), 291–306, shows that many of Thoreau's later studies anticipated those of ecologists, and argues that he was one in all but name.

46. Badè, ed., *Thousand-Mile Walk,* pp. 138–39; Muir, "Wild Wool," *Overland Monthly, 14* (1875), 364.

velop a sense of "earth righteousness" which would transfer man's dominion from the realm of commerce to that of morals.[47]

Schweitzer was a German from Alsace who approached the problem of man's relation to the living world from the standpoint of philosophy and theology. In 1905, after extensive training in these subjects, he suddenly decided to become a medical doctor and serve the natives of equatorial Africa. Ten years later, while on a river journey into the interior of that continent, it occurred to him that the foundation for all ethical systems must be "reverence for life." Previous philosophers, Schweitzer pointed out, had taken too narrow a view. "The great fault of all ethics hitherto has been that they believed themselves to have to deal only with the relations of man to man." According to Schweitzer "a man is ethical only when life, as such, is sacred to him, that of plants and animals [as well] as that of his fellow men."[48] All beings along the great chain were equally deserving of respect, even reverence, simply because they were alive.

The science of ecology came of age during Leopold's lifetime. In rapid succession a series of breakthroughs revealed the way in which land and the life that shared it constituted a complex organism functioning through the interaction of its components.[49] In Leopold's eyes this was "the outstanding discovery of the twentieth century," comparable in import to Darwinism.[50] Ecology enabled him to conceive of nature as an intricate web of interdependent parts, a myriad of cogs and wheels each essential to the healthy operation of the whole. Men had only a walk-on part in the larger drama of the sustenance of life that went on about him. We are, Leopold remarked, "only fellow-voyageurs with other creatures in

47. Liberty Hyde Bailey, *The Holy Earth* (New York, 1915), pp. 14, 24, 31. An extended discussion appears in Philip Dorf, *Liberty Hyde Bailey: An Informal Biography* (New York, 1956), pp. 107–15. Leopold cited Bailey's work in *Game Management* (New York, 1933), pp. 21, 422. Another anticipation of Leopold's ideas was Henry Frederick Fletcher's *Ethics of Conservation* (Rockville, Conn., 1910).

48. Albert Schweitzer, *Out of My Life and Thought: An Autobiography,* trans. C. T. Campion (New York, 1933), pp. 156–59. An earlier statement, with which Leopold may well have been acquainted, appeared as *Civilization and Ethics: The Philosophy of Civilization Part II,* trans. John Naish (London, 1923).

49. See Richard Brewer, *A Brief History of Ecology: Part I—Pre-nineteenth Century to 1919.* Occasional Papers of the C. C. Adams Center for Ecological Studies, 1. (Kalamazoo, Mich., 1960).

50. *Round River: From the Journals of Aldo Leopold,* ed. Luna B. Leopold (New York, 1953), p. 147.

the odyssey of evolution." Yet there was one important difference: technology had given man the "whip-hand over nature," the ability to bring about extensive changes in the environment. This power had not always been used wisely: land had been laid waste, waters polluted and, in extreme cases of what Leopold termed the "impertinence of 'civilization,'" entire species exterminated. As an ecologist, Leopold regretted his own youthful contributions to campaigns against predators. Not only did the elimination of beasts of prey remove a desirable check on the population of other species, but the whole idea of an undesirable species was entirely synthetic. Leopold told classes at the University of Wisconsin that "when we attempt to say that an animal is 'useful,' 'ugly,' or 'cruel' we are failing to see it as part of the land. We do not make the same error of calling a carburetor 'greedy.' We see it as part of a functioning motor."[51]

The extension of this attitude to the land mechanism was difficult for most men to make. Leopold realized that unless a change in attitude toward the natural world could be brought about, disharmony and sickness would continue to characterize those parts of the earth man had civilized. Initially necessary was an "ecological conscience" teaching man his true place as a dependent member of the biotic community. It would encourage people "to see land as a whole . . . to think in terms of community rather than group welfare, and in terms of the long as well as the short view."[52] Leopold hoped that from this understanding would spring a sense of the moral wrong of regarding the environment as man's slave. Like Schweitzer, he had in mind the extension of ethics to wider spheres.

As an approach to his problem, Leopold traced the history of ethics, which he defined as self-imposed limits on the struggle for existence. At first the ethical sense pertained only to a man's relation with his family, but in time it broadened to include the members of his society. Chattels or prisoners of war, however, were still excluded. Ideally, ethics encompassed all men. Leopold pleaded

51. Leopold, *Sand County Almanac*, p. 109; Leopold, "Conservation Economics," *Journal of Forestry, 32* (1934), 537; Leopold, untitled, undated fragment, Leopold Papers, Box 9; Leopold, "Thinking Like a Mountain" (typescript dated April 1, 1944), Leopold Papers, Box 4; Leopold, "Wherefore Wildlife Ecology?" (undated lecture notes), Leopold Papers, Box 8.

52. Leopold, "The Ecological Conscience," *Bulletin of the Garden Club of America, 46* (1947), 49.

that they be extended even further—to the natural world. "The land ethic," he explained, "simply enlarges the boundaries of the community to include soils, waters, plants, and animals, or collectively the land."[53] It demanded that each question of man's relation to his environment be studied "in terms of what is ethically and esthetically right, as well as what is economically expedient." And according to the land ethic, "a thing is right when it tends to preserve the integrity, stability, and beauty of the biotic community. It is wrong when it tends otherwise."[54]

Summarizing his ideas, Leopold pointed out that an ecological conscience makes possible the extension of an ethical attitude toward nature. This, in turn, "changes the role of *Homo sapiens* from conqueror of the land-community to plain member and citizen of it. It implies respect for his fellow-members, and also respect for the community as such."[55]

Leopold knew that an intellectual as well as an emotional revolution was necessary for these ideas to take hold. "Recreational development," he observed in 1938, "is a job not of building roads into lovely country, but of building receptivity into the still unlovely human mind." It was inconceivable to Leopold that the land ethic could exist, "without love, respect, and admiration for land."[56] He had no illusions about the speed with which "harmony between men and land"[57] could be expected to become reality. "It required 19 centuries," Leopold pointed out, "to define decent man-to-man conduct and the process is only half done; it may take as long to evolve a code of decency for man-to-land conduct."[58] Still he was willing to start, to be the prophet of the new order.

Wilderness had an important place in Aldo Leopold's land ethic as a model of ecological perfection. Civilization altered the environment so drastically that unmodified, wild country assumed sig-

53. Leopold, *Sand County Almanac,* p. 204. The first statement of these ideas occurred in "The Conservation Ethic," *Journal of Forestry, 31* (1933), 634–43.

54. Leopold, *Sand County Almanac,* pp. 224–25. See also "Ecology and Economics in Land Use" (undated typescript), Leopold Papers, Box 8.

55. Leopold, *Sand County Almanac,* p. 204.

56. Leopold, "Conservation Esthetic," *Bird-Lore, 40* (1938), 109; Leopold, *Sand County Almanac,* p. 223.

57. Leopold first used the phrase in a typescript of Nov. 23, 1938, "Economics, Philosophy and Land," Leopold Papers, Box 8, and frequently in his later writings.

58. Leopold, "The Ecological Conscience," 53.

nificance as "a base-datum of normality, a picture of how healthy land maintains itself as an organism." Wild places, Leopold remarked in 1934, reveal "what the land was, what it is, and what it ought to be." Evolution operated there without hindrance from man, providing "standards against which to measure the effects of violence."[59]

In the second and third decades of the twentieth century, professional ecologists such as Victor E. Shelford, G. A. Pearsons, Barrington Moore, W. W. Ashe, F. B. Sumner, and Charles C. Adams published articles calling for wilderness preserves.[60] The Ecological Society of America, founded in 1915, became a force for preservation through its Committee on the Preservation of Natural Conditions.[61] Subsequently, Aldo Leopold became president of the Society and expanded his arguments for a system of wilderness areas to include science as well as recreation. "Each biotic province," he declared, "needs its own wilderness for comparative studies of used and unused land." In 1941 he went so far as to state that "all wilderness areas . . . have a large value to land science . . . recreation is not their only or even their principal utility."[62]

In his later thought Leopold also recognized wilderness as a pointed reminder for modern man of his actual relation to the natural world. "Civilization has so cluttered this elemental man-earth relation with gadgets and middlemen," he observed in a 1941 address, "that awareness of it is growing dim. We fancy that indus-

59. Leopold, "Wilderness as a Land Laboratory," *Living Wilderness, 6* (1941), 3; Leopold, "The Arboretum and the University," *Parks and Recreation, 78* (1934), 60; Leopold, "A Biotic View of Land," *Journal of Forestry, 37* (1939), 730.

60. Victor E. Shelford, "Preserves of Natural Conditions," *Transactions of the Illinois State Academy of Science, 13* (1929), 37–58; G. A. Pearsons, "The Preservation of Natural Areas in the National Forests," *Ecology, 3* (1922), 284–87; Bennington Moore, "Importance of Natural Conditions in the National Parks," *Hunting and Conservation: The Book of the Boone and Crockett Club,* eds. George Bird Grinnell and Charles Shelden (New Haven, 1925), pp. 340–55; W. W. Ashe, "Reserved Areas of Principal Forest Type as a Guide in Developing an American Silviculture," *Journal of Forestry, 20* (1922), 276–83; F. B. Sumner, "The Responsibility of the Biologist in the Matter of Preserving Natural Conditions," *Science, 54* (1921), 39–43; Charles C. Adams, "The Importance of Preserving Wilderness Conditions," *New York State Museum Bulletin, 279* (1929), 37–44.

61. Ecological Society of America, *Preservation of Natural Conditions* (Springfield, Ill., 1921); *Naturalist's Guide to the Americas,* ed. Victor E. Shelford (Baltimore, 1926).

62. Leopold, *Sand County Almanac,* p. 196; Leopold, "Wilderness as a Land Laboratory," 3.

try supports us, forgetting what supports industry."[63] Contact with wilderness was a corrective, emphasizing man's dependence on his environment and removing the illusion that his welfare and even survival were distinct from that of the whole. Moreover, the presence of wilderness prompted the development of an ethical relation toward land. Leopold regarded the preservation of wild country as "an act of national contrition" on the part of a people who had been so careless in the past. As a remnant of stable, healthy land with its full complement of life-forms, the preserve was "a token of things hoped for." In this sense the wilderness preservation movement was "a disclaimer of the biotic arrogance of *homo americanus.* It is one of the focal points of a new attitude—an intelligent humility toward man's place in nature." For this reason Leopold believed that "the richest values of wilderness lie not in the days of Daniel Boone, nor even in the present, but rather in the future."[64]

Finally, wilderness was significant to Leopold as the essential source, the departure point for man and his civilization. "Shallow-minded modern man . . . who prates of empires, political and economic" lacked the humility to perceive this truth. "It is only the scholar," Leopold explained, "who appreciates that all history consists of successive excursions from a single starting-point, to which man returns again and again to organize yet another search for a durable scale of values." This initial bedrock was "raw wilderness."[65] To possess it, he thought, but most importantly to understand it ecologically as well as aesthetically, was the key to health—of land and also of culture. So persuasively and eloquently did Leopold press these points that they quickly became gospel among preservationists and were woven into the fabric of the justification of the continued existence of wilderness.

63. Leopold, "Wildlife in American Culture," *Journal of Wildlife Management,* 7 (1943), 1.

64. Leopold, "The Last Stand," *Outdoor America,* 7 (1942), 9; Leopold, "Why the Wilderness Society," *Living Wilderness, 1* (1935), 6; Leopold, "Wilderness Values," *Living Wilderness,* 7 (1942), 25.

65. Leopold, *Sand County Almanac,* pp. 200–201.

CHAPTER 12

Decisions for Permanence

> There is just one hope of repulsing the tyrannical ambition of civilization to conquer every niche on the whole earth. That hope is the organization of spirited people who will fight for the freedom of the wilderness.
>
> Robert Marshall, 1930

FOLLOWING the Hetch Hetchy setback in December 1913 and the death of John Muir a year later, wilderness preservation rallied strongly. New leaders such as Aldo Leopold, Robert Marshall, Sigurd Olson, Howard Zahniser, and David Brower, along with new organizations, notably the Wilderness Society, took up the crusade. They benefitted from careful reformulations of the rationale for the continued existence of wild country in modern civilization as well as from a firmer grasp of the techniques of influencing the political process. But their efforts would have been fruitless without the responsive chords they struck throughout American society. Public appreciation of wilderness increased steadily as the nation's pioneer past receded, and the promise of the wilderness cult and the Hetch Hetchy protest was fulfilled in a series of successful defenses of wild regions. The most important blocked construction of Echo Park Dam in Dinosaur National Monument and, in effect, reversed the Hetch Hetchy verdict. The Echo Park victory also gave preservationists the momentum necessary to launch a campaign for a national policy of wilderness preservation. Its establishment under the Wilderness Act of September 3, 1964, did not end the conflict between wilderness values and those of civilization, as the climactic struggle over dams in the Grand Canyon proved. But the Wilderness System did accord wild country unprecedented national recognition as a desirable component of the American landscape.

"As a boy," recalled Robert Marshall, "I spent many hours in the heart of New York City, dreaming of Lewis and Clark and their glorious exploration into an unbroken wilderness. Occasionally," he added, "my reveries ended in a terrible depression, and I would imagine that I had been born a century too late for genuine excitement."[1] In part, of course, he was right. The wilderness Lewis and Clark knew vanished long before his birth in 1901. But Marshall underestimated his own spirit. Although he died at thirty-eight, he not only found excitement in abundance but confronted a challenge equal to Lewis and Clark's: the retention of wilderness in an expanding American civilization.

Marshall is a case in point of the tendency of wilderness enthusiasts to arise from refined, urban situations. The family lived in New York City, where Louis Marshall's practice of constitutional law placed him among the renowned and wealthy of his time. The Marshalls also owned a comfortable "camp" on Lower Saranac Lake in the heart of northern New York's Adirondack region, and Bob spent his first twenty-one summers at "Knollwood."[2] From his vacationer's point of view the surrounding wilderness meant delight, not hardship or terror. He jumped at the chance to explore the mountains, and in the company of his brother George and a guide climbed *all* the surrounding peaks higher than four thousand feet—a total of forty-six.[3] It was typical of Marshall not to be content with half loaves.

Wilderness preservation also figured prominently in Marshall's youth: his father frequently brought his legal talents to the defense of New York's Adirondack State Park. In 1915, when Bob was fourteen, New York held a constitutional convention; years later he still remembered his father's successful fight to retain the clause guaranteeing the sanctity of wilderness in the Park.[4] Later, after Marshall received a master's degree in forestry from Harvard, his father urged him to continue the "missionary work" for wilder-

1. Marshall, "Impressions from the Wilderness," *Nature Magazine, 44* (1951), 481. Marshall wrote the essay about 1930.

2. Marshall to Paul Brandreth, April 23, 1935, Robert Marshall Papers, Wilderness Society, Washington, D.C. The best biographical notice of Marshall is in Roderick Nash, "The Strenuous Life of Bob Marshall," *Forest History, 10* (1966), 18–25, and in two essays by his brother George, "Adirondacks to Alaska: A Biographical Sketch of Robert Marshall," *Ad-i-ron-dac, 15* (1951), 44–45, 59, and "Robert Marshall as a Writer," *Living Wilderness, 16* (1951), 14–20. Marshall's bibliography is appended to the last, 20–23, with a supplement in *Living Wilderness, 19* (1954), 34–35.

3. Robert Marshall, *High Peaks of the Adirondacks* (Albany, 1922); Russell M. L. Carson, *Peaks and People of the Adirondacks* (Garden City, N.Y., 1928), pp. 231–34.

4. Marshall to Russell M. L. Carson, Jan. 14, 1937, Marshall Papers. For the circumstances of the Adirondack controversy see Chapter 7. A new biography of Marshall's prominent father is Morton Rosenstock, *Louis Marshall: Defender of Jewish Rights* (Detroit, 1965).

ness.[5] Little persuasion was needed. As early as his junior year in high school, Marshall declared: "I love the woods and solitude. . . . I should hate to spend the greater part of my lifetime in a stuffy office or in a crowded city."[6] He devoted much of his subsequent thought to explaining this attraction and to generalizing from his own emotions to a philosophy of the value of wilderness for modern man. The basic importance of wilderness, Marshall decided, was its capacity for meeting human needs that civilization left unsatisfied. In 1925 he wrote that "in these days of overcivilization it is not mere sentimentalism which makes the virgin forest such a genuine delight." On the simplest level, contact with wild country benefitted health. Marshall explained that the physical demands of the trail produced "a soundness, stamina, and élan unknown amid normal surroundings." The wilds, moreover, demanded self-sufficiency: away from "the coddling of civilization" men had to depend on their own resources, and this was of no small value for a country that coveted "individuality."[7]

For Marshall the greatest values of wilderness were mental. In making this point the new science of psychology came to his assistance. When John Muir wrote about the adverse effects of city life on the human spirit, scientific understanding of the mind was incipient in Europe and largely unknown in the United States. But in Marshall's time the work of Sigmund Freud, William James, and their colleagues lent substance to the idea that a repressive civilization was responsible for much of modern man's tension and unhappiness.[8] Marshall believed that "one of the most profound discoveries of psychology has been the demonstration of the terrific harm caused by suppressed desires." And since civilized society was the primary suppressing force, the importance of wilderness followed. Marshall was his own best example for his contention that some men had a "psychological urge" for challenge, adventure and, above all, for "the freedom of the wilderness." These individuals

5. Louis Marshall to Robert Marshall, March 19, 1927 in *Louis Marshall: Champion of Liberty, Selected Papers and Addresses,* ed. Charles Reznikoff (2 vols. Philadelphia, 1957) 2, 1047.

6. Quoted in George Marshall, "Robert Marshall as a Writer," 19.

7. Marshall, "Recreational Limitations to Silviculture in the Adirondacks," *Journal of Forestry, 23* (1925), 173; Marshall, "The Problem of the Wilderness," *Scientific Monthly, 30* (1930), 142–43.

8. This idea, implicit in most of Freud's work, is made forcefully in *Civilization and its Discontents,* trans. Joan Riviere (New York, 1930).

deplored the "horrible banality" and "drabness" of civilized existence; their very sanity depended on periodically renouncing society and pushing into the blank spaces on the map. Without wilderness, Marshall warned, these "malcontents" might turn for "thrills" to crime and war.[9]

Another "psychological necessity for escape to the primitive" concerned the human need for peace. According to Marshall a complex, mechanized existence produced almost unbearable pressures. Wilderness offered a sanctuary; its solitude and silence eased strains and encouraged "contemplation."[10] Here again the basic idea was old, but psychology and a greater understanding of mental health gave it enlarged meaning.

Finally Marshall stressed "the esthetic importance of the wilderness." He felt wild scenery compared to great works of art. When asked how many wilderness areas America needed, he replied, "how many Brahms symphonies do we need?"[11] Indeed in some respects natural beauty took precedence over synthetic varieties. In the presence of wilderness, Marshall noted, all the senses came into play. The observer was literally "encompassed by his experience, lives in the midst of his esthetic universe." No object of art, he thought, could claim as much, nor could it compare to the sheer size and awe of wild landscapes. In brief, "wilderness furnishes perhaps the best opportunity for . . . pure esthetic rapture."[12]

While Robert Marshall does not rank among the most original students of the meaning of the American wilderness, few have exceeded his zeal and effectiveness in crusading for its preservation. Although he was a scholar with a Ph.D. in plant pathology from Johns Hopkins, his forte was translating ideas into action. He knew that the keystones were the government agencies which administered the public domain. In 1931, after thirteen months above the Arctic Circle exploring unmapped territory and collecting data on tree growth under severe conditions,[13] Marshall returned fired

9. Marshall, "The Problem of the Wilderness," 143–44; Marshall, "The Forest for Recreation," *A National Plan for American Forestry*, 73rd Cong., 1st Sess., Senate Doc. 12, 2 vols. (March 13, 1933) *1*, 469–70.

10. Marshall, *National Plan*, 466, 469.

11. As quoted in Elizabeth C. Flint, "Robert Marshall, the Man and His Aims," *Sunday* [Montana] *Missoulian*, Nov. 19, 1939, in Pinchot Papers, Box 1961.

12. Marshall, "The Problem of the Wilderness," 144–45.

13. Marshall's Alaskan journals, maps, and photographs have been collected in *Arctic Wilderness*, ed. George Marshall (Berkeley, 1956).

with enthusiasm. He agreed to write the recreation sections of the massive *National Plan for American Forestry* (1933) and took the opportunity for stating the case for wilderness in the National Forests. In the same year he assumed direction of the Forestry Division of the United States Office of Indian Affairs. From this vantage point he besieged government personnel with letters, telephone calls, and personal visits on behalf of wilderness, rapidly gaining recognition in Washington as the champion of preservation.

Indicative of Marshall's activity was a lengthy memorandum of February 27, 1934, directed to Secretary of the Interior Harold L. Ickes, pleading that roads be kept out of undeveloped areas within his jurisdiction. It was vital, Marshall maintained, to preserve a "certain precious value of the timeless, the mysterious, and the primordial . . . in a world overrun by split-second schedules, physical certainty, and man-made superficiality." He readily conceded that in 1934 more pressing problems than protecting wilderness faced the nation. "Yet to a vast number of American citizens," he pointed out, "life's most splendid moments come in the opportunity to enjoy undefiled nature." Marshall hoped that as an advocate of national planning Ickes would help lead a coordinated preservation effort by all federal land agencies.[14] In a subsequent paper he recommended the establishment of a "Wilderness Planning Board" to be free of "stuffed shirts" and able to select areas for reservation by Congressional action "just as National Parks are today set aside." Such ideas marked Marshall as a radical, especially among professional foresters, but they proved to be harbingers of subsequent national policy.[15]

During the height of the New Deal, communications from Marshall's desk pointed out the threat public works projects posed to wild country. It was a difficult stand to take. "What makes wilderness areas most susceptible to annihilation," Marshall conceded, "is that the arguments in favor of roads are direct and concrete, while those against them are subtle and difficult to express."[16] He even admitted that with the arguments fully stated, only a small number would opt for the wild. The masses either resented the

14. Robert Marshall to Harold Ickes, Feb. 27, 1934, Record Group 79 [National Park Service], National Archives, Washington, D.C.

15. Marshall to Ickes, "Suggested Program for Preservation of Wilderness Areas: The Reason for Wilderness Areas" (April, 1934), ibid.

16. Marshall to Ickes, "Immediate Problems of Wilderness Preservation" (April 25, 1935), Marshall Papers.

economic loss involved in preserving wilderness or, if they placed recreation first, wanted roads and hotels rather than trails and campsites. To meet this obstacle Marshall turned to the concepts of comparative values and minority rights. A democratic society, he believed, ought to respect the preferences of those who coveted wilderness. The majority already had its roads and hotels; wild places, on the contrary, were vanishing rapidly. To be sure, many would welcome their extinction. But, Marshall argued, "there is a point where an increase in the joy of the many causes a decrease in the joy of the few out of all proportion to the gain of the former." To explain the point, Marshall reminded skeptics that only a small minority enjoyed art galleries, libraries, and universities. Yet no one would suggest making these facilities into bowling alleys, circuses, or hot-dog stands just because more people would use them. Quality had a claim as well as quantity, and Marshall felt the principle applied equally well to the allocation of land.[17]

This was not to say that all remaining wildernesses must be inviolable. Marshall only insisted that careful scrutiny precede every decision concerning undeveloped regions. He recognized that preservation involved a conflict "between genuine values." Irrigation projects, lumbering operations, and highway plans were not inherently wrong. But of every one it must be asked if the increased benefits of this proposed extension of civilization really compensated for the loss of wilderness. The answer, Marshall realized, would never be simple; still he hoped that fair-minded and far-sighted Americans could through careful planning make possible both "a twentieth-century and a primitive world."[18]

Gradually Marshall made headway. John Collier, his immediate superior in the Office of Indian Affairs, found himself caught up in the enthusiasm of his Director of Forestry. On October 25, 1937, Collier approved an order, drafted by Marshall, designating sixteen wilderness areas on Indian reservations.[19] But Marshall knew

17. Marshall, "The Problem of the Wilderness," 146, 147; Marshall, "The Universe of the Wilderness is Vanishing," *Nature Magazine, 29* (1937), 235–40; Marshall, "The Wilderness as a Minority Right," [United States Forest] *Service Bulletin, 12* (1928), 5–6.

18. Marshall, "The Universe of the Wilderness is Vanishing," 240; Marshall, "A Plan for the Old Wilderness," *New York Times Magazine*, April 25, 1937.

19. John Collier, *From Every Zenith: A Memoir and Some Essays on Life and Thought* (Denver, 1963), pp. 270–75; Marshall, "Wilderness Now on Indian Lands." *Living Wilderness, 3* (1937), 3–4.

that the National Forests contained the bulk of federally controlled wilderness, and he took pains to place inventories, proposals, and exhortations before Chief Forester Ferdinand A. Silcox. In May 1937 Silcox brought Marshall into the United States Forest Service as head of the Division of Recreation and Lands. Taking up where Aldo Leopold left off, he pressed forward plans to increase the number of wilderness reserves in the National Forests.[20] On September 19, 1939, two months before Marshall died of a heart failure—to which his punishing backpacking trips probably contributed—new Forest Service "U" regulations restricted roads, settlement, and economic development on some 14,000,000 acres.[21]

At the same time that Marshall was being "the most efficient weapon of preservation in existence"[22] in government circles, he also provided a pillar of inspiration and monetary support around which gathered a group of private citizens interested in the wilderness movement. As early as 1930, Marshall forecast the formation of the Wilderness Society when he warned that the only hope of resisting an all-conquering civilization was an "organization of spirited people who will fight for the freedom of the wilderness."[23] Four years later he visited Knoxville, Tennessee, and met with Benton MacKaye, a regional planner and originator of the Appalachian Trail concept (Chapter 11), then employed by the Tennessee Valley Authority. Together with Harvey Broome, a Knoxville lawyer, MacKaye reminded Marshall of his 1930 proposal and suggested action for the purpose of resisting plans for skyline drives in the Appalachians. Marshall responded enthusiastically but declared that the organization should not confine itself to a single region.[24]

20. For an indication of the extent of his efforts see "Subject Classified Files, Division of Recreation and Land Use, U Recreation," Record Group 95 [United States Forest Service], National Archives, Box 1655.

21. Gilligan, "Forest Service Primitive and Wilderness Areas," pp. 174–204, is the definitive discussion. Marshall's prowess as a wilderness hiker was legendary. According to his brother he had by October 1937 taken over two hundred hikes of thirty miles in a day, fifty-one of forty miles, and several up to *seventy:* George Marshall, "Robert Marshall as a Writer," 17.

22. Robert Sterling Yard to Bernard Frank, Sept. 13, 1937 (carbon), Marshall Papers.

23. Marshall, "The Problem of the Wilderness," 148.

24. Harvey Broome, "Origins of the Wilderness Society," *Living Wilderness,* 5 (1940), 10–11; Broome to Robert Sterling Yard, Sept. 7, 1939, Marshall Papers; interview with Harold C. Anderson, Dec. 20, 1963, Washington, D.C.

Later in 1934 Marshall returned to Knoxville. This time Bernard Frank, a forester associated with TVA, joined the original nucleus in laying definite plans. The men mailed an "Invitation to Help Organize a Group to Preserve the American Wilderness" to those known to be deeply concerned. It expressed the founders' desire "to integrate the growing sentiment which we believe exists in this country for holding wild areas *sound-proof* as well as *sight-proof* from our increasingly mechanized life" and their conviction that such wildernesses were "a serious human need rather than a luxury and plaything."[25]

On January 21, 1935, the organizing committee published a folder stating that "for the purpose of fighting off invasion of the wilderness and of stimulating . . . an appreciation of its multiform emotional, intellectual, and scientific values, we are forming an organization to be known as the WILDERNESS SOCIETY."[26] Marshall launched it financially with an anonymous contribution of a thousand dollars—the first of his many gifts climaxed by a bequest of close to $400,000.[27] Aldo Leopold was invited to assume the presidency, but, hoping to confine his association to an advisory capacity, declined in favor of Robert Sterling Yard, a long-time preservationist and former colleague of Stephen T. Mather in the National Park Service.[28] Membership grew steadily, despite the Society's policy of limiting it at first to a hard core of believers in what Yard once termed "the gospel of wilderness."[29] From its Washington headquarters the Wilderness Society participated in a series of controversies involving wild regions throughout the country from Florida's Everglades to Washington's Olympic Peninsula. Its periodical, *Living Wilderness,* publicized threatened areas and attempted to arouse public resistance on the grounds that "wilderness is a natural resource having the same basic relation to man's

25. The "Invitation" was attached to Robert Marshall to John C. Merriam, Oct. 26, 1934, John C. Merriam Papers, Library of Congress, Box 118.

26. Harold C. Anderson, et al., *The Wilderness Society* (Washington, D.C., 1935), p. 4.

27. Marshall to Robert Sterling Yard, June 8, 1935, and Yard to Marshall, Nov. 23, 1938, Marshall Papers; "Last Will and Testament" (July 12, 1938), Marshall Papers. He left the money specifically to "increase the knowledge of the citizens of the United States of America as to the importance and necessity of maintaining wilderness conditions in outdoor America for future generations."

28. Robert Marshall to Aldo Leopold, March 14, 1935, Wildlife Management Department Files, University of Wisconsin Archives, Madison, Wis., Box 4.

29. Yard to Frank, Sept. 13, 1937.

ultimate thought and culture as coal, timber and other physical resources have to his material needs."[30] In the face of both success and failure, President Yard explained his philosophy: "applying wilderness doctrine behind a local cause makes a flare, big or little, which may start hundreds or thousands talking wilderness, but when the area is lost or the highway defeated, nineteen out of twenty shouters drop away. . . . The flare has left its half a dozen permanents."[31]

One of the most important "causes" involved the Quetico-Superior country in Minnesota. Sprawling in a network of lakes and connecting rivers north and west of Lake Superior, the region had been recommended as a wilderness preserve by Arthur Carhart as early as 1919. Seven years later the Forest Service designated portions of the Superior National Forest as roadless and off limits to private development. But water power, lumber, and highway interests continued to threaten its primitive character. Preservationists in the region, organized after 1927 as the Quetico-Superior Council, resisted. Ernest C. Oberholtzer and Sigurd F. Olson, both of whom lived a few-hours' paddle from the wilderness, campaigned vigorously and enlisted Robert Marshall in the battle. A skillful writer, Olson became the canoe country's philosopher. As modern men discovered "that there is a penalty for too much comfort and ease, a penalty of lassitude and inertia and the frustrated feeling that goes with unreality," he wrote in 1938, they sought places like the Quetico to recover both mental and physical well being. Wilderness areas, according to Olson, were also "living pictures of . . . the type of continent our forefathers knew" and valuable for showing modern Americans "the road over which we have come."[32]

Olson and his colleagues were particularly concerned at the use of hydroplanes in the Quetico-Superior. In the 1940s elaborate resorts, serviced entirely by air, appeared on remote lakes. Led by the Izaak Walton League of America, preservationists protested effectively enough to persuade President Harry S. Truman to issue an executive order of December 17, 1949, prohibiting the use of aircraft over the region below an altitude of four thousand feet.

30. "The Wilderness Society Platform," *Living Wilderness, 1* (1935), 2. The Wilderness Society Records, Wilderness Society, Washington, D.C. suggest the range of the group's activities.

31. Yard to Frank, Sept. 13, 1937.

32. Olson, "Why Wilderness?" *American Forests, 44* (1938), 395, 396; Olson, "The Preservation of Wilderness," *Living Wilderness, 13* (1948), 4.

Thereafter defenders of the wilderness focused their attention on extending the boundaries of the reserved area and tightening restrictions governing its use. In the 1950s Sigurd Olson's books about the Quetico, *The Singing Wilderness* and *Listening Point,* enjoyed considerable popularity and helped create a climate of opinion in which Secretary of Agriculture Orville L. Freeman could issue a directive to National Forest officers on January 12, 1965, giving unprecedented protection to its wilderness qualities.[33]

A half century after the Hetch Hetchy controversy the wilderness rationale and the political skill of preservationists were again tested in a nationwide debate over the future of another part of the United States National Park System. This time the proposal of a dam on the Green River at Echo Park threatened wilderness values in the 320-square mile Dinosaur National Monument on the Colorado-Utah border. In 1915 Woodrow Wilson had designated eighty acres in Utah as a monument for the purpose of protecting a deposit of dinosaur skeletons imbedded in a shale and sandstone ledge. When Franklin D. Roosevelt enlarged the reservation to over 200,000 acres in 1938, it acquired interest for wilderness enthusiasts as well as paleontologists. Added to the original preserve were approximately one hundred miles of the deep, isolated canyons of the Green and Yampa Rivers plus the surrounding benchland. But as with the Hetch Hetchy Valley, the deep, narrow gorge of the Green attracted the attention of irrigationists and hydropower engineers. In the 1940s the federal Bureau of Reclamation began to plan a ten-dam, billion-dollar Colorado River Storage Project which included an Echo Park Dam. (Initial plans also called for a second dam in the Monument at Split Mountain.) On learning that the canyons in the Monument might be flooded by

33. Herman H. Chapman, *A Historic Record of the Development of the Quetico-Superior Wilderness and of the Chippewa National Forest, Minnesota* (n.p., 1961); Russell P. Andrews, *Wilderness Sanctuary,* Inter-University Case Program: Cases in Public Administration and Policy Formation, 13 (rev. ed. University, Ala., 1954); Baldwin, "Historical Study of the . . . Wilderness Concept," pp. 133–50, 186–227; Robert C. Lucas, "The Quetico-Superior Area: Recreational Use in Relation to Capacity" (unpublished Ph.D. dissertation, University of Minnesota, 1962), pp. 70–111; Sigurd Olson, "Voyageur's Country: The Story of the Quetico-Superior," *Wilson Bulletin, 65* (1953), 56–59; Olson to the author, Sept. 14, 1961; Izaak Walton League of America, *The Boundary Waters Canoe Area* (Glenview, Ill., 1965); New York *Times,* Jan. 13, 1965; interview with George S. James, Regional Forester (in charge Superior National Forest), Hanover, N.H., May 11, 1966.

the resulting reservoir, friends of the wilderness and the National Parks protested. With the support of the water-conscious Southwest, reclamationists defended their proposal. The controversy quickly assumed major proportions, dominating conservation politics in the 1950s. Not since Hetch Hetchy had so many Americans so thoroughly debated the wisdom of preserving wilderness.

The Echo Park controversy acquired added significance from the fact that many people on each side of the question regarded it as a test case. By midcentury the material needs of a rapidly growing population had darkened prospects for the continued existence of the American wilderness. At the inception of the debate over Dinosaur a number of other reserves faced similar pressure for development. The Olympic National Park had only barely escaped lumbering during World War II, and its thick stands of Douglas fir still tempted loggers. Dams were pending in both Glacier and Grand Canyon National Parks. Los Angeles had designs on Kings Canyon, wildest of the national parks which the Sierra Club unsuccessfully sought to have named in John Muir's honor, for a source of municipal water supply. In the East, the Adirondack State Park's status as wilderness was in jeopardy from plans for dams on the Moose River at Panther and Higley Mountains.[34] Consequently Echo Park had the characteristics of a showdown. In the opening phases of the battle one participant made the point clear: "let's open this to its ultimate and inevitable extent, and let's settle . . . once and for all time . . . whether we may have . . . wilderness areas . . . in these United States."[35]

34. Irving M. Clark, "Our Olympic Heritage and Its Defense," *Living Wilderness, 12* (1947), 1–10; "Olympic National Park," *National Parks Magazine, 74* (1943), 30; Ise, *National Park Policy,* pp. 470 ff.; "News Items of Special Interest," *Living Wilderness, 13* (1948–49), 25–28; Sierra Club Archives, Sierra Club, San Francisco; E. T. Scoyen, "Kilowatts in the Wilderness," *Sierra Club Bulletin, 37* (1952), 75–84; Thompson, "Doctrine of Wilderness," pp. 248 ff.

35. William Voigt, Jr., "Proceedings before the United States Department of the Interior: Hearing on Dinosaur National Monument, Echo Park and Split Mountain Dams" (April 3, 1950), p. 415, Department of the Interior Library, Washington, D.C.

It should be noted that wilderness preservation was not the only issue in the Dinosaur controversy. There was criticism of the entire Colorado River Storage Project on economic grounds. Discussion also involved engineering, irrigation and hydroelectric considerations, and frequently opposition to the dam stemmed from these sources alone. For a full treatment of the interplay of issues, with special reference to the shaping of executive policy in the federal government, see Owen Stratton and Phillip Sirotkin, *The Echo Park Controversy,* Inter-University Case Program; Cases in Public Administration and Policy Formation, 46 (University, Ala., 1959). Less useful is

On April 3, 1950, Secretary of the Interior Oscar L. Chapman held a public hearing to ascertain the positions of the two schools of thought concerning Dinosaur National Monument. It was indicative of the difficulty of the decision that most statements were ambivalent. While a few supporters of the dam used the traditional pioneer justification of "conquering the wilderness," most hesitated to condemn wilderness outright. Senator Arthur V. Watkins of Utah, for instance, confessed that "I am as much interested in beauty, in rugged scenery and preservation of nature's great wonders [as anyone] . . . but I want to point out . . . that to my mind, beautiful farms, homes, industries and a high standard of civilization are equally desirable and inspiring."[36] The wilderness advocates who testified were also caught in a conflict of values. "We recognize thoroughly the importance of water," a representative of the Izaak Walton League declared, and added that "no one in his right mind can be opposed to sound and logical development of that prime resource." But in this case, preservationists hoped to demonstrate, beneficial river development worked against the benefit of having wilderness. And given the scarce and irreplacable nature of wild country, the balance should be tipped in its favor. Perennial difficulties of finding a common scale for aesthetic and material values complicated their task. As a member of the National Audubon Society remarked at Chapman's hearing, "no one has ever been able to place a dollar sign on wilderness values."[37]

Late in June 1950 Secretary Chapman directed a memorandum to the Bureau of Reclamation and the National Park Service stating that "in the interest of the greatest public good" he was approving Echo Park Dam.[38] Friends of the wilderness realized that their only hope lay in carrying their case before Congress and the public. The Colorado River Storage Project still required legislative authorization, and the controversial dam could be deleted. "Per-

---

James J. Brady II, "An Analysis of the Echo Park Dam Controversy" (unpublished M.A. thesis, University of Michigan, 1956).

36. Ray P. Greenwood, "Proceedings," p. 555; Watkins, "Proceedings," p. 62.

37. Joseph W. Penfold in a statement read by Will B. Holton, "Proceedings," p. 406; Kenneth D. Morrison, "Proceedings," p. 299.

38. *Annual Report of the Secretary of the Interior* (1950), p. 305. Stratton and Sirotkin, *Echo Park Controversy*, 46–47, suggest that the Chapman decision may have had political overtones. Several Democratic Congressmen from the West were convinced that the defeat of the dam would ruin them politically. They allegedly spoke to President Truman who in turn instructed Chapman to approve it.

haps the stage is set," one preservationist remarked, "for a full dress performance by all those . . . who are protecting the West's recreational and wilderness values."[39] There certainly were enough actors! When John Muir led the Hetch Hetchy protest, he could have called on only seven national and two state conservation organizations. Fifty years later the figures had jumped to seventy-eight and two hundred thirty-six.[40] On Dinosaur's behalf a number of the larger groups pooled their efforts in several lobbying agencies: the Emergency Committee on Natural Resources (later the Citizens Committee on Natural Resources), the Trustees for Conservation, and the Council of Conservationists.[41]

David R. Brower, Executive Director of the Sierra Club, and Howard C. Zahniser, who served the Wilderness Society in a similar capacity, led the way in applying this wealth of organized conservation sentiment. During the course of two sets of Congressional hearings, the opponents of Echo Park Dam defended wilderness with an unparalleled combination of vigor and skill. Hard-hitting, illustrated pamphlets, prepared for mass distribution, asked the public: *"Will you DAM the Scenic Wild Canyons of Our National Park System?"* and *"What is Your Stake in Dinosaur?"*[42] A professional motion picture, in color, received hundreds of showings throughout the country. Wallace Stegner, novelist and historian, edited a book-length collection of essays and photographs showing the importance of keeping Dinosaur wild.[43] Conservation periodicals featured numerous articles on the Monument.[44] More impor-

39. John N. Spencer to Richard M. Leonard, Nov. 30, 1950 (carbon), Olaus Murie Papers, Conservation Library Center, Denver Public Library, Denver.

40. E. Arnold Hanson and C. W. Mattison, *The Nation's Interest in Conservation 1905 and 1955* (Washington, D.C., 1955), p. 1.

41. David R. Brower to the author, Feb. 18, 1962; Stratton and Sirotkin, *Echo Park Controversy*, pp. 21–22.

42. The first was published in Washington in 1951; the second in San Francisco in 1954. Extensive collections of material revealing the preservationists' strategy in the controversy may be found in the Wilderness Society Records, Wilderness Society, Washington, D.C. and the Sierra Club Archives.

43. Stegner, ed., *This Is Dinosaur: Echo Park Country and Its Magic Rivers* (New York, 1955). Alfred A. Knopf, an enthusiastic supporter of wilderness, published the book and contributed an essay.

44. Arthur H. Carhart, "The Menaced Dinosaur Monument," *National Parks Magazine, 108* (1952), 19–30; Devereaux Butcher, "In Defense of Dinosaur," *Audubon Magazine, 53* (1951), 142–49; Margaret Murie, "A Matter of Choice," *Living Wilderness, 15* (1950), 11–14; Harvey Broome, "Dinosaur National Monument," *Nature Magazine, 44* (1951), 34–36, 52; "Trouble in Dinosaur," *Sierra Club Bulletin, 39* (1954), 1–12; "Rugged Beauty of Dinosaur," *American Forests, 57* (1951), 16–17, are only a sample.

tant from the standpoint of national opinion was the extensive coverage the controversy received in *Life, Collier's, Newsweek,* and the *Reader's Digest* as well as in influential newspapers like the New York *Times.*[45]

A campaign of this scope obviously required considerable financial support, and in this respect preservationists were strikingly successful. In the course of defending the Adirondacks in the 1940s, Howard Zahniser became acquainted with the wealthy St. Louis chemical manufacturer and Sierra Club member Edward C. Mallinckrodt, Jr. When the defense of Dinosaur moved into the conservation spotlight, Zahniser persuaded him to become its patron.[46]

While publicity and money were vital in the Echo Park battle, it was also essential to have convincing arguments to publicize. Spokesmen for preservation brought the fruit of a century of thought about the meaning and value of wilderness to bear on the problem. Some arguments rested on the need of civilized man for wilderness sanctuaries which had precedents in the ideas of Thoreau, Muir, and Marshall. In 1950 General Ulysses S. Grant III, grandson of the President and himself president of the American Planning and Civic Association, defended Dinosaur because "our industrial civilization is creating an ever greater need for the average man . . . to reestablish contact with nature . . . and to be diverted from the whirling wheels of machinery and chance." It would be a tragedy, he added, to sacrifice the canyons for "a few acre-feet of water and a few kilowatt hours." George W. Kelley, representing the Colorado Forestry and Horticultural Association at the 1950 hearing, agreed that the "original pioneer wilderness" had value as one of the "things that make it worth while to live after we have gotten our bread and butter." Pointing out that "wilderness areas have become to us a spiritual necessity, an antidote to the strains of modern living," Kelley argued that Americans needed them periodically "to renew their souls and gain a fresh perspective on life."[47] Olaus Murie, president of the Wilderness Society, also pronounced a wild Dinosaur essential "for our happi-

45. For example, "Sounds of Anguish from Echo Park," *Life, 36* (1954), 45–46; "Are You For or Against Echo Park Dam?" *Collier's, 135* (1955), 76–83; John B. Oakes, "Partisan Feeling Running High on Colorado River Project," New York *Times,* June 14, 1955.

46. Interview with Howard Zahniser, Sept. 10, 1963, Washington, D.C.

47. "Proceedings," pp. 319, 322, 323, 377–78.

ness, our spiritual welfare, for our success in dealing with the confusions of a materialistic and sophisticated civilization." And in *This Is Dinosaur: Echo Park Country and Its Magic Rivers* Wallace Stegner followed Thoreau in suggesting the importance of wilderness not only as a sanctuary for rare birds and animals but for "our own species" hard-pressed by "twentieth-century strains and smells and noises."[48]

Aldo Leopold suffered a fatal heart attack on April 21, 1948, while fighting a brush fire near his Wisconsin camp, but the ecological significance he accorded wilderness figured prominently in the resistance to Echo Park Dam. Bernard DeVoto, a free-lance writer and historian, first applied it to the controversy in an influential article in *Saturday Evening Post.* He declared that Dinosaur was important "as wilderness that is preserved intact . . . for the field study of . . . the balances of Nature, the web of life, the interrelationships of species, massive problems of ecology—presently it will not be possible to study such matters anywhere else."[49] Benton MacKaye discussed the same theme in *Scientific Monthly,* referring specifically to Leopold's notion that wild country provided "an exhibit of normal ecologic process." Dinosaur National Monument and other wildernesses, MacKaye continued, constitute *"a reservoir of stored experiences in the ways of life before man."*[50]

The land ethic was another Leopold concept which opponents of the dam put into action. Speaking in Montana in 1952, Charles C. Bradley estimated that the amount of paved land in the United States equalled the amount of wilderness. This dramatized for him the fact that Americans were in danger of losing their sense of the "man-earth relationship." Quoting Leopold as his authority, Bradley pleaded for the retention of Dinosaur in an unaltered condition as a gesture of human respect for the biotic community. Howard Zahniser also believed that "we deeply need the humility to know ourselves as the dependent members of a great community of life." He pointed out that such knowledge was "one of the spiritual benefits of a wilderness experience" because "to know the wilderness is to know a profound humility, to recognize one's littleness,

48. Murie, "Wild Country as a National Asset: Beauty and the Dollar Sign," *Living Wilderness, 18* (1953), 27; Stegner, ed., *This Is Dinosaur,* pp. 15, 17.

49. DeVoto, "Shall We Let Them Ruin Our National Parks?" *Saturday Evening Post, 223* (1950), 44. A condensation appeared under the same title in the *Reader's Digest, 57* (1950), 18–24.

50. MacKaye, "Dam Site vs. Norm Site," *Scientific Monthly, 81* (1950), 244.

to sense dependence and interdependence, indebtedness and responsibility."[51]

In 1954 both the House and Senate Subcommittees on Irrigation and Reclamation held hearings on the Colorado River Storage Project. Echo Park Dam dominated discussion. Preservationists believed, as the New York *Times* recognized editorially, that if pressures for development prevailed in the case of Dinosaur, the sanctity of the entire National Park System would be shaken and the end of the American wilderness hastened.[52] One tactic used to alert the legislators to the fallacy of reclamationists' arguments for a dam was a revival of the memory of Hetch Hetchy. Realizing the value of pictorial evidence, David Brower took photographs of the Hetch Hetchy reservoir and combined them with older pictures of the wild valley and explanatory text into a striking display. The lush grass, trees, and spectacular cliffs of the pre-dam Hetch Hetchy contrasted sharply with the stumpy, mud-rimmed banks of the artificial lake.[53] Brower and David Bradley, a doctor and author of Hanover, New Hampshire who had floated through Dinosaur's canyons, used the photographs as part of their testimony. "If we heed the lesson learned from the tragedy of the misplaced dam in Hetch Hetchy," Brower told the Senate's subcommittee, "we can prevent a far more disastrous stumble in Dinosaur National Monument." In the tradition of John Muir and Robert Underwood Johnson, Bradley informed the Representatives that "we have had money changers in our temples before. We have thrown them out in the past, and with the help of this good committee we shall do it again."[54]

In spite of these and other efforts, both subcommittees favorably reported the Colorado River Storage Project, including Echo Park Dam. Their action was understandable since Western Congress-

51. Bradley, "Wilderness and Man," *Sierra Club Bulletin, 37* (1952), 59–67; Zahniser, "The Need for Wilderness Areas," *National Parks Magazine, 29* (1955), 166.

52. "No Dam at Dinosaur," New York *Times,* Dec. 22, 1953.

53. The photographs are reproduced in *Living Wilderness, 18* (1953–54), 36, and in literature prepared specifically for the Echo Park battle such as *What Is Your Stake in Dinosaur?* (San Francisco, 1954) and Robert K. Cutter, "Hetch Hetchy—Once is Too Often," *Sierra Club Bulletin, 39* (1954), 11 ff.

54. U.S. Congress, Senate, Committee on Interior and Insular Affairs, Subcommittee on Irrigation and Reclamation, Hearings, *Colorado River Storage Project,* 83d Cong., 2d Sess. (June 28–July 3, 1954), p. 503; U.S. Congress, House, Committee on Interior and Insular Affairs, Subcommittee on Irrigation and Reclamation, Hearings, *Colorado River Storage Project,* 83d Cong., 2d Sess. (Jan. 18–23, 25, 28, 1954), p. 851.

men, whose constituents generally favored the dam, were in the majority in both bodies. Wilderness appeared to be heading for a decisive defeat, but preservationists worked frantically. Appealing to the public with flyers, articles, editorials, and open letters, they succeeded in arousing a storm of protest. The House mail showed a ratio of those who would keep Dinosaur wild to those in favor of the dam of eighty to one. The result was a postponement of Congressional consideration of the Project. "Controversy over the proposed Echo Park Dam," said Speaker of the House Joseph Martin, "has killed any chance for . . . approval this year."[55]

In preparation for the renewal of the Echo Park controversy in the Eighty-Fourth Congress in 1955, the Council of Conservationists met in New York to plan strategy. In a series of resolutions it emphasized that while preservationists were opposed to the alteration of designated wilderness areas, they sympathized with the need of the Southwest for water and supported the idea of the Colorado River Storage Project.[56] Such a stand invited compromise, but as the Senate hearings opened in March, exchanges were heated. Supporting the dam were Western interests: Congressmen, governors, civic clubs, chambers of commerce, utility companies, water-users associations, the Bureau of Reclamation, and a tribe of Navajo Indians. On the other side were some Eastern Congressmen, many educational institutions, conservation and nature organizations, and a mounting tide of public opinion expressed in letters, telegrams, and editorials.

As the hearings proceeded, the preservationists used two kinds of tactics. One stemmed from the familiar idea of the importance of the aesthetic and spiritual values of wilderness in materialistic America. Charles Eggert, director of motion pictures for the National Parks Association, testified that wild country was "the place we . . . rediscover ourselves" when "troubled, confused or dismayed." Sigurd Olson also appeared before the Senate subcommittee. In a lengthy, thoughtful statement he questioned the wisdom of extending the pioneer compulsion to conquer wilderness into the twentieth century. He pointed out that frontiersmen "did the job that had to be done" but wondered if "in our mad rush to

55. Stratton and Sirotkin, *Echo Park Controversy*, p. 21; United Press dispatch as quoted in *Living Wilderness, 19* (1954), 26–27.

56. *Congressional Record*, 84th Cong., 1st Sess., *101* (April 19, 1955), pp. 4651–52; Sigurd Olson to the author, Nov. 11, 1961.

dam every river, chop down every tree, utilize all resources to the ultimate limit . . . we might not destroy the very things that have made life in America worth cherishing and defending?" In conclusion, Olson warned the Senators that a dam at Echo Park endangered an entire philosophy of appreciation of wilderness, and of intangible qualities generally, that had gradually evolved through American history.[57]

The wilderness advocates also endeavored to challenge reclamationists and engineers with their own tools: statistical data concerning the efficiency of a dam at Echo Park. David Brower's testimony presented the mathematics supporting his contention that the Bureau of Reclamation had erred in its calculation of the water that would be lost by evaporation from an Echo Park reservoir. Using the Bureau's own base figures, he showed that the lake would actually be far more costly in terms of water loss than advertised and that alternative dam sites, outside wilderness areas, were preferable in this respect. In the face of angry cross-examination, Brower defended his views successfully enough to raise questions about the economics of the entire Colorado River Storage Project.[58]

When the bill authorizing the Colorado River Storage Project reached the floor of the Senate in April 1955, Richard L. Neuberger of Oregon offered an amendment deleting Echo Park Dam. A member of the Wilderness Society, Neuberger declared that wilderness was priceless as "the last place where Americans can see what our country must have been like as the first white men camped there." The present generation also needed it, he continued, as a sanctuary from "the tensions and anxieties of the civilization we have created." Paul H. Douglas of Illinois rose to support his colleague. "Certainly, Mr. President," he argued, "we should keep some wild places" to "benefit the human spirit." Echo Park Dam, Douglas alleged, would contribute to transforming the nation "into a placid, tepid place, greatly unlike the wild and stirring

57. U.S. Congress, Senate, Committee on Interior and Insular Affairs, Subcommittee on Irrigation and Reclamation, Hearings, *Colorado River Storage Project*, 84th Cong., 1st Sess. (Feb. 28, March 1–5, 1955), pp. 696, 679–84.

58. Ibid., 634 ff. U.S. Congress, House, Committee on Interior and Insular Affairs, Subcommittee on Irrigation and Reclamation, Hearings, *Colorado River Storage Project*, 84th Cong., 1st Sess. (Part 1: March 9, 10, April 18, 20, 22, 1955; Part 2: March 11, 14, 16–19, 28, 1955), pp. 751 ff.; David R. Brower to the author, Feb. 18, 1962.

America which we love and from which we draw inspiration." After claims that a dam and reservoir would beautify Dinosaur National Monument, Hubert H. Humphrey of Minnesota pointed out that "where once there was the beautiful Hetch Hetchy Valley . . . there is now the stark, drab reservoir of O'Shaughnessy Dam."[59]

When Senator Arthur V. Watkins of Utah gained the floor, he demanded that the discussion "get back to fundamentals." Then for half an hour he reiterated the advantages of the Echo Park dam site from the standpoint of irrigation, hydropower, and cost. Just before the vote on the Neuberger amendment, Senator Douglas arose again to plead for wild canyons "where man may acquire some humility and see how little he is in comparison with the great works of nature." Neuberger added that if his proposal were defeated, it would be a "backward step for recreation, for scenic and aesthetic values, and for other similar areas throughout the Nation."[60]

With all but three Western Senators voting in a bloc against the Neuberger amendment, it failed to pass, and the Colorado River Storage Project received Senate approval with Echo Park Dam intact. But the arguments of the leading preservationists and the pressure of public opinion were beginning to tell. On July 8, 1955, the report of the House Committee on Interior and Insular Affairs endorsed a version of the Project *without* the controversial dam.[61] "We hated to lose it," Representative William A. Dawson of Utah explained, but "the opposition from conservation organizations has been such as to convince us . . . that authorizing legislation could not be passed unless this dam was taken out." He added that the proponents of the dam had "neither the money nor the organization to cope with the resources and mailing lists" of the preservationists.[62]

Still many supporters of wilderness did not feel victory was

59. *Congressional Record*, 84th Cong., 1st Sess., *101* (April 19, 1955), pp. 4657, 4641, 4689. Howard Zahniser contended that he wrote most of the speeches which these and other congressmen delivered on behalf of Dinosaur: interview with Zahniser, Sept. 10, 1963.

60. *Congressional Record*, 84th Cong., 1st Sess., *101* (April 20, 1955), pp. 4800, 4804, 4805.

61. U.S. Congress, House, Committee on Interior and Insular Affairs, *Colorado River Storage Project*, 84th Cong., 1st Sess., House Rpt. 1887 (July 8, 1955).

62. *Congressional Record*, 84th Cong., 1st Sess., *101* (June 28, 1955), p. 9386.

secure. In confirmation of their fears, Congressmen and governors from the Colorado Basin states met in Denver on November 1 to discuss ways of restoring Echo Park Dam to the Project. Learning of the meeting, the Council of Conservationists rushed a full-page open letter into the Denver *Post* of the day before. It made clear that unless the dam were irrevocably deleted, the wilderness lobby would use every legal means to block the entire Project. The open letter hastened to add, however, that preservationists "are NOT anti-reclamationists, and are NOT fighting the principle of water use in the west."[63] Thus put in the awkward position of defeating their own interests, the Denver strategists promised not to attempt to reinstate Echo Park Dam. With Howard Zahniser's Washington office bearing the brunt of the work, the final details of the compromise were completed before the Eighty-Fourth Congress reconvened for its second session. As a result a new sentence appeared in the Colorado River Storage Project bill stating the intention of Congress "that no dam or reservoir constructed under the authorization of the Act shall be within any National Park or Monument."[64]

On April 11, 1956, the new bill became law, and the American wilderness movement had its finest hour to that date. The development of a convincing justification for the existence of wild country along with an increase in the number of Americans who subscribed to it were basic to the triumph. But equally important was the growth in political weight of preservation. In part this stemmed from wider public support of an intensity that vote-conscious Congressmen could not ignore. It was also a result of improvements in the skill of preservationists as political infighters. A wild Hetch Hetchy had been lost largely because San Francisco lobbied so effectively in Washington; Dinosaur's wilderness remained intact thanks to the success of Zahniser, Brower, and their colleagues in putting enough pressure on Congress to overcome the arguments of other interest groups.

63. The letter is reproduced in its entirety in *Living Wilderness, 20* (1955–56), 24.

64. U.S. Congress, House, Committee on Interior and Insular Affairs, *Supplemental Report on HR 3383*, 84th Cong., 2d Sess., House Rpt. 1087, pt. 2 (Feb. 14, 1956), p. 3. The details of the final settlement of the controversy are described in full in "Echo Park Controversy Resolved," *Living Wilderness, 20* (1955–56), 23–43; David Perlman, "Our Winning Fight for Dinosaur," *Sierra Club Bulletin, 41* (1956), 5–8; and Stratton and Sirotkin, *Echo Park Controversy*.

The successful defense of Dinosaur National Monument encouraged preservationists to press for a still more positive affirmation of wilderness in American civilization. Attention centered on the possibility of a national system of wilderness preserves with full legal endorsement. As early as 1921 Benton MacKaye advocated a nationwide system of wilderness belts along mountain ridges, and throughout the 1930s Robert Marshall dreamed of a federal land-management policy that would protect wild country permanently.[65] The concept of a wilderness system also received support at this time from Franklin D. Roosevelt's secretary of the interior, Harold L. Ickes. Eager to convince Congress that his department, rather than the Department of Agriculture and the United States Forest Service, should be the exclusive custodian of the nation's wildernesses, Ickes declared his allegiance to systematic wilderness preservation. To underscore the point, he proposed in 1939 that the inchoate national park in the Kings Canyon region of California's Sierra be named "Kings Canyon National Wilderness Park." The legislators did not approve the idea, but Ickes's agitation played a major role in persuading the Forest Service to counter with the 1939 "U" regulations (see above, p. 206). The following year a bill for a wilderness system was introduced in Congress, but in the mood of growing concern over World War II it died quietly.[66]

Wilderness Society director Howard Zahniser revived the campaign for a wilderness preservation law late in the 1940s. At the Sierra Club's First Biennial Wilderness Conference in 1949, Zahniser led discussion of the idea. The same year the Library of Congress's Legislative Reference Service, at a Zahniser-inspired suggestion of several Congressmen, published an extensive study of the status of the American wilderness.[67] It was intended, at least by

65. See *Living Wilderness*, 2 (1946), 5.

66. The authoritative study of early attempts at statutory wilderness preservation is Douglas Scott's "The Origins and Development of the Wilderness Bill, 1930–1956," which is being prepared for submission to the University of Michigan's School of Natural Resources as a Master's thesis in the Department of Forestry. Also useful on the bureaucratic tension between the Forest Service and the National Park Service that inadvertently advanced wilderness preservation, are Cate, "Recreation and the United States Forest Service," and Gilligan, "Forest Service Primitive and Wilderness Areas."

67. C. Frank Keyser, *The Preservation of Wilderness Areas: An Analysis of Opinion on the Problem,* Committee on Merchant Marine and Fisheries, Subcommittee on Fisheries and Wildlife Conservation, Committee Print 19 (Aug. 24, 1949).

Zahniser, as a prelude to action. In 1951 Zahniser formally proposed a national wilderness preservation system in an address at the Sierra Club's Second Biennial Wilderness Conference. He spoke of how the National Park Service, United States Forest Service, and other federal agencies might be made legally responsible for preserving the wilderness under their jurisdiction. Only an act of Congress or a presidential proclamation could alter the wild character of such an area.[68]

Four years later Zahniser reiterated his ideas at the National Citizen's Planning Conference on Parks and Open Spaces for the American People and at the Fourth Biennial Wilderness Conference of the Sierra Club. The latter meeting resolved in favor of federal legislation for wilderness protection.[69]

At this juncture the Echo Park victory gave promise that statutory wilderness preservation might be more than a dream. Immediately after the 1956 defeat of Echo Park Dam, an elated Howard Zahniser dashed off a four-page draft of a plan for a national system of wilderness preservation. He circulated it to Robert Marshall's brother George, and then to a widening circle of friends and conservation colleagues. Finally Zahniser and other preservationists persuaded Senator Hubert Humphrey and Representative John P. Saylor to introduce bills to the Second Session of the Eighty-Fourth Congress. As written in large part by Zahniser, the bill stated that it was the intent of Congress "to secure for the American people of present and future generations the benefits of an enduring reservoir of wilderness."[70] It went on to itemize over 160 areas in the National Forests, National Parks and Monuments, National Wildlife Refuges and Ranges, and Indian reservations that would constitute the National Wilderness Preservation System. A National Wilderness Preservation Council of federal administrators and citizen conservationists would be created to gather information concerning wilderness and make recommendations for the maintenance and possible expansion of the system.

68. Zahniser, "How Much Wilderness Can We Afford to Lose?" in *Wildlands in Our Civilization,* ed. David Brower (San Francisco, 1964), pp. 50–51.

69. Zahniser, "The Need For Wilderness Areas," *National Parks Magazine, 29* (1955) 161 ff.; "Recommendations: Fourth Biennial Wilderness Conference," *Sierra Club Bulletin, 42* (1957), 6.

70. The text cited is that of S. 1176, a revised version introduced in the Senate on Feb. 11, 1957, as printed in *Living Wilderness, 21* (1956–57), 26-36.

This original proposal was big and bold. Zahniser determined to capitalize on the momentum of the Echo Park decision even at the risk of engendering opposition that less ambitious proposals would have avoided.[71]

The concept of a wilderness system marked an innovation in the history of the American preservation movement. It expressed, in the first place, a determination to take the offensive. Previous friends of the wilderness had been largely concerned with defending it against various forms of development. But the post-Echo Park mood was confident, encouraging a bold, positive gesture. Second, the system meant support of wilderness in general rather than of a particular wild region. As a result debate focused on the theoretical value of wilderness in the abstract, not on a local economic situation. Finally, a national wilderness preservation system would give an unprecedented degree of protection to wild country. Previously, preservation policy in the National Forests had been only an administrative decision subject to change at any time by Forest Service personnel. Even the laws creating National Parks and Monuments deliberately left the way open for the construction of roads and tourist accommodations. The intention of the wilderness bill, however, was to make any alteration of wilderness conditions within the system illegal.

Congress lavished more time and effort on the wilderness bill than on any other measure in American conservation history. From June 1957 until May 1964 there were nine separate hearings on the proposal, collecting over six thousand pages of testimony. The bill itself was modified and rewritten or resubmitted sixty-six different times. One reason for the extraordinary delay in reaching a decision was the vigorous opposition to the permanent preservation of wilderness from wood-using industries, oil, grazing, and mining interests, most professional foresters, some government bureaus, and proponents of mass recreation with plans for mechanized ac-

71. Interview with Howard Zahniser, Sept. 10, 1963. Also extremely valuable are Scott, "Origins and Development of the Wilderness Bill," and Jack M. Hession, "The Legislative History of the Wilderness Act" (unpublished Master's thesis, San Diego State College, 1967). Albert Dixon, "The Conservation of Wilderness: A Study in Politics" (unpublished Ph.D. dissertation, University of California, Berkeley, 1968) and Joel Gottlieb, "The Preservation of Wilderness Values: The Politics and Administration of Conservation Policy" (unpublished Ph.D. dissertation, University of California, Riverside, 1972) both approach their subjects from the standpoint of political science.

cess to outdoor areas. At the root of their dissent was the feeling that a wilderness preservation system would be too rigid and inflexible. Adhering to the multiple-use conception of the function of the public domain, they contended that the bill locked up millions of acres in the interests of a small number of campers.[72] It was not that the critics of the system opposed wilderness preservation on principle. They agreed for the most part with W. D. Hagenstein, executive vice president of the Industrial Forestry Association, that wilderness had its place. "The only question," he asserted, "is where and how much. To dedicate, willy-nilly, millions of acres of land to wilderness before they are adequately studied to determine their highest uses to society, cannot be justified under either multiple- or single-use concepts."[73] The ambivalence such a statement reflects is understandable in the light of the history of American attitudes toward wilderness: appreciation is so relatively new that it is difficult to deny the claims of civilization—especially with the finality of the wilderness system.

In defense of the bill, preservationists hastened to assure men like Hagenstein that it did not consist of "willy-nilly" removal of land from productive purposes but only gave legal sanction to areas already administered as wilderness. They pointed out that the most land the system would ever include was about fifty million acres, or roughly two percent of the nation. And they added, in David Brower's words, that "the wilderness we now have is all . . . men will ever have."[74] A century had brought greatly changed conditions. "If the year were 1857 instead of 1957," one supporter of the legislation wrote, "I'd say definitely no." But given the almost

72. For example, Richard W. Smith, "Why I Am Opposed to the Wilderness Preservation Bill," *Living Wilderness, 21* (1956–57), 44–50; "Minority Views on S. 174," U.S. Congress, Senate, Committee on Interior and Insular Affairs, *Establishing a National Wilderness Preservation System*, 87th Cong., 1st Sess., Senate Rpt. 635 (July 27, 1961), pp. 36–43; and the testimony of Radford Hall of the American National Cattlemen's Association, U.S. Congress, Senate, Committee on Interior and Insular Affairs, Hearings, *National Wilderness Preservation Act*, 85th Cong., 1st Sess. (June 19, 20, 1957), pp. 397–401.

73. Hagenstein, "Wilderness Bill Favors a Few," *Pulp and Paper, 34* (1960), 100. Hagenstein testified similarly at a Senate hearing in 1963: U.S. Congress, Senate, Committee on Interior and Insular Affairs, Hearings, *National Wilderness Preservation Act* (Feb. 28, March 1, 1963), p. 104.

74. U.S. Congress, Senate, Committee on Interior and Insular Affairs, Hearings, *National Wilderness Preservation Act*, 85th Cong., 2d Sess. (Nov. 7, 10, 13, 14, 1958), p. 573.

total dominance of civilization, he was compelled to work for saving the remnants of undeveloped land.[75] Repeatedly, preservationists explained that they were endeavoring to protect the right of future generations to experience wilderness.[76] Answering the argument that only a tiny minority actually went into wild country for recreation, they declared that, for many, just knowing wilderness existed was immensely important.[77] As for the objection on multiple-use grounds, wilderness advocates exposed as fallacious the assumption that this doctrine must apply to every acre. True multiple use, they contended, made sense only for the public domain as a whole, providing for economic uses on some portions and wilderness recreation on others.[78]

The testimony at Congressional hearings and the treatment of the bill in the press revealed an acquaintance with the history of the American discussion of wilderness. The names and ideas of Thoreau, Muir, Marshall, and especially of Leopold, appeared time and again. Senator Clinton P. Anderson of New Mexico, chairman of the crucial Committee on Interior and Insular Affairs, stated that his support of the wilderness system was the direct result of having come into contact almost forty years before with Leopold, who was then in the Southwest with the Forest Service.[79] In a major statement in favor of the legislation in the New York *Times,* Secretary of the Interior Stewart L. Udall discussed ecology and a land ethic and referred to Leopold as the instigator of the modern wilderness movement.[80] At a Senate hearing in 1961,

75. Roy Hoff, "Should Our Wilderness Areas Be Preserved?" *Archery* (1957) as quoted in *Living Wilderness, 21* (1956–57), 60. See also "The Wilderness Bill," *Christian Science Monitor,* July 3, 1956.

76. David Brower in Senate, Hearings (1958), p. 581; Howard Zahniser in Senate, Hearings (1957), pp. 153.

77. Howard Zahniser and Sigurd Olson in Senate, Hearings (1957), pp. 154, 322; David A. Collins in U.S. Congress, House, Committee on Interior and Insular Affairs, Subcommittee on Public Lands, Hearings, *Wilderness Preservation System,* 88th Cong., 2d Sess. (Jan. 9, 1964), p. 56.

78. Hubert Humphrey in U.S. Congress, Senate, Committee on Interior and Insular Affairs, Hearings, *The Wilderness Act,* 87th Cong., 1st Sess. (Feb. 27, 28, 1961), pp. 133–38; Wayne Morse in *Congressional Record,* 87th Cong., 1st Sess., *107* (Sept. 6, 1961), p. 18355.

79. Anderson, "The Wilderness of Aldo Leopold," *Living Wilderness, 19* (1954–55), 44–46; *Congressional Record,* 87th Cong., 1st Sess., *107* (Jan. 5, 1961), pp. 191–93.

80. Udall, "To Save the Wonder of the Wilderness," New York *Times Magazine,* May 27, 1962.

Brower went so far as to allege that "no man who reads Leopold with an open mind will ever again, with clear conscience, be able to step up and testify against the wilderness bill."[81] For others, the philosophies of Thoreau and Muir provided a justification for the wilderness system, particularly the idea that man's happiness and strength depend on blending periodic contact with the primitive into a civilized existence.[82] Finally, some supported preservation "because of the central role which the wilderness, the frontier, has played in our history" and the importance of maintaining a distinctive American national character.[83]

The succession of hearings on the wilderness bill revealed a remarkable volume of sentiment for preservation. The professionals spared no effort in their advocacy. Howard Zahniser attended every Congressional hearing on the matter, including those conducted in various Western states, making his final appearance on April 28, 1964, a week before his death. Even more impressive from the legislators' viewpoints was the extent of grassroots support. Thousands of citizens with no greater commitment to wilderness than having enjoyed a pack or canoe trip took the time to communicate their opinions either personally or by mail. In the Senate hearings conducted in Oregon, California, Utah, and New Mexico during November 1958, for instance, 1,003 letters were received favoring the bill and only 129 in opposition.[84] And even that dissent virtually ceased when the wilderness bill was altered, in 1962 and 1963, to eliminate a National Wilderness Preservation Council, to exclude temporarily from the system all but fifty-four areas (slightly over nine million acres) in the National Forests, and to make every addition to the system dependent on a special act of Congress. Moreover, mineral prospecting and mining development were to be permitted in the designated wildernesses until January 1, 1984. Even after that date prior valid claims could be developed, and the president retained the right to authorize dams, power plants, and

81. Brower in Senate, Hearings (1961), p. 347.

82. Sigurd Olson in Senate, Hearings (1957), pp. 319–20; John P. Saylor, "Saving America's Wilderness," *Living Wilderness, 21* (1956–57), 2, 4, 12.

83. Kenneth B. Keating in the *Congressional Record,* 87th Cong., 1st Sess., *107* (Sept. 6, 1961), p. 18396.

84. Senate, Hearings (1958), p. 1060. See also the list of communicants in favor and opposed to the bill in U.S. Congress, House, Committee on Interior and Insular Affairs, Subcommittee on Public Lands, Hearings, *Wilderness Preservation System,* 87th Cong., 2d Sess. (May 7–11, 1962), pp. 1749–62.

roads in the wildernesses if he deemed them in the national interest. This hedging was a classic instance of Americans' ambivalence about the relative merits of wilderness and civilization.

In this revised form the wilderness bill passed in the Senate on April 10, 1963, by a vote of 73 to 12. The House vote was 373 to 1 on July 30, 1964. In August 1964, a Senate-House conference committee adjusted the more liberal Senate version to meet the Representatives' requirements, and on September 3 President Lyndon B. Johnson's signature established the National Wilderness Preservation System.[85]

Preservationists were disappointed at the discrepancy between the Wilderness Act and their original conceptions. Zealots like Howard Zahniser had hoped to include in the initial Wilderness System all federal lands managed as wilderness, as well as so-called de facto wildernesses in the public domain—a total of about 60 million acres instead of the 9 million approved by the act. But there were grounds for encouragement in the opportunity the act provided to add much of this area to the Wilderness System over the designated ten-year review period. Realists understood that additions would not be automatic. Reflecting the American uncertainty about wilderness, the act deliberately created a cumbersome system of government bureau reviews, local public hearings, Congressional committee reviews, and finally a separate act of Congress for each addition. A dogged citizen effort on behalf of wilderness would be crucial, especially since many federal administrators (particularly in the National Park Service) tended to regard the Wilderness System as unnecessary. Preservationists were greatly encouraged, however, by the knowledge that the United States had formally expressed its intent to keep a portion of its land permanently wild.[86]

85. Public Law 88–577 in U.S., *Statutes at Large*, 78, pp. 890–96. The act is printed and analyzed in *Living Wilderness*, *28* (1964), and further discussed in: Michael McCloskey, "The Wilderness Act of 1964: Its Background and Meaning," *Oregon Law Review*, *45* (1966), 288–321; Hession, "The Legislative History of the Wilderness Act"; Delbert V. Mercure, Jr. and William M. Ross, "The Wilderness Act: A Product of Congressional Compromise" in *Congress and the Environment*, eds. Richard A. Cooley and Geoffrey Wandesforde-Smith (Seattle, 1970), pp. 47–64; and James L. Sundquist, *Politics and Policy: The Eisenhower, Kennedy, and Johnson Years* (Washington, D.C., 1968), pp. 337 ff.

86. Steward M. Brandborg (Zahniser's successor as executive director of the Wilderness Society) to the author, May 2, 1966 and May 24, 1966. Brandborg, "New Chal-

Passage of the Wilderness Act of 1964 did not, of course, terminate the American debate over the meaning and value of wild country. Celebrations occasioned by the passage of the act were still under way when proposals for more dams on the Colorado River created a whole new front for defenders of wilderness. This time the Grand Canyon itself was involved, and for that reason many observers regarded the controversy as climactic.

The idea of building dams in the Grand Canyon was not new with the 1960s. Two sites in particular had long attracted the attention of engineers: Bridge Canyon and Marble Canyon, both within Grand Canyon. Both places had been fully surveyed in the 1920s as part of the process that resulted in the selection of Boulder Canyon, downstream from the Grand, as the site of Hoover Dam. A bill authorizing construction of a dam at Bridge Canyon actually passed the Senate in 1950, only to be summarily defeated in the House. There were also elaborate plans of long standing for bringing water from a reservoir in Marble Canyon through a forty-mile tunnel under the Kaibab Plateau to hydropower facilities in Kanab Creek. Ninety percent of the Colorado River would have been diverted from its normal course through Grand Canyon. Serious consideration of such projects was possible because of a loophole deliberately left in the act of February 26, 1919, establishing Grand Canyon National Park. "Whenever consistent with the primary purposes of said park," it declared, "the Secretary of the Interior is authorized to permit the utilization of areas therein which may be necessary for the development and maintenance of government reclamation projects."[87] The obvious inconsistency in this state-

---

lenges for Wilderness Conservationists" (mimeographed address, 1968); Brandborg, "The Job Ahead Under the Wilderness Act" (March, 1967), Wilderness Society print; Michael McCloskey (executive secretary of the Sierra Club), "How to Make a Wilderness Study" and "Organizing Support for a Wilderness Proposal" (mimeographed papers distributed by the Sierra Club, March 20 and 31, 1967). Also indicative of the way wilderness advocates responded to the Wilderness Act is the Wilderness Society's "Wilderness Conservation Leader's Background Information Kit" (1967), and conferences like the Southern California Wilderness Workshop sponsored by the Sierra Club, the Wilderness Society, and the Southern California Environmental Coalition, Oct. 29, 30, and 31, 1971. See also *Action for Wilderness,* ed. Elizabeth Gillette (New York, 1972), which contains papers from the 12th Biennial Wilderness Conference of the Sierra Club, and Michael McCloskey, "Is the Wilderness Act Working?" *Trends, 9* (1972), 19–23, along with McCloskey's "Wilderness Movement at the Crossroads," *Pacific Historical Review, 41* (1972), 346–61.

87. Public Law 277 in U.S., *Statutes at Large,* 40, pp. 1175–78. The best history

ment left the way open for widely varying interpretations of the legality of dams in the Grand Canyon.

The controversy began to gather momentum in 1963 when Secretary of the Interior Udall made public the Bureau of Reclamation's billion-dollar Pacific Southwest Water Plan.[88] Its scope was unprecedented. To solve the growing Southwest's water shortage, the reclamationists proposed diverting water from the water-rich Pacific Northwest, including northern California, through a series of tunnels, ducts, and canals to the arid lower Colorado River basin. The increased flow would be utilized with aid of a series of new dams and diversion facilities. The Central Arizona Project, for instance, proposed to transport water from the Lake Havasu impoundment on the lower Colorado to the booming Phoenix-Tucson area. To finance this massive undertaking and to generate hydroelectric power to pump water into central Arizona, dams would be built at Bridge and Marble canyons in the Grand Canyon. As proposed by the Bureau of Reclamation, the Marble Canyón Dam would flood fifty-three miles of river, while the impoundment behind Bridge Canyon Dam would be ninety-three miles long. Forty miles of Grand Canyon National Monument would be affected and thirteen miles of the National Park. Eventually, sedimentation would mean still further encroachments on the wilderness conditions of the inner canyon.

The Bureau of Reclamation anticipated the opposition of preservationists, and it was not disappointed. Wilderness defenders were primed for vigorous resistance by the closing on January 21, 1963 of the gates of Glen Canyon Dam. Immediately upstream on the Colorado from Grand Canyon, Glen Canyon was a little-known region of incredible beauty and wildness extending over a hundred river miles. It was not a national park or monument, and for that reason preservationists had not offered resistance when the dam was approved in 1956 as part of the Colorado River Storage Project. Their main concern in that proposal, of course, was Echo Park Dam *in* Dinosaur National Monument. But after rejoicing in the

of the Colorado River region, including the Grand Canyon, is *The Grand Colorado: The Story of a River and Its Canyons*, ed. T. H. Watkins (Palo Alto, Calif., 1969). Ise, *National Park Policy*, pp. 230–38, treats the history of Grand Canyon National Park and Monument.

88. U.S. Department of the Interior, Bureau of Reclamation, *Pacific Southwest Water Plan* (August, 1963).

salvation of Dinosaur, preservationists suddenly awoke to the fact that Glen Canyon was also worth protecting as wilderness. The Sierra Club led the way in the belated protest with a volume in its lavishly illustrated Exhibit Format Series, *The Place No One Knew: Glen Canyon on the Colorado* (1963). Eliot Porter's photographs and David Brower's editing drove home the moral: a needless reservoir was inundating one of the wonders of the New World simply because enough Americans had not cared. Dinosaur, it was clear, had been saved by vigilance and stubbornness; Glen Canyon was lost through apathy. The hand-wringing increased when it became evident that Lake Powell, rising behind Glen Canyon Dam, would back water up to and, ultimately, through Rainbow Bridge National Monument in clear violation of Colorado River Storage Project agreements.

Congressional hearings on the Pacific Southwest Water Plan in 1965 and 1966,[89] and the official backing of President Johnson and Secretary of the Interior Udall, led most observers to expect that the Grand Canyon dams would be approved despite the preservationists' wrath. Construction sites in the canyon were already being prepared for the almost certain authorization. But the tide turned on June 9, 1966. The New York *Times* and Washington *Post* for that day carried a full-page advertisement about the dams. Placed by the Sierra Club at a cost of $15,000 and designed by David Brower with professional public relations assistance, the ad declared, in headlines, "NOW ONLY YOU CAN SAVE GRAND CANYON FROM BEING FLOODED . . . FOR PROFIT." The body of the ad described the dam projects and their liabilities. It concluded, "remember, with all the complexities of Washington politics and Arizona politics, and the ins and outs of committees and procedures, there is only one simple, incredible issue here: this time it's the Grand Canyon they want to flood. *The Grand Canyon.*"[90] A second version of the ad, which appeared in several runs of the June 9 *Times,* was an open letter to Secretary Udall.

89. U.S. Congress, House, Committee on Interior and Insular Affairs, Subcommittee on Irrigation and Reclamation, Hearings, *Lower Colorado River Basin Project,* 89th Cong., 1st Sess. (Aug. 23–27, 30, 31, Sept. 1, 1965) and U.S. Congress, House, Committee on Interior and Insular Affairs, Subcommittee on Irrigation and Reclamation, Hearings, *Lower Colorado River Basin Project,* 89th Cong., 2d Sess. (May 9–13, 18, 1966) are valuable collections of opinion for and against the Grand Canyon dams.

90. New York *Times,* June 9, 1966, p. 35.

The Sierra Club advertisements paid remarkable dividends. Mail deploring Bridge and Marble Canyon Dams flooded key Washington offices in one of the largest outpourings of public sentiment in American conservation history. Senator Thomas Kuchel of California called it "one of the largest letter-writing campaigns which I have seen in my tenure in the Senate."[91] Hundreds of thousands of Americans, it appeared, had marveled at the Grand Canyon and were concerned about its future as wilderness. Unlike Glen Canyon, the Grand was a place everyone knew, at least by reputation. David Brower realized that in defending the Grand Canyon, the American wilderness movement was playing its trump. "If we can't save the Grand Canyon," he remarked, "what the hell can we save?"[92]

The June 9, 1966, advertisement achieved its greatest success for an unexpected reason. At 4 P.M., June 10, a special Internal Revenue Service messenger hand-delivered a warning to the club that henceforth it could no longer be certain about the tax deductibility of the donations it received. In the opinion of the IRS the club was engaging in "substantial" efforts to influence legislation, something the law did not permit tax-exempt organizations to do. If the IRS warning and subsequent official revocation of the tax-exemption were designed to help the cause of the Grand Canyon dam builders by muzzling the Sierra Club, they were backfires of colossal proportions.

In the public mind, at least, it appeared that the club was being punished by the federal government for altruistic efforts on behalf of Grand Canyon. An explosion of protest immediately followed. The controversial advertisements had appeared on an inside page of two newspapers, but the Internal Revenue Service's criticism of the Sierra Club became front-page news across the country. People who did not know or care about the threat to the Grand Canyon as wilderness now rose in its behalf in the name of civil liberties. Could the government intimidate citizen protest? Were only well-connected and well-heeled lobbyists tolerated? The tax action made the issue of Grand Canyon dams transcend conservation and prompted protest letters from thousands who might never

91. As quoted in *Congressional Quarterly Fact Sheet*, Nov. 1, 1968, p. 3024.

92. Interview with David Brower, Nov. 6, 1969. The records of the Sierra Club's involvement in the Grand Canyon dams controversy are available in the Sierra Club Archives, San Francisco, California.

have written about wilderness alone. One index of the public's concern was the rise in Sierra Club membership from 39,000 in June 1966 to 67,000 in October 1968 and 135,000 by 1971.

With the tide of national opinion running in their favor, defenders of an undammed Grand Canyon pressed their case. Another Sierra Club advertisement appeared in nationally important newspapers on July 25, 1966. Later in the summer a number of newspapers and magazines carried still a third, this one headlined: "SHOULD WE ALSO FLOOD THE SISTINE CHAPEL SO TOURISTS CAN GET NEARER THE CEILING?". The gist of the preservationists' argument was simple: like the Sistine Chapel, the Grand Canyon was one of the world's treasures. It should be kept in its pristine condition. "Wilderness," the advertisements made clear, "has all but disappeared." Armed with technology, man seemed bent on obliterating the "forces which made him." The limits had been reached. Now it fell to the lot of wilderness advocates in the 1960s to make sure "that something untrammeled and free remains in the American earth." Keeping the Grand Canyon wild would be evidence "that we had love for the people who follow." At the essence of the argument were questions of priorities, definitions of progress. Mankind would be poorer, it was implied, if the Grand Canyon were dammed.

In answer to the Bureau of Reclamation's rebuttals that the Grand Canyon dams and impoundments would not even be visible from most places on the rims, wilderness advocates replied that it was essential on psychological and emotional grounds to *know* that the free-flowing river that had cut the chasm was still at work. Dams, moreover, would eliminate the possibility of one of the world's supreme wilderness adventures—running the Colorado by boat through Grand Canyon. Supporting these points was the charge that the Grand Canyon dams served no purpose other than to finance water development elsewhere. Was the United States so poor, preservationists wondered, that it had to convert the Grand Canyon into a "cash register"? Turning to their slide rules and calculators, opponents of the dams endeavored to convince Congress and the public that coal-fired thermal plants or nuclear generators could supply the requisite electric power at less cost than the dams. Another line of attack stemmed from evidence that the dams would actually waste the Colorado's limited supply of water through evaporation and seepage. In this way the dams were represented as working against the very purpose of the Pacific Southwest Water Plan. But for most Americans the simple plea to "SAVE GRAND CANYON"—as bumper stickers proclaimed—was argument enough.[93]

As a result of the furor in the summer of 1966, the Department of the Interior and the Bureau of Reclamation brought revised proposals to the January 1967 opening of the 90th Congress. They would abandon Marble Canyon Dam entirely. But Bridge Canyon (renamed "Hualapai") Dam would remain, and, in order to avoid trespassing on a part of the national park system, Grand Canyon National Monument would be abolished. Preservationists were not impressed with the compromise. One bullet in the heart, they maintained, was just as deadly as two. And changing names or jurisdictions on maps did not alter the fact that a dam was being placed in the Grand Canyon. Compromise was out of the question. Having seen Glen Canyon dammed as part of a compromise that saved Dinosaur National Monument, the preservationists tended toward skepticism and caution. Besides, there was a growing consciousness of the muscle in wilderness preservation. The Wilderness System was a reality. Perhaps there was no need to bargain for part of the Grand Canyon. A power play, the kind developers had used for years, might save it in its entirety.

This mentality was reflected in the March 1967 hearings of the House Interior and Insular Affairs Committee on the Grand Canyon dams. At one point in the testimony Representative Morris K. Udall of Arizona, brother of the secretary of the interior, questioned David Brower on the uncompromising position of the Sierra Club. Udall found the club's stand incredible. Suppose, he proposed to Brower, we have "a low, low, low Bridge Canyon Dam, maybe 100 feet high, is that too much? Is there any point at which you compromise here?" Responding, Brower pointed out that "you are not giving us anything that God didn't put there in the first place." Later he explained that "we have no choice. There have to be groups who will hold for these things that are not replaceable.

93. For a summary of the Sierra Club's arguments against the dams, see the *Sierra Club Bulletin, 51* (1966), the May number of which is a special on Grand Canyon, and, in the July-August issue, "Why Grand Canyon Should Not Be Dammed." See also an undated Sierra Club brochure, *Dams in Grand Canyon—A Necessary Evil?*

If we stop doing that, we might as well stop being an organization, and conservation organizations might as well throw in the towel." Taken aback and clearly moved, Representative Udall replied: "I know the strength and sincerity of your feelings, and I respect them."[94]

Adding greatly to the preservationists' cause in 1967 was François Leydet's *Time and the River Flowing: Grand Canyon*. Published three years previously in the Sierra Club's Exhibit Format Series, the book was by this time a subject of considerable public attention. Leydet's text described a river trip through Grand Canyon, and the accompanying color photographs conveyed a sense of what would be lost if a dam were built. Selections from Aldo Leopold and other exponents of wilderness reinforced the point that if wonder and humility in the earth's presence were to continue to exist in modern civilization, man needed places like a wild Grand Canyon. A quotation from Howard Zahniser summarized the message. "Out of the wilderness," he wrote, "has come the substance of our culture, and with a living wilderness . . . we shall have also a vibrant, vital culture, an enduring civilization of healthful, happy people who . . . perpetually renew themselves in contact with the earth." Here was a concept with which Henry David Thoreau would have sympathized and which, given Zahniser's high regard for the Transcendentalist, he probably inspired. "We are not fighting progress," Zahniser's statement concluded, "we are making it."[95]

On February 1, 1967, Secretary of the Interior Stewart Udall announced that the Johnson administration had changed its mind about the Grand Canyon dams. For the time being, Udall suggested, the Central Arizona Project would plan to receive its money and pumping power from a coal-fired steam plant. Later in the year Udall took his family on a raft trip through the Grand Canyon. Overwhelmed by the experience, Udall declared at its conclusion that he had erred in making an "armchair" judgment about

94. U.S. Congress, House, Committee on Interior and Insular Affairs, Subcommittee on Irrigation and Reclamation, Hearings, *Colorado River Basin Project*, 90th Cong., 1st Sess. (March 13, 14, 16, 17, 1967), pp. 458–59. Also important as a source of preservationist sentiment is U.S. Congress, Senate, Committee on Interior and Insular Affairs, Subcommittee on Water and Power Resources, Hearings, *Central Arizona Project*, 90th Cong., 1st Sess. (May 2–5, 1967).

95. Howard Zahniser in François Leydet, *Time and the River Flowing: Grand Canyon* (San Francisco, 1964), p. 139.

the canyon and the dams. "The burden of proof," he now believed, "rests on the dam builders."[96]

Preparing for the final stages of the fight, the Sierra Club scheduled frequent showings of two sound-and-color motion pictures. "The Grand Canyon" dramatized what could still be saved while "Glen Canyon" showed what had been lost. A Grand Canyon Task Force, representing a coalition of conservation clubs and individuals, was charged with national leadership of the campaign. Another full-page advertisement (March 13, 1967) also appeared. Washington mailboxes again filled, and the pressure began to tell. In June 1967 the Senate Interior and Insular Affairs Committee voted to authorize the Central Arizona Project *without* either of the controversial dams. On August 8, 1967, the Senate accepted its committee's recommendation and passed a damless Central Arizona Project. In the House, however, Representative Wayne Aspinall of Colorado retained the chairmanship of the Interior and Insular Affairs Committee that he had held during the Wilderness System discussions. Aspinall supported the Grand Canyon dams and constituted a formidable obstacle to preservationist hopes. But by early 1968 even proponents of Bridge Canyon Dam sensed the change in national mood. Representative Morris K. Udall announced in January that he had given up on the dam idea. "I must tell you bluntly," he sadly declared, "that no bill providing for a so-called 'Grand Canyon Dam' can pass the Congress today."[97]

Political consequences followed in due course. On July 31, 1968, Senate and House conferees on the $1.3 billion Central Arizona Project agreed on a bill specifically prohibiting dams on the Colorado River between the Hoover and Glen Canyon dams. Another stipulation precluded the possibility that any state, city, or group such as an Indian tribe could obtain a license under the Federal Power Act to construct a dam in the Grand Canyon. On September 30, 1968, President Johnson signed a damless Central Arizona Project bill into law.[98]

96. Stewart Udall in *Grand Canyon of the Living Colorado,* ed. Roderick Nash (New York, 1970), p. 87. (The article appeared originally in the February 1968 issue of *Venture* magazine.)

97. Quoted ibid., p. 105.

98. The legislative history of the Central Arizona Project is the subject of the *Congressional Quarterly Fact Sheet* (Nov. 1, 1969), pp. 3019–31. For a critical discussion of the project see Richard L. Berkman and W. Kip Viscusi, *Damming the West* (New York, 1973), pp. 105–30. A more objective account may be found in

Reflecting on the Grand Canyon dam controversy a Congressman, who preferred anonymity, observed that "hell has no fury like a conservationist aroused."[99] The wilderness cause, he added, was irresistible. The Congressman should, of course, have added a chronological qualifier to his assertion. Conservers of wilderness values had been aroused repeatedly since the Hetch Hetchy era, but not until the 1950s and 1960s did the quantity and quality of their fury become sufficiently potent to influence the political process. The result, in terms of the Grand Canyon, was unprecedented. Dams that originally had the full backing of the administration, the personal enthusiasm of the secretary of the interior, and nearly unanimous support from senators and representatives of the seven Colorado Basin states, as well as the determined boosting of water and power users' lobbies—dams, in other words, that seemed virtually certain of authorization—were stopped.

But the decision to save the Grand Canyon, like any other political act, was not final. Congress could give and Congress could take away. As long as Colorado water flowed downhill proposals for dams and generators would remain alive. The energy crises of the 1970s and the growing realization that the burgeoning West was running out of water spawned several renewals of plans for Colorado River dams.[100] The state of Arizona, the city of Los Angeles, and the Hualapai Indians (who owned part of the Bridge Canyon dam site) kept pressure on the federal government for construction permits. Congress, however, held firm and on January 3, 1975, enlarged Grand Canyon National Park to include all non-Indian lands adjacent to the 279-mile Grand Canyon.[101] On an international level the Canyon became, in 1981, a United States addition to the United Nation's "World Heritage List." Established

---

Norris Hundley, Jr., *Water and the West* (Berkeley, 1975), *passim*. Valuable insights into the emotions, pro and con, that the Grand Canyon dams generated are available in John McPhee's account of a trip with David Brower and Floyd Dominy through the Canyon: *Encounters with the Archdruid* (New York, 1971).

99. Quoted in *Grand Canyon of the Living Colorado,* ed. Nash, p. 105.

100. John Boslough, "Rationing a River," *Science 81, 2* (1981), 26–37; Russell Martin, "The Mighty Colorado," *Rocky Mountain, 3* (1981), 35–40; Steve Comus, "The Colorado River Could Provide L.A. with 5 Billion Watts of Power," Los Angeles *Herald-Examiner,* Dec. 4, 1973. An excellent book-length discussion is Philip S. Fradkin, *A River No More* (New York, 1981), esp. Chapter 1.

101. Public Law 93–620 in U.S., *Statutes at Large, 88,* 2089–93. Regarding the land added to the national park see *National Parks and Conservation Magazine, 48* (1974), 5–10.

in 1972 the list recognizes for special protection certain natural and historic features that have importance to all mankind.[102] But laws and lists only express values. The only certain safeguard of wilderness areas like the Grand Canyon is in the attitudes that inspired the dam protest. And these depend on an intellectual revolution concerning wilderness that is not yet complete.

While the free-flowing character of the Colorado River in the Grand Canyon grabbed headlines, Congress moved in a quieter way to institutionalize river protection. On October 2, 1968, just two days after the final defeat of the Grand Canyon dams, the President signed a bill establishing the National Wild and Scenic Rivers System. Modeled on the National Wilderness Preservation System, it created a legislative category of protection which could be accorded to any free-flowing river Congress designated. The Wild and Scenic Rivers Act instantly created eight components of the system in 1968, and the state of Maine added the Allagash two years later. By the end of the 1970s there were nineteen rivers, totaling more than 1600 miles, under protection. In addition over fifty rivers or segments of rivers were under study as potential additions. The Wild and Scenic Rivers Act explicitly accepts the concept of balance which underlies the recent wilderness movement. The legislation states that "the established national policy of dam and other construction at appropriate sections of the rivers of the United States needs to be complemented by a policy that would preserve other selected rivers . . . in their free-flowing condition."[103] Some feared this policy was too little, too late. By 1980 wild rivers were one of the nation's rarest resources, an endangered species

102. See Roderick Nash, "The Exporting and Importing of Nature," *Perspectives in American History, 12* (1979), 558–59; Russell E. Train, "An Idea Whose Time Has Come: The World Heritage Trust," in Hugh Elliott, ed., *Second World Conference on National Parks* (Morges, Switzerland, 1974), pp. 378–79. See also below, Chapter 16, pp. 377.

103. Public Law 90–542 in U.S., *Statutes at Large, 82*, pp. 906–18. The act is conveniently reprinted and discussed in Jack G. Utter and John D. Schultz, *A Handbook on the Wild and Scenic Rivers Act* (Missoula, Mt., 1976). See also River Conservation Fund, *Flowing Free* (Washington, D.C., 1977) and "Preserving Our Wild and Scenic Rivers," *National Geographic, 152* (1977), pp. 2–59. A useful political analysis of the meaning of the act is to be found in Dennis G. Asmussen and Thomas P. Bouchard, "Wild and Scenic Rivers: Private Rights and Public Goods" in *Congress and the Environment*, ed. Cooley and Wandesforde-Smith, pp. 163–74. On the rareness of whitewater rivers see Robert O. Collins and Roderick Nash, *The Big Drops: Ten Legendary Rapids* (San Francisco, 1978).

comparable in some opinions to condors and grizzlies. Unlike many wilderness areas, all undeveloped rivers had utilitarian value as potential hydropower sources. The emergence of higher national priorities, such as energy or water or population growth, could swing the political pendulum back toward river development.

But for the time being American culture appears at ease with the balance between wilderness and civilization struck on the Colorado River. Parts of it "work"; parts flow wild and free. Hoover and Glen Canyon dams symbolize civilization and its material needs. Free-flowing rivers in Dinosaur National Monument and Grand Canyon National Park represent antipodal values. Seeking a balance, American political institutions worked against extremists who would have kept the Colorado River as John Wesley Powell found it in 1869, a 2,000-mile river flowing unchecked to the sea. But thus far the nation has also turned from the vision of a Mississippi-like chain of interconnected dams and reservoirs extending from Wyoming to Mexico. The legitimate ambivalence American culture feels between wilderness and civilization is quite accurately expressed in the present pattern of resource use on the Colorado.

CHAPTER 13

Toward a Philosophy of Wilderness

I'd rather be a forest than a street.

Paul Simon and Arthur Garfunkel, 1970

If the *Saturday Evening Post*'s guest editorial was any indication, wilderness hatred was alive and well on November 6, 1965. "Why shouldn't we spoil wilderness?" Robert Wernick asked. Everything good, in his view, depended on beating back and holding at bay the power of wilderness both in nature and in the human heart. As for wilderness lovers, "they affect old rumpled clothes, unshaved jaws, salty language; they spit and sweat and boast of their friendship with aborigines." But underneath this backwoods veneer, Wernick found "decadents, aristocrats, and snobs." If such people wanted wilderness, he concluded, let them take "excursion rockets to Mars and Alpha Centauri."[1]

In response to critics of the wilderness idea, like Robert Wernick, and to developers who attacked more tangible targets, twentieth-century defenders of wild things struggled to formulate a philosophy. This meant finding and articulating the underlying principles in the defense of wilderness. It was not an easy task. In the American past, wilderness advocacy characteristically took the form of highly emotional and often frantic defenses of particular places, species, or experiences: "Save the Grand Canyon!" or "Stop Slaughtering Baby Seals!" Such exhortations passed for argument. No one, at least no one in the movement, was supposed to ask "Why?" Wilderness appreciation was a faith. Its unexamined premises might have great importance to an individual, yet that did not help much in the brass tacks political and economic arenas that largely determined the future of wilderness. Implicitly admitting as much, preservationists resorted to arguments unrelated to their central concern. Thus, opponents of dams frequently argued over benefit-cost ratios, discussing kilowatt-hours, acre-feet and the prime rate of interest,

1. Robert Wernick, "Speaking Out: Let's Spoil the Wilderness," *Saturday Evening Post*, 238 (November 6, 1965), 12, 16.

instead of explaining the values of wild rivers and their canyons. The need was for ideas that defend wilderness in general in the way that the philosophy of human freedom underlies the many specific defenses of civil liberty. Wilderness defenders tended to reinvent the wheel time and again. But with the approach of the 1990 centennial of the ending of the frontier, they began to think in more general and systematic terms.

As the viewpoint that had to be answered, the modern case *against* wilderness deserves more scrutiny. Robert Wernick's editorial is representative of the belief in civilization as a beneficent tide that our hardworking ancestors extended over the earth. But like a tide, civilization could recede. Man must continually work at controlling the opposing force: wildness. To relax is to risk undoing the primary human achievement. As noted in an earlier chapter (above, p. 27), Wernick's ideas are very much in the pioneer tradition that could only see wilderness and man in an adversary relationship. The battle, moreover, is never won. Wilderness, Wernick feels, is always out there, just beyond the clearing, a dark presence actively seeking revenge on man the controller. Like the Puritans, Wernick is also frightened by the wilderness within man. Civilization tries to tame this power but it still lurks and occasionally breaks loose, according to Wernick, in "wars and oppressions and crimes."

Believing that civilization is an unalloyed good, Wernick's advice is straightforward. Humans should "look after our own interests as best we can, and no more consider the feelings of the eagle and the rhinoceros than they consider ours." If such a policy means the end of wild animals, Wernick is prepared to accept that conclusion. His feeling about wilderness recreation is similar. There is, he concedes, a small minority which has a taste for "desolate landscapes" and "a mosquito-clouded view." Nothing is inherently wrong with this according to Wernick, but he advises people who covet an "exultant thrashing through the wilderness" to "bow gracefully to the inevitable."[2] The kings of ancient England lost their royal hunting preserves to farms and factories, he concludes, and today's wilderness will and should give way to civilization.

2. Ibid. Another, representative, diatribe against wilderness is Allan May, *Voice in the Wilderness* (Chicago, 1978).

Many contemporary opponents of wilderness share Wernick's assumption that even in the middle of the twentieth century it was still a matter of civilization *versus* wilderness. From this point of view wilderness preservationists were not just locking up valuable natural resources but somehow reducing modern man to a degraded and uncomfortable primitive state. William H. Hunt, head of a Pacific coast lumber company, lashed out in 1971 at the "woodsy witchdoctors of a revived ancient nature cult" who sought to "restore our nation's environment to its disease-ridden, often hungry wilderness stage."[3] The same idea appeared in land developer Charles Fraser's characterization of wilderness advocates as druids, the ancient Celtic wizards who sacrificed human lives to the spirits thought to dwell in oak trees. "Modern druids," Fraser said, "worship trees and sacrifice human beings to those trees." John McPhee picked up this theme when he labeled Friends of the Earth president David Brower "the archdruid."[4] Sometimes the characterization seemed apt as when ecologist Garrett Hardin remarked that in view of their relative numbers he would, if forced to choose, support the existence of one redwood tree over one baby.[5] Hardin was quite serious, and his well-publicized remark exacerbated anti-wilderness biases.

More often than not opponents of wilderness were people whose lifework consisted of hard physical efforts to control nature. Thus Floyd E. Dominy, chief of the Bureau of Reclamation and proponent of the Grand Canyon dams in the 1960s, grew up in central Nebraska and northeastern Wyoming where water management was the key to human survival. "Nature," Dominy declared, " is a pretty cruel animal."[6] Dams, as a consequence, ranked at the top of his scale of priorities. A wild river was an insult to man's capacity to modify his environment. The longshoreman-philosopher Eric Hoffer held similar views. As a migratory farm laborer and placer miner, he found wild nature "ill-disposed and inhospitable." When he tried to rest on the ground, untamed nature poked and pricked

3. As quoted in Brock Evans, "Representatives' Reports," *Sierra Club Bulletin,* 57 (1972), 20.

4. John McPhee, *Encounters with the Archdruid* (New York, 1971), p. 95.

5. In discussion at the Sierra Club's Tenth Biennial Wilderness Conference, San Francisco, March 15, 1969. A published statement of similar import is Garrett Hardin, "Destroying Wildlife in the People's Name," *Defenders,* 56 (1981), 22, 24.

6. McPhee, *Encounters,* p. 156.

him. Indeed, any contact with unmodified nature left man with "scratches, bites, torn clothes, and grime." Hoffer described how he learned to use a mattress "to make life bearable," interposing "a protective layer between myself and nature." On a larger scale, Hoffer thought of civilization as just such a "protective layer." He confessed to feeling more of a "sense of kinship" with it than with wilderness. Like Wernick, Hoffer hoped technological man would conquer wilderness completely. In his paradise scenario man would "wipe out the jungles, turn deserts and swamps into arable land, terrace barren mountains, regulate rivers, eradicate all pests, control the weather, and make the whole land mass a fit habitation for man." Wilderness had no place in this vision. "The globe," in Hoffer's estimation, should be man's and not nature's.[7]

A much more sophisticated statement of the same thesis appears in the recent writings of René Dubos. A famous microbiologist, Dubos taught the world the principles of antibiotics, and the idea of a fruitful collaboration between nature (microbes, in this case) and man is the hallmark of his thinking. With regard to land use, Dubos does not believe in wild nature as a criterion. "The natural channels," he wrote in 1976, "are not necessarily the most desirable, either for the human species or for other species." He thinks of a gardenlike earth, shaped and controlled by man, as the logical fulfillment of the human potential. As an example of this kind of environment Dubos offers his homeland, northern France, where two thousand years of human occupation have produced a landscape more beautiful, productive, and ecologically balanced than the primeval forest Neolithic settlers encountered. He sees Europe as a "semiartificial landscape," the result of "converting primeval nature into an orderly arrangement of farmlands, pastures, and wooded areas," and he calls it a "work of art."[8] The same reasoning appears in Martin Krieger's 1973 essay, "What's Wrong with Plastic Trees?" "Artificial . . . wildernesses," Krieger opines, "have been created and there is no reason to believe that these . . . need be unsatisfactory." Drawing on an earlier edition of *Wilderness and the American Mind,* Krieger argues that if wilderness is a state of mind, why not "proxy environments" and the manipulation

7. Eric Hoffer, *The Temper of Our Time* (New York, 1967), pp. 79, 94.

8. Dubos, "Symbiosis Between the Earth and Humankind," *Science, 193* (1976), 461; Dubos, *A God Within* (New York, 1972), pp. 135, 138. See also Dubos, *The Resilience of Ecosystems* (Boulder, Co., 1978), p. 1.

of the way we think about them? As with Dubos, Krieger's implication is that nature does not always know best.[9]

In 1980 Dubos brought his ideas together in a book significantly entitled *The Wooing of Earth.* He begins his first chapter with the thought that "some of the landscapes that we most admire are the product of environmental degradation." Dubos goes on to celebrate man's ability to woo the earth by creating "new environments that are ecologically sound, aesthetically satisfying, economically rewarding, and favorable to the continued growth of civilization." Dubos cites an earlier edition of *Wilderness and the American Mind,* and concedes that wild places have some values. He would not turn national parks into farmland. But he professes considerable difficulty understanding why anyone would want to be in wilderness environments that are so "fundamentally alien to our biological nature . . . that we can function and survive in them only with the accoutrements of civilization."[10] When man stopped hunting and gathering, Dubos thinks, he forever severed his biological relationship with wilderness. The love of the wild that remains is purely intellectual—a posture—and it is very rare. "For one John Muir . . . trying to remove himself as far as possible from human settlements," he writes in *A God Within,* "there are millions of nature lovers for whom the country means humanized nature." Around the world, he insists, most people prefer "landscapes which have been modified by human intervention." For this reason Dubos expresses no regret that by "about 1985 . . . practically all the earth's surface compatible with human life will be . . . humanized." His chief concern is that manipulation of the earth be done intelligently and reverently.[11]

The pastoral, European origins of René Dubos help to explain his attitudes toward wilderness. So does his penchant, both as a microbiologist and a landscape gardener, for imposing his "own sense of order upon the natural process."[12] But antiwilderness views also arose from quite different circumstances. Eric Julber, whom Dubos quotes approvingly in *A God Within,* is a Los Angeles attorney and, as he styles himself, "a former member of the Sierra

9. Krieger, "What's Wrong with Plastic Trees?," *Science, 179* (1973), p. 453.

10. Dubos, *The Wooing of Earth* (New York, 1980), pp. 1, 159, 132.

11. Dubos, *A God Within,* pp. 140, 141, 149, 174, 45. Similar ideas are expressed in Dubos's "Humanizing the Earth," *Science, 179* (1973), 769–72.

12. Dubos, *A God Within,* p. 168.

Club." He was also, formerly, a wilderness "purist" who hiked the two hundred miles of the John Muir Trail with a fifty-pound pack "feeling vastly superior to the rest of humanity." But Julber visited Switzerland and "that was the end of my purist ethic." What he discovered was that the Swiss Alps were readily accessible by mechanized conveyances, heavily used by people, and still beautiful and satisfying. Julber rode the aerial tramways; lunched at 10,000 feet on cheese fondue, white wine, and pastry; and found that his thoughts were "just as beautiful" as they had been on an isolated Sierra peak with a peanut-butter sandwich. Returning to the United States, Julber was disturbed that his own country's system of wilderness preservation excluded 99 percent of the people. "What," he asked, "of the too-old, the too-young, the timid, the inexperienced, the frail, the hurried, the out-of-shape or the just-plain-lazy . . . ?" Their taxes, Julber reasoned, acquired and maintained the established wilderness areas but because of the access problem wilderness users tended to be a small, wealthy, young, and leisured elite. While not as vitriolic as Robert Wernick's charge of elitism, Julber's was a staple of the antiwilderness school of thought.[13]

As an alternative to the "purist" position, Eric Julber proposed an " 'access' philosophy." He called, for example, for several tramways "within easy driving distance of Los Angeles" that would wisk the public into the heart of the Sierra wilderness within minutes. At Half Dome, a summit overlooking Yosemite Valley, Julber envisioned a restaurant and hotel "so that ordinary people could spend a spectacular night on a mountain top and watch the sun come up over the Sierra Nevada." The Grand Canyon, Julber felt, was also inaccessible, and he proposed a cable car down from each rim so that visitors could get "a feel for its immense depths."

Julber stated clearly, however, that his philosophy of access was not to be construed as a denial of the value of wilderness for American civilization. On the contrary, he declared it his "firm belief that if Americans were permitted access to wilderness areas

13. Eric Julber has expressed his philosophy in "Let's Open Up Our Wilderness Areas," *Reader's Digest, 100* (1972), 125–28 and "The Wilderness: Just How Wild Should It Be?" *Trends, 9* (1972), 15–18. William Tucker in "Is Nature Too Good for Us?" *Harper's* (March, 1982), 27–35, seconds both Julber and Dubos, arguing that a wilderness area is a "reserve set up to keep people *out*," that a pro-wilderness stance is inevitably antihuman, and that constructive intervention in natural processes is better than "letting nature take its course."

in the manner I have suggested, we would soon create a generation of avid nature lovers." The problem with Julber's philosophy is that, according to most definitions, the wilderness quality of a place would vanish when the tramways and hotels arrived. The confusion stems from equating "scenery" and "natural beauty" with "wilderness." The nature Julber liked was not wild.

Humanity's "best interest" has figured prominently in the modern debate over the value of the American wilderness. Robert Wernick used the term in arguing for the extension of control over wild nature, and René Dubos had the concept in mind in his paean to beneficent pastoralism. The contemporary defense of wilderness began with the assumption that it was *not* in the best interest of human beings or of their civilization to eliminate wilderness. Benton McKaye, an environmental planner, approached the subject from the standpoint of human nature. "The first thing to understand," declared MacKaye, "is not the wilderness but the human." He began his own understanding by labeling two tendencies: the "gregarious" and the "solitary." MacKaye recognized that these categories applied not to two groups of people but to "two human states of mind." At times the individual craves the society of his fellows; on other occasions he seeks solitude.[14]

The relationship some felt existed between these impulses was stated poetically in the *Living Wilderness* in 1946: "Gregarious man has a lonesome soul, / And wilderness ways lead back to a crowd."[15] MacKaye endeavored to suggest some reasons for this. Man had evolved, he thought, from a primitive to a rural and, finally, to an urban environment. In America the process was condensed into three centuries. The result was the implantation in human nature, especially that of Americans, of a desire to be simultaneously "the pioneer, the husbandman, [and] the townsman." MacKaye concluded that effective environmental planning must permit man to indulge the "three sides of [his] inward nature."[16] Speaking for himself, in a manner reminiscent of Thoreau, MacKaye asserted, "I enjoy the high lights of Broadway as also the aroma of the new-mown hayfield, and with them both the frog chorus in the dank and distant muskeg." It followed that wilderness preserves were an "integral part of a balanced, civilized territory

14. MacKaye, "The Gregarious and the Solitary," *Living Wilderness, 4* (1939), 7.
15. Anonymous, "Nothing More?," *Living Wilderness, 11* (1946), 24.
16. MacKaye, "A Wilderness Philosophy," *Living Wilderness, 11* (1946), 2.

just as tilled land and city blocks are for the other integral parts." Wilderness enthusiasts, MacKaye patiently explained, had no intention of reverting "from clerks to cavemen, nor from Times Square to Plymouth Rock." Their interest was in preserving the opportunity "to recharge depleted human batteries directly from Mother Earth." Periodic recourse to wilderness, MacKaye argued, "is not to retreat into secret silent sanctums to escape a wicked world; it is to take breath amid effort to forge a better world."[17]

The northland explorer and defender of the Quetico-Superior canoe country, Sigurd Olson, joined MacKaye in examining man's need for both wilderness and civilization. Although Olson wrote many books, most of his ideas on this subject were distilled into a chapter of *Listening Point* (1958), entitled "The Whistle," where he expressed his thoughts on hearing the sound of a distant locomotive while camping alone in the wilderness. Initially, Olson recalled, he was greatly disturbed by the intruding sound. But after it had passed, he reflected on the whistle as the symbol of civilization. "Without that long lonesome wail and the culture that had produced it, many things would not be mine." Those included music, books, and cars—all of which Olson used and enjoyed. Moreover, it was his life in civilization that ultimately explained his appreciation of wilderness. Olson realized that without the experience of living amidst cities and cars and whistling locomotives, he would never have understood the deepest significance of wilderness as a stabilizer and sustainer. The Cree Indians whom Olson had encountered in the Athabasca wilderness lacked the civilized perspective and remained oblivious to the meaning and value of their wild environment. "Only through my own personal contact with civilization," Olson concluded, "had I learned to value the advantages of solitude."[18]

A popular writer on the Southwest, J. Frank Dobie pinpointed Olson's message when he wrote that "the greatest happiness possible to a man . . . is to beome civilized, to know that pageant of the past, to love the beautiful, to have just ideas of values and proportions, and then, retaining his animal spirits and appetites, to

17. MacKaye, as quoted in Murie, *Living Wilderness, 18* (1953), 24; MacKaye, "A Wilderness Philosophy," 4.

18. Olson, *Listening Point* (New York, 1958), pp. 150–53. Further statements of Olson's philosophy occur in *Open Horizons* (New York, 1969) and *Reflections From the North Country* (New York, 1976).

live in a wilderness."[19] This was, of course, exactly the kind of blending that Thoreau and Emerson had idealized a century earlier (see above, pp. 92–93). Its modern expression formed an important part of the justification of the remaining American wilderness. Charles A. Lindbergh, for example, wrote about the "wisdom of wilderness" and wondered if man could tap it "without experiencing the agony of reverting" to the wilderness condition Wernick, for one, detested. For his own part, Lindbergh described how his career as an aviator had permitted him to see the world's great wild places: "I loved bringing qualities of science and wilderness together." He added that the human future depended on the same combination.[20]

Joining Thoreau and, particularly, Olson, John P. Milton felt that a way of life which alternated between wilderness and civilization was the solution to ambivalence. Milton refined his thinking on a 1967 hike across Alaska's Brooks Range and down to the Arctic Ocean. He was on the trail continually for six weeks with a pack that started out weighing ninety pounds, and the experience was not uniformly thrilling. Milton was frank to admit that "over periods of time, deficiencies in life appear—in either the wholly civilized life or a life constantly in the wilderness." The key is balance, proportion. "It is a life spent contrasting and living alternately in both worlds," Milton concluded, "that seems best to me." And, with an accurate understanding of the origin of the terms, he added that the very concepts of civilization and wilderness require each other to have real meaning.[21]

The same idea of balance figured prominently in the philosophy of poet Gary Snyder. Repeatedly, Snyder explained that his defense of wilderness did not constitute a rejection of civilization. The point was to identify man's best interests (the elusive good life) on the spectrum between the wild and the civilized. The proper condition for people, Snyder thought, resulted from blending nature and technology, spirit and science, the Indian's way and the white man's, wilderness and civilization. Dramatically,

19. Dobie as quoted in Joseph Wood Krutch, *Grand Canyon: Today and All Its Yesterdays* (New York, 1958), p. 270.

20. Charles A. Lindbergh, "The Wisdom of Wildness," *Life*, *63* (1967), 8, 10.

21. Milton, "Arctic Walk," *Natural History*, *78* (1969), 51. See also Milton's book-length description, *Nameless Valleys, Shining Mountains* (New York, 1970), and *Earth and the Great Weather: The Brooks Range*, ed. Kenneth Brower (New York, 1971), which concerned the same trip.

Snyder stated as his ideal: "computer technicians who run the plant part of the year and walk along with the elk in their migrations during the rest."[22] One result of such a Thoreau-like ambivalence could be Snyder's ideal of a technology scaled to human needs and realistic environmental capacities. While not denying the tension between wilderness and civilization, ideas such as these made wilderness an important component of the vitality of civilization. They recognized that man needs solitude and society, freedom and order, beauty and bread, or—as Katherine Lee Bates wrote in "America the Beautiful"—the purple mountain's majesty above the fruited plain.

When bringing the wilderness cause to the political arena, preservationists took care not to dismiss the values of civilization. After making a case for what would become the Wilderness Act of 1964, Howard Zahniser quickly added that permanent, legal protection of wilderness "is not a disparagement of our civilization—no disparagement at all—but rather an admiration of it to the point of perpetuating it" in a healthy, happy condition. Advocates of the wilderness, according to Zahniser, were not recommending a return to cave dwelling on a permanent basis: "We like the beef from cattle grazed on the public domain. We relish the vegetables from the lands irrigated by virtue of the Bureau of Reclamation. . . . We nourish and refresh our minds from books manufactured out of the pulp of our forests."[23] Colin Fletcher, the high priest of backpacking, agreed that wilderness recreation offered a way of benefitting from a temporary return to the primitive. "The last thing I want to do," he explained, "is knock champagne and sidewalks and Boeing 707s. Especially champagne. These things distinguish us from the other animals. But they can also limit our perspectives."[24] For Fletcher and Zahniser the proper solution lay in a balance of environment and way of life. As the subtitle of a Sierra Club leaflet stated: "Sound Development and Unimpaired Parks: A Way to Have Both". David Brower echoed the same idea when he told a Senate committee collecting testimony on the Wilderness System that "true multiple use will accommo-

22. Gary Snyder, *Turtle Island* (New York, 1974), p. 100. See too Snyder's, *The Real Work: Interviews and Talks, 1964–1979* (New York, 1980).

23. Zahniser, "The Second Wilderness Conference," *Living Wilderness, 16* (1951), 31.

24. Fletcher, *The Complete Walker* (New York, 1970), p. 9.

date both civilization and wilderness."[25] Supreme Court Justice William O. Douglas, in reference to the Olympic Peninsula, agreed, "We can have the road and a stretch of wilderness both."[26] Congressman John P. Saylor, long time champion of the National Wilderness Preservation System, recognized most precisely the source of this ambivalence in a national pride that stemmed both from having and destroying wilderness. "We are a great people," he said, "because we have been so successful in developing and using our marvelous natural resources, but also, we Americans are the people we are largely because we have had the influence of the wilderness on our lives."[27]

Wilderness advocates thus recognized and assimilated ambivalence into their philosophies. The strategy involved showing that wilderness deserved a place within the totality of American civilization as one of its distinguishing and valuable assets. The wild no longer posed a threat to civilization in the United States. Robert Wernick was answered with the observation that in the 1980s it was absurd to think of wilderness and civilization locked in an adversary relationship. Wernick's lizards and eagles and creeping jungle vines were really not major problems to modern mankind. One way to dramatize this was to point out that in the forty-eight states, wilderness constituted about (problems of definition always made the figure tentative) two percent of the total area. The frontier was long gone. Especially in the East, wilderness existed only as islands in a growing sea of civilization. With realities like this in mind, spokesmen for wilderness were not persuaded by arguments based on the alleged demands of civilization. The wilderness of the New World had met these for three centuries. The compromises with civilization had already been made. Some ninety-eight percent of the nation, excluding Alaska, had been altered by technological man. Wilderness partisans entered the 1980s with the idea of saving *all* the wild country that remained. Given the relative proportions of wilderness and civilization, they felt there could no longer be good reasons for any new development in

25. Sierra Club, *Upper Colorado Controversy* (San Francisco, 1955); Brower in U.S. Cong., Senate, Committee on Interior and Insular Affairs, Hearings, *National Wilderness Preservation Act*, 85th Cong., 2d. Sess. (Nov. 7, 10, 13, 14, 1958), p. 586.

26. Douglas as quoted in Grant Conway, "Hiking the Wild Olympic Shoreline," *National Parks Magazine, 33* (1959), 8.

27. *Congressional Record*, 84th Cong., 2d Sess., *102* (July 12, 1956), p. 12589.

wilderness areas. It was precisely this conviction that energized Edward Abbey's 1975 novel, *The Monkey Wrench Gang,* in which a band of environmental guerrillas sabotaged the technology of industrial development in the Southwest.

A simple scarcity theory of value, coupled with the shrinking size of the American wilderness relative to American civilization, underlies modern wilderness philosophy. Opinion of wilderness in America also depended to a considerable extent on opinion of civilization but change occurred here as well. While the nation was expanding westward, confidence in the virtues of American culture ran high. Appreciation of the wilderness sputtered fitfully in such an optimistic atmosphere. By the end of the nineteenth century, however, enough doubts had arisen about the benefits of civilization to make possible widespread popular enthusiasm for the uncivilized (see above, Chapter 9).

Subsequent developments in the twentieth century did little to alter the trend toward discontent with civilization and the related growth in the attractiveness of wilderness. Involvement in two inconclusive global wars and a severe economic depression lent substance to the ideas of Brooks and Henry Adams, Oswald Spengler, and Arnold Toynbee, that America, along with the entire Western world, was declining and perhaps falling.[28] The individual seemed stripped of his autonomy by an overorganized society.[29] Science and technology appeared to have gotten out of control, particularly in the grisly light of the first atomic bombs and subsequent arms testing. Psychologists, led by Sigmund Freud,

28. H. Stuart Hughes's *Oswald Spengler* (New York, 1962) discusses Spengler's *The Decline of the West,* which became available in English in the 1920s. The pessimism of the Adams brothers and other Americans is treated in Frederic C. Jaher, *Doubters and Dissenters: Cataclysmic Thought in America,* 1885–1918 (New York, 1964). Toynbee's major statements are *A Study of History* (12 vols., London, 1934–61) and *The World and the West* (New York, 1953).

29. Among the best-known examinations of this social phenomenon are David Riesman, *The Lonely Crowd: A Study of the Changing American Character* (Garden City, N.Y., 1953); William H. Whyte, *The Organization Man* (New York, 1956); and Vance Packard, *The Naked Society* (New York, 1964). George Orwell, *Nineteen Eighty-four* (New York, 1949) and Aldous Huxley, *Brave New World* (New York, 1932) suggested in fictional form the conditions to which it could lead.

30. Fitzgerald's, *The Great Gatsby* (New York, 1925), pp. 217–18. Edwin S. Fussell's "Fitzgerald's Brave New World," *English Literary History, 19* (1952), 291–306, offers a relevant interpretation.

revived the primitivistic notion that man had been less repressed, and consequently happier, in an uncivilized condition.

Novelists also joined the attack. It was the garish hollowness of Jay Gatsby's Long Island, New York, society that moved F. Scott Fitzgerald to write about the "fresh green breast of the new world" —the wilderness that three centuries before confronted Dutch sailors with "something commensurate to [man's] capacity for wonder."[30] For William Faulkner the unrelenting rapacity of the civilizing process in the Deep South undermined confidence in the value of American culture. The lush bottomlands had degenerated, in Faulkner's view, into "the untreed land warped and wrung to mathematical squares of cotton for the frantic old-world people to turn into shells to shoot at one another." This spectacle compelled him to believe that the conquest of the wilderness had been unjustified.

Faulkner expressed his ideas symbolically in describing Ike McCaslin's thoughts on killing his first buck: "I slew you; my bearing must not shame your quitting life. My conduct forever onward must become your death." The point was that American civilization, in Faulkner's estimation, had shamed the death of the American wilderness. The New World, once so ripe with promise, had become a "gilded pustule." Americans had not proved worthy of their opportunity. They had turned predatory, feeding on their fellows, and giving Faulkner grim satisfaction that "the people who have destroyed [the wilderness] will accomplish its revenge."[31] This according to Faulkner, was the final tragedy in the interaction of wilderness and civilization in America. The pioneer did not comprehend that pioneering was self-defeating.

31. Faulkner, *Go Down Moses* (New York, 1942), pp. 193, 351, 353–54, 364; Faulkner, *Big Woods* (New York, 1955), [p. 7]. Faulkner has commented personally on this subject in Frederick L. Gwynn and Joseph L. Blotner, *Faulkner in the University* (Charlottesville, Va., 1959), pp. 271–72, 277, 280. Among the most useful secondary commentaries are William Van O'Connor, "The Wilderness Theme in Faulkner's 'The Bear,' " *Accent, 13* (1953), 12–20; Otis B. Wheeler, "Faulkner's Wilderness," *American Literature, 31* (1959), 127–36; R. W. B. Lewis, "The Hero in the New World: William Faulkner's 'The Bear,' " and Francis Lee Utley, "Pride and Humility: The Cultural Roots of Ike McCaslin" in *Bear, Man and God: Seven Approaches to William Faulkner's "The Bear,"* ed. Francis Lee Utley, Lynn Z. Bloom, and Arthur F. Kenney (New York, 1964), pp. 233–60 and 306–23; Ursula Brumm, "Wilderness and Civilization: A Note on William Faulkner" in *William Faulkner: Three Decades of Criticism,* ed. Frederick J. Hoffman and Olga W. Vickery (East Lansing, Mich., 1960), pp. 125–34; and John W. Hunt, *William Faulkner: Art in Theological Tension* (Syracuse, N.Y., 1965), pp. 137–68.

He could not moderate his success before he destroyed himself along with the wilderness. Beneficial up to a point, civilization in excess proved a liability.

In the 1960s, wilderness benefitted from the most intense and widespread questioning of established American values and institutions in the nation's history. The new mood emanated from young people, and in the mid-1960s half of the total population of the United States was under twenty-five. These Americans did not venerate success and security with the intensity of their depression- and war-scarred parents' generation. Neither did they celebrate technology, power, profit, and growth—the gods to which wilderness had traditionally been sacrificed in United States history. From their perspective the gross national product was not the best criterion of national progress. Centralization, urbanization, and industrialization appeared as devourers rather than saviors of mankind. "Can it be," Charles Lindbergh asked in the early 1970s, "that civilization is detrimental to human progress?" By the end of a decade marred by war, riots, and assassinations, such disenchantment was widespread. By that time, too, enough older Americans had joined the social and intellectual rebellion to make the terms "youth culture" and "generation gap" inadequate. "Counterculture" seemed more appropriate. Vague and inclusive as it was, the label at least expressed the fact that the critical energies were directed against the core of traditional American values.[32]

Given its general orientation, the counterculture inevitably found value in wilderness which was, after all, diametrically opposed to a civilization many had come to distrust and resent. Indeed many Americans in the 1960s began to think of wilderness and, parenthetically, of Indians, as victims of the same fixation on progress, growth, and competition which threatened countercultural values such as peace, freedom, and community. It followed that defending wilderness was a way of resisting the so-called

32. Lindbergh as quoted in Dubos, *Wooing of Earth*, p. 141. Standard sources on the counterculture are: Theodore Roszak, *The Making of a Counter Culture: Reflections on the Technocratic Society and Its Youthful Opposition* (New York, 1969); Herbert Marcuse, *Counterrevolution and Revolt* (Boston, 1972); Charles A. Reich, *The Greening of America* (New York, 1971); William L. O'Neill, *Coming Apart: An Informal History of America in the 1960's* (Chicago, 1971), pp. 233–71; Roderick Nash, "Bob Dylan" in Nash, *From These Beginnings: A Biographical Approach to American History* (New York, 1973), pp. 513–38.

establishment. It was no accident that Charles Reich used the phrase "greening of America" in the title of a 1971 book calling for a revolution in American priorities. The green world was the wild world, and it contained essential truths. Paul Simon and Arthur Garfunkel sang, "I'd rather be a forest than a street." Granted, one object of the counterculture was to change the "street," but being a "forest" appeared to many to be the proper means to that end.

By 1970 "wild" had become an approbative adjective in American popular speech. The counterculture identified it with freedom, authenticity, and spontaneity or, in the common parlance, with "letting it all hang out." Gary Snyder urged his countrymen to delight in wild country and wild thoughts. With people like Robert Wernick in mind, Snyder remarked that there was too much "fear of one's deepest natural inner-self wilderness areas, and the answer [was], relax. Relax around bugs, snakes, and your own hairy dreams."[33] Wernick abhorred such wildness in nature, and in human nature, because it could not be controlled. The counterculture celebrated it for the same reason. In a significant aside in *Earth House Hold* (1969), Snyder associated the countercultural symbol of long hair with wilderness. The establishment, he felt, preferred trimmed, shaved, controlled hair just as it liked an environment ordered in the interests of man. Cut hair was like a pastoral landscape. Wild, unkempt, and free hair endorsed naturalness. "Long hair," Snyder concluded, means "to accept, to go *through* the power of nature."[34] The alternative course, which mankind had tried for centuries, involved conquering or circumventing nature. It was time, Snyder and his countercultural colleagues believed, for a change. Specifically, they hoped for the emergence of "a new ecologically-sensitive harmony-oriented wild-minded scientific-spiritual culture" and for "new ways of living based on proximity to nature."[35] Charles Reich and Theodore Roszak joined Snyder in hoping this could entail a rejection of overdependence on science, reason, and technology and a renewal of the importance of magic, intuition, mystery, and awe.[36] This

33. Snyder, *Turtle Island*, p. 96.

34. Snyder, *Earth House Hold* (New York, 1969), p. 133.

35. Snyder, *Turtle Island*, p. 99.

36. Roszak, *Counter Culture*, pp. 249–53, 258. For additional indications of the importance of magic and mystery to the countercultural perspective, see Charles Reich and Douglas Carroll III, "After the Gold Rush," *National Parks and Conservation Magazine*, 45 (1971), 5.

neoromanticism accorded wilderness, as the epitome of the unknown and uncontrolled, new importance. At stake in such redirections, they felt, was nothing less than the survival of civilization because, in Snyder's words again, "a culture that alienates itself from the . . . wilderness outside . . . and from that other wilderness, the wilderness within, is doomed to a very destructive behavior, ultimately perhaps self-destructive behavior."[37]

Criticism of American civilization reached massive proportions during the zenith of the counterculture, and wilderness was a major beneficiary. "There are no real values left in society," several campers in Yosemite National Park told a reporter. "We came here because it is beautiful, it is real."[38] Conversely, the modern urban lifestyle was unbearable for many of this persuasion. Asked why he backpacked in the wilderness, a young Californian gestured at the city surrounding his apartment and responded, "Because I want to get the hell out of here." Colin Fletcher agreed. "I go to the wilderness," he declared, "to kick the man-world out of me." Actor Steve McQueen said, "I'd rather wake up in the middle of nowhere than in any city on earth."[39] The point was that wilderness trips were escapes from a culture that, in the jargon of the time, "alienated" some of its members. Wild places demanded dependency on self rather than on society. For a junior at Utah State University wilderness meant an opportunity of "confronting yourself with [your] own uniqueness."[40] Under wilderness conditions decisions were simple, vital, personal, and satisfying. "Up there with the trees for four months, I learned my head," one young man offered. For Terry Russell, principal author of the Sierra Club's popular paperback *On the Loose* (1967): "City life is the scary life, inane, tiny and alone. Learn wilderness and you don't fear anything."[41] The enormously popular singer of the early 1970s, John Denver, knew what Russell meant. Articulating one of his generation's most compelling dreams, Denver described in "Rocky Mountain High" (1972) how at the age of twenty-seven he renounced city life to

37. Snyder, *Turtle Island,* p. 106.

38. Gilbert F. Stucker, "Youth Rebellion and the Environment," *National Parks and Conservation Magazine, 45* (1971), 8.

39. Susan Sands, "Backpacking: 'I Go to the Wilderness to Kick the Man-World Out of Me,'" New York *Times,* May 9, 1971, p. 7; McQueen quoted in Terry and Renny Russell, *On the Loose* (San Francisco, 1967), p. 20.

40. Richard F. Carter, "Common Carrier: Give Man Wilderness," *Salt Lake Tribune,* Oct. 17, 1971.

41. Sands, "Backpacking," p. 7; Russell, *On the Loose,* p. 111.

find simplicity, sincerity, and serenity with friends around a campfire high in Colorado. It is significant that Denver's updated back-to-nature philosophy made him the best-selling songmaker in the world in 1973 and 1974. The political crusades of the 1960s had apparently given way to internal quests for personal happiness, and wilderness seemed to many a necessary ingredient. As Gilbert Stucker explained it, wilderness is "a perpetual beginning in which youth . . . finds both substance and symbol."[42]

Along with countercultural unrest, a new-style environmental movement helps explain the vogue of wilderness in modern American thought. In the 1960s and 1970s "environment" and "ecology" became household words. They reveal as much about that time as faith does about the Puritans, efficiency about Progressives, and security about the generation that experienced the Great Depression.

Fear underlay the upswell in what used to be called "conservation," but was increasingly known as "environmentalism." It was not the old fear of running out of resources and losing the competitive edge in international politics that had alarmed the generation of Theodore Roosevelt and Gifford Pinchot. Neither did the fear stem from the prospect of ugliness in the world. The "cosmetic" conservation implicit, for instance, in highway beautification and much of the quality-of-life and quality-of-environment ideas lost momentum rapidly as the 1960s ended. The new driving impulse, based on ecological awareness, transcended concern for the quality of life to fear for life itself. Americans suddenly realized that man is vulnerable. More precisely, they began to see man as part of a larger community of life, dependent for his survival on the survival of the ecosystem and on the health of the total environment. Man, in a word, was rediscovered as being part of nature. The ecological perspective also entailed recognition that civilized man has placed heavy strains on the delicate balances that support life on earth. This, of course, was not a new idea in American environmental history. What was new in the 1960s and 1970s was the volume and intensity of public concern and the tendency to define the issue in ethical rather than economic terms.[43]

42. Stucker, "Youth Rebellion," p. 9.

43. For a review of American conservation history that extends to the 1970s see Roderick Nash, *The American Environment: Readings in Conservation History* (Reading, Ma., 1976).

The reality, but especially the idea, of wilderness played an important role in the new ecology-oriented environmentalism. It was a pointed reminder of man's biological origins, his kinship with all life, and his continued membership in and dependence on the biotic community. We need wilderness, Howard Zahniser reflected, to get away from the technology that gives us the illusion of mastering rather than belonging to the environment. In wilderness, he pointed out, "we sense ourselves to be dependent members of an interdependent community of living creatures that together derive their existence from the sun."[44] Wilderness areas, according to a 1970 observer, were meccas for a "pilgrimage into our species' past." In these "sanctuaries of reorientation" we can "reduce life to the essentials of food and shelter." From this perspective of dependency on the environment came a view of man "as part of the system of nature, not demigods above or outside it."[45]

This idea of a continuous and interrelated web of living things and natural processes, and of man's total dependency on it, characterized the new environmentalism. Wilderness underscored the message. The wild world, according to David Brower, fills man's need for an environment "where he can be reminded that civilization is only a thin veneer over the deep evolutionary flow of things that built him." It is a setting "where we consider our beginnings and our beyondings, where we learn to absorb, and to respect and love and remember."[46] For Edward Abbey, interpreter of the slickrock wilderness of the Southwest, wild country has the power to remind civilized people "that out there is a different world, older and greater and deeper by far than ours, a world which surrounds and sustains the little world of men."[47]

The ecological point of view seemed to be instinctive with contemporary wilderness defenders. William O. Douglas wrote that his contact with wild places helped him to see all living things "as links in a chain of which [man] too is part."[48] In the opinion of

44. Zahniser, "Our Wilderness Need," *Living Wilderness, 20* (1955), [1].

45. F. Bodsworth, "Wilderness Canada: Our Threatened Heritage" in *Wilderness* Canada, ed. Borden Spears (Toronto, 1970), p. 28.

46. Brower in *Gentle Wilderness: The Sierra Nevada,* ed. David Brower (San Francisco, 1967), p. 12; Brower in Eliot Porter, *Summer Island* (San Francisco, 1966), p. 12.

47. Abbey, *Desert Solitaire: A Season in the Wilderness* (New York, 1968), pp. 41–42.

48. Douglas, *My Wilderness: East to Katahdin* (New York, 1961), p. 299.

Douglas Burden, a wilderness experience brings "an awareness that we are part of a great continuum, for within the vast panoply of divergent life lies fundamental unity."[49] And Colin Fletcher, whose descriptions of epic hikes became best sellers in the 1970s, wrote that after being in contact with wilderness "you know deep down in your fabric . . . that you are part of the web of life, and the web of life is part of the rock and air and water of pre-life. You know the wholeness of the universe, the great unity." And as a result of this knowledge, you abandon "the crass assumption that the world was made for man."[50]

The lesson most frequently drawn from both ecology and wilderness was the need for humility on the part of man. Having gained the power to modify nature on a massive scale, man now had to develop the restraint prerequisite to responsible environmental citizenship.[51] This, in turn, depended on extending ethics from man-to-man relationships to those involving man and the environment—the kind of "land ethic" that Aldo Leopold advocated in the 1930s and 1940s.[52] Given the long-established blindness of man to the rights of the nonhuman, this would be neither quick nor easy. Wilderness, however, could help. As Howard Zahniser put it, man's deepest need for wilderness is as an aid in "forsaking human arrogance and courting humility in a respect for the community and with regard for the environment."[53] Barbara Ward and René Dubos, the latter temporarily contradicting his pastoral biases, contended that human beings "may find the wilderness a great teacher of the kind of planetary modesty man most needs if his human order is to survive."[54] Loren Eiseley, the anthropologist, felt that encounters with the wild world helped civilized man develop a badly needed reverence for life and for the idea of life.[55]

An appreciation of the meaning and importance of restraint is another contribution many felt wilderness could make in the quest

49. Burden, *Look to the Wilderness* (Boston, 1956), p. 249.

50. Fletcher, *Complete Walker*, pp. 322, 7.

51. For further development of these ideas, see Roderick Nash, "Can We Afford Wilderness?" in *Environment—Man—Survival*, eds. L. H. Wullstein, I. B. McNulty, and L. Klikoff (Salt Lake City, 1971), pp. 97–111.

52. See above, Chapter 11, especially pp. 195–97.

53. Zahniser, "Our Wilderness Need," p. [1].

54. Ward and Dubos, *Only One Earth: The Care and Maintenance of a Small Planet* (New York, 1972), p. 114.

55. Eiseley, *The Unexpected Universe* (New York, 1969), pp. 86 ff.; also pertinent is Eiseley, *The Invisible Pyramid* (New York, 1970).

for environmental responsibility. Preserving wilderness means establishing limits. We say, in effect, we will go this far, and no farther, for development. We agree to do without the material resources the wilderness might contain. David Brower was fond of saying in the late 1960s that if stopping dams in the Grand Canyon meant economic sacrifice, then the United States should choose to be that much poorer. For Americans, especially, this kind of self-limitation does not come easily. The traditional association of progress and prosperity with growth and development was a major obstacle. In the 1960s environmentalists joined forces with the counterculture in arguing that bigger was not always better. Less could be more. Preserving wilderness became an important symbol of a revolutionary new way of thinking about man's relationship to the earth. It recognized limits and the need for restraint. It acknowledged the rights of nonhuman forms of life. Wilderness seemed to be the best evidence that, in the last analysis, the earth did not belong to man. It helped people see themselves as part of the earth. In this way wilderness spearheaded the shift in direction of the recent American conservation movement, from what Bill Devall calls a "shallow" utilitarianism, to a "deep" nonanthropocentric concern for the entire ecosystem.[56]

Within the favorable context created by the counterculture and the environmental movement, several additional ideas about the value of wilderness today deserve special attention. Few, in fairness, were brand new. Wilderness defenders frequently returned to the concepts of Aldo Leopold, John Muir, and Henry David Thoreau among others. What was new as the end of the twentieth century approached was the realization that the future of wilderness on earth depended as never before on the promulgation of a convincing philosophy.

One cluster of arguments that appears again and again in contemporary defenses of wilderness centers on its importance as a reservoir of normal ecological processes and of a diversity of genetic raw material. Wild places, biologists say, are models of unmodified nature which science can use as criteria against which to measure the changes made by civilization. Following in the intellectual foot-

56. Devall, "Streams of Environmentalism," *Natural Resources Journal*, 20 (1980), 299–322. I have also benefitted from Devall's "Why Wilderness in a Nuclear Age?" (unpublished manuscript, 1982) which discusses several values of wild country as perceived by contemporary thinkers.

steps of Aldo Leopold modern ecologists claim to need wilderness as medical scientists need normal, healthy people. One result of this idea was the United Nations Man and the Biosphere Program (see below, p. 375) which set as its goal in the 1970s the preservation of representative samples of the world's major ecosystems. Especially in the well-populated temperate latitudes, this depended on the designation of wilderness reserves.

Ecology held it axiomatic that wild environments were biologically diverse and that diversity contributed to stability. Wilderness afforded sanctuary to all life, even these varieties man thought useless. As Michael Frome has written, wilderness was "the last home ground of countless species that would otherwise be doomed."[57] Certainly, the species preservation argument could take a very utilitarian slant, and, realistically, it carried the most weight. In *The Sinking Ark* (1979) Norman Myers described the many benefits medicine and agriculture received from allegedly "useless" species that had persisted without man's care, and often without his prior knowledge, in wildernesses.[58]

But Myers, like most contemporary ecologists, believed there was more at stake in the preservation of biotic diversity than mankind's present material interests. The whole evolutionary process seemed to be involved. The argument began with the self-evident proposition that the origin and shaping of life on earth had infinitely much more to do with wilderness than with the controlled order man began to impose on nature with the beginnings of herding and agriculture. "Remember," David Brower told dozens of audiences, "that all the essential creative capability of DNA was shaped in the wilderness, not in civilization." Wilderness was the crucible of evolution. Only in the last tiny fraction of a geological tick of time has man sailed out on the uncertain seas of controlling what once controlled him. End wilderness, Brower explained, and you end a condition responsible for all life, including human life. When we save wilderness, he added, we save "the life force, the

57. Frome, *Battle for the Wilderness* (New York, 1974), p. 63.

58. Myers, *The Sinking Ark: A New Look at the Problem of Disappearing Species* (Oxford, 1979), Chapter 5. Defenses of diversity may also be found in Raymond F. Dasmann, *A Different Kind of Country* (New York, 1968) and in Paul and Anne Ehrlich, *Extinction: The Cause and Consequence of the Disappearance of Species* (New York, 1981). A dramatic discovery of the wild ancestor of corn by Hugh H. Iltis is reported in Noel D. Vietmeyer, "A Wild Relative May Give Corn Perennial Genes," *Smithsonian, 10* (1979), 68–76.

unbroken living chain that extends back to the beginning of life on earth . . . a force that made us possible and that is essential, in its wonderful complexity, to our staying aboard the planet."[59] Perhaps, as René Dubos believed, man could build a better world than nature. Yet, many of his contemporaries were not sure enough of this to sever the biological roots wilderness constituted. The physicist A. J. Rush spoke for them when he wrote: "When man obliterates wilderness, he repudiates the evolutionary force that put him on this planet. In a deeply terrifying sense, man is on his own."[60]

Fears arising from these thoughts frequently centered on the rate of species extinction in the modern world. Biologists calculated that of the approximately ten million species that currently share the planet with *Homo sapiens,* as many as one-fifth could be gone within a century. This represents a rate of extinction thousands of times greater than before the rise of technological civilization. For better or for worse, natural selection was no longer the driving force behind evolution. Man was, and his responsibilities were awesome. The Nature Conservancy thought in terms of depleting "the ecological library"; Brower of tearing pages from "the Creator's great encyclopedia"; Myers of a "sinking ark."[61] But Aldo Leopold, characteristically, may have given the concept its most meaningful form when he told his wildlife ecology students at the University of Wisconsin that the first law of successful tinkering is to save all the parts.[62]

From this perspective wilderness assumed importance as an environment where the full complement of life forms remained intact. Edward O. Wilson, in fact, defined wilderness as a region of biological complexity as opposed to man-modified environments

59. Brower, "Individual Freedom in Public Wilderness," *Not Man Apart, 6* (1976), 2. Brower in Robert Wenkam, *Kauai and the Park Country of Hawaii* (San Francisco, 1967), p. 25.

60. Rush as quoted in *Voices for the Wilderness,* ed. William Schwartz (New York, 1969), p. xvi.

61. The Nature Conservancy, *The Preservation of Natural Diversity: A Survey and Recommendations* (Washington, D.C., 1975), p. 25; Brower, "Individual Freedom," 2; Myers, *Sinking Ark.*

62. Aldo Leopold, "Lecture Notes," Leopold Papers, Box 8. In the Sierra Club—Ballantine edition of *A Sand County Almanac* (New York, 1970), p. 191, Leopold stated the same idea: "To keep every cog and wheel is the first precaution of intelligent tinkering."

like a field of hybridized corn or a cattle feedlot. Wilson reported that a single mountain in South America's undisturbed tropical rainforest supported two hundred *species* of ants. To clear cut such a place for agriculture, he maintained, was to pull apart a biological miracle a billion years in the making.[63] Of course some modification of nature, including species extinction, could be defended on the grounds of legitimate human need. But as the world's population approached five billion, biologists like Wilson wondered if the civilizing process had gone far enough. Again, it was a matter of balance and proportion and of the scarcity value of wilderness which, in Nancy Newhall's words, "holds answers to questions man has not yet learned how to ask."[64] Wilderness, in the final analysis, was thought to keep options open; it seemed a hedge against the human potential to make mistakes.

Another way of defending wilderness emphasized its importance to history. Wild places could be valued as documents, sources of information about the human past. As a "library," wilderness had more than ecological importance; it preserved potential historical knowledge, providing opportunities to know first-hand how most of the people who had ever occupied the planet felt about themselves and their world. Of course, the scarcity value of wilderness plays a role. With most of the temperate latitudes modified by civilization, wilderness areas in those regions were like rare books. Lose them and you risked cultural amnesia.

As a historical document wilderness has meaning to any nation, but Americans claimed an especially intimate relationship to the wild. Following Frederick Jackson Turner and Theodore Roosevelt, philosophers of wilderness have contended that American culture bore the imprint of close and prolonged association with wilderness. In 1935 Thomas Wolfe wrote that America's roots run "back through poverty and hardship, through solitude and loneliness and death and unspeakable courage into the wilderness." The wild, he went on, is the nation's "mother" because "it was in the wilderness that the strange and lonely people who have not yet spoken . . . first knew themselves." For Wolfe the real history of America was "a history of solitude, of the wilderness, and of the

63. Interview with Edward O. Wilson, Brookline, Ma., Jan. 31, 1981. Wilson's studies are published as *The Insect Societies* (Cambridge, Ma., 1971) and *Sociobiology: The New Synthesis* (Cambridge, Ma., 1975).

64. As quoted in *Earth and the Great Weather: The Brooks Range* ed. Kenneth Brower, p. 15.

eternal earth."[65] Gertrude Stein put it another way: "In the United States there is more space where nobody is than where anybody is. That is what makes America what it is."[66] Wolfe and Stein were one in thinking that if there exists a national character, the wilderness explained America's. It also constituted the best place to learn about—and perhaps sustain—what was distinctively American. As Gerard Piel said, "the wilderness was there to recall the dream."[67]

The debt American thought and culture owed to wilderness was noted as early as the 1890s in Turner's "frontier thesis." The lengthening distance from frontier conditions produced new and more eloquent articulations. One of the best was made in 1960 by the novelist and historian Wallace Stegner. He began his statement to the Outdoor Recreation Resources Review Commission with the observation that his argument for wilderness had nothing to do with recreation. What Stegner wanted to discuss was American history and the role of wilderness in it. He understood wilderness to be the essential formative influence because "an American, insofar as he is new and different at all, is a civilized man who has renewed himself in the wild." To lose contact with wilderness, in Stegner's view, was to risk losing what was characteristically American. "Something will have gone out of us as a people," he continued, "if we ever let the remaining wilderness be destroyed." That "something" was the promise of a new start in a new world which, for Stegner, was the essence of the "American dream." What worried Stegner and prompted his 1960 letter was the prospect of losing "the thing that helped to make an American different from, and, until we forget it in the roar of our industrial cities, more fortunate than other men." He urged the commission to recommend keeping the remaining American Wilderness as "a sort of wilderness bank" in which a collective experience—pioneering on a frontier—could be safeguarded. Stegner knew that museums, roadside pioneer villages, and frontierlands were sorry substitutes for the opportunity of knowing wilderness first hand.[68]

65. Wolfe, *Of Time and the River* (New York, 1935), as quoted in Roderick Nash, "American Space" in Smithsonian Exposition Books, *The American Land* (New York, 1979), p. 48.

66. Gertrude Stein, *The Geographical History of America* (New York, 1936), pp. 17–18.

67. Piel in *Wilderness: America's Living Heritage,* ed. David Brower (San Francisco, 1961), p. 30.

68. Stegner, *The Sound of Mountain Water* (Garden City, N.Y., 1969), pp. 146, 148.

Mark Sagoff, a philosopher and lawyer, took Stegner's argument a step further; in 1974 he proposed a nonutilitarian rationale for preserving wilderness based on its importance as a central symbol of American nationality. According to Sagoff the obligation to preserve nature is an obligation "to our cultural tradition . . . to our national values, to our history, and, therefore, to ourselves." He contends that a legal and political "right" is at stake. Just as he has a right to vote, every citizen has "a right to participate in the *culture* of the nation." This "right of our citizens to their history, to the signs and symbols of their culture" makes preserving wilderness as necessary to American nationhood as maintaining institutions such as trial by jury and public education. Take away wilderness and you take away the opportunity to be American.[69]

A related line of thinking about the historical value of wilderness stressed its special relationship to human freedom. Stegner expressed the relationship when he described wild country as "a part of the geography of hope."[70] The Puritans understood this when they found in the wild New World a sanctuary in which to worship as they pleased. When Roger Williams dissented from the Puritan oligarchy, he too headed for the wilderness of Naragansett Bay, later Rhode Island. In the 1840s the Mormons also found freedom in wilderness, and so did some countercultural communities in the 1960s.

While ecologists recognized the contribution of wilderness to biotic diversity, social scientists and humanists underscored its importance in maintaining intellectual diversity. Wilderness, by definition, is the uncontrolled and unorganized—the antipode of civilization. As such it is fertile ground for deviancy, eccentricity, and idiosyncrasy in the positive sense of those terms. Raymond Dasmann called wilderness areas "reservoirs of freedom," and he meant that without them "there would be no place left for that last wild thing, the free human spirit."[71] Joseph Wood Krutch agreed, writing that "the wilderness and the idea of wilderness is one of the permanent homes of the human spirit."[72] Thoreau, of course, was an important precursor of this line of thinking, as was Aldo Leopold, whose aphorism, "of what avail are forty freedoms

69. Sagoff, "On Preserving the Natural Environment," *Yale Law Journal, 84* (1974), 264–67.

70. Stegner, *Mountain Water*, p. 153.

71. Dasmann, *The Destruction of California* (New York, 1966), pp. 197, 199.

without a blank space on the map" (see above, p. 189), became a common quote in contemporary wilderness philosophy.

Implicit in many defenses of wilderness as a free and unstructured environment lay fear of the kind of totalitarian society of the future described in George Orwell's *Nineteen Eighty-four* (1949) and Aldous Huxley's *Brave New World* (1932). "When we think of the book *1984*," Sigurd Olson noted, ". . . we realize that we are in danger of losing the spiritual values which have been part of us."[73] He was well aware that the rulers of Orwell's futuristic police-state abolished wilderness because they knew it supported freedom of thought and action. This importance of wilderness preservation transcends mere recreation. Evidence comes from the fact that rebelling guerrilla bands still head for the hills. Without them the possibility, and even the idea, of resistance loses considerable meaning. Supreme Court Justice William O. Douglas felt that with the wilderness gone man would more easily become an "automaton." Consequently, "roadless areas are one pledge of freedom." Edward Abbey offered "political reasons" for keeping places like the Grand Canyon and the High Sierras wild. He saw them as "a refuge from authoritarian government, from political oppression [and] . . . as a base for resistance to centralized domination."[74] Wallace Stegner put this idea succinctly: "Without any remaining wilderness we are committed wholly, without change for even momentary reflection and rest, to a headlong drive into our technological termite-life, the Brave New World of a completely man-controlled environment."[75] Gary Snyder entertained a similar fear when he observed that "there is not much wilderness left to destroy, and the nature in the mind is being logged and burned off."[76]

The concept of creativity became the point of departure for yet another recent exploration of the value of wilderness in modern

72. Krutch, *Grand Canyon,* p. 275.

73. Olson in *Wilderness: America's Living Heritage,* ed. David Brower, pp. 138–39. Compare Olson's remarks entitled "The Spiritual Aspect of Wilderness" in *The High Sierra,* ed. Ezra Bowers (New York, 1972), p. 156.

74. Douglas, *My Wilderness: The Pacific West,* p. 101. As a jurist and a lifelong champion of both wild country and liberal causes, Douglas's defense of wilderness as a bulwark of freedom carried special weight. His *A Wilderness Bill of Rights* (Boston, 1965) was widely read and cited; Abbey, *Desert Solitaire,* p. 149.

75. Stegner, *Mountain Water,* p. 147.

76. Snyder, *The Back Country* (London, 1967), dustjacket.

civilization. On one level there were reiterations of the thesis of nineteenth-century cultural nationalists that great nature inspired great art and literature.[77] For modern illustrations, defenders of wilderness offered the music of John Denver, the essays of Edward Abbey, the photography of Ansel Adams and Eliot Porter, and the poetry of Gary Snyder, which won the Pulitzer Prize in 1975. But some thinkers wondered if, on a deeper level, there might be a link between wilderness and the creative process. Thoreau, once again, started this inquiry when he referred to wilderness as the "raw-material of life" (see above, p. 88). Aldo Leopold understood the entire history of human thought as consisting of "successive excursions from a single starting-point" which was the "raw wilderness" (see above, p. 199). Edward Abbey developed this idea in *Desert Solitaire* (1968) when he observed that in wild country we "confront, immediately and directly, . . . the bare bones of existence, the elemental and fundamental."[78]

If the springs of artistic and intellectual creativity depend on fresh penetrations to and interpretations of this elemental reality, so the argument runs, then wilderness is vital to fresh thinking. It makes possible what Emerson referred to as an original relationship to the universe. The alternative is synthesis derived from synthesis. Or, as the Russell brothers put it in 1967, "After the first Artist / Only the copyist." Discovery, this implies, demands the unknown, the unmodified, the wild.[79] It is no accident that characterizations of scholarship like "pathfinding," "trailblazing," and "pioneering" originated in a wilderness context. In the absence of wilderness, creativity might not disappear but it would, at least, take different directions.

77. Chapter 4, above, treats this relationship. More recent investigations of the dependency of American art on the wild American environment may be found in J. Gray Sweeney, *Themes in American Painting* (Grand Rapids, Mi., 1977); Barbara Novak, *Nature and Culture: American Landscape and Painting, 1825–1875* (New York, 1980); and John Wilmerding, ed., *American Light: The Luminist Movement, 1850–1875* (New York, 1980).

78. Abbey, *Desert Solitaire*, p. 6.

79. Russell and Russell, *On the Loose*, p. 71. John G. Mitchell has asked important questions about the human intellectual and emotional need for the uncertainty of wildness in "Why We Need Our Monsters," *National Wildlife, 16* (1978), 12–15. Another illuminating analysis is J. R. L. Anderson, *The Ulysses Factor: The Exploring Instinct in Man* (New York, 1977). Anderson, a solo-oceanic sailor, argues that throughout human evolution wild places elicited the creative qualities necessary for the survival and progress of the race.

The contributions that the wilderness experience could make to mental health provided preservationists with another line of argument. Sigmund Freud laid the foundation with his work on the repressive effects of civilization. The Minnesota guide, Sigurd Olson, gave substance to Freud's theories with his accounts of the effect of wilderness canoe trips on himself and his clients. He came to understand that millions of years of wilderness living left marks on the human psyche that the relatively short history of civilization had not erased. Psychologically, man is "still attuned to woods and fields and waters." He has come "a long way from the primitive, but not far enough to forget." As a consequence of this background of racial experience, civilized man actually misses contact with the wild world. Deprived of the physical challenge of surviving through his own abilities, he feels frustrated, unhappy, and vaguely repressed. As a corrective measure some people seek the wilderness "once a month or once a year as a sick man might go to his physician." In wild country they slip back into the ancient grooves and regain perspective, which Olson defined as simplicity, serenity, and "the longtime point of view so often lost in the towns." Wilderness outings permit a temporary exchange of the artificial for the natural; a way of finding a "spiritual backlog in the high speed mechanical world in which we live." Civilized people, Olson concluded, "will aways be drawn to the last frontiers, where they can recapture some of the basic satisfactions and joys of the race."[80] He described how, time and again, he saw listless, almost desperate, city people made whole and happy in the course of a wilderness trip. Such experiences, Olson came to feel, were not merely vacations but psychological holidays essential to healthy minds.

Professional psychologists and psychiatrists have begun to supply clinical evidence in support of Olson's feelings. Two different, but not necessarily contradictory, theories emerged. One emphasized the ability of a wilderness experience to simplify and slow down lives made overly complicated by civilization. In wild country people could find relief from noise, stress, and, especially, from the

80. Olson "Why Wilderness?," *American Forests, 44* (1938), 396 and "We Need Wilderness," *National Parks Magazine, 84* (1946), 19, 20–21, 28. More recent statements of Olson's philosophy are: "The Meaning of Wilderness for Modern Man," *Carleton Miscellany, 3* (1962), 99–113; "The Spiritual Need" in *Wilderness in a Changing World,* ed. Bruce M. Kilgore (San Francisco, 1966), pp. 212–19; and Olson, *Listening Point.* A recent summation of Olson's ideas is found in his *Reflections From the North Country* (New York, 1970).

presence of too many other people. Solitude was said to be a great healer. "The parklands of America," neurologist William C. Gibson told a Sierra Club conference, "are the greatest mental health guardians we have."[81] On purely economic criteria, several psychiatrists observed, one wilderness area might save society the cost of several mental health hospitals. Indeed the phrase "wilderness therapy" came to have increasing prominence in mental health literature of the 1970s.[82]

For some psychologists, stress was the enemy, whereas its use, in moderation and in wilderness contexts, seemed to others to be the key to recuperation. It was believed that the complexity of civilization overwhelmed some individuals, rendering them helpless and afraid. But a wilderness challenge—even one as simple as carrying a pack and following a trail—required self-sufficiency and could generate self-confidence. Many recognized that the single most vital component of mental health was to devise reasonable challenges for an individual. Outward Bound's wilderness courses featured a succession of activities that demanded just a little more of students than they thought themselves capable of doing. Some Outward Bound programs included a "solo." For three days, and with a minimum of equipment and food, students coped with the wilderness and with themselves. Outward Bound president Hank Taft thought of the "solo" as less a survival exercise and more an "experience in self-consideration and contemplation."[83] Students

81. William C. Gibson, "Wilderness—A Psychiatric Necessity" in Kilgore, ed., *Wilderness in a Changing World,* p. 228. See also Donald McKinley, "A Psychiatrist Examines Wilderness's Worth" in *Crisis in Wilderness, Proceedings of the Fifth Biennial Conference on Northwest Wilderness,* ed. J. Michael McCloskey (Portland, Or., 1965), pp. 13–17 and J. Berkeley Gordon, "Psychiatric Values of the Wilderness," *Welfare Reporter, 6* (1952), 3–4, 15, 16.

82. A bibliography for this growing field may be found in *Wilderness Psychology Newsletter,* n.v. (Feb., 1979). Key articles are A. Bernstein, "Wilderness as a Therapeutic Behavior Setting," *Therapeutic Recreation Journal, 6* (1972), 160–161, 185; Andrew L. Turner, "The Therapeutic Value of Nature," *Journal of Operational Psychiatry, 12* (1976), 64–74; and an unpublished paper by Eric S. Gebelein, "The Curative Potential of the Wilderness Experience," delivered at the Wilderness Psychology Symposium of the American Psychological Association, Aug., 1977.

83. Taft as quoted in Phil Patton, "Outward Bound—Again," *Mainliner* (Sept., 1981), 65. For more on Outward Bound's program see Kristi Kistler et. al., "Outward Bound: Providing a Therapeutic Experience for Troubled Adolescents," *Hospital and Community Psychiatry, 28* (1977), 807, 812 and Joseph Nold and Mary Wilpers, "Wilderness Training as an Alternative to Incarceration" in *A Nation Without Prisons,* ed. Calvert R. Dodge (Lexington, Ma., 1975).

returned to civilization better able to cope with their problems. For some people at least taking risks and responding to challenges in wilderness situations were principal ingredients of health and happiness. As reported in a leading journal of wilderness adventure, Dr. Sol R. Rosenthal conducted empirical studies on the effect of risk and concluded that "risk exercise" was a valuable tool for preventative medicine.[84]

On a more philosophical level, this value of wilderness is thought to stem from its ability to strip away the securities of civilization that normally intervene between humans and elemental challenges. One of civilization's supreme ironies concerns the elimination of challenges, including fear, hardship, and pain, that merely surviving in the precivilized world entailed. For thousands of years after our race opted for a civilized existence, we dreamed of and labored toward an escape from the anxieties of a wilderness condition only to find, when we reached the promised land of supermarkets and air conditioners, that we had forfeited something of great value. In wild places, surrounded by what is uncontrolled, modern man can once again cope with the old uncontrived challenges. Some people need this for complex psychological reasons. "It must be [a] poor life," Aldo Leopold remarked after a lightning bolt narrowly missed him on a New Mexico ridgetop, "that achieves freedom from fear." From his point of view, "too much safety seems to yield only danger in the long run."[85] J. R. L. Anderson explored this point in 1977 in *The Ulysses Factor,* reasoning that danger and fear were the energizing forces of evolution long before financial success and social status entered the picture. In *Desert Solitaire,* Edward Abbey also spoke for those who required the "taste of danger" in their lives and went to the toughest, wildest country to find it.

One of the most ambitious experiments in wilderness therapy occurred in 1972 when Dr. Dean Brooks of the Oregon State Hospital arranged a two-week wilderness trip for fifty-one chronic mental patients. "We haven't picked the easiest cases," Brooks noted at the outset. There were schizophrenics, sex offenders, and narcotic addicts, some of whom had been hospitalized for more than ten years. Lute Jerstad, the Mount Everest climber, arranged

84. William Barry Furlong, "Doctor Danger," *Outside,* 5 (1980–81), 40–42, 92–96.

85. Leopold, *A Sand County Almanac* (New York, 1949), pp. 126, 133.

a combination of backpacking, river rafting, and rock climbing for the group. The idea was to offer opportunities for physical achievement and pride to people who, in Brooks's words, were "drained of self-confidence and respect through the dehumanization and depersonalization that inevitably creep into every social institution." The hospital hoped that in wilderness situations the patients would feel comfortable about releasing their "back stage" personalities and simply being themselves. The results exceeded expectations. Asked why she was crying after completing a four-day hike with a forty-pound pack, one woman said, "It's the best I've ever done." Another patient touched the ground after a difficult rappel down a cliff face and exclaimed, "If I can do this, I can solve my own problems." A motion picture record of every participant was made so that these moments of achievement could be relived back at the hospital. But for more than half the allegedly hopeless group there was no more hospital. And many of the remaining patients seemed markedly improved.[86]

The concept of wilderness as a church, as a place to find and worship God, helped launch the intellectual revolution that led to wilderness appreciation. The logic was that if nature embodies moral law and spiritual truth, then wild nature provides the most direct link to the deity. Thoreau and Emerson absorbed this axiom from European romantics and Asian mystics, and Muir brought it into the American West. His trips into the Sierra Nevada became acts of worship.

In the last several decades the course of American thought on the subject of wilderness and religion has swung away from a direct linking of God and wilderness. As early as 1913, when John Muir was still characterizing trees as "psalm-singing," George Santayana commented that "primeval solitudes . . . teach no transcendental logic . . . and give no sign of any deliberate morality seated in the world."[87] Robert Frost, Wallace Stevens, and Robinson Jeffers were among later writers who agreed that wild places were inscrutable,

86. Margaret C. McDonald, "Adventure Camping at Oregon State Hospital" in *Camping Therapy: Its Uses in Psychiatry and Rehabilitation,* ed. Thomas Power Lowry (Springfield, Ill., 1974), pp. 17, 19, 22, 30. The Oregon experiment is also discussed in McDonald's "Hospital Patients and Staff Share a Wilderness Trip in Oregon," *Psychiatric News,* 7 (Sept. 20, Oct. 4, and Oct. 18, 1972), n.pag. and in "Roughing It Back Toward Sanity," *Life,* 72 (1972), 60–69.

87. Santayana, *Winds of Doctrine* (New York, 1913), pp. 213–14.

inhuman, and indifferent.[88] From this perspective the association of God and wilderness was just as much a myth—as much an anthropomorphic fallacy—as the earlier tendency to link wilderness and evil. The wilderness, modern philosophers tended to believe, was neither moral nor immoral, but amoral. It might still, of course, be sacred in the sense of inspiring reverence and providing meaning.[89] What is new is that these emotions are based, to a much greater extent than ever before, on what wilderness was rather than on what human beings feared or hoped it might be. Wilderness could be sacred but in its own right and not as sign or symbol of some overarching divinity.

So it is that Edward Abbey can call wilderness "paradise" but quickly explain that he does not mean "the banal Heaven of the saints . . . a garden of bliss and changeless perfection." Abbey's paradise was the "real earth" and particularly the desert which he characterized as "spare, sparse, austere, utterly worthless, inviting not love but contemplation." Abbey never reported finding evidence of God in the desert. What he found was "a dangerous and terrible place . . . of rock and heat, sand dunes and quicksand, cactus, thornbush, scorpion and rattlesnake." Repeatedly he warned nature lovers and God seekers to stay away. "The desert," he made clear, "says nothing." But for those who might persist in their desire to visit this "fearsome land," he offered succinct advice: "Enter at your own risk. Carry water. Avoid the noonday sun. Try to ignore the vultures."[90]

Why, then, go to the desert, or any wilderness? Abbey offered an answer in 1977 in the form of an account of a hike in northern Arizona. Scrambling up a canyon wall to a mesa, he reached a

88. For analyses of these and other thinkers who turned to wilderness for inspiration, see Wilson O. Clough, *The Necessary Earth: Nature and Solitude in American Literature* (Austin, 1964), pp. 143 ff. A suggestive analysis of Frost in James P. Dougherty, "Robert Frost's 'Directive' to the Wilderness," *American Quarterly, 18* (1966), 208–19.

89. I have benefitted here from Linda H. Graber's *Wilderness as Sacred Space,* "Monograph Series of the Association of American Geographers, No. 8" (Washington, D.C., 1976). Graber defines wilderness as the "Wholly Other," sacred because of and not despite its antipodal relation to man and his ideas. The "sacred power" of wilderness, Graber concludes, has nothing to do with churches and traditional faiths.

90. Abbey, *Desert Solitaire,* pp. 190, 270 and *The Journey Home* (New York, 1977), p. 87.

point he supposed no one had ever visited before. "But someone had. Near the summit I found an arrow sign, three feet long, formed of stones and pointing off into the north." Looking that way, even with field glasses, revealed only "more canyons, more mesas and plateaus, more mountains, more cloud-dappled sun-spangled leagues of desert sand and desert rock." A walk in the direction the arrow pointed led to a sheer cliff; Abbey returned to the arrow. He concluded "there was nothing out there. Nothing at all. Nothing but the desert. Nothing but the silent world." And then it struck him: "That's why."[91] In pointing at nothing, the arrow on the mesa in fact pointed at something of great value. It had to do with emptiness and otherness and the way that wilderness was the antipode of civilization and all its myths, including those concerning wilderness. If this was a religious value, as Abbey implied, it differed greatly from the simple, if sincere pantheism of a John Muir.

Finally some preservationists have attempted to defend wilderness based on nonanthropocentric reasons. They have argued that wilderness has a right to exist for its own sake, independent of whether mankind values it or not. One root of this idea is the so-called process philosophy of Alfred North Whitehead. Everything in the world, Whitehead suggests, is meaningful in the total scheme of things regardless of its usefulness to any other component.[92] There are several problems with this approach to defending wilderness. For one thing, as explained earlier, wilderness is an entirely human concept, an invention of civilized man. Objects that compose a wilderness, such as wild animals, virgin forests, even rivers, might be thought of as having rights to exist independent of man's interests, but it is difficult to use the same logic for a concept that exists solely in the human mind.

91. Abbey, *Journey Home,* pp. 21–22. A perceptive analysis of Abbey's work is Peter Wild's *Pioneer Conservationists of Western America* (Missoula, Mt., 1979), Chapter 16 and also Garth McCann, *Edward Abbey* (Boise, Id., 1977).

92. Whitehead's relevant works are *The Concept of Nature* (Cambridge, Eng., 1920) and *Process and Reality* (Cambridge, Eng., 1929). More recent statements of the rights of nature independent of human interests are John Rodman, "The Liberation of Nature?," *Inquiry, 20* (1977), 83–145, and Kenneth H. Simonsen, "The Value of Wildness," *Environmental Ethics, 3* (1981), 259–63. Also insightful is Thomas H. Birch, "Man the Beneficiary: A Planetary Perspective on the Logic of Wilderness Preservation" in *International Dimensions of the Environmental Crisis,* ed. Richard Barret (Boulder, Co., 1982).

Other philosophers offer a related objection.[93] Wilderness, they contend, is not a sensate being with definable interests and thus capable of being injured or benefitted. Consequently, it can not have rights as we commonly understand that term. Injury to wilderness is best understood as injury to people who value wilderness. The rights of those people are really at issue. For instance, when William O. Douglas set forth a "wilderness bill of rights" in 1965 he was really thinking about the right of people to experience wilderness. Similarly, in the 1972 litigation concerning a ski development in California's Mineral King Valley, Supreme Court Justice Douglas wrote an opinion stating that the valley, and any wilderness, had a right to legal standing in courts. But he could think of no way to proceed from this premise other than to say that people who have an "intimate relation with the inanimate object about to be injured . . . are its legitimate spokesmen."[94] It was not clear in the balance whether the valley, or the people who loved it, had the standing. And since a natural object had no way to represent itself, since human spokesmen were always necessary, the line between the rights of nature and the rights of people appeared fine indeed.

Giving rights to wilderness is an appealing idea which has proven useful in recruiting supporters for wilderness preservation. But in the political and legal arenas where the future of wilderness is shaped, it makes a minimal contribution to a philosophy of wilderness. The most effective defenses of wildness seem to be rooted squarely in the needs and interests of civilized people. The essential premise is that wilderness and civilization are no longer in an adversary relationship. Modern civilization, it is said, needs wilderness, and if wilderness is to exist it surely needs the protection of a self-restraining civilization.

93. For example, Joel Feinberg, "The Rights of Animals and Unborn Generations" in *Philosophy and Environmental Crisis,* ed. William Blackstone (Athens, Ga., 1974), pp. 43–67 and Scott Lehmann, "Do Wildernesses Have Rights?," *Environmental Ethics, 3* (1981), 129–46. The issue is further explored in Roderick Nash, "Do Rocks Have Rights?," *Center Magazine, 10* (1977), 2–12.

94. As quoted in Christopher D. Stone, *Should Trees Have Standing?: Toward Legal Rights for Natural Objects* (Los Altos, Ca., 1974), p. 76.

CHAPTER 14

Alaska

> To the lover of pure wildness Alaska is one of the most wonderful countries in the world.
>
> John Muir, 1879

> For God's sake, don't tell people where *you* went. Don't make it one of those how-to-do-it, where-to-go tourist guides.... The idea of wilderness in Gates of the Arctic should be fundamentally different than what we call wilderness in the Lower 48.
>
> Anonymous Alaskan guide to Michael Rogers, 1979

On December 2, 1980, President Jimmy Carter consummated the greatest single act of wilderness preservation in world history. In signing the Alaska National Interest Lands Conservation Act, Carter protected 104 million acres of federal land, or 28 percent of the state, an area larger than California. Of this total the National Wilderness Preservation System received 56 million acres which more than tripled its size. The National Park Service doubled the area it administered. The now famous, or notorious, "d(2)" clause of Section 17 of the Alaska Native Claims Settlement Act of 1971 created this opportunity for the federal government to designate "national interest" lands and opened a decade-long debate. Substantial portions of it did not concern wilderness but rather issues such as native rights, the meaning of Alaskan statehood and subsistence lifestyles. But the future of Alaska's enormous wilderness was never far from the center of public discussion. It was said, continually, that Alaska was America's last frontier. Some hoped this meant opportunity for settlement and development as had been the rule on earlier American frontiers. Others relished the idea of Alaska as a permanent frontier where Americans could visit their past both in person and as an idea. "Armchair" tourists, intellectual importers of Alaska's wilderness, were among the most vocal in defending land they never expected to see. They said that Alaska represented the nation's last chance to do things right the first time. Most Alaskans, on the other hand, were suspicious of the rules and restrictions associated with wilderness preservation. They might like living near wild country, but they decidedly did not like the thought of a federally managed wilderness system. Their resistance to d(2) designations set the stage for nearly ten years of intense and revealing controversy.

Writing in 1977, Robert Jones of the Los Angeles *Times* reacted to the contention that Alaska was too big, too isolated, and too rugged to ever be spoiled by tourism. "I can only think," he wrote, "that that's exactly what was said about Yellowstone when it was created."[1] The remark invites a comparison of the American West of the late nineteenth century and the American North a hundred years later. At both times these parts of North America were largely wilderness; indeed, white eyes had not seen much of the land. In 1869 John Wesley Powell floated a thousand miles down the Colorado River through largely unexplored canyons. Exercising the explorer's prerogative, he named the geographical features he saw. Sixty years later Robert Marshall did the same in Alaska's Brooks Range. When Montana became a state in 1889, civilization existed as tiny specks and thin strings along railways and a few roads. The matrix was wild; civilization, not wilderness, was fragile. When Alaska gained statehood in 1959 the same held true. Although definitions differed, more than ninety-five percent of the state could be called wilderness. The total white population in an area twice the size of Texas was under 150,000.

This situation gave rise in both the West and the North to pioneer opinions of wilderness just as it had in Massachusetts in the 1620s and Michigan in the 1820s. The scarcity theory of value favored civilization. Wilderness was the threat, not the threatened. Walter J. Hickel, governor of Alaska in the late 1960s, had a clear sense of this relationship and the priorities it engendered: "The cold can kill you. The tundra can kill you. The beautiful sky can kill you. . . . It's tough up here. This country can kill you. . . . So the light you want to see, the finest light you can possibly see, is that first glimmer from a Coleman lantern in somebody's cabin." Substitute a candle for a Coleman lantern, and many felt the same way a century before in Colorado or Idaho. Wilderness preserva-

1. Jones, "Alaska: Hidden Land to Most Americans," Los Angeles *Times*, Sept. 5, 1977, pt. 1, p. 3.

tion simply did not make much sense to pioneers. They tended to be much more concerned about preserving themselves. The change in attitude of other Americans mystified them. Hickel overheard a statement in 1970 in an Anchorage bar: "Two years ago it was the hostile frozen North. Now all of a sudden it's the goddamned delicate tundra."[2]

Yet the United States' northern frontier, and the way modern Americans think about it, is unique in several important respects:

1. *Environment.* From the perspective of settlers in the seventeenth century, Maryland was big, wild, rugged land. So was Kentucky and, later, Kansas. But Alaska represents inhospitable environmental qualities in extremes unprecedented in previous American experience. University of Alaska biologist Robert Weeden points out that half of Alaska is treeless, and where trees do grow, apart from the narrow southeastern panhandle, they do so very slowly. The growing season is only forty-five to ninety days. In the Brooks Range Robert Marshall found knee-high spruce over a century old. Timberline in Alaska tends to be a function of latitude and not altitude as is the case in, say, California's Sierra Nevada. On the treeless tundra, shrubs and grasses do all their annual growing in about three weeks. In 85 percent of Alaska living things, man included, must contend with permanently frozen ground called permafrost. Beneath the few inches of soil that melts briefly in the summer there can be a half mile of ice. Traditional forms of construction are impossible. And of a total of 376 million acres in Alaska only 20 million are considered fit for agriculture and grazing.[3]

While Alaska is reputed to be a paradise for hunters and fishermen, its per-acre productivity of fish and game is far less than, for example, Oregon's. Actually, the relative scarcity of sportsmen, not the abundance of game, explains the reputation. As an old prospector told Weeden, "It's a hungry country."[4]

Added to these biological realities are Alaska's formidable weather and seasons. North of sixty degrees latitude the sun does not shine

2. As quoted in Jack Hope, "The Question of Alaska" in Smithsonian Exposition Books, *The American Land* (New York, 1979), p. 252; Hickel, *Who Owns America?* (Englewood Cliffs, N.J., 1971), p. 124.

3. Weeden, *Alaska: Promises to Keep* (Boston, 1978), Chapter 3; also useful is Orlando Miller, *The Frontier in Alaska and the Matanuska Colony* (New Haven, Conn., 1975).

4. Weeden, *Alaska,* p. 45.

at all in the heart of the winter, and temperatures of minus forty degrees are routine in all interior locations for months at a time. Alaska is unquestionably less subject to human control and modification, and in this sense wilder, than the rest of the United States. Americans can irrigate their southwestern deserts and thereby nourish cities like Phoenix and San Diego each of which had in 1980 a greater population than all of Alaska. The far North resists this kind of development.

One consequence is heightened determination, most common among "boomer" Alaskans, to conquer the last frontier—to make the hard land bend to allegedly harder superpioneers. The 1977 completion of the Trans-Alaska Pipeline through the heart of the hardest and hungriest country strengthened this point of view. Another consequence is impatience with people, especially "outsiders," who regard Alaska as endangered. "Anybody who says the ecology is fragile is an ignoramus or a goddamn liar," shouts Joe Vogler of the Alaskan Independence Party. In his view the wilderness ecosystems of Alaska need no legislative protection. "Our climate protects the ecology," he continues, "our geography protects it." And then the hard-land hard-men concept: "It's a struggle up here, all the way! . . . Our country has a way of weeding out the weak!"[5]

Another reaction to the extraordinary wildness of the Alaskan environment comes mainly from non-Alaskans. John Muir started a tradition in 1879 by characterizing Alaska's wilderness as "pure," subsequent tourists used adjectives such as "absolute" and "ultimate." The words "nameless," "trackless," and "unknown" figure repeatedly in descriptive prose, and they are meant to be laudatory. The image of Alaska that emerges from the accounts of recreation-seekers and environmentalists is that of a wilderness mecca, a qualitatively wilder country than any that exists or, perhaps, ever existed in the lower forty-eight states.

2. *Technology.* The flowering of the industrial revolution created another difference between the western and northern American frontiers. When the West was settled the nation's technological capabilities were modest. Horsepower and manpower chipped away at wilderness conditions—slowly. But by 1959 when statehood opened the doors to the development of Alaska, science and technology were ready to condense time. What required a

5. As quoted in Hope, "The Question of Alaska," p. 253.

decade in the West could be done in a few months in the North. The Trans-Alaska Pipeline is a good example of something completely beyond the technological capabilities of the mid-nineteenth century. The same could be said about huge hydropower dams such as the one proposed for Rampart Canyon on the Yukon River. The Old West did not even dream in these terms, but powered by modern technology dreams could become realities in Alaska.

No technology is more important in Alaska than that associated with aviation. The bush plane is Alaska's covered wagon. Helicopters have replaced horses. Air travel has, in effect, condensed distance in the forty-ninth state. In terms of time and trouble required to traverse wilderness, it is arguable that Alaska in 1972 was smaller than Yellowstone National Park at the time of its creation a century before. The congregation of thirty hydroplanes at a favored salmon lake 200 miles from the nearest road illustrates the point. Alaska may be the wildest country an expanding United States encountered, but the availability of technology made its wilderness more vulnerable. For a time in the history of the West, lack of technology held in check human desire to modify the land. Wilderness was the beneficiary. But when Alaska took its turn as the final American frontier, technological progress had largely removed these restraints.

3. *Natives.* Over the course of three centuries the Indians of the contiguous forty-eight states lost their land, their political rights, their cultural existence, and often their lives. The forced removal of natives from the land that became the United States amounted to one of the greatest quantitative displacements of one people by another in world history.[6] But in Alaska no such systematic extinguishing of native interests occurred. The Eskimos and Indians of the northern frontier were never fought, hence never conquered, and never made to sign treaties relinquishing their rights to the land. The natives were simply ignored for a century after the United States' 1867 purchase of Russia's interest in Alaska. So it was that when the oil strikes of the 1960s made clarification of land titles in Alaska imperative, the natives spoke for their rights and the federal government hurriedly prepared to deal for the first time

6. Wilbur R. Jacobs, *Dispossessing the American Indian* (New York, 1972) and "The Indian and the Frontier in American History—A Need for Revision," *Western Historical Quarterly, 4* (1973), 43–56, are instructive on this point.

with native land claims that were very much intact. Adding to the pressure was the fact that the 1960s was a time of widespread liberal support of minority interests. In the context of the burgeoning black civil rights movement, it was impossible to follow the only-good-Indian-is-a-dead-Indian formula that had cleared the western frontier of natives and native claims.

The government's response to this situation was the Alaska Native Claims Settlement Act (ANCSA) of December 18, 1971. With a degree of generosity unprecedented in American history, it allowed Alaskan natives to choose forty-four million acres of federal land for outright ownership, awarded them a billion dollars, and established a series of native-run regional and village corporations to manage and promote native lifestyles. As inconceivable in the America of Andrew Jackson or Ulysses S. Grant as such legislation was, times and ideas had changed. John McPhee called ANCSA an attempt to make a "great, final and retributive payment" in compensation for "twenty decades of national guilt."[7]

In regard to the wilderness issue federal recognition of native rights created a situation in Alaska markedly different from that which had obtained in the rest of the nation. From the natives' perspective the whole concept of wilderness was a curious, white myth that ignored history.[8] Tony Vaska, an Eskimo from the Bering coast, phrased the issue succinctly: white people, he pointed out, "think there's nothing out there. They are only vaguely aware that our people are already there, using the land for hunting and fishing and trapping, as we have for 15,000 years. . . . They think the native people and our lifestyle are part of the nothingness of the frontier. . . ."[9] Those "nameless" valleys and that "unknown" country had been habitat and home territory. As anthropologist William Brown recognized, the whole concept of wilderness in Alaska is "ethnocentric to the point of being insulting."[10] Understandably, natives consistently avoided the word "wilderness," preferring

7. McPhee, *Coming Into the Country* (New York, 1977), p. 145.

8. As noted in the Preface (see above, p. xiii), Chief Standing Bear made this point in reference to his homeland on the Great Plains.

9. As quoted in Hope, "The Question of Alaska," p. 259.

10. Interview with William Brown, National Park Service, Anchorage, Alaska, Aug. 26, 1980. See also Arctic Environmental Information and Data Center, *Nuiqsut Heritage: A Cultural Plan* (Anchorage, 1979) and North Slope Borough Contract Staff, *Native Livelihood and Dependence: A Study of Land Use Values Through Time* (Anchorage, 1979), pp. 3–46.

"land." They also insisted that any federal reserves created under ANCSA's d(2) clause be open to natives who wished to live off the land by hunting and gathering (the so-called subsistence lifestyle). Tony Vaska explained that he favored protecting land in parks and reserves "for all its usual values—aesthetic, recreational, wildlife—and to those values or systems that the land supports, I would add, *people*."[11] Willie Hensley, the Eskimo rights leader who sat in the Alaska House of Representatives, agreed. If what the white man called "wilderness" could be used for subsistence purposes, he had no problem with preservation. Better a park than, say, a mine with its network of roads and its armies of white sportsmen competing with the natives for a limited amount of game. But Hensley had serious doubts about the perspective of some preservationists. "The environmentalists—the posey sniffers from the Dartmouth Outing Club—come up here and talk about the flora and the fauna and the scenery and never mention the people. Us! They act like *we* are the violators here."[12]

Given the climate of opinion of the 1970s respecting native rights, it was probable that the Alaska National Interest Lands Conservation Act of 1980 would respect feelings like Vaska's and Hensley's and permit subsistence activities even in designated wildernesses. When this happened, another break with the precedent of the nineteenth-century West occurred. No Indians hunt or fish or gather in Yosemite or Yellowstone national parks or in wilderness areas under the jurisdiction of the Forest Service. Western Indians live on reservations assigned them by the federal government, but in Alaska, where the reservation concept finally died, native economic use was incorporated with wilderness preservation.

4. *Wilderness.* Settlement of the American West occurred a century before the intellectual and political ripening of the wilderness movement. The debate over land use policy in Alaska, on the other hand, took place right in the middle of the greatest wave of conservation enthusiasm in American history. Appreciation of wilderness was at its zenith. A well-developed philosophy, detailed in Chapter 13, was available to provide ammunition in the fight for

11. As quoted in Hope, "The Question of Alaska," p. 259.

12. As quoted in Susan Hackley Johnson, "Profiles of the North: Willie Hensley," *Alaska Journal*, 9 (1979), 29. See also Hensley's comments in McPhee, *Coming Into the Country*, pp. 82–83.

wilderness in Alaska. Some of its central concepts had not been formulated even a half-century before. But more significant, at least politically, was the degree of popular enthusiasm for wilderness values. Alaska easily became a celebrated cause, an opportunity to make up, if only symbolically, for the near-total elimination of wilderness in the rest of the nation. Here was a last American chance to do things right—at least from the perspective of wilderness advocates—and they leaped at the chance in numbers that would have astonished John Muir during his comparatively lonely defense of Hetch Hetchy Valley. In contrast even to Glen Canyon in the 1950s, Alaska was definitely not a place no one knew. Sensing the popularity of the subject, writers, publishers, and filmmakers produced a flood of material. Professional wilderness preservationists knew how to use this public interest. An Alaska Coalition, consisting of the nation's strongest conservation organizations, formed to defend Alaska's wilderness in Washington, D.C. The greatest wilderness lobby ever organized influenced Congressmen to lead the fight in the hearing rooms and on the floor of both houses. Wildernesss never had more friends.

Wilderness recreation also flourished while Alaska's future hung in the balance. A revolution in transportation, outdoor equipment, and information (see below, pp. 317–19) made it easier than ever before for Americans to go to the wilderness. Even Alaska's formidable climate was no longer an insurmountable obstacle to pleasure seekers. Wilderness had the clientele in the 1970s that it had lacked a century earlier. Significantly, many non-native Alaskans liked wilderness too. The chance to live close to wild land was a major reason why many of them had moved north. Alaskans might differ with "outsiders" over what should be permitted in a designated wilderness (cabins, for example), but many of them would support some kind of preservation policy if properly conditioned. Essentially, they did *not* want Alaska to become like the rest of the United States. Almost the opposite sentiment motivated pioneers on earlier American frontiers.

John Muir was in all likelihood the first American to become interested in Alaska for its wilderness. As Chapter 8 explains, he had gone west in 1868 to find in California's Sierra Nevada an environment wilder than his Wisconsin boyhood home. But by 1879 he was ready to strike out for new frontiers. The idea of going to

Alaska may have originated with, and was certainly encouraged by, the visit to Yosemite of Dr. Sheldon Jackson. A presbyterian missionary, Jackson had only moved to Alaska two years before, but he was already bursting with enthusiasm for America's most recent territorial acquisition.[13] On June 7, 1879, Muir and Jackson met at a conference in Yosemite, and July found the men sailing northward on the steamship *California*. Jackson was returning to his home base in Sitka, but Muir's itinerary was characteristically vague. He wanted primarily to see the country, and after a tour up the Stikine River, he and S. Hall Young continued north via Indian canoe. The highlight of their trip was the second-known entrance into the ice plugged fiord that came to be called Glacier Bay.[14]

Having become an expert on glaciation in the Sierra Nevada, Muir's scientific curiosity exploded in the presence of the huge glaciers that spilled directly into salt water. But the major theme in his writings about Alaska was the way that wilderness symbolized divinity. He wrote about the "harvests of revealed glory" to be gathered on every hand and repeatedly called the Alaskan wilderness a temple. On a later trip to Glacier Bay and Muir Glacier, Muir remarked that in such surroundings "divine influences, however invisible, are showered down on us thick as snowflakes in a snowstorm." Ralph Waldo Emerson would have been proud of his disciple's extension of Transcendentalism to Alaska.[15]

At several points John Muir used the adjective "pure" to describe the wilderness he encountered in Alaska. The idea became a staple in subsequent tourists' accounts. Other places might have wilderness, but Alaska was *real* wilderness. Certainly there was nothing in Muir's previous experience to match what he found in the North. When he entered the Sierra Nevada in 1868, grazing and lumbering were already widespread and Yosemite was rapidly becoming a mecca for tourists. But Alaska's forests seemed

13. Jackson's best-known work is *Alaska and Missions on the North Pacific Coast* (New York, 1880). A useful secondary study is Ted C. Hinckley, "Sheldon Jackson, Presbyterian Lobbyist for the Great Land," *Journal of the Presbyterian Historical Society, 40* (1962), 3–23.

14. The definitive history is Dave Bohn, *Glacier Bay: The Land and the Silence* (San Francisco, 1967).

15. Muir, *Travels in Alaska* (Boston, 1915), pp. vii, 153; Linnie Marsh Wolfe, ed., *John of the Mountains: The Unpublished Journals of John Muir* (Boston, 1938), p. 315. See also Jed Dannenbaum, "John Muir and Alaska," *Alaska Journal, 2* (1972), 14–20.

"trackless" to Muir and its mountains "seem never before to have been even looked at." Indeed in all Alaska it appeared to be "still the morning of creation." Perhaps this assumption led Muir, and many later visitors, to deplore even the few evidences of white civilization they encountered. Muir described Wrangell as "the most inhospitable place . . . I had ever seen . . . a lawless draggle of wooden huts." Its residents, miners, struck him as crude, hostile, and oblivious to the "grand wild country in which they lived."[16] Here was the beginning of a tendency on the part of non-Alaskan defenders of Alaskan wilderness to distrust Alaskans. The consequence of this attitude was the d(2) controversy.

John Muir ranks as one of the most florid describers of wilderness in American letters, and the Alaskan scene called forth his full literary energies. Everything was "glorious" or "sublime" or "grand" or "glowing." He wrote of "snowy falls booming in splendid dress; colossal domes and battlements . . . their bases laved by the blue fiord water; green ferny dells . . . and glaciers above all." In such a wilderness Muir felt himself near to "the very paradise of poets, the abode of the blessed."[17]

In regard to American attitudes toward Alaska it is important to bear in mind that Muir's effusions came only a dozen years after the 1867 purchase. At this time the prevailing American image of Alaska was unflattering in the extreme. Secretary of State William Seward was still being derided for the "folly" that had bought America a huge hunk of worthless ice, a wasteland. Even defenders of the acquisition could only muster vague references to potential resources and to the strategic benefits. No one in the 1870s valued Alaska's wilderness or appreciated its scenery. Muir was the first to chip away at the iceberg image.

This situation began to change in the late 1880s and 1890s. Thanks to Muir's publications, which initially appeared in newspapers and periodicals such as *Century,* and the writings of Sheldon Jackson and Eliza Ruhamah Scidmore, tourists began to cruise what was being called the "Inside Passage."[18] In 1890 five thousand peo-

16. Muir, *Travels,* pp. 13, 67, 207–08.

17. Ibid., pp. 13, 222, 14.

18. Scidmore's *Alaska, Its Southern Coast and Sitkan Archipelago* (Boston, 1885) became the standard tourist guide. Ted C. Hinckley discusses the development of the cruise industry in "The Inside Passage: A Popular Golden Age Tour," *Pacific Northwest Quarterly,* 56 (1965), 67–74.

ple made the thirty-day, round trip from San Francisco. Glacier Bay was the highlight. Several hundred tourists poured out of the posh ships for a few hours on the moving river of ice. It was, one tourist's journal stated, "the great event of my life."[19] Muir, understandably, was amused and somewhat disgusted by the clientele of the cruise ships. "Only by going alone in silence, without baggage," he wrote to his wife in 1888, "can one truly get into the heart of the wilderness. All other travel is mere dust and hotels and baggage and chatter."[20] But at this time boats were the only way to reach Alaska, and few had Muir's talent for wilderness travel. Ironically, Muir had much more in common with recent trends in Alaska nature tourism, yet his writings did much to publicize and promote the cruises.

The most grandiose of all the cruises to Alaska took place in June, 1899, when Edward H. Harriman, the railroad king, chartered the 250-foot *George W. Elder* and invited the foremost scientific, literary, and artistic talents in the country to join him on a trip to Glacier Bay. Muir was present along with his nature-writing colleague John Burroughs. Also in the party were scientists of the stature of Grove Karl Gilbert, William Healey Dall, and C. Hart Merriam. Edward Curtis's photographs and R. S. Gifford's paintings created a visual record of the journey. The written record ultimately amounted to twelve published volumes.[21] Here was abundant evidence in refutation of the wasteland image of Alaska. Although it was conducted in the luxurious surroundings of a cruise ship, the Harriman Alaska Expedition marked a high point of nineteenth-century enthusiasm for the American wilderness.

Among the more interesting comments of members of the Harriman expedition were those of Henry Gannett. A geographer who helped survey Wyoming in the 1870s and later assumed directorship of the United States Geological Survey, Gannett quickly realized the potential of Alaska's scenery for tourism. He knew the territory's mountains, fiords, and glaciers had no equal in the western Hemisphere. The prestigious *National Geographic Magazine,* in 1901, published an essay by Gannett. "The Alaska coast," he stated, "is to

19. Septima M. Collis, *A Woman's Trip to Alaska* (New York, 1890), p. 150.

20. As quoted in Dannenbaum, "John Muir and Alaska," p. 19.

21. *Harriman Alaska Expedition* (12 vols., New York, 1902–14). Volume 1 lists the members and gives the details of the trip. For interpretation see Morgan B. Sherwood, *Exploration of Alaska, 1865–1900* (New Haven, Conn., 1965), pp. 182 ff.

become the showplace of the earth and pilgrims, not only from the United States, but from far beyond the seas, will throng in endless procession to see it." Gannett understood the economics of this situation. The economic value of Alaska's "grandeur, . . . measured by direct returns in money received from tourists, will be enormous." Moreover, Gannett continued, scenery "is more valuable than the gold or the fish or the timber, for it will never be exhausted." This was one of the earliest statements of a later, repeated argument for nature preservation in Alaska.

Gannett's essay concluded with a much-quoted "word of advice and caution" for tourists to Alaska.

> If you are old, go by all means, but if you are young, stay away until you grow older. The scenery of Alaska is so much grander than anything else of the kind in the world that, once beheld, all other scenery becomes flat and insipid. It is not well to dull one's capacity for such enjoyment by seeing the finest first.

Closer examination of Gannett's ideas suggests that what excited him most about Alaskan scenery was the newness of the country. At one point the *George W. Elder* found a glacier just receded enough to permit passage into an unexplored fiord. The idea of being a discoverer thrilled Gannett, and he quoted a poet: "We were the first that ever burst / Into that silent sea." This idea, too, would echo frequently in reactions of subsequent visitors to Alaska's wilderness.[22]

The Harriman expedition was the final one to Glacier Bay for many years because on September 10, 1899, a huge earthquake jolted southeastern Alaska. Miles of ice broke away from the glaciers and clogged the bay thereby preventing access by ship. For the next half-century Glacier Bay was little visited and the establishment in 1925 of Glacier Bay National Monument went almost unnoticed except by the scientists for whom the reserve was largely intended. So it was that interior Alaska began to receive attention. Inaccessible, mysterious, and more rugged than the relatively temperate coastal regions, the interior could be valued as a reservoir of wilderness which was rapidly draining away from the rest of the United States. Perhaps, some Americans began to think, the frontier

22. Gannett, "The General Geography of Alaska," *The National Geographic Magazine, 12* (1901), pp. 182, 196.

had not died in 1890 after all. Perhaps pioneering, and temporary pioneering by vacationers, could continue in Alaska.

The event that crystallized these ideas and focused unprecedented attention on wild land and frontier lifestyles in Alaska was the gold rush of 1898. As David Wharton's monograph makes clear, the series of mineral stampedes of the late 1890s partly involved Canada's Yukon Territory but were generally known as the "Alaska gold rush."[23] Wharton also points out that this frenzied pursuit of gold represented the final chapter in a myth as old as European knowledge of the New World. But the timing of the Alaska stampede was special. When the forty-niners rushed to California's gold fields in the mid-nineteenth century, the United States was still a developing nation with a wild West. The miners did not seem picturesque and romantic so much as uncouth and a bit embarrassing to a society trying to mature.[24] But with the frontier officially dead (according to the 1890 census), the time was ripe for a myth that accorded cowboys and hunters and miners legendary proportions. Americans of the early twentieth century were prepared to romanticize the "ninety-eighters" and paint their rush to the gold of the north in glowing colors. In fact the Alaskan "sourdoughs" were no more glamorous than their predecessors in Colorado and California, but the nation was intellectually more prepared to regard them as heroes as Chapter 9, above, attempts to explain.

A related observation is that many of the participants in the Alaska gold rush sought excitement in the wilderness rather than gold. They were not frontiersmen so much as city folks seeking a frontier experience. Many were, in effect, tourists. Gold provided an excuse to leave urban situations in the lower forty-eight and heed, for a time, the call of the wild. Afterwards many returned, usually penniless, to quiet civilized ways of life in San Francisco or St. Louis. The prospector who in 1896 discovered and named Mount McKinley, for example, was, on closer examination, a

23. Wharton, *The Alaska Gold Rush* (Bloomington, Ind., 1972), especially Chapter 1. In Sherwood, *Exploration of Alaska,* Chapter 10 also provides factual background.

24. The classic study of attitudes toward nineteenth-century frontiersmen is Henry Nash Smith, *Virgin Land: The American West as Symbol and Myth* (Cambridge, Mass., 1950), especially Chapters 5–9. Also insightful is Arthur K. Moore, *The Frontier Mind: A Cultural Analysis of the Kentucky Frontiersman* (Lexington, Ky., 1957).

Princeton graduate who resided in Seattle. His self-styled "summer outing" amounted to a wilderness vacation.[25]

The appeal of Alaska's wilderness in the era of the gold rush was its savageness. A man could be a man there, and only the strong survived. Jack London recognized and gave extraordinary circulation to this theme in *The Call of the Wild* (1903), which drew upon his winter on the Yukon River in 1898. Robert Service came north in 1904 and succeeded in creating the images with which numerous Americans would thereafter interpret the North. In *The Spell of the Yukon* (1907) Service makes the land itself the protagonist. It was "the cussedest land that I know" with "big, dizzy mountains" and "deep, deathlike valleys," an "outcast land," a "leper land," a "land God forgot." Gold might draw men north, Service believed, but the "nameless" and "unpeopled" land had the most powerful hold on their lives and imaginations. Significantly, neither London or Service attempted to portray Alaska as beautiful or spiritual or fragile in the manner of interpreters later in the century. Like Walter Hickel, they stressed its toughness, but unlike Hickel they saw value in that toughness for people in search of challenge and, in a special sense, peace.

Charles Sheldon took a different view of wilderness in Alaska. A Yale graduate, he made a fortune in Mexican silver mines and retired at age thirty-five to pursue an interest in the hunting, study, and protection of big game animals. In 1906 he penetrated to the foothills of the Alaska Range, and the following year he wintered in a cabin hundreds of miles from civilization at the base of Mount McKinley. For Sheldon the Alaskan wilderness was not a tooth-and-claw setting for the defiance of death as it had been to Jack London and Robert Service. He saw it as a frontier, but, especially in regard to big game habitat, a perishable frontier that needed protection. Even John Muir did not move from a recognition of Alaska's beauty to a perception of its fragility. But Sheldon came north a quarter of a century after Muir. By that time miners

25. William A. Dickey, "Discoveries in Alaska," *New York Sun,* Jan. 24, 1897, which is reprinted in Bradford Washburn, *Mount McKinley and the Alaska Range in Literature* (Boston, 1951), pp. 81–88. Information on Dickey is gathered in the library of the National Park Service, Mount McKinley National Park. A fuller discussion of Dickey appears in Roderick Nash, "Tourism, Parks and the Wilderness Idea in the History of Alaska," *Alaska in Perspective, 4* (1981), 11.

26. Service, *The Spell of the Yukon* (New York, 1958), pp. 11, 15–18.

in the Kantishna region north of Mount McKinley were decimating game and the construction of the Alaska Railroad just east of the area promised to reduce its wilderness still more. On January 12, 1908, his journal mentions national park status for the McKinley region. Subsequently Sheldon worked with Belmore Browne of the Camp Fire Club of America and John Burnham of the American Game Protective Association to establish a park. Finally, on February 26, 1917, Woodrow Wilson signed a bill creating Mount McKinley National Park. Charles Sheldon received the pen used in the signing ceremony. It was appropriate recognition because Sheldon had been the first to understand that Alaska was not too big or too rugged to be transformed by civilization.[27]

The first waves of American tourists who followed Charles Sheldon to Alaska in the 1920s and 1930s lacked his taste and talent for wilderness living. Their preference was for a room with a view and an abundance of wild animals close to the roads. To serve this resort-oriented clientele the Curry Hotel opened in 1923 near Mount McKinley on the route of the Alaska Railroad. There was a scenic viewpoint, the "Regalvista," plus golf, tennis, and a swimming pool.[28] If such things did not have much to do with wilderness, it is only fair to recall that visitors of this era to Yosemite and Grand Canyon national parks had similar tastes (see below, p. 325). Apart from a few harbingers such as Muir and Sheldon, recreational interest in wilderness simply did not exist at that time. But times and tastes changed and so, gradually, did the mission and meaning of protected wild land in Alaska.

27. Sheldon's *The Wilderness of the Upper Yukon* (New York, 1911) and *The Wilderness of Denali* (New York, 1930) stimulated interest in Alaskan scenery and wildlife. Denali is the native name for Mount McKinley. The story of the establishment of the national park is contained in James B. Trefethen, *Crusade for Wildlife* (New York, 1961), pp. 179 ff. and John Ise, *Our National Park Policy: A Critical History* (Baltimore, 1961), pp. 226 ff. Morgan Sherwood's *Big Game in Alaska* (New Haven, Conn. 1981) is relevant. Additional material on Sheldon and the park are available in the Charles Sheldon Papers, University of Alaska Archives, Fairbanks, Alaska.

28. Details on the early history of the park may be found in Grant H. Pearson, *A History of Mount McKinley National Park* (Washington, D.C., 1953); Chalon A. Harris, *Highlights in the History of Mount McKinley National Park* (n.p., 1974); and Alaska Travel Publications, *Exploring Alaska's Mount McKinley National Park* (Anchorage, 1967), pp. 62 ff. For the comments of a representative tourist see William N. Beach, *In the Shadow of Mount McKinley* (New York, 1931). A useful discussion of the railroad, tourism, and the national park is William H. Wilson, "The Alaska Railroad and Tourism, 1924–1941," *Alaska Journal*, 7 (1972), 18–24.

On July 22, 1929, Noel Wein landed a seven-passenger Hamilton on the dirt strip at Wiseman, and a new era in Alaska tourism began. One innovation concerned the use of aircraft for access to wilderness. The cruise ship and railroad henceforth had a competitor that could quickly and easily bring visitors of sufficient affluence into some of the wildest places on earth. The other fact of importance had to do with Wein's passenger: rich, twenty-eight year old, New York City born and Harvard educated Robert Marshall (see Chapter 12). The previous winter, impatient with the shrinking opportunities for wilderness recreation in the lower forty-eight, Marshall had taken a world atlas and looked for blank spaces. The map of Alaska showed a huge one in the central Brooks Range. Wiseman, in Marshall's words, was "two hundred miles beyond the edge of the Twentieth Century,"[29] and northward lay, as far as white men knew, terra incognita. At one point, facing three grizzlies on a tributary of the Koyukuk River, it occurred to Marshall that he was "eleven miles from the closest gun, [a] hundred and six from the first potential stretcher, and three hundred from the nearest hospital."[30] Marshall liked it that way. "There is something glorious," he wrote in 1934, "in traveling beyond the ends of the earth, in living in a different world which men have not discovered, in cutting loose from the bonds of a world-wide civilization."[31] In the course of four trips into the Brooks Range, Marshall spent more than two hundred days in country no white men had ever mentioned visiting. The names he placed on the maps became official. Amazingly, he had found in America in the twentieth century a chance to emulate his boyhood heroes: Lewis and Clark.

After experiencing Alaska, Bob Marshall turned his extraordinary energies from exploration to politics in an effort to protect what he appreciated. The "U" regulations of the United States Forest Service were largely his responsibility, but they applied to a part of the nation that Marshall realized could never match Alaska's wildness. Even his idea of keeping portions of the Ameri-

29. Marshall, *Arctic Village* (New York, 1933), p. 9. Acclaimed by sociologists and anthropologists, this description of Marshall's year in Wiseman helped Americans understand Alaskan natives and their problems.

30. Marshall, *Alaska Wilderness,* ed. George Marshall (1956; reprint ed., Berkeley, 1970), p. 50. See George Marshall, "Bob Marshall and the Alaska Arctic Wilderness," *Living Wilderness, 34* (1970), 29–32.

31. As quoted in *Alaska Wilderness,* p. xxxii.

can West in a "super wilderness" condition (see below, p. 322) would not be the equivalent of protecting an unknown land. But in the North there was still the chance of prolonging what Marshall called "the possibility of exploration."[32] He was the first American to recognize that wilderness preservation in Alaska could involve whole watersheds, entire mountain ranges, and intact ecosystems. Instead of wilderness being islands in a sea of civilization, the proportions were reversed, and Marshall hoped to keep them that way—permanently.

In 1938, a year before his untimely death at the age of thirty-eight, Marshall consolidated his ideas in comments to a Congressional committee studying Alaska's recreational resources. Why not, he argued, look upon Alaska as a source of not merely wilderness recreation but of "pioneer conditions" and "the emotional values of the frontier." This would involve prohibiting roads, industry, and agriculture in all Alaska north of the Yukon River. About half of the future state was involved. No American had thought about wilderness preservation in such grandiose terms, but Marshall was entirely in earnest. Anticipating the thought of Robert Weeden (see below, p. 314), he explained to the federal government that his proposal really did not demand major economic sacrifices. Northern Alaska was unfit for agriculture and roads and, in the pre-oil era, Marshall could add industry. Its greatest use might be as wilderness. As for the natives, whom Marshall knew and admired from his months in Wiseman, they "would be much happier, if the United States experience is any criterion," without white civilization. "Alaska," Marshall concluded, "is unique among all recreational areas belonging to the United States because Alaska is yet largely a wilderness. In the name of a balanced use of American resources, let's keep northern Alaska largely a wilderness!"[33] Here was the first, inevitably controversial, call not just for wilderness preservation but for a permanent American frontier.

Over the next two decades the United States Corps of Engineers and some non-native Alaskans formed quite different visions of the

32. Ibid., p. xxxii.

33. Marshall, "Comments on the Report of Alaska's Recreational Resources Committee," *Alaska—Its Resources and Development*, U.S. Congress, House Doc. 485, 75th Cong., 3d Sess., Appendix B, p. 213. For a discussion of how Marshall's remarks angered Alaskans see Miller, *The Frontier in Alaska*, p. 164.

future of northern Alaska. The key to their plans was the mighty Yukon River and the possibility of damming it at Rampart Canyon a hundred miles south of Bob Marshall's mecca, Wiseman. Proposed by the Corps of Engineers about the time of Alaskan statehood in 1959, Rampart Dam was taken by many Alaskans to be something of a federal birthday gift. At a cost of over a billion dollars, the Yukon Flats would have become the largest artificial lake in the world, bigger than Lake Erie.[34] The objective was hydroelectric power and the consequent attraction of industry to northern Alaska. Vast areas would be opened to mining and logging. Just as important, to Alaskans, however, was evidence that the Rampart project would provide an end to the long night of colonialism.

Ernest Gruening, territorial governor for fourteen years and later one of Alaska's first United States Senators, was especially sensitive on this point. He saw Rampart Dam as a way for Alaska to catch up to the rest of the nation after years of federal neglect and indifference. Moreover, according to Gruening, "the site of the proposed dam was a wasteland."[35] Gruening's assistant, George Sundborg, went further when he wrote in the mid-1960s: "Search the whole world and it would be difficult to find an equivalent area with so little to be lost through flooding." The entire site of the reservoir, an area larger than New Jersey, contained "not more than ten flush toilets."[36]

Wilderness preservationists felt Sundborg was wrong about the toilets. "The Yukon Flats," observed Paul Brooks in 1965, "are wholly without plumbing. This is wild country and its values are wilderness values."[37] One element that figured most prominently in the statements against Rampart Dam was wildlife habitat. The vast marshes of the Yukon Flats were a major North American breeding ground for waterfowl, a salmon spawning area, and a

34. The factual and political background of Rampart Dam is sketched in Janet R. Klein, "Some Environmental Issues in Alaska's Past and Present," *Alaska in Perspective*, 4 (1981), p. 11–13. For representative statements of opposition see Ginny Hill Wood, "The Ramparts We Watch," *Sierra Club Bulletin*, 50 (1965), 13–15 and Terry T. Brady, "The Rampart Dam Project: Power and a Land Ethic," *Sierra Club Bulletin*, 48 (1963), 8–9, 12.

35. Gruening, *The State of Alaska* (New York, 1968), p. 538.

36. Sundborg as quoted in Paul Brooks, *The Pursuit of Wildness* (Boston, 1971), pp. 90, 83.

37. Ibid., p. 83.

prime moose, mink, and wolf habitat. Twelve hundred natives lived there too. Sundborg brushed such considerations aside. The reservoir would not be harmful, he pointed out with a questionable understanding of wildlife ecology, because ducks like water. Gruening felt that Rampart Dam's opponents ignored "the economic needs of *Homo sapiens,* who needs the wherewithal to make use of the natural resources of the earth to ensure his survival."[38] The *Anchorage Daily Times* voiced a widespread Alaskan attitude on July 31, 1962, when it observed that "Alaska is more than 99 percent wilderness. The threat of dissipating such a vast area by economic development must be several generations away."

Americans had, of course, heard this all before. On every frontier in the nation's past, man's economic interest had been pitted against wilderness in an either-or relationship. And wilderness, in general, had fared poorly. Ohio, as Alaskans liked to point out, had no wilderness reserves. But the Rampart controversy occurred in the 1960s when changing geographical and intellectual conditions had altered for Americans the meaning of both wilderness and civilization. The defeat of Echo Park Dam in 1956 was a harbinger, as was the Wilderness Act of 1964. And the Rampart controversy reached its crucial stages just at the time that opponents of dams in the Grand Canyon were gaining the upper hand, as chapter 12 shows. Still, from the standpoint of many Alaskans, the 1967 decision of the Department of the Interior to drop consideration of Rampart Dam seemed unfair and discriminatory. What these Alaskans only partially understood was their misfortune to be advocating frontier-style development at a time when wilderness appreciation had come of age.

On the eve of the North Slope oil strike of 1968, the Rampart controversy climaxed and established two principles that would influence debates in the 1970s. The first was that many outsiders saw Alaska's wilderness not as a wasteland suitable for reservoirs but as a reservoir of a scarce, and hence valuable, environmental condition. Second, the Rampart defeat demonstrated that the wilderness movement was capable of heavily influencing, if not determining, Alaska's future. If this constituted colonialism as Ernest Greuning feared, it had as a new main objective preservation not exploitation.

38. Gruening, *State of Alaska,* p. 539.

It would be a mistake, however, to use the Rampart issue as an illustration that outsiders and Alaskans held diametrically opposite positions with regard to wilderness. Contemporary Alaskans were, after all, Americans of the 1960s and 1970s. As such they were not oblivious to the value of wilderness and to the enviable uniqueness of their state in being largely wild. A quick look at Project Chariot bears this out.[39] In 1958 the Atomic Energy Commission, seeking peaceful applications of nuclear devices, proposed to use a series of atomic bombs to excavate a deep-water harbor near Point Hope at the western extremity of the Brooks Range. While some Alaskan boomers applauded Project Chariot as they did Rampart Dam, many others were not enthusiastic. Natives, who had occupied the area continuously for at least five thousand years, expressed dismay at the effect of the blasts on traditional hunting, fishing, and gathering grounds and, consequently, on their entire culture. A significant number of non-native Alaskans, including major businessmen and Governor William A. Egan, opposed the plan for its destructive impact on wildlife, wilderness, and native lifestyles. Not only were the economic benefits of Project Chariot dubious, but twentieth-century economic objectives were inappropriate a hundred miles above the Arctic Circle. In the ultimately successful Alaskan opposition to the project there was recognition that Alaska could be different; that it did not have to emulate Texas and California. "Do we really want to make Alaska over in the image of Los Angeles?" Ginny Hill Wood, an Alaskan, asked in 1965. The implication was that an alternate economic and social order, one based on proximity to an abundance of permanent wilderness, might work better in the North. As Wood recognized, her state's most valuable resource might simply be "space—spectacularly beautiful space that is not all filled up with people and industry as is so much of the rest of the world."[40] The existence of this idea among Alaskans brought them close to the position of outside

39. The Project Chariot story is told in Brooks, *Pursuit of Wildness*, pp. 59–74 and in Klein, "Environmental Issues," pp. 14–15. It is relevant that in 1965, 1969 and 1971, the federal government detonated nuclear bombs on Amchitka Island in the Aleutian Chain. Protests against the blasts were vigorous both in Alaska and elsewhere. Although Amchitka was uninhabited, wildlife and wilderness values were cited by the opposition. In 1973 the Atomic Energy Commission announced there would be no more tests.

40. Wood, "Ramparts We Watch," p. 15.

preservationists and lay the basis for the compromises that the Alaska National Interest Lands Conservation Act of 1980 embodied.

The opportunity that the Alaska Native Claims Settlement Act created in 1971 to protect wilderness coincided with and was strongly influenced by the increasing popularity of the Alaskan wilderness for recreation. By the 1970s first hundreds and then thousands of people were ready to follow the lead of Charles Sheldon and Bob Marshall. Cruise ships, trains, buses, and hotels continued to handle the bulk of the tourist traffic, but many, Alaskans as well as outsiders, wanted closer contact with wild Alaska. The opening in 1948 of the Alaska Military Highway to the public facilitated this trend. For the first time it became possible to drive to Alaska for a vacation. Also important in the encouragement of the new style tourism was the appearance of a wilderness-oriented recreation industry.

Celia Hunter and Ginny Wood pioneered in this field in 1952 when they opened Camp Denali just north of Mount McKinley National Park for what they called the "adventurous fringe" of the traveling public.[41] A hundred miles from the railroad and the resort-style hotels of the National Park Service, their tent-cabins appealed to people who put wilderness and wildlife ahead of comfort and convenience. Although they were a gamble in the 1950s, backcountry tourist operations like Camp Denali and Thayer Lake Lodge on Admiralty Island proved popular. In 1960 Ginny Wood went a step further, instituting Tundra Treks, a twelve-day backpack with no hunting allowed, which was the first commercial venture of its kind in the history of Alaskan tourism. In advertising it, Wood relied on what was becoming the dominant theme in the American understanding of the Alaskan wilderness. "With wilderness fast disappearing in the 'first 48' states," she wrote, "Alaska . . . offers the last large unspoiled outdoor laboratory for the study and appreciation of undisturbed nature." Join her trek and have "the experience of the frontiersmen and explorers who first gazed on unbroken prairies, unharnessed rivers and undiminished wildlife."[42]

41. Celia Hunter, "From My Corner," *Living Wilderness,* (1977), 61–63; Susan Hackley Johnson, "Celia Hunter: Portrait of an Activist," *Alaska Journal, 4* (1979), 30–35; interview with Celia Hunter and Ginny Wood, Fairbanks, Alaska, Sept. 3, 1980.

42. Privately printed brochure of 1960, in the possession of Ginny Wood, Fairbanks, Alaska.

Beginning in the 1950s, and increasing in the subsequent two decades, a flood of publicity called attention to the values of wild Alaska. From 1951 to 1953 the National Park Service surveyed recreational opportunities on what it termed "our last frontier." Lowell Sumner supplemented the official report with articles in the *Sierra Club Bulletin* and argued that Alaska's leading industries—hunting, fishing, and tourism—depended on preserving wilderness. Excellent photographs helped Sumner make his points.[43] Sally Carrighar's *Icebound Summer* (1951) attracted many readers with its lyrical description of the change of seasons in a "land of delicate loveliness and violence."[44] A comparable book, Lois Chrisler's *Arctic Wild* (1958), told about her months in the Brooks Range and her success in raising wolves from pups. In 1956 Olaus and Margaret Murie, along with Supreme Court Justice William O. Douglas, made the first of their well-publicized trips to the eastern portion of the Brooks Range.[45] Their enthusiasm for this region aided in its establishment four years later as the nine million acre Arctic National Wildlife Range. Robert Marshall's *Alaska Wilderness* also appeared in 1956.

The publicity continued with books such as Frank Dufresne's *My Way Was North* (1960) and Booton Herndon's *The Great Land* (1971). John Milton described a 1967 backpack across the Brooks Range in *Nameless Valleys, Shining Mountains* (1970), while another member of the expedition, Kenneth Brower, contributed the magnificently illustrated *Earth and the Great Weather* (1973). The Sierra Club made Alaska the central subject of its 1969 Wilderness Conference and subsequently published the papers under the title *Wilderness: The Edge of Knowledge* (1970). In *One Man's Wilderness: An Alaskan Odyssey* (1973), Sam Keith described the quintessential Alaskan dream: building a log cabin and living alone forty miles from the nearest settlement. John McPhee's national best seller *Coming Into the Country* (1977) intrigued hundreds of thousands of readers with an account of neopioneers in the "bush"

43. William J. Stanton, Alaska Recreation Survey (2 vols., Washington, D.C., 1953); George L. Collins and Lowell Sumner, "Northeast Arctic: The Last Great Wilderness," *Sierra Club Bulletin, 38* (1953), 13–26; Sumner, "Your Stake in Alaska's Wildlife and Wilderness," *Sierra Club Bulletin, 41* (1956), 54–71.

44. Carrighar, *Icebound Summer* (New York, 1951), p. 221. Indicative of the continued interest in this kind of book, a paperback edition appeared in 1971.

45. Olaus J. Murie, *Journeys to the Far North* (Palo Alto, Ca., 1973); William O. Douglas, *My Wilderness: The Pacific West* (New York, 1960), Chapter 1. Another Murie, Adolph, contributed *A Naturalist in Alaska* (Old Greenwich, Conn., 1961).

near Eagle, Alaska. For the sportsman there was *Alaska: The Magazine of Life on the Last Frontier,* which revised its format in 1969 and benefitted from the surge of interest in the Alaskan wilderness. Jim Repine's similar product, *Alaska Outdoors Magazine,* jumped on the bandwagon in the late 1970s. Time-Life Books' American Wilderness Series brought out Dale Brown's *Wild Alaska* in 1972, and there were numerous picture books, featuring wilderness, such as Paul C. Johnson's *Alaska* (1974), Paul M. Lewis's *Beautiful Alaska* (1977), and Boyd Norton's *Alaska, Wilderness Frontier* (1978). *National Geographic's* June, 1975, issue featured Alaska under the now trite title "America's Last Great Wilderness." The Alaska Geographic Society published a superbly illustrated edition of *Alaska Geographic* in 1977 concerning the lands proposed for wilderness status. If anything remained to be described or photographed, the travel industry filled the gap with special supplements.[46]

Films added to the popular estimation of Alaska. The Sierra Club's "Alaska: Land in the Balance" (1976) combined extraordinary footage of wilderness and wildlife with a plea to refrain from further development. The National Park Service distributed a film portraying Alaska as, once again, the "last great wilderness." "This is Jack London country," the script read, "and men in it have heard the call of the wild." In the late 1970s John Denver made an important film, "Alaska: America's Child," filled with bears and Dall sheep and whitewater rivers. His central idea was implicit in the film's title: Alaska was both a living reminder of the nation's past and a hope for keeping the wildness of young America alive. In Denver's song, "America's Child" (1977), which the film featured, he captured the classic image of Alaska's wilderness: "American Child does the call of the wild / Ever sing through the mist of your dreams? / Can you picture the time / When a man had to find / His own way through an unbroken land?"

The words and pictures created a huge "armchair" clientele for Alaska's wilderness, and they also inspired unprecedented numbers of tourists to go north. Visitor statistics provide ample evidence. In 1962 Mount McKinley National Park recorded 57 backcountry visitors. The 1971 total was 5,500. In 1977 an astonishing 32,000

46. For example, "Advertising Supplement," *Travel, 147* (1977) and Alaska Travel Specialists, *The 1980 Alaska Adventure Catalog* (n.p., 1980).

individuals spent one or more nights away from the lodges and roadside campgrounds.[47] "I came," one visitor told Sigurd Olson, "to see Alaska before it was too late." When the man pulled a worn copy of Robert Service's poems from his pack, Olson understood what he meant.[48]

Meanwhile the summit of Mount McKinley became inundated with climbers who rarely found themselves alone on the routes during periods of good weather. One party even carried hang gliders up and flew down.[49] It was not that the climb of the continent's highest peak had become easy, but rather that more and more people were willing to pay the physical price for the experience. Wilderness was calling as never before.

In another corner of the state, Glacier Bay National Monument's cold, wet backcountry attracted only five visitors in 1972, but seven years later the total was 2,913, and the National Park Service was contemplating measures to disperse or restrict kayakers and hikers.[50] The Alsek River, which enters the Pacific on the northern edge of Glacier Bay, was not run with inflatable rafts until 1976. Only four years later a dozen river outfitters competed for permits to conduct commercial trips on the river. Articles about the trip by well-known writers such as Edward Abbey did much to stimulate visitation.[51] The same situation occurred on the remote Noatak River which drains the western part of the Brooks Range. A year after *National Geographic's* 1977 illustrated feature story and map of the river,

47. Statistical records are available at National Park Service headquarters, Anchorage, with supplemental data at Mount McKinley National Park headquarters. Peter Womble, "Survey of Backcountry Users in Mount McKinley National Park, Alaska: A Report for Management" (December, 1979), mimeographed copy in the library, National Park Service, Mount McKinley National Park. Interviews with William Nancarrow, William Truesdell, and Gary Brown, of the National Park Service, Mount McKinley National Park, Aug. 29, 30, 1980.

48. Sigurd F. Olson, "Alaska: Land of Scenic Grandeur," *Living Wilderness, 35* (Winter, 1971–72), 10.

49. Dennis Cowals, "The Expedition that Fell from the Sky," *Mariah, 1* (Winter, 1976), pp. 41 ff.

50. Interview with Bonnie Kaden, Alaska Discovery, Gustavus, Ak., Sept. 6, 1980; interview with Don Chase, National Park Service, Glacier Bay National Monument, Sept. 6, 1980. Statistics are available in the libraries of the National Park Service headquarters, Anchorage and Glacier Bay National Monument.

51. Richard Bangs, "Tatshenshini Trial," *Mountain Gazette* (Winter, 1976–77), 12–19; Edward Abbey, "Down the Tatshenshini: Notes from a Cold River," *Mariah/Outside, 4* (Dec. 1979–Jan. 1980), 18–24, 66, 68; Jack H. Evans, "Alaskan Run," *Westways, 70* (1978), 24–27, 67.

more people boated it than in previous history.[52] If a wilderness experience in Alaska was to remain "fundamentally different"[53] from the one obtainable in the rest of the United States, land managers would have to solve the unprecedented problems occasioned by sudden popularity.

In the 1970s much of the American discussion of Alaskan wilderness centered on what came to be called the Alaska National Interest Lands Conservation Act of 1980. The political history of this landmark legislation needs a brief description.[54] Responding to pressure from prospective oil developers, natives, and the State of Alaska to settle the land ownership issue, Congress, through the Alaska Native Claims Settlement Act of 1971, set a deadline of exactly eight years (or December 18, 1978) for federal action. It appears that the idea of attaching a comprehensive land use plan

52. John Kauffmann, "Our Wild and Scenic River: The Noatak," *National Geographic, 152* (1977), 52–59. Sepp Weber's *Wild Rivers of Alaska* (Anchorage, 1976), pp. 20–27, also featured the Noatak. Interview with Ray Bane, Chief Ranger, National Park Service, Bettles, Ak., Aug. 23, 1980. Other examples of guidebooks that lured tourists north are Helen Nienhueser and Nancy Simmerman, *55 Ways to the Wilderness in Southcentral Alaska* (Seattle, 1972) and Margaret Piggot, *Discover Southeast Alaska with Pack and Paddle* (Seattle, 1974).

53. See the epigraph to this chapter from Michael Rogers, "Alaska: Dividing Our Last Wilderness," *Outside, 3* (1979), 40 and 41. Chapter 15, below, details the ways in which managers have approached the problem of keeping wilderness wild in the face of increased use.

54. The most useful descriptions of the shaping and passage of the Alaska National Interest Lands Conservation Act are: Eugenia Horstman Connally, "D-2: Saving Our Last Frontier," *National Parks, 55* (1981), 5–8; Julius Discha "How the Alaska Act Was Won," *Living Wilderness, 44* (1981), 4–9; "Congress Clears Alaska Lands Legislation," *CQ Almanac, 36* (1980), 575–84; Joint Federal-State Land Use Planning Commission for Alaska, *"The D-2 Book": Lands of National Interest in Alaska* (n.p., 1977); Final Report of the Joint Federal-State Land Use Planning Commission, *Some Guidelines for Deciding Alaska's Future* (Anchorage, 1979); Robert Cahn, "Alaska: A Matter of 80,000,000 Acres," *Audubon, 76* (1974), 3–13, 66–81; and Cahn's "The Race to Save Wild Alaska," *Living Wilderness, 41* (1977), 13–43. Eugenia Horstman Connally, *Wilderness Parklands in Alaska* (Washington, D.C., 1978) and "Wilderness Proposals," *Alaska Geographic, 4* (1977), 81–113. Mary Clay Berry, *The Alaska Pipeline: The Politics of Oil and Native Land Claims* (Bloomington, Ind., 1975); John Hanrahan and Peter Gruenstein, *Lost Frontier: The Marketing of Alaska* (New York, 1977); Richard Cooley, *Alaska: A Challenge in Conservation* (Madison, Wi., 1966); Robert D. Arnold, *Alaska Native Land Claims* (Anchorage, Ak., 1976); and Weeden, *Alaska,* contain additional information of importance in understanding land history and politics in Alaska. An excellent unpublished history that puts land use issues in perspective is Jonathan M. Nielson's "Focus on Interior History: Alaska's Past in Regional Perspective" (prepared for the Alaska Historical Commission, 1980, 531 pp.).

for Alaska to the native claims settlement legislation began with Representative Morris Udall. The Arizona congressman had previously been asked by the Wilderness Society and other environmental lobbies to think comprehensively about Alaska's future. When he introduced ANCSA, the time was ripe for such an endeavor. Wilderness areas in the continental United States were being studied at this time for inclusion in the National Wilderness Preservation System. And in 1970 the report of the Public Land Law Review Commission recommended identifying all nationally significant lands in Alaska. But the most telling pressure to plan Alaska's future came from potential native and non-native owners of Alaskan lands. Alaska, it must be kept in mind, was 99 percent federal land at the time of the statehood act in 1958 and very little of it changed hands in the next decade. Indeed in the late 1960s Stewart Udall, Morris's brother and secretary of the interior, put a freeze on further disposal of federal holdings. Then ANCSA made it clear that the claims of all interest groups would be unconfirmed until "national interest" lands were located and protected.

This process proved slow, laborious, and controversial. The new secretary of the interior, Rogers C. B. Morton, began to identify land for permanent federal ownership in 1972, but his relatively small recommendations of December 1973 (eighty-three million acres) disappointed preservationists. Further delays stemmed from the preoccupation of the nation with the Watergate scandals and the forced resignation of President Richard M. Nixon. When Jimmy Carter became president in 1977 less than two years remained before the ANCSA deadline.

In an effort to speed the process along, Morris Udall introduced a bill, H.R. 39, to the Ninety-fifth Congress on January 4, 1977. It called for the protection of 115 million acres and acquired 73 cosponsors in the House. But Alaskans expressed strong criticism of the measure. Governor Jay Hammond demanded that the reserved land be reduced to twenty-five million acres and be managed by a new federal–state partnership. After nationwide hearings and consideration of the Carter administration's ninety-two million acre proposal, Udall brought his bill to the floor of the House on May 17, 1978. "In a way not generally true of the day-to-day legislation which comes before this body," he said, "H.R. 39 poses an opportunity of historic dimensions. As long as any of us serves in this House, we shall vote on no more vital, more far-reaching, more memorable conservation measure . . . this will indeed be the land and wildlife vote of the century."[55]

On May 19, 1978, the House approved the bill by a margin of 246 votes, but in the Senate a threatened filibuster by Mike Gravel of Alaska brought deliberations to a halt. By November, as the Ninety-fifth Congress ended, it became evident that the December 18 deadline would not be met. In that event, state and private land claims could be filed anywhere in Alaska. The task of establishing parks and wilderness areas would be hopelessly complicated. But on November 16, Secretary of the Interior Cecil Andrus withdrew 110 million acres of federal land from mineral entry and state selection. On December 1, President Carter used authority granted him by the Antiquities Act of 1906 to give national monument status to fifty-six million acres. Carter also directed Andrus to create forty million new acres of wildlife refuge and had Secretary of Agriculture Bob Bergland withdraw eleven million acres of Alaskan national forest from mineral claims. These designations covered almost all the critical lands being considered under the stalled bill. Only Theodore Roosevelt's establishment of millions of acres of national forest in the West compared with Carter's action. *Living Wilderness* called it "the strongest and most daring conservation action by any president in American history."[56] But everyone, with the exception of the most rabid anticonservationists, recognized that Carter's actions were emergency, stopgap measures intended to last only until Congress passed a bill. The President did not leave any doubt about his personal feelings: "The top environmental priority of my administration, perhaps my entire life," he stated, "has been a carefully considered, proper protection of the wild and precious land of Alaska." By proper, Carter indicated, he meant balanced. "We have the imagination and the will as a people," he noted on December 1, 1978, "to both develop our last great natural frontier and also preserve its priceless beauty for our children and grandchildren."[57] This ambivalence put Carter squarely in the tradition of historic and contemporary American thought about wilderness. It was not so much a politician's instinct

55. *Congressional Record,* 95th Cong., 2nd Sess., *124* (May 17, 1978), p. H4089.
56. *Living Wilderness, 44* (1981), 36.
57. As quoted in White House Press Office, "Alaskan Lands Status Report" (July 12, 1980), p. 3.

for evasiveness as a genuine desire to make a place for both wilderness and civilization in the future of Alaska.

The opening of the Ninety-sixth Congress in January 1979 saw Morris Udall, with the strong assistance of Ohio's John F. Seiberling, once again start an Alaskan lands bill on its involved way through the legislature. By this time strong lobbies had developed on both sides of the issue. Oil, timber, and mining interests, along with chambers of commerce, made sure that Alaska's sole congressman, Don Young, had a full war chest. Commonwealth North, an allegedly nonpartisan organization headed by two former Alaskan governors, produced an eight-page insert for key American magazines. Its cover featured an oil barrel, natural gas flame, and lump of coal superimposed over a map of Alaska while the heading read: "The 49th state is a potential world power in the energy area." But, ambivalently, another drawing showed caribou walking past an oil drilling rig. The text explained that "the Arctic's energy resources can be tapped without harming the land or the wildlife."[58] No one could mistake the message of the publication: don't lock up Alaska's energy potential in wilderness reserves. Full-page advertisements appeared regularly in newspapers. They began with the headline "Kentucky [or the relevant state] You Need Alaska." And the need, it quickly became evident in the body of the ad, was not as wilderness.

Those who disagreed succeeded in constructing what became the largest and most powerful citizen conservation organization in American history. The Alaska Coalition began as the combined effort of the nation's five leading wilderness protection groups: the Wilderness Society, the Sierra Club, the National Audubon Society, Friends of the Earth, and the National Parks and Conservation Association. Under the leadership of the Sierra Club's Charles M. Clusen it grew to include 1,500 national, state, and local associations with membership totalling ten million persons. Obviously the coalition cut across regional, institutional, and philosophical differences that in the past had divided and weakened environmental movements. Born a quarter-century earlier in resistance to Echo Park Dam and developed in the struggles for the Wilderness Act of 1964 and against Grand Canyon dams, a concerted, massive

58. The insert summarized a longer report by Commonwealth North entitled *Why Not Alaska?* (Anchorage, ca. 1979).

movement for preservation came of age at the time Alaska's wilderness most needed it. The public pressure that the Alaska Coalition first generated and then applied, with skill, in the capital proved irresistible. The effort convinced Congress that the Alaska lands issue had national importance, that people in every state—whether personally familiar with Alaska or not—cared deeply about its future. In a significant departure from the norm in American politics, the 1980 act passed over the consistent and heated objections of Alaska's entire congressional delegation. The decision, in the end, was a national one.[59]

Morris Udall was again eloquent on the occasion of his May 1979 recommendation of the new Alaska lands bill to his colleagues. "Americans will never see a buffalo herd again," he declared, "and if we are not wise today, our grandchildren will not be able to see a caribou herd. This is the test of our congressional careers. This will be the most important vote we cast."[60] The House responded on May 24 by passing, 268 to 157, a prowilderness bill itemizing 127.5 million acres of national interest lands, including 67.5 million acres of designated wilderness. But just as it had in 1978, the Senate, and particularly its Energy Committee, resisted. Finally, on August 19, 1980, it approved by 64 votes a substantially less protective measure. House leaders initially refused to compromise with the Senate and vowed to start yet another Alaska bill through the legislative process. On November 4, 1980, however, a Republican landslide swept Ronald Reagan into the White House, Secretary James Watt into the Department of the Interior, and a less restrictive philosophy into American natural resource policy. In a televised October debate Reagan attacked Carter on the basis that the federal government "has in the last year or so taken out of multiple use millions of acres of public lands." It angered Reagan that potential oil producing lands were removed from exploration and development, and he singled out the "shut down" of Alaska for special criticism.[61] Recognizing that the political climate favoring the protection of Alaskan lands was changing rapidly, House

59. For information about the organization and function of the Alaska Coalition see Stephen T. Young, "The Success of the Alaska Coalition," *National Parks, 55* (1981), 10–13.

60. As quoted in Discha, "How the Alaska Act Was Won," p. 8.

61. As quoted by Rebecca Wodder, "The Alaska Challenge Ahead," *Living Wilderness, 44* (1981), 13.

leaders reluctantly approved the Senate bill on November 12 without any alterations. Still, as Morris Udall noted, the final bill "does accomplish 85–90 percent of the things the House wanted."[62] Alaska's governor, Jay Hammond, similarly felt the bill was not perfect but that it gave his state most of what it wanted. Once again the American political system's ability to compromise accommodated ambivalent American ideas concerning wilderness.

As signed by Jimmy Carter on December 2, 1980, the Alaska National Interest Lands Conservation Act set the pattern for future use of 375 million acres.[63] The act revoked the President's 1978 stopgap establishment of national monuments and gave final approval to most of the 105 million acres that the State of Alaska selected under the terms of statehood legislation. It also assured Alaska's natives of the forty-four million acre entitlement granted them under ANCSA. The rest of Alaska would remain federal property. From preservationists' viewpoint the great achievement of the 1980 act was that it set aside for permanent protection 104 million acres or 28 percent of the state, an area larger than California. Of this, Congress placed a little more than half, 56.7 million acres, in the National Wilderness Preservation System. Twenty-six additions were made to the National Wild and Scenic Rivers System. The amount of land in national parks and in wildlife refuges in the United States doubled upon passage of the Alaska lands act. It was, indeed, the most expansive action ever taken for wilderness and associated values at any one time in world history.

The principal dissatisfactions of preservationists with the 1980 act concerned the omission of ecologically important areas and the permission of noncompatible activities in protected lands. Time and again in the decade-long discussion of the act, wilderness advocates pointed to the unique opportunity Alaska afforded to protect "complete ecosystems" rather than just bits and pieces of a once wild environment as had occurred in the lower forty-eight. In California, for example, portions of the headwaters of rivers in the Sierra Nevada were designated wilderness, but downstream one found dams, agriculture, towns, and large cities. Some Alaskan watersheds of comparable size were almost completely unaltered, and preservationists hoped that areas as large as say, Tuolumne Meadows to San Francisco Bay, would be set aside. But the lines

62. As quoted in Connally, "D-2: Saving Out Last Frontier," p. 7.
63. Public Law 96–487 in U.S., *Statutes at Large*, 94, 2371ff.

drawn on the map of Alaska in 1980 generally omitted lower, level land and sometimes excluded important ranges of migratory animals such as caribou. Some ecologically significant areas like the Yukon Flats and the delta of the Copper River were, from a preservationist perspective, badly fractured. There was also concern over the use of legal and de facto wilderness in the national interest lands for subsistence hunting, fishing, and gathering. The primary beneficiary of this provision were native people but non-native (white) residents of the Alaskan backcountry were also permitted to live off protected lands. Most preservationists favored this marked departure from wilderness policy elsewhere in the nation, but the use of snowmobiles, motorboats, and complex rifles by modern-day hunters and gatherers occasioned considerable misgivings. One concession to preservation interests was the establishment of a procedure for monitoring wildlife populations and, when necessary, restricting subsistence consumption.[64]

Another acknowledgement of Alaska's special circumstances was a section of the act permitting cabins, symbols of the Alaskan style of bush living, in much of the protected acreage under renewable five-year leases. The provision for reindeer grazing and established commercial and sport hunting in the same area had been a central concern of the debates, and the final legislation permitted it in all the reserved lands with the exception of most national parks. A new land management category, "national preserves," facilitated sport hunting in places that would otherwise have been part of a park.[65] Another compromise involved mining and particularly oil and gas exploration. The 1980 act allowed prospecting in national interest lands known to have mineral or oil potential. Preservationists especially regretted the opening of 1.4 million acres of the Arctic National Wildlife Refuge and the lack of any restrictions in the twenty-two million acre Naval (National) Petroleum Reserve No. 4 adjacent to the producing wells at Prudhoe Bay. But the decisions with respect to energy development and mining in Alaska only extended the compromises that had been made with preservationists and built into the 1964 wilderness act. In Alaska, as in the

64. John T. Shively, "Subsistence Hunting in Alaskan Parks," *National Parks*, 55 (1981), 18–21. For a criticism of high technology subsistence hunting see George Reiger, "Subsistence Hunting: Fact or Fiction?" *Field and Stream*, 84 (1979), 20.

65. For a criticism of this policy see Devereux Butcher, "Is Sport Shooting a Responsibility of the National Park Service?" *National Parks*, 55 (1981), 13–15.

rest of the nation, it appeared that the only wilderness *certain* to be preserved was that which contained no valuable resources.[66]

The d(2) controversy, including two sets of Congressional hearings in 1977 and 1979, generated thousands of pages of documentation on the American attitude toward Alaskan wilderness. In general there were few surprises. Those opposed to the protection of significant amounts of wilderness in Alaska centered their protests on the way preservation closed development options. "Lock up" was the key idea in their argument. "I believe," said Robert Dilger of the Washington State Construction Trades Council, "it is unwise to lock up for the future 146 million acres of land [that] . . . has hardly been surveyed, let alone thoroughly analyzed for its resources."[67] Variations of the same theme occurred numerous times in the Congressional hearing records. Almost no one spoke against wilderness in and of itself; the objections were invariably that one good thing (environmental protection) stood in the way of a greater good (obtaining oil, minerals, lumber and, in a sense, progress). At almost every House hearing, Alaska's only congressman, Don Young, called attention to the inconsistency of his congressional colleagues. They would not dare, he said, support H.R. 39 type legislation for their own states. It struck Young as discriminatory: "Why a wilderness Alaska? Why not Arizona? The people back home wouldn't stand for it, that why." In Young's opinion "voting to lock up Alaska is a politically easy way for a member [of Congress] to gain an environmental record—but at the expense of the people of Alaska and the nation . . . America is running short of a lot of things that Alaska has."[68]

Former Alaska governor Walter J. Hickel shared this view. "Don't lock the people away from their land with this wilderness category," he pleaded. "When you lock up the land you lock up the human mind. You lock up the human spirit." Wilderness protection in Alaska, Hickel felt, was unnecessary. The vastness and harshness of the land would keep civilization at bay. "When God

66. On the idea that only "worthless" lands are ever protected as wilderness or national parks in the American context see Alfred Runte, *National Parks: The American Experience* (Lincoln, Neb., 1979), Chapter 3.

67. U.S. Congress, House, Committee on Interior and Insular Affairs, Hearings, *Inclusion of Alaska Lands in National Park, Forest, Wildlife Refuge, and Wild and Scenic Rivers Systems,* 95th Cong., 1st Sess. (June 18, 1977), p. 23.

68. As quoted in Don Dedera, "Will a Law Lock Up Alaska" *Exxon USA, 17* (1978), 22.

made this country," Hickel explained, "He zoned it Himself."[69] The fact that non-Alaskans, the outsiders who had neglected their northern colony for decades, were influencing the use of Alaskan lands added insult to alleged injury. "I hate those bastards down in the Lower 48 who think they own Alaska," screamed the leader of the Alaska secession movement, Joe Vogler. "Anybody who tells me this land was not put here to use is a socialist enemy of mine! Anybody who tells me trees shouldn't be cut, I'd use the axe on him."[70]

Homesteaders and squatters on public lands in Alaska were especially suspicious of the entire d(2) process. It seemed to them that the nation was systematically eliminating, in John McPhee's words, "the last place in the United States where the pioneer impulse can leap from confinement." The neopioneers McPhee talked to along the Yukon River thought their simple cabins, dozens or hundreds of miles from the nearest roads, were harmless. "It's not as if we're building fifty-thousand-dollar houses with asphalt driveways and stinking cesspools," one explained. In the interest of social diversity and individual freedom, why not allow the few who wished to go back to nature the chance to do so in Alaska. Otherwise, another homesteader pointed out, "Alaska is going to be just like every other state." These arguments, and the hardships the homesteaders voluntarily faced, even convinced as strong a preservationist as McPhee: "If I were writing [the legislation], I would say that anyone at all is free to build a cabin on any federal land in the United States that is at least a hundred miles from the nearest town of ten thousand or more."[71] This position, of course, discounted the desires of wilderness travelers who might not wish to find a permanent human habitation a hundred miles from town. The issue boiled down to whether the handful of people who wanted to be pioneers in the twentieth century should be subsidized at the expense of the nation's last vast wildernesses. In the end McPhee's view prevailed. The 1980 legislation permitted backwoods cabins and subsistence lifestyles in most of the national interest lands.

Alaska's native people also worried that federal land legislation would prohibit them from lands used for subsistence purposes for

69. As quoted in Hope, "The Question of Alaska," p. 252.
70. Ibid, p. 253.
71. McPhee, *Coming Into the Country*, pp. 235–36, 415–16.

not just tens but thousands of years. At the hearings held in Alaska's small native towns and villages, congressmen listened attentively as Eskimos and Indians, some speaking broken English, told of their desire to continue living off the land.[72] "The land," Chuck Hunt of the Kuskokwim River delta explained, "is our supermarket." If its use for hunting and gathering was to be curtailed, "you lose your livehood. . . . you lose your identity. You go on a long slide, take to firewater."[73] Most natives, it appeared, had no objection to designating land "wilderness" although many found it hard to understand this white man's concept applied to their homeland. What did concern them was how the new preserves would be managed. Ultimately, the natives, too, got most of what they wanted.

An interesting variation of the "lock up" argument came from professional hunting guides. Clare Engle, for instance, feared the d(2) decisions would put him out of a business three decades in the making. He was not, after all, engaged in subsistence hunting, and H.R. 39 would close, by his estimation, "two thirds of the hunting country in the state." This objection aside, Engle had no problem with designated wilderness. He disliked mines and lumber operations (particularly, he said, those which sold their output to Japan) as much as any environmentalist. And, as a caterer to sophisticated American and European hunters, Engle especially resented new roads that would bring "every cowboy and his brother . . . dropping beer cans and blasting away at the moose." In addition, if the national interest lands limited use by sport hunters, Engle predicted violence. "If the Feds come up here," he declared, they'd better bring bullet-proof vests and a priest!"[74]

The Alaskan most opposed to wilderness preservation was, arguably, Robert Atwood, and as editor and publisher of the Anchorage *Times* his influence was considerable. Atwood's lifelong

72. See U.S. Congress, House, Committee on Interior and Insular Affairs, Hearings, *Inclusion of Alaska Lands in National Park, Forest, Wildlife Refuge, and Wild and Scenic Rivers Systems,* 95th Cong., 1st Sess., (Aug. 8–11, 13, 14, 17–19, 1977).

73. As quoted in Hope, "The Question of Alaska," p. 260. An excellent source for native opinion in the 1970s is the *Tundra Times,* a native newspaper published in Fairbanks, Alaska. The issue of Jan. 11, 1978, contained a special supplement, "Subsistence: Tradition and a Way of Life." An insightful analysis of the subsistence issue is John G. Mitchell, "Where Have All the Tuttu Gone?" *Audubon, 79* (1970), 3–15.

74. As quoted in Hope, "The Question of Alaska," p. 258.

dream was to reproduce American civilization, lower forty-eight style, in Alaska. He felt that vast amounts of wilderness were no more appropriate in Alaska than they were in Ohio or Massachusetts. "The ultimate destiny of Alaska," Atwood believed, "is to help the nation be self-sufficient." Every oil and mineral deposit should be exploited. "We should preserve wilderness," Atwood contended, "only in areas that are without other resources.... Locking up the land is unfair to future generations."[75] Like many opponents of d(2), Atwood's concern was that the size of the area in question and the speed of the classification process made it impossible to make a careful inventory. He wondered why there was a rush to "lock [resources] up in a park that only environmentalists with their planes can get to?"[76] This was a subject of considerable sensitivity to the opponents of wilderness. Since the days of Charles Sheldon and Robert Marshall, both of whom were millionaires, visitors to the Alaskan wilderness were generally either rich or (like John McPhee and representatives of environmental groups and federal bureaus) traveling on expense accounts. According to Donald Simasko, spokesman for the Alaska Oil and Gas Association, the average Alaska vacation cost $3,000 per person. Chartered air travel to roadless wildernesses would increase that figure. Moreover, Simasko continued, maintaining wilderness like that found in Alaska would eliminate its use by large groups of Americans. "Are we setting this area aside for the very healthy and young people who have the fortunate circumstances to find themselves with the time and ability to backpack?"[77] Alaska Senator Mike Gravel agreed that "for the older, less agile, and less affluent" most national interest lands in Alaska will forever be "nothing more than lines on a map."[78] Wilderness preservationists had always faced this kind of objection, but the remoteness, severity, and undeniable dangers associated with backcountry travel in Alaska made elitism more of a reality.

The preservationist response to these arguments focused on several now familiar themes. Alaska, it was said over and over again

75. As quoted in McPhee, *Coming Into the Country*, pp. 81–82. Hanrahan and Gruenstein, *Lost Frontier*, devote a chapter to Atwood, pp. 42–65.

76. As quoted in Hope, "The Question of Alaska," p. 255.

77. U.S. Congress, House, Committee on Interior and Insular Affairs, Hearings, *Inclusion of Alaska Lands in National Park, Forest, Wildlife Refuge, and Wild and Scenic Rivers Systems*, 95th Cong., 1st Sess., (June 4, 1977), pp. 45–46.

78. *Congressional Record*, 96th Cong., 2nd Sess., *126* (Aug. 19, 1980), p. S11186.

in the course of the d(2) debates, was America's last frontier. People appeared anxious to preserve Alaska as a living link to the national past and to the roots of the national character. The wilderness cult, expanding since the demise of the first frontier in 1890 (see above, Chapter 9), came to the assistance of the final frontier. Alaska offered a second chance to learn from history and to build a balance between man and nature so notable for its absence a century before. Sierra Club spokesman Edgar Wayburn called Alaska "the last great first chance" and added that "in Alaska we have an unparalleled opportunity to learn from our past mistakes."[79] Some preservationists implied that the United States bore a burden of guilt that could only be expiated by protecting Alaska. At the 1977 Chicago hearings, a biology teacher said that preserving Alaska's wilderness would "in some measure compensate for our past follies."[80] When the hearings moved to Seattle, a witness explained that Americans "have squandered resources and polluted the environment in the name of progress." Alaska was "our last chance not to . . . exploit the land."[81]

Others who supported H.R. 39 in its several versions, were excited by the opportunity Alaska afforded to preserve wilderness of an unprecedented scale and quality. The phrase "complete ecosystems" occurred in the testimony of hundreds of witnesses. Drawing on the importance of wilderness as a biological resource (see above, pp. 257–60), they defended the preservation of, in the words of John Kauffmann of the National Park Service, "whole ecosystems, whole ranges, whole watersheds." In Kauffmann's view modern man desperately needed places "where we can learn how . . . to live in close harmony with the earth," and Alaska was such a place.[82] Citing the need for genetic material and biological diversity, a witness testified in Denver that "the preservation of complete ecosystems, or collections of ecosystems . . . is essential." There remains, he added, "but one opportunity for the United States to do so."[83]

79. Wayburn, "Alaska, The Last Great First Chance," *Sierra Club Bulletin, 62* (1977), 42.

80. U.S. Congress, House, Committee on Interior and Insular Affairs, Hearings, *Inclusion of Alaska Lands in National Park, Forest, Wildlife Refuge, and Wild and Scenic Rivers Systems,* 95th Cong., 1st Sess., (May 7, 1977), p. 88.

81. Ibid. (June 18, 1977), p. 185.

82. McPhee, *Coming Into the Country,* p. 84.

83. House, Hearings (June 4, 1977), p. 140.

If Robert Atwood represented one end of the spectrum of opinion on Alaska's future, John Kauffmann spoke for the antipode. Kauffmann was bitter that the nation had not followed the advice of Henry David Thoreau in the 1850s and made much of Maine and New Hampshire a permanent wilderness. His efforts were directed at avoiding the same mistake in Alaska. What Kauffmann really championed was "the chance to go adventuring in country so wild that valleys and mountains are without names." Kauffmann, like Marshall, was independently wealthy, yet charges of elitism did not bother him. "The day will come," he predicted, "when people will want to visit such a wilderness—saving everything they have in order to see it, at whatever cost." Alaska was special, continued Kauffmann, because in fifty years "there may be nowhere else to go to a place that is wild and unexplored."[84] At other times Kauffmann turned philosophical and, in a passage read into the *Congressional Record* in the final minutes of the 1980 Senate debate, declared: "Alaska is our ultimate wilderness, the last remnant of what the New World used to be. If we lose the freshness and the beauty there, something essential to North America will have died out forever."[85]

John Kauffmann was enraged when he perceived that Alaskans, like older-style frontiersmen, were totally oblivious to these considerations. In fact Kauffmann redesigned the state coat of arms featuring the four foundations of Alaskan attitude toward land: "Dig It Up," "Chop It Down," "Fish It Out," and "Shoot It." Moreover, he pointed out, along with many other preservationists, Alaskans did not even own much of the land they wished to exploit. It was national property, federal land, and American citizens were not "meddlers" but legal owners. Clever with figures, Kauffmann tried to demonstrate that in reality Alaskans had little to complain about. According to the federal proposals, the state received 250 acres for each non-native citizen, and 600 acres for each native. That left about one acre of Alaska for each resident of the other forty-nine states.[86] In Kauffmann's opinion this was none too much.

While some prowilderness spokesmen, like Kauffmann, traveled frequently in wild Alaska, the majority of those who testified in favor of H.R. 39 admitted they had never seen, or even expected to

84. McPhee, *Coming Into the Country*, pp. 85, 27.
85. *Congressional Record*, 96th Cong., 2d Sess., *126* (Aug. 19, 1980), p. S11202.
86. McPhee, *Coming Into the Country*, p. 83.

see, the places they wished to preserve. The Alaskan wilderness appealed to them primarily as a symbol. Edward Abbey understood that "man could be a lover and defender of the wilderness without ever in his lifetime leaving the boundaries of asphalt, powerlines, and right-angled surfaces. . . . I may never in my life get to Alaska . . . but I am grateful that it's there. We need the possibility of escape as surely as we need hope."[87] Congressman John Seiberling thought that an important reason many worked for the Alaska bill was "the mere knowledge that somewhere in this world there are pristine areas comparable to what this whole North American continent was like when the first Europeans landed on its shores."[88] Sally Ann Ranney of the American Wilderness Alliance offered another perspective: "There are many of us that are never going to see the treasures of Michelangelo, . . . but, that . . . does not mean that we advocate burning them, . . . and I think the same thing can apply to Alaska."[89] Seiberling agreed that the Alaskan wilderness was "part of the heritage of mankind," something that transcended individual interest. He also knew, with reference to the world's natural treasures, that the American decision regarding Alaska would be closely scrutinized and used, for better or for worse, as a precedent for other nations' undeveloped areas.[90]

Another common tactic of the preservationists was to counter the opposition's argument with posters that read, "Development is the Greatest Lock Up." In their opinion, wilderness preserved resources that, after all, were still there, still available if the nation needed them. Striving for a metaphor to make his hopes for Alaska understandable, Morris Udall observed that "the day may come in 200 years when we are in bad trouble and . . . we are going to have to mine in the middle of Yellowstone Park, . . . but I say let's do that last."[91] He implied that the United States was not so desperate that it had to exploit its last wilderness. By the 1970s some Americans were willing to go even a step further and contend that wilderness was just as valuable as minerals, oil, and lumber. From their perspective wilderness did not block utilization of valuable resources; it

87. Abbey, *Desert Solitaire*, pp. 148–49.

88. U.S. Congress, House, Committee on Interior and Insular Affairs, Hearings, *Inclusion of Alaska Lands in National Park, Forest, Wildlife Refuge, and Wild and Scenic Rivers Systems*, 95th Cong., 1st Sess. (May 14, 1977), p. 2.

89. Ibid. (June 4, 1977), p. 53.

90. Ibid. (May 7, 1977), pp. 100–01.

91. Ibid. (June 4, 1977), p. 53.

was a valuable resource. "I support H.R. 39," one witness declared, "because it recognizes the fact that only within my lifetime has undeveloped land become as rare as and more valuable than molybdenum."[92] Copper, said a witness from Arizona, was the major resource of his state; in Alaska the most important resource from a world prespective was wilderness. "Arizona," he concluded, "supplies the world with much of its copper. . . . Alaska can supply . . . vast and pristine wilderness."[93] In a few minds, even this kind of comparison did not wholly express the value of wild Alaska. As John Denver's July 1980 invitation to join him in Washington, D. C., to lobby the senate put it: "Wilderness is not just a resource; it is the source."[94]

While tempting as a way to order history, it would be much too simple to see the Alaska lands controversy of the 1970s as a battle between northern frontiersmen who despised wilderness and outside preservationists who would make a national park out of most of the state. The life of Jay Hammond, who was elected governor of Alaska in 1974 and again in 1978, illustrates some of the complexities. In 1946 at the age of twenty-four Hammond came to Alaska to make his living in the backwoods. He trapped, homesteaded, fished commercially and, for a time, shot wolves from airplanes as part of a predator control effort. Hammond has a fifty-inch chest, shoulders to match, a full beard and a deep, bear-like voice. "Hammond is Alaska," a colleague declared, "he . . . looks like a goddam Alaska mountain." But Jay Hammond resists attitudinal stereotyping. He is not opposed to wilderness preservation, and the fact of his governorship suggests that he is not alone in these views in Alaska. "Environment," Hammond explained, "is not an obscene, four-letter word. It has eleven letters, just as does the word 'development.' "[95] As for wilderness, Hammond understood that it is essential to the appeal of Alaska. Speaking in 1977 to the House committee conducting hearings in Fairbanks, Hammond said, "Ask yourselves why Alaskans came here, or why they stay. The great

92. As quoted by John Seiberling in "John Seiberling on the Future of Alaska," *Living Wilderness, 41* (1977), 16.

93. House, Hearings (June 4, 1977), p. 38.

94. Pamphlet distributed by the Windstar Foundation, Snowmass, Co., July, 1980.

95. The quotations are from an interview, "Jay S. Hammond," published in *Mariah, 3* (Dec., 1978), 14, 16. The eleven-letter statement is from Hammond's 1975 inaugural address. A useful biography appears in Hanrahan and Gruenstein, *Lost Frontier*, pp. 66–81.

beauty and wilderness of our State is a prime reason."[96] In a subsequent interview Hammond professed frustration with outsiders who did not think Alaskans could be trusted with the Alaskan environment. "There is a great misapprehension on the part of people who live elsewhere that they have to protect Alaska from Alaskans," he declared, and added that "most Alaskans are here because of those very values that many outsiders are so concerned we are insensitive to." He felt that boomers like Robert Atwood who wanted to reproduce Southern California in the arctic were a lunatic fringe. Most Alaskans, Hammond thought, would agree that "we can and should have both development and wilderness."[97]

Governor Hammond did oppose the Alaska National Interest Lands Conservation Act, but his resistance did not stem from indifference about wilderness. Hammond disliked federal land management; instead, he wanted a cooperative arrangement in which federal, state, native, and private interests would plan the future of Alaska together. He hoped that the state could be an equal partner with the nation in managing the national interest lands.

Many Alaskans agreed with their governor that the media and outside preservationists misunderstood the attitudes of Alaskans toward wilderness. In 1978 Ginny Wood, an early advocate of wilderness oriented tourism attempted to correct the oversimplifications: "Give or take the boomers, . . . the Secessionists, . . . and even a few nature buffs who would like to see all Alaska a national park, the great majority who are in between—no matter which side of the fence they shout from—are not basically that far apart on what kind of an Alaska they want to continue to live in." The majority, Wood thought, wanted to sustain, not destroy, "our unique quality of life," and they realized that that depended on preserving wilderness. For Mike Miller, an Alaskan for twenty-three years and member of the state legislature, "wilderness . . . provides . . . the dynamic differ-

96. U.S. Congress, House, Committee on Interior and Insular Affairs, Hearings, *Inclusion of Alaska Lands in National Park, Forest, Wildlife Refuge, and Wild and Scenic Rivers Systems*, 95th Cong., 1st Sess. (Aug. 20, 1977), p. 14. According to Robert Weeden, a hundred Alaskan "opinion leaders," meeting in 1969 at the invitation of the state legislature, concluded that "the special feel of Alaska emanated from nature and from human experiences in nature." Wildness, beauty, and freedom, or what in 1963 Governor William A. Egan called "elbow room," dominated the discussion of Alaska's assets: Weeden, *Alaska*, pp. 32–33. The Egan statement is quoted in Cooley, *Alaska*, p. 129.

97. "Jay S. Hammond," *Mariah*, *3* (Dec., 1978) 16, 37.

ence that sets Alaska apart from any of the other forty-nine states." In his view "it would be tragic, in the extreme, if we were to eliminate or emasculate that dynamic difference."[98] Miller had prefaced his testimony at the Juneau hearings with the observation that he would be in the minority, but the record revealed that many Alaskans, whether they liked the particulars of H.R. 39 or not, were of a similar mind.

Even Don Young, a die-hard opponent of the bill's land withdrawals, bemoaned "the tendency of almost everyone (especially the media) to portray the issue as a battle between the forces of unchecked development and those who wanted to save the land." He added, "I'll put my state's environmental record up against that of any state in the union." In Young's view, "the real issue, the issue that was for the most part ignored, was the preservation of the Alaskan lifestyle." A former trapper, Young knew that this required the right to live off wild land. He opposed the national interest lands not because they protected wilderness but because, in his view, they kept Alaskans from using, economically, a wilderness they had long prized and desired to maintain.[99]

Sue E. Liljeblad, an eleven-year resident of Anchorage, felt that most Alaskans had come north, as she had, to escape the environment and way of life of the rest of the United States, not to recreate it. This, she realized, set modern Alaskans apart from pioneers of the past. For Liljeblad the last frontier image was a major obstacle to understanding how Alaskans actually felt about wilderness. "The outsider has to realize," she observed, "that Alaskans are not 'hell bent for leather' to rape, pillage and ruin the land. They don't want to 'californicate' Alaska." They differ from other Americans in their understanding of what activities are appropriate in wild country. Cabins, she felt, and even occupied homesteads were not incompatible with the Alaskan definition of wilderness. Neither were airplanes, small mining operations, sport and subsistence hunting, and the presence of native people. The Alaskan wilderness, Liljeblad continued, was so wild and so extensive that it could easily

98. Wood, "Woodsmoke," *Alaska Conservation Review, 19* (1978), 15; Miller in U.S. Congress, House, Committee on Interior and Insular Affairs, Hearings, *Inclusion of Alaska Lands in National Park, Forest, Wildlife Refuge, and Wild and Scenic River Systems,* 95th Cong., 1st Sess. (July 7, 1977), p. 6.

99. Young as quoted in "Political Protagonists in the D-2 Drama," *National Parks, 55* (1981), 15.

absorb and dilute influences that might ruin wilderness elsewhere. The failure of the outside to understand this wrongly made the d(2) controversy seem to be a fight between love and hatred of wilderness. Most Alaskans, Liljeblad concluded, like moose in their backyards. This was what made Alaska special. Consequently, Alaskans accepted the designation of vast amounts of land as permanent wilderness. Their concern was what would be permitted in these wilderness lands.[100] As it turned out, the Alaska National Interest Lands Conservation Act adopted a less restrictive philosophy of wilderness management that was consistent with Alaskan thinking.

One way to avoid forcing a dichotomy in analyzing the recent discussion of wilderness in Alaska is to understand that the state's economic interests, that is, development, would best be served by the permanent preservation of wilderness. Robert Marshall hinted at this in 1938, as did Lowell Sumner in the 1950s, and it became even more apparent with the growth of tourism. In 1962 a University of Alaska economist, George Rogers, described how wilderness could make money for Alaska—as a mecca for tourists and a necessary habitat for harvestable fish and game. Owning land and developing it, he explained, was not a great economic advantage in most parts of the North, as it has been in much of the lower forty-eight. It made economic sense to Rogers to keep Alaska wild, and he recommended including wilderness "within the meaning of the term 'development' in Alaska."[101] Richard Cooley had the same thing in mind in 1966 when he recommended discarding the "old mythology" that wilderness always had to give way if civilization were to progress. Why not a future, Cooley asked, in which wilderness was a permanent and economically significant part of civilization?[102]

100. Interviews with Sue E. Liljeblad, Aug., 1980, and Sept., 1981, in Anchorage, Ak. and Santa Barbara, Ca.

101. Rogers, "Wilderness and Development" in *Alaska Public Policy: Current Problems and Issues,* ed. Gordon Scott Harrison (College, Ak., 1971), p. 232. Also relevant is Rogers's *The Future of Alaska: The Economic Consequences of Statehood* (Baltimore, 1962) and his "Alaska in Transition: Wilderness and Development" in Maxine E. McCloskey, ed., *Wilderness: The Edge of Knowledge* (San Francisco, 1970), pp. 143–53.

102. Cooley, *Alaska,* pp. 129–30. See also George W. Rogers and Richard A. Cooley, *Alaska's Population and Economy: Regional Growth, Development and Future Outlook* (College, Ak., 1963).

In recent years Robert Weeden, a University of Alaska biologist who advised Jay Hammond's administration, continued this discussion. He called for acceptance of the fact that Alaska is not suitable for development characteristics of more temperate climates. The North needed a new land use philosophy in which wilderness was not a museum piece with "Don't Touch" signs but a working wilderness, "an integral part of the human environment." Weeden understood that if large amounts of wilderness were to be part of Alaska's future the state's population would have to be stabilized at a low level (he recommended 500,000) and technology restrained. But if small, as the counterculture thought, was beautiful, the payoff could be human happiness, land health, and the knowledge that "there is a place where men live amidst a balanced interplay of the goods of technology and the fruits of nature."[103] Yet Margaret Murie, who grew up in Fairbanks not far from where Weeden taught, may have made his point more succinctly: "In the long view, all Alaska needs to do is be Alaska. That will be her economy."[104]

In 1978, with the d(2) controversy in full stride, Weeden published *Alaska: Promises To Keep*. He again called on Alaska to find and follow the middle way between the extremes of hands-off preservation and destructive exploitation. The promises Weeden felt Alaska should keep concerned the demonstration of a viable alternative to the philosophy that bigger was always better. The way to begin keeping them was to maintain the quantity and quality of wilderness presently in Alaska and to build a culture and an economy upon it. This meant using wilderness carefully, both for recreation and for resources, and with special attention to the biological limits imposed by the land. Weeden's dream for the permanent coexistence of civilization and wilderness in Alaska included both resolution and final expression of the oldest American ambivalence.

The division of Alaska confirmed in 1980 found 12 percent of the state in native hands. The State of Alaska had 27 percent. National interest lands, the parks, preserves, and refuges, constituted 27 percent, and the federal government retained title to another 33

103. Weeden, "Man in Nature: A Strategy for Alaskan Living," in Harrison, ed., *Alaska Public Policy*, pp. 261, 269. See also Weeden's "Can Economics Save Wildlands?" *Alaska Conservation Review, 18* (1977), 7 and his "Letter from Alaska," *Living Wilderness, 35* (1971), 35–40.

104. House, Hearings (June 4, 1977), p. 26.

percent of Alaska as simply public domain. Private holdings in 1980 amounted to only 1 percent, but this figure was expected to increase as state lands were sold to individuals. Significantly, in view of the repeated cries of discrimination and colonialism, Alaska emerged from two decades of controversy with almost exactly the same pattern of land ownership as a typical Western state. Arizona, for instance, had even more land in the native and federal categories. What was different about Alaska was the amount of wilderness. In addition to the 56.7 million acres of land added to the National Wilderness Preservation System, the Alaska National Interest Lands Conservation Act mandated review for preservation of over 70 million additional acres of federal land. Probably about 33 percent of the state will eventually be designated wilderness. Another third of Alaska will, in the foreseeable future, be wild by default of development.

This comes close to creating the permanent American frontier preservationists desired. It will, inevitably, be a modern frontier with airplanes taking the place of horses and chain saws substituting for axes. Preserving the unique qualities of wild Alaska will demand the best efforts of the still young and tentative profession of wilderness management. Saving the Alaskan wilderness from its friends may prove a more formidable task than protecting it from boomers and developers. Managing the managers is part of that challenge. Ray Bane, an officer of the new Gates of the Arctic National Park, understood the difficulties involved: "The goal is to manage this land in such a way that a visitor one hundred years from now could experience the same feeling of discovery . . . that Bob Marshall felt more than forty years ago."[105] And so it was, as Ginny Wood realized, that the legislative triumphs began, rather than concluded, the struggle for wilderness in Alaska. "Ironically," Wood told a House hearing in Fairbanks, "I know that after a d(2) bill is passed I will then be fighting to protect the d(2) lands from . . . the very agencies instructed to protect them."[106]

105. As quoted in Boyd Norton, "A Gentle, Welcoming Wilderness," *Audubon, 79* (1977), 45.

106. House, Hearings (Aug. 20, 1977), p. 83. For a related view see Edgar Wayburn, "All Quiet on the Alaska Front?" *Sierra, 66* (1981), 59.

CHAPTER 15

The Irony of Victory

The woods are overrun and sons of bitches like me are half the problem.

Colin Fletcher, 1971

IRONY, literary critics tell us, occurs when a result is opposite that which was intended or expected. Success turns out to be failure. It is a case of too much of a good thing becoming a bad thing. Wilderness appreciation offers a classic instance of irony in our own time. For more than a century the Thoreaus, Muirs, Leopolds, and Browers labored to attract American attention to wild country as a recreational resource. Preserving wilderness seemed dependent on building a clientele for it. Hetch Hetchy Valley was lost, Muir felt, because so few knew its glories firsthand. Glen Canyon disappeared under a reservoir in Brower's time because it was the place no one knew. And then, in the late 1960s and 1970s, victory! Wilderness was suddenly "in." An increasingly urban population turned to the nation's remaining empty places in unprecedented numbers. Although hard to document precisely, visits to wilderness areas grew 12 percent annually, doubling in a decade. Projections, which may be conservative, looked for a tenfold increase by the year 2000.[1] In highly publicized wildernesses such as the Grand Canyon of Arizona the rate of visitor growth was almost exponential until stopped by the National Park Service (see below, p. 331). Popularity like this contributed to saving wilderness areas from development. In publicizing wilderness Muir and his colleagues had succeeded spectacularly. But even as preservationists were celebrating their apparent victory, the more perceptive among them saw a disturbing new threat to wilderness in their own enthusiasm. Ironically, the very increase in appreciation of wilderness threatened to prove its undoing. Having made extraordinary gains in the public's estimation in the last century, wilderness could well be loved to death in the next.

1. Wildland Research Center, *Wilderness and Recreation*, pp. 213–54 and especially pp. 236–37; Ezra Bowen, *The High Sierra* (New York, 1972), p. 156.

The problem, of course, was people. Dams, mines, and roads are not the basic threat to the wilderness quality of an environment. Civilized people are, and whether they come with economic or recreational motives is, in a sense, beside the point. Wilderness values are such that even appropriate kinds of recreational use can, in sufficient quantity, destroy the wildness of a place. As ecologist Stanley A. Cain puts it, "innumerable people cannot enjoy solitude together."[2]

In retrospect it appears that four revolutions contributed to what Colin Fletcher called the overrunning of the woods. The *intellectual revolution* is, essentially, the subject of this book. As Chapter 13 suggests, a fully developed philosophy of the value of wilderness emerged by 1970. More importantly, from the standpoint of popularity, the reasons for wilderness appreciation filtered down from intellectuals to a broader base of acceptance in American society. The success of the Sierra Club's and David R. Brower's "Exhibit Format Series" of coffee-table books extolling wilderness is an instance. So, on a less expensive level, is Time-Life's series of books entitled "The American Wilderness." In the 1970s wilderness oriented magazines such as *Backpacker, Wilderness Camping,* and *Outside* spread the message to still wider circles. From another perspective, Henry David Thoreau and Aldo Leopold, who were known to only a small circle of associates during their lifetimes, became celebrated savants of the wilderness movement. A revolutionary change in attitude explains the difference.

But ideas by themselves could not cause the woods to be overrun. A *revolution in equipment* has facilitated the implementation of love for wilderness. It is not easy today to examine, or even imagine, the kind of gear earlier generations of outdoorspeople used when they went into the wilderness.[3] Tents in the 1920s were made of white canvas and weighed fifty pounds. People slept in bulky woolen bedrolls fastened at the end with giant safety pins. Food came wet-packaged in cans. Understandably, horses and mules trans-

2. As quoted in Ann and Myron Sutton, *The Wilderness World of the Grand Canyon* (Philadelphia, 1971), p. 204.

3. For help look at the early editions of the book regarded as the campers "bible" in the early twentieth century: Horace Kephart, *The Book of Camping and Woodcraft: A Guide For Those Who Travel in the Wilderness* (New York, 1910). See also Louis Bignami, "Past and Present Tents," *Westways, 73* (1981), 34–37.

ported camping outfits.[4] Wilderness travelers who carried their equipment on their backs were so rare as to be considered eccentric. As recently as 1934, David Brower could complete a ten-week backpack in the Sierra Nevada and fill two pages of a journal with a list of the places he had seen that no one had previously visited.[5] But the technological breakthroughs at the time of the Second World War began to change all that. Plastic, nylon, aluminum, and foam rubber appeared along with the freeze-dried process for preserving food. By the 1950s it was possible for the average person to contemplate a backpacking trip of more than a few days.[6] Improvements in insulated clothing and cross-country skis opened the woods to winter visitors. Fiberglass and synthetic rubber revolutionized whitewater boating. The pace of the improvement is astonishing. In 1972, an early issue of *Backpacker* reviewed the nineteen backpacks then on the market. Five years later the magazine found 129 to evaluate. The figures are comparable for tents, sleeping bags, and hiking boots. Such rapid proliferation is both a response to and a cause of the popularity of wilderness.

Before the era of modern paved highways getting to the wilderness was almost as difficult as traveling in it. In 1916 it took three days of tough driving on dirt roads to go from the San Francisco area to Sierra Nevada trailheads such as Donner Summit. For easterners of that era who rode the rails it was virtually impossible to fit a vacation in a western national park into two weeks. As late as the 1950s the edges of Utah's canyonlands were several days' travel from transportation centers such as Denver, Salt Lake City, and Las Vegas. Today, by way of contrast, air travel and fast roads make wilderness a realistic objective for millions even for a long weekend.[7] The impact of the *transportation revolution* on wilderness use patterns is indisputable. It can be argued that the piece of technology with the most devastating effect on the American wilderness was the family automobile.

4. A revealing account of an 1890 trip with packstock in the Sierra Nevada is Joseph N. LeConte, *A Summer of Travel in the High Sierra* (Ashland, Or., 1972).

5. David R. Brower, "Individual Freedom in Public Wilderness," *Not Man Apart*, 6 (1976), p. 2.

6. Colin Fletcher, *Complete Walker* discusses modern equipment. A comparable volume is John Hart, *Walking Softly in the Wilderness: The Sierra Club Guide to Backpacking* (San Fancisco, 1977).

7. In this regard see Charles Jones and Klaus Knab, *American Wilderness: A Gousha Weekend Guide to Our Wild Lands and Waters* (San Jose, Ca., 1973).

The fourth and final factor in bringing wilderness to the point of being loved to death is the *information revolution.* A half century ago wilderness was indeed unknown country. Once in the wilderness, one learned by trial and error. John McPhee reports that by the end of the 1930s David Brower could have been left off at night anywhere in the Sierra Nevada, and in the morning he would have known where he was.[8] But that kind of intimacy with a piece of wild country resulted from ten years of almost constant travel in it. Brower carried maps and guidebooks in his head. Today aids to wilderness travel are published in pack-size paperback editions. The ancestor of western hiking guidebooks is *Starr's Guide to the John Muir Trail,* originally published by the Sierra Club in 1934. Newer ones take the beginning wilderness traveler by the hand, providing equipment lists and suggestions for routes that are "leisurely," "moderate," or "strenuous."[9] What took Muir, Brower, and John Wesley Powell a lifetime to acquire is available today for $2.95. Along with the detailed 7.5 minute United States Geological Survey topographic maps, the guidebooks allow thousands of first-time wilderness explorers to plan wilderness trips in their living rooms. Those desiring more assistance can turn to the dozens of commercial guiding and outfitting operations that have sprung up in the last decade. According to the *Adventure Trip Guide,* over fifteen companies include wilderness in their titles.[10] The Sierra Club offers more than 300 outings each year. Confirming Muir's prediction (see p. 140), "thousands of tired, nerve-shaken, over-civilized people" *had* come to the wilderness and discovered that "wildness is a necessity."[11] Some also discovered that in the process the wildness had vanished.

This is most dramatically illustrated in the Grand Canyon (see p. 331), but there are surprising statistics all around the nation. Consider the East with little wilderness and lots of wilderness

8. McPhee, *Encounters,* p. 34.

9. Karl Schwenke and Thomas Winnett, *Sierra South: 100 Back-country Trips in California's Sierra* (Berkeley, 1968). George S. Wells, *Handbook of Wilderness Travel* (Denver, 1968) is nationwide in focus. Step-by-step "how to" books abound as, for instance, Mary Scott Welch, *The Family Wilderness Handbook* (New York, 1973).

10. *Adventure Trip Guide,* ed. Pat Dickman (New York, 1972).

11. A typical contemporary statement is Susan Sands, "Backpacking: 'I Go to the Wilderness to Kick the Man-World Out of Me,'" New York *Times,* May 9, 1971, p. 1.

lovers. A 1940 study divided the number of users into trail miles to show that in the White Mountains of New Hampshire a backpacker could expect to encounter one other person every four and one-half miles. In the early 1970s that figure had shrunk to seventy-three yards![12] It was not much better in highly publicized parts of the once-wild West. One hiker described a trip to California's Mount Whitney with his father on August 6, 1949. Proudly they signed the register on the summit of the highest peak in the forty-eight states, the sixth and seventh persons to do so that year. Twenty-three years later to the day, the hiker took *his* son to Mount Whitney. When they signed in they noted they were the 259th and 260th persons to do so that *day!*[13] Fortunately, they avoided the Labor Day weekend when an estimated two thousand enthusiasts jammed the mountain. "You literally can't find a square yard of ground without human feces on it," a Forest Service officer declared after an inspection of Mirror Lake midway through the climb. "The smell is just horrible."[14] In 1974 the Forest Service limited the number of climbers permitted on Mount Whitney on a given day to seventy-five. In the case of Mount San Jacinto, California, however, the number was not restricted and in the late 1970s Round Valley recorded five thousand visitors in a single day. A ranger let them up to the peak two-by-two every few seconds. Across the valley in the San Gorgonio Wilderness (also too near Los Angeles for its own good) a thousand people tried to camp in one small mountain meadow at once. Meanwhile, forty miles to the east on the Mojave Desert, several thousand off-road vehicles, lined up for hundred-mile races across some of the best remaining desert wilderness in California.[15] Clearly, it is not wilderness but people who need management.

Wilderness management rests on the assumption that uncontrolled wilderness recreation is just as much a threat to wilderness

12. "We're Loving our Wilderness to Death," *Audubon,* 75 (1973), 111. An excellent examination of crowding of eastern wilderness is contained in Laura and Guy Waterman, *Backwoods Ethics* (Boston, 1979), pp. 158–70.

13. Interview with Ivan Maxwell, February 10, 1973.

14. Interview with Ed Waldapful, U.S. Forest Service Information Officer, October 6, 1978.

15. Edward Hay, "Wilderness Experiment," *American Forests,* 80 (1974), 26–29; Jack Quigg, "Our Desert Being Killed with Love," *Santa Barbara* [Ca.] *News Press,* March 28, 1970; U.S. Department of the Interior, Bureau of Land Management, *The California Desert Conservation Area: Draft Plan Alternatives and Environmental Impact Statement* (Riverside, Ca., 1980).

qualities as economic development. The history of this idea is not long, but then neither is the problem. For the first three decades of this century no one believed that wilderness preservation meant more than simple designation. You drew a circle on a map and concentrated on keeping things like roads and buildings out. What happened inside the wilderness boundary did not seem important by comparison. It was not a matter of oversight. In fairness to federal land managers of the 1920s and 1930s, there was really little to manage. Relatively few Americans ventured into the backcountry. Most park visitors in this era wanted some degree of civilization: a room with a scenic view and entertainments such as scheduled bear feedings and Yosemite's famous firefall.[16]

The attitude toward management of Chief Forester, William B. Greeley, is representative. In 1926 he asked an assistant, L. F. Kneipp, to inventory the wilderness remaining in the national forests. Three years later some of the seventy-four areas Kneipp identified were placed in protective categories by the "L-20" regulations. Greeley stopped at this point. He made no attempt to determine what a wilderness experience should be and then manage in a positive way to attain this goal for visitors. In fact, Greeley explicitly disavowed any intent to regulate the numbers or behavior of recreational users of national forest wilderness. "I have no sympathy," he wrote in a directive to his field staff, "for the viewpoint that people should be kept out of wilderness areas because the presence of human beings destroys the wilderness aspect." According to Greeley the only factor limiting public use should be "the natural one set up by the modes of travel possible" in the area. Greeley concluded that "public use and enjoyment were the only justification for having wilderness reserves at all."[17]

One of the first recognitions that unrestricted public enjoyment could threaten wilderness appeared as a 1926 cartoon in the New York *Herald Tribune*. It was a before-and-after view of a mountain lake. In the first frame a lone horseman approached the lake, which

16. The emphasis on "carnivalism" in the national parks is well covered in Alfred Runte, *National Parks: The American Experience* (Lincoln, Neb., 1979), especially Chapter 8.

17. As quoted in Roderick Nash, "Historical Roots of Wilderness Management" in *Wilderness Management,* ed., John Hendee, George H. Stankey, and Robert Lucas, "U.S. Forest Service Miscellaneous Publication No. 1365" (Washington, D.C., 1978), p. 35.

was surrounded by pines and full of leaping trout. In the "after" view, a few years later, the trees were almost gone, the fish dead, and the shoreline jammed with fishermen's camps. L. F. Kneipp, for one, was worried about the trend. He did not like the constructed trails, elaborate shelters, latrines, and corrals that his Forest Service colleagues were placing in the backcountry. Writing to the field staff on May 30, 1930, Kneipp stated "there should be no need for developing [wilderness] . . . areas to take care of the large numbers of people who are capable of exploring wild country without considerable aid." He recommended that "primitive simplicity" be used as a guideline in managing wilderness because the areas were intended for people "who seek almost absolute detachment from the evidences of civilization."[18]

When in 1931 Robert Marshall emerged from over a year in Alaska's Brooks Range to begin a career in the Forest Service advocating wilderness, he cheered Kneipp's discouragement of recreational development in wild country. In his contribution to *A National Plan for American Forestry* (1933), Marshall added the warning that wilderness could be overused. Campsites could deteriorate into dustbowls. A need existed, he concluded, to educate recreational users in wilderness etiquette.[19]

In 1937 Marshall turned again to this theme. The occasion was a fact-finding trip to California's Sierra Nevada with members of the Sierra Club. Marshall, now the Forest Service's top recreation administrator, saw national forest wilderness severely damaged by parties of as many as 200 campers and their pack stock. At the conclusion of the trip he asked Sierra Club president Joel Hildebrand to think about ways of lessening visitor impact in the mountains. Marshall wanted to investigate the feasibility of managing land so that "certain areas may still be preserved in what might be termed a super-wilderness condition." For him this meant no constructed trails or trail signs, no established campgrounds and, most importantly, the feeling on the part of the visitor of being "where no one has ever been before."[20] In Alaska Marshall had personally traveled in such "super wilderness," but the chance of preserving those conditions in the other states was rapidly slipping away.

18. Ibid., p. 36.
19. Marshall, "The Forest for Recreation," pp. 466.
20. Joel H. Hildebrand, "Maintenance of Recreation Values in the High Sierra," *Sierra Club Bulletin*, *23* (1938), 85–96.

Robert Marshall assumed that a combination of careful conduct on the part of visitors and restraint in building trails and shelters would keep wild country wild. He did not take the next logical step: limitation on numbers of visitors. But in 1936 Lowell Sumner, a wildlife technician with the National Park Service, asked "how large a crowd can be turned loose in a wilderness without destroying its essential qualities?" Here was the first explicit recognition that wilderness "cannot hope to accommodate unlimited numbers of people."[21] By 1947 Sumner was talking about "oversaturation of wilderness" and suggesting limits on the length of stay permitted one camping party at one site.[22] This concept of distributing use dominated early wilderness management efforts. No one was quite ready to consider an absolute visitor quota that would turn some potential visitors away altogether.

By the 1950s the Sierra Club clearly understood that its members were part of the problem of wilderness preservation. The club's Biennial Wilderness Conferences, which began in 1949, brought together state and federal land managers, professional guides and outfitters, and wilderness recreation enthusiasts to consider the implications.[23] A consensus existed that the designation of wilderness areas was meaningless without management policies that maintained wilderness conditions.

Increasingly in the 1950s and 1960s wilderness preservationists, faced with the new problem of too much popularity for wilderness, turned to the idea of carrying capacity. Originally a stockman's term, it referred to the number of head of sheep or cattle that could graze a specific range without causing its permanent deterioration as grassland. This policy would keep the number from exceeding the carrying capacity and ruining the range. Pack stock caused a large part of the recreational impact on fragile mountain meadows which may explain the switch in application of the concept. Applied to people in wilderness, carrying capacity came to mean the ability of an environment to absorb human influence and still retain its wildness.

21. E. Lowell Sumner, "Special Report on a Wildlife Study in the High Sierra in Sequoia and Yosemite National Parks and Adjacent Territory," unpublished report, U.S. National Park Service Records, National Archives, Washington, D.C.

22. Richard M. Leonard and E. Lowell Sumner, "Protecting Mountain Meadows," *Sierra Club Bulletin, 32* (1947), 53–62.

23. Summaries of the five conferences may be found in Brower, ed., *Wildlands in Our Civilization,* pp. 130 ff.

As early as 1942 Lowell Sumner used carrying capacity to refer to the "maximum degree of the highest type of recreational use which a wilderness can receive, consistent with its long-term preservation." By "highest type of recreational use" Sumner meant the kind of camping practiced by careful, experienced wilderness travelers. Today we would call this minimum impact or no-trace camping. Significantly, Sumner realized that even with every visitor camping carefully there was a maximum use level. "Managers," he continued, "should determine . . . the . . . maximum permissible use" of a wilderness and stick to that limit.[24]

In 1942 Lowell Sumner's main concern as a wildlife biologist was the impact of people on nature. The *biological carrying capacity* of wilderness refers to the ability of life forms and processes in the area to withstand alteration as the result of human presence. When a lake is "fished out" or a mountain meadow beaten to dust, there has been a transgression of carrying capacity limits. The same situation exists when the presence of too many people in a region causes a falcon to vacate its nest or a neurotic grizzly to attack a campsite. The problem, Sumner would say, lies not with the bear but with the manager who allowed the carrying capacity of the bear for people to be exceeded. *Physical carrying capacity* is perhaps a more appropriate concept for the impact of visitors on the nonliving environment. The ability of certain soils to resist trail erosion is a case in point. More difficult to assess, but ultimately most important to the wilderness idea, is *psychological carrying capacity:* the impact of people on people. The focus here is not on the land so much as on the human mind. Psychological carrying capacity assumes that wilderness is an experience best defined in terms of a human perception. Managers can allow so many visitors to enter a wilderness that none of them perceives it as wilderness. Tolerances, to be sure, vary with the individual just as does definition. At one extreme are those for whom the sight or sound of another camper, or even the knowledge that one is in the area, spoils the wilderness experience completely. But social scientists have discovered that for many wilderness users contact with other users does not prevent a place from being perceived as wilderness. There are limits, of course. As visitation increases there is a point at which the wilder-

24. E. Lowell Sumner, "The Biology of Wilderness Protection," *Sierra Club Bulletin*, 27 (1942), 14–22.

ness quality of a place disappears. This impact of wilderness lovers upon other wilderness lovers is the main reason why wilderness can be loved to death. It also provides the philosophical basis for controlling the numbers of even highly sensitive, skilled backcountry campers allowed to enter a particular wilderness at a given time.[25]

One of the most sensitive issues in wilderness management is the debate over anthropocentrism *versus* biocentrism.[26] Behind the big words is the very old problem of whether parks, reserves, and wildernesses are for man (anthropocentric) or for nature (biocentric). Gifford Pinchot and John Muir clashed on this point in the 1890s (see above, pp. 136–38). The National Park Service Act of 1916 tried to sidestep it by declaring the parks' mission to be both preserving nature and facilitating public recreation.[27] In general before 1960 the national parks leaned toward anthropocentrism. Hotels were built, roads extended, trails improved, toilets provided, and lakes stocked with fish—all in the name of aiding the recreating

25. Since the first (1967), and particularly since the second (1973), edition of this book, literature of wilderness management has grown prodigiously. Bibliographic guidance may be found in George H. Stankey and David W. Lime, *Recreational Carrying Capacity: An Annotated Bibliography,* "U.S. Forest Service General Technical Report, INT-3" (Ogden, Ut., 1973) and in Nina Brew, *Biological-Sociological Investigations: Backcountry Recreation—An Annotated Bibliography,* "Grand Canyon National Park Colorado River Research Series, No. 15" (Grand Canyon, Az., 1976). The definitive textbook in the field is *Wilderness Management,* ed. Hendee, Stanley, and Lucas (see fn. 17) which also contains an extensive bibliography current to 1978.

Several works deserve special mention for providing early definition of the carrying capacity idea. J. Alan Wagar's "The Carrying Capacity of Wild Lands for Recreation" (unpublished Ph.D. dissertation, University of Michigan, 1961) was a seminal study, part of which received publication, under the same title, by the Society of American Foresters as "Forest Science Monograph, No. 7" (Washington, D.C., 1964). In 1962 Robert C. Lucas made the first extensive application of carrying capacity strategy to a specific area in "The Quetico-Superior Area: Recreational Use in Relation to Capacity" (unpublished Ph.D. dissertation, University of Minnesota). Part of Lucas's findings were published in 1964 as *The Recreational Capacity of the Quetico-Superior Area,* "U.S. Forest Service Research Paper LS-15" (St. Paul, Mn.) Arthur H. Carhart, *Planning for America's Wildlands* (Harrisburg, Pa., 1961) contains a very early treatment of the principles behind contemporary wilderness management philosophy and practice. Also of historical importance as a harbinger is J. V. K. Wagar, "Some Major Principles in Recreation Land-use Planning," *Journal of Forestry,* 49 (1951), 431–35.

26. A good summary of the issue is available in *Wilderness Management,* ed. Hendee, Stankey, and Lucas, pp. 16 ff.

27. See Runte, *National Parks,* pp. 103–04 and William C. Everhart, *The National Park Service* (New York, 1972). The famous organic act creating the National Park Service may be found in U.S., *Statutes at Large,* 39 (1916), p. 535.

public in its pursuit of what the 1916 act called "enjoyment." An especially ambitious program of park improvement called "Mission 66" operated according to this philosophy from 1956 to 1966. With regard to wilderness, anthropocentrism frowned at any restriction on recreational use. Instead its adherents called on management to provide more facilities to take care of the crowds. The idea was to let technology help more people enjoy wilderness. Eric Julber pointed out how backcountry chalets, tramways, and cog railways allowed large numbers of visitors to experience the Alps without, in his opinion, adverse effects on the quality of the environment or the experience.[28]

The first major departure from the access-resort (anthropocentric) philosophy associated with national parks was resistance to trans-Sierra roads in California. John Muir had favored roads, reasoning after the loss of the little-known Hetch Hetchy Valley in 1913 that easier access meant more visitors and therefore more supporters of the national park idea.[29] In the infancy of motor travel, Muir failed to anticipate the problem of loving wilderness to death. By the 1930s, however, some Sierra Club leaders began to entertain second thoughts about roads and crowds. The campaign for a national park in the Kings Canyon area south of Yosemite focused the issue. The drainage of the Kings River was roadless, and a young Sierra Club member and photographic genius named Ansel Adams wished it to remain so. His book of wilderness photographs, *Sierra Nevada: The John Muir Trail* (1938), played a major role in convincing Franklin Roosevelt's administration to support a new kind of park. Roads stopped at the edge of Kings Canyon National Park, established in 1940. No hotels, restaurants, gift shops, and visitor services would be constructed. Adams applauded this revolt against what he termed "resortism" in the national parks. In 1948, with the cluttered condition of Yosemite Valley in mind, Adams responded to those who saw biocentrism as elitist: "Is it a matter of 'snobbery' that the priest does not permit the sale of peanuts in the aisles of the church? Is it snobbery that the Metropolitan

28. Eric Julber, "Let's Open Up Our Wilderness Areas," *Reader's Digest, 100* (1972), 125–28 and Julber, "The Wilderness: Just How Wild Should It Be?" *Trends, 9* (1972), 15–18.

29. Richard Lillard, "The Siege and Conquest of a National Park," *American West,* (Jan., 1968), 28–31, 67, 69–71, discusses Muir's role in the debate over admitting cars to Yosemite National Park.

Museum of Art objects to my playing my portable radio in the Egyptian Room?"[30]

At the root of Ansel Adams's protest was a biocentric philosophy of national parks and wilderness. Along with Sierra Club colleague David Brower, he was among the first to face the fact that national parks should not try to be all things to all people. Specialization in unmodified nature was the proper mission for parks, and Adams endorsed this concept in the full realization that it would entail a loss in mass appeal. There were enough Americans, he reasoned, who preferred nature without embellishments and conveniences to justify a new approach to park management. In the 1950s Adams joined Brower in opposing improvement of the old Tioga Road across the Sierra Nevada in the northern part of Yosemite National Park. Let the road be slow and, in parts, dangerous; there were those who liked it that way. In 1958 Adams went so far as to accuse the National Park Service of "criminal negligence" in its ultimately successful effort to upgrade the Tioga Road.[31]

A biocentric management philosophy puts the preservation of naturalness first and recreation second in a ranking of the purposes of parks and wildernesses. Secretary Rogers Morton was quoted on September 25, 1972, in the New York *Times* as saying: "Parks are for people." Exponents of biocentrism responded that parks are for nature and for people who like nature unmodified. The biocentric position held that wilderness managers should have the courage to make decisions against people and especially against those people unwilling to take the wilderness on its own terms. This idea stemmed from the conviction that what gave wilderness its value, what was unique about it in the twentieth century, was the presence there of ecological forces operating with little or no human influence. Eric Julber, biocentrists reasoned, was confusing scenic beauty with wildness. There was nothing wrong with the European-style experience in the Alps if the visitors were willing to forgo a wilderness experience.

A seminal document in the difficult struggle of biocentrism for parity with anthropocentrism in national park policy was a 1963

30. Robert Turnage, "Ansel Adams: The Role of the Artist in the Environmental Movement," *Living Wilderness*, 43 (1980), 8, 9.

31. Ibid., 9; "David R. Brower: Environmental Activist, Publicist, and Prophet" (unpublished transmission of an oral history interview conducted by Susan Schrepfer, Regional Oral History Office, Bancroft Library, Berkeley, 1980), pp. 53 ff.

report from an advisory board on wildlife to Secretary of the Interior Stewart Udall. The chairman of the Board was A. S. Leopold, son of Aldo Leopold and subscriber to his wilderness ethic. Leopold's report opened with a review of national park policy concerning wild animals. For a half century the federal government had, in effect, weeded out "good" animals from "bad" ones, protecting the former (deer, for example) and attempting to eliminate predators such as wolves, bears, and mountain lions. A. S. Leopold and his committee proposed major policy changes. "As a primary goal," they said, "we would recommend that the biotic associations within each park be maintained, or where necessary recreated, as nearly as possible in the condition that prevailed when the area was first visited by the white man."[32] If this meant re-establishing populations of big, wild animals that frightened some visitors, so be it. The parks, Leopold and his colleagues implied, were for people who liked big, wild animals. If a visitor was on occasion killed and eaten, that was the way of the wilderness that was being preserved. Eliminate the risk and you eliminate the wildness.

The revolt against anthropocentrism continued in the 1972 report of a task force of citizens organized to advise the National Park Service on the centennial of the establishment of Yellowstone. The gist of the document was that parks should have the courage to specialize in wilderness and wilderness-dependent activities. The confusion of purpose that had resulted in golf courses, tennis courts, and ski lifts in national parks should be ended by defining the kind of recreation appropriate for them as wilderness oriented. The centennial report did not go so far as to advocate the termination of all motorized access in the parks, but it urged that in the next century private automobiles, hotels, and restaurants be phased out in favor of backpacking and camping. The report defended its findings as discrimination in favor of those who appreciated wilderness. Those who needed aids to enjoy wilderness were invited to seek alternate locales for their vacations. With this logic the task force attempted to resolve the chronic preservation *vs* enjoyment dilemma. Parks and wildernesses were to be preserved for those who derived their enjoyment *from* wild nature. Guided by such a phi-

32. A. S. Leopold, et. al., "Wildlife Management in the National Parks," in U.S. Department of the Interior, National Park Service, *Administrative Policies for Natural Areas of the National Park System* (Washington, D.C., 1968), p. 92. The report also appeared in *National Parks Magazine*, 37 (1963).

losophy, wilderness areas could be biocentric and, at least for a select clientele, anthropocentric too. Recognition of the importance of wilderness for humans resolved the dilemma.[33]

In 1980 Joseph Sax, a professor of law at the University of Michigan, published what amounts to a culmination of the opinion that national parks should specialize in wilderness.[34] *Mountains Without Handrails* argues that the parks should dare to be different. They should endeavor, says Sax, to offer the public an experience that contrasts with the kind available in civilization. This means as little human control of the parks, and of people in them, as possible. Sax understands that emphasizing the uncontrolled (scenic overlooks without handrails, for example) means danger, but he welcomes it as a way of challenging visitors and encouraging prudence. According to Sax, hotels and roads and a myriad of visitor services should be phased out of the national parks. If this means occasional discomfort for people, it is a small price to pay for the higher quality experience those who camp and hike receive. Those who cannot forgo the conveniences are invited to stay away, but Sax would prefer to see the National Park Service engage in a program of teaching self-sufficiency in wilderness environments. Let park personnel lead from the front in introducing overcivilized Americans to wilderness.

Implicit in all Sax's arguments is the conviction that the national parks and the American wilderness in general, have come of age. They are popular, indeed too popular. There is no need to encourage visitation, as there was in the era of John Muir and Stephen T. Mather, by providing accommodations and a circus atmosphere. The parks, Sax believes, can afford to eliminate such civilized forms and functions as being inappropriate for an institution specializing in natural environments.

Contemporary recreational pressure on wilderness, and the challenges managers face in making biocentrism work, acquire meaning from specific instances. The most sought-after and most intensely managed wilderness in the United States and, arguably, the world is the Grand Canyon of Arizona. The future of wilderness every-

33. Conservation Foundation, *National Parks for the Future* (Washington, D.C., 1972), esp. pp. 9–39. An anticipation of the conclusion of this report appeared in 1967 as a Conservation Foundation publication: F. Fraser Darling and Noel D. Eichhorn, *Man and Nature in the National Parks* (Washington, D.C., 1967), esp. pp. 73–78.

34. Joseph Sax, *Mountains Without Handrails: Reflections on the National Parks* (Ann Arbor, Mi., 1980).

where could well be on display now in Grand Canyon National Park. Day hiking and mule trips excepted, there is no free (non-permit) access to the area. Backpackers must make reservations for the most popular trails months in advance. Opportunities to backpack during the traditionally popular Easter holidays are determined by lottery seven months in advance. Only twenty percent of the requests are filled. Successful applicants are issued tags to attach to their packs. Rangers check campsites and follow groups on the trails with binoculars, searching for the appropriate tickets. Tagless campers are subject to fine and immediate removal from the canyon.[35]

River running on the Colorado through Grand Canyon National Park is even more in demand. The twenty-one commercial rafting companies who boat the river fill their trips a year in advance at prices ranging from $700 to $1200. Noncommercial river runners (persons who prefer a do-it-yourself type of trip) faced in 1981 an eight-year wait for the chance to make a trip. The waiting list, moreover, is growing several years longer each year.[36] Given this growth in demand, the noncommercial trip could become a once-in-a-lifetime opportunity. Once on the river, visitors must comply with the strictest minimum-impact camping regulations in the nation. It is mandated, for instance, that human feces be containerized and carried out of the Grand Canyon for disposal.[37]

Thanks to the expeditionary nature of early Grand Canyon river trips and to the way topography assists current patrol programs (there is only one feasible launch and departure point in the canyon's first 225 miles), a complete record of visitation exists. The data in the table below are unique in that they represent the total visitation to an American wilderness.[38]

35. Interview with Richard Marks, Superintendent, Grand Canyon National Park, Aug. 8 1981.

36. Interview with Marvin Jensen, River Unit Manager, Grand Canyon National Park, Aug. 10, 1981.

37. U.S. National Park Service, *Draft Colorado River Management Plan* (Washington, D.C., 1977), p. 24.

38. These figures have been compiled from the records of individual expeditions and, after 1941, from the archives of Grand Canyon National Park. Recent statistics are available in "Boating Use on the Colorado River, Grand Canyon" (unpublished annual release of the River Unit, Grand Canyon National Park). The Otis Marston Papers, The Huntington Library, San Marino Ca., contain the most complete compilation of early river trips in the Grand Canyon.

Travel on the Colorado River Through the Grand Canyon of Arizona

Year	*Number of People*	*Year*	*Number of People*
1867	1?	1960	205
1869–1940	73	1961	255
1941	4	1962	372
1942	8	1963–64	44
1943	0	1965	547
1944	0	1966	1,067
1945	0	1967	2,099
1946	0	1968	3,609
1947	4	1969	6,019
1948	6	1970	9,935
1949	12	1971	10,885
1950	7	1972	16,432
1951	29	1973	15,219
1952	19	1974	14,253
1953	31	1975	14,305
1954	21	1976	13,912
1955	70	1977	11,830
1956	55	1978	14,356
1957	135	1979	14,678
1958	80	1980	15,142
1959	120		

Possibly the first traveler, in 1867, was the prospector James White who, if he was not totally confused or shamelessly lying about his itinerary, must have floated through the Grand Canyon clinging to a makeshift log raft.[39] John Wesley Powell and five companions completed an undisputed "first" descent in 1869. In the next seventy years only sixty-seven individuals took the water route through the canyon. But by the early 1950s military surplus inflatable rafts, some as long as thirty-three feet, began to change the Grand Canyon river run from a high risk expedition to a family vacation.[40] Yet improved equipment would have had little effect on

39. Robert Collins and Roderick Nash, *The Big Drops: Ten Legendary Rapids* (San Francisco, 1978), pp. 191–93; Harold A. Bulger, "First Man Through the Grand Canyon," *Missouri Historical Society Bulletin, 17* (1961), pp. 321–31; R. C. Lingenfelter, *First Through the Grand Canyon* (Los Angeles, 1958). Discredit of White's feat appears in Robert Brewster Stanton, *Colorado River Controversies,* ed. James M. Chalfont (New York, 1932).

40. Collins and Nash, *The Big Drops,* esp. pp. 94–96.; Roderick Nash, "River Recreation: History and Future" in *River Recreation Management and Research,* "U.S. Forest Service General Technical Report NC-28 (St. Paul, Mn., 1977), pp. 2–7.

the amount of visitation without a simultaneous growth in appreciation of wilderness recreation. Just as in the case of backpacking, technology and ideas have combined to bring the pressure of popularity to bear on wildernesses like the Grand Canyon.

The marked drop in river travel in 1963 and 1964 was due to the completion of Glen Canyon Dam, just upstream of the Grand Canyon, and the need to begin filling Lake Powell. Very little water passed through the dam in these years. But an explosion of interest in the trip was just ahead. The year 1965 saw the start of near-exponential increases in visitation. One explanation was the publicity the river trip received as part of the effort to stop dams in the Grand Canyon (see above, pp. 227–36). Glen Canyon was inundated by Lake Powell, preservationists believed, because it was "the place no one knew."[41] Vowing not to make the same mistake with the inner gorge of the Grand Canyon, the Sierra Club led the way in producing books, articles, and a film. Well-publicized river runs by celebrities such as Robert Kennedy also created a clientele for the canyon. One of the supreme ironies in American wilderness history was the appearance of a new problem (loving the Grand Canyon to death) as a result of solving an old one (the dam threat). Having been saved from the dam builders, the canyon's wildness became threatened by the saviors themselves.

After the 1972 season when an astonishing 16,432 persons floated through the Grand Canyon, the National Park Service realized it had a problem on its hands as potentially damaging to the wilderness qualities of the place as dams and reservoirs.[42] Not only were

41. Eliot Porter, *The Place No One Knew: Glen Canyon on the Colorado* (San Francisco, 1963).

42. Examples of the literature discussing human impact on the wilderness qualities of the Colorado River in the Grand Canyon are: Peter Cowgill, "Too Many People on the Colorado River," *National Parks and Conservation Magazine, 45* (1971), pp. 10–14; Robert Dolan, Alan Howard, and Arthur Gallenson, "Man's Impact on the Colorado River in the Grand Canyon," *American Scientist, 62* (1974), 392–401; W. E. Garrett, "Grand Canyon: Are We Loving it to Death?" *National Geographic, 154* (1978), 16–51; Roy R. Johnson, et al., "Man's Impact on the Colorado River in the Grand Canyon," *National Parks and Conservation Magazine, 51* (1977), 13–16; Robert Dolan, et. al., "Environmental Management of the Colorado River Within the Grand Canyon," *Environmental Management, 1* (1977), 391–400.

The proceedings of two symposia bear directly on these issues: Lawrence Royer, William H. Becker, and Richard Schreyer, *Managing Colorado River Whitewater: The Carrying Capacity Strategy* (Logan, Utah, 1977) and *River Recreation Management and Research* (cited above, fn. 40). Also useful is Dorothy H. Anderson,

the physical and biological carrying capacity of the canyon's inner gorge being exceeded, in addition, no matter how careful visitors were to minimize their impact, their very presence diluted the wilderness experience. Indeed by the mid-1970s many familiar with conditions in the canyon were prepared to write it off as a wilderness. Thinking of the big motor-powered rafts on which 80 percent of the visitors traveled, guide John Husing remarked that the river run "isn't a wilderness trip, it's a carnival-style thrill ride."[43] Others pointed to the way the Glen Canyon Dam totally controlled the flow of the Colorado River in the Grand Canyon and concluded that the place could not be considered wild. Old timers, such as Ken Sleight, who knew the canyon in the uncrowded, pre-Glen Canyon Dam days had understandably lower tolerances of hordes of river runners. "There's no wilderness left, only scenery," Sleight declared, "but it's still worth fighting for."[44] On the other hand, research based on questionnaires revealed that 91 percent of a sample of one thousand 1975 river runners considered the area wilderness. But almost all respondents were new to the Grand Canyon and many had never camped out before.[45] The data substantiated the axiom that in the last analysis wilderness is a matter of perception—part of the geography of the mind.

Reviewing the extraordinary visitor statistics, the National Park Service concluded that wilderness values were threatened in the Grand Canyon. There was little room for any other conclusion when as many as five hundred persons left the Lee's Ferry launching site on a single day. Downstream, there was congestion at the major rapids and points of interest. In the peak-use summer months it was hard to escape from the sight of other river parties or the sound of their outboard motors for more than a few hours. Grand Canyon National Park responded to these conditions by freezing use at the

---

Earl C. Leatherberry, and David W. Lime, eds., *An Annotated Bibliography on River Recreation* (St. Paul, Mn., 1978).

43. As quoted in "Troubled Waters," *Newsweek, 81* (1973), 62.

44. Interview with Ken Sleight, Marble Canyon, Arizona, March 30, 1979.

45. Joyce M. Nielson and Bo Shelby, "River Running in the Grand Canyon: How Much and What Kind of Use" in *River Recreation Management and Research,* p. 172. The full report of Nielsen's and Shelby's contract research is available as "Colorado River Research Series, Contribution No. 18" (1976) at the library of Grand Canyon National Park. Its findings are summarized in Grand Canyon National Park, *Final Environmental Statement: Proposed Colorado River Management Plan* (Washington, D.C., 1979), pt. 8, pp. 7 ff.

1972 level and setting as a management goal the restoration and perpetuation of "the wilderness river-running experience."[46] One of the most important means toward this end was the decision to phase out motorized watercraft used by 80 percent of the river travelers. In the opinion of the National Park Service and of most wilderness advocates, the ban on motors would make for trips more consistent with a wilderness experience. Supporting this conclusion was research demonstrating that 87 percent of the river runners familiar with both kinds of trips preferred oars to motors.[47]

The 1979 National Park Service decision to ban motors in favor of oars or paddles in order to enhance wilderness values aroused a storm of controversy. Commercial river outfitters, who used outboards to power their heavy inflatable rafts, had a big economic stake in the issue. These outfitters argued that motors were traditional on the Colorado River and that the public should have the right to choose between kinds of trips. Pointing out that oar-powered trips took more time and used smaller boats, the pro motor Professional River Outfitters Association issued a form letter urging that citizens "tell . . . [the National Park Service] that river trips belong to everyone, not just athletes, the idle rich, and park rangers and their friends."[48] The motor outfitters' lobby attempted to sidestep the wilderness issue by arguing, correctly, that no portion of the Colorado River in the Grand Canyon was designated wilderness under the 1964 Wilderness Act. This reasoning, however, ignored the intent of the National Park Service to recommend wilderness status for the canyon backcountry. It also ignored the fact that fast-paced, motor-powered commercial trips involving ten thousand persons a season conflicted with wilderness conditions.

46. Grand Canyon National Park, *Final Environmental Statement,* pt. 1, p. 1. It should be noted that a very few voices pointed out the incompatibility of these policies. The 1972 use levels, they contended, were far too high both for the wilderness and the wilderness experience. The National Park Service was reluctant to cut visitation in either the commercial or noncommercial sector. Since the Grand Canyon did not vote, it was the easiest party in the controversy to injure but perhaps the least appropriate.

47. Nielsen and Shelby, "River Running," p. 174; National Park Service, *Draft River Management Plan,* pp. 18–19; Bo Shelby, "Contrasting Recreational Experiences: Motors and Oars in the Grand Canyon," *Journal of Soil and Water Conservation, 35* (1980), 129–31; Steve Martin, "Dilemma in Grand Canyon," *National Parks and Conservation Magazine, 50* (1976), 15–17.

48. Professional River Outfitters Association, mimeographed form letter, August, 1979.

The motor outfitters, facing the need to convert to oar-powered boats, also pleaded economic hardship. Park personnel responded with a delay in the phaseout from 1981 to 1985. But late in 1980 motor advocates Fred Burke and Gaylord Staveley caught the ears of Senators Orrin Hatch and Jake Garn of Utah, and Barry Goldwater of Arizona. On November 14, 1980, Hatch introduced a rider on the 1981 appropriations bill for the entire Department of the Interior that forbade any of the money being used to implement a plan that banned motors from the Grand Canyon or that cut back commercial traffic below the 1978 level. Defending his amendment on the floor of the Senate, Hatch stated that unless motors were retained only a "hardy, young, wealthy elite" would be able to experience the river trip. The American wilderness had frequently fallen victim to such reasoning despite substantial evidence to the contrary, and it was no different this time. The Hatch Amendment slid through the few Senators present on a consent basis (no vote was taken). It wiped out in minutes six years of planning and research into the nature of the wilderness experience in the Grand Canyon.[49]

Chances of overturning the pro motor Hatch Amendment did not appear good in early 1981. James G. Watt, the Secretary of the Interior in the incoming Ronald Reagan administration had, in his previous job with the Mountain States Legal Foundation, already recommended filing a suit to keep motors in the canyon.[50] Then, on March 9, 1981, Watt told a meeting of national park concessioners about his boat trip through the Grand Canyon the previous September. "The first day was spectacular, . . . The second day started to get a little tedious, but the third day I wanted bigger motors to move that raft out. There is no way you could get me on an oar powered raft on that river–I'll tell you that. On the fourth day we were praying for helicopters and they came." As for means

49. *Congressional Record,* 96th Cong., 2d Sess., *126* (Nov. 14, 1980), pp. S14467–70. The amendment appeared in Public Law 96–514, U.S., *Statutes at Large,* 94, p. 2972. The National Park Service responded at once: U.S. Department of the Interior, "To Permit Motor/Oar Options on the Colorado River in Grand Canyon National Park," *News Release 81–2,* Jan. 14, 1981. An example of the ensuing protest is Shirley Fockler, 'Running the Colorado By Oar or Roar," *San Francisco Examiner and Chronicle,* April 19, 1981, p. 3. "Tour Operators Gut Grand Canyon Plan," *Currents, 3* (1981), 1.

50. James G. Watt to Board of Litigation, Mountain States Legal Foundation, Feb. 27, 1980 (duplicated copy distributed by Western River Guides Association, Salt Lake City, Utah).

of travel more appropriate to wilderness, Watt remarked, "I don't like to paddle and I don't like to walk."[51] Reluctantly taking this cue from its chief, Grand Canyon National Park drafted alternatives for the Colorado River Management Plan that accepted large numbers of motorized trips. But the introduction to the June 1981 draft indirectly went against the Hatch and Watt point of view by defining the principal value of a Grand Canyon experience as a time to "sense another rhythm, something older and more stable than what controls our normal, hurried lives."[52]

For many who had fought hard for the continued existence of wilderness in modern American civilization the philosophy of Secretary Watt, a high-ranking federal guardian of wilderness, was discouraging and frightening. Watt, along with many other elected and appointed federal officials, interpreted the landslide Reagan victory in November 1980 as a mandate for resource development. Any wilderness not legally protected, and some that were, appeared to be fair game for both resource and recreational exploitation.[53] The old biases—against wilderness and for civilization—seemed alive and well. Hope, in some minds, lay in the possibility that Watt and his colleagues might perish politically by virtue of their own excesses. The Reagan administration's championing of the frontier perspective might be a final flare-up of values approaching obsolesence.

The annual quota that Grand Canyon National Park established after the 1972 season for boating on the Colorado River created the "allocation" controversy. For the first time in the short history of American wilderness management, recreational users were turned away in the interest of preserving wilderness.[54] With the quota sys-

51. As quoted in Nathaniel P. Reed, "Why Watt Must Go," *Not Man Apart, 11* (1981), 10. A slightly different version appears in Michael Frome, "Park Concessions and Concessioners," *National Parks, 55* (1981), 18.

52. Grand Canyon National Park, "Draft Alternatives for the Colorado River Management Plan" (mimeographed format, June, 1981), p. 1.

53. See Reed, "Why Watt Must Go," pp. 10–11, and "James Watt's Land Rush," *Newsweek, 97* (1981), 22–24, 29–32; and Jeffrey Klein, "Man Apart: James Watt and the Marketing of God's Green Acres," *Mother Jones, 6* (1981), 21–27. A petition to replace Watt as Secretary of the Interior circulated among environmentalists in the summer of 1981 and was published in *Not Man Apart, 11* (1981), 15.

54. At about the same time the United States Forest Service began enforcing visitor quotas on "name" peaks such as Mount Whitney and Mount San Gorgonio in California and Mount Rainier in Washington. Prior to 1973 wilderness permits had been used to gather information rather than to limit use. By the 1975 summer season visitors quotas were being enforced by permit at many national park and national forest locations.

tem in effect competition to float through the Grand Canyon became increasingly intense. The major competitors were twenty-one commercial river outfitters, who had 92 percent of the permitted annual use and a gross annual income of $10 million, and noncommercial boaters with the remaining 8 percent of the quota. This ratio derived from actual 1972 use percentages but quickly became outdated as demand for noncommercial river trips skyrocketed. Noncommercial permit applicants saw their chances for success in the annual lottery drop to one in fourteen (37 trips and 515 applications for trips) in 1977.[55] Conceivably, an applicant unlucky in lotteries could *never* get on the river. At the same time a telephone call and a check could secure a place immediately on a commercial Grand Canyon trip. In fact, a small percentage of the commercial allocation went unused in any given year. Arguing that the commercial sector had too large a share of the total number of wilderness visitors on the Colorado River in Grand Canyon, noncommercial interests sought redress through the National Park Service. When that proved unproductive, law-suits and illegal protest trips were initiated.[56] At the center of the issue was the question of the purpose of national parks and other public wildernesses. Commercial outfitters contended that they served the public; the noncommercial sector responded that as part of the public they were being denied access.[57] The root of the problem, of course, was that the public had become too large for the wilderness.

55. River use data, Grand Canyon National Park Archives: Randy Frank, "The River Allocation Problem: A Brief History," *River Rights Action Newsletter* (Summer, 1977), 5.

56. *Wilderness Public Rights Fund* v. *Thomas F. Kleppe, Secretary of the Interior . . . and Merle Stitt, Superintendent of Grand Canyon National Park,* Ninth Circuit Court of Appeals, 77–1606 (1977) and *Frederick B. Eiseman, Jr. et. al.,* v. *Cecil Andrews, Secretary of the Interior, et. al.,* Ninth Circuit Court of Appeals, 77—3693 (1979). In a combined ruling on both suits, the courts ruled that the National Park Service had a duty to make rules respecting visitation in the national parks. See also Robert A. Jones, "Whitewater Rights: Running Out of River," *Outside* (Sept., 1977) and Bo Shelby and Joyce Nielsen, "Private and Commercial Trips in the Grand Canyon" (unpublished research report, Grand Canyon National Park, 1976). The definitive report on allocating recreational opportunities on rivers is Bo Shelby and Mark Danley, *Allocating River Use,* "United States Forest Service, Region 6, Recreation Report 059–1981" (Dec. 1980). The assertion of noncommercial rights to river recreation has been spearheaded since 1979 by the National Organization of River Sports and its periodical *Currents.*

57. For succinct summaries of the commercial and noncommercial positions on this issue see "What Are 'Wilderness Public Rights'?" and "What Do You Say, John Muir? Would You Have Wanted to Pay a Commercial Guide in Order to Walk the

Under the management plan published in 1979, Grand Canyon National Park expanded the noncommercial share of the quota from 8 percent to approximately 25 percent of the total number of persons allowed to boat the Grand Canyon.[58] The National Park Service also replaced the annual lottery system of allocating noncommercial river trips with one consolidated waiting list that, by 1982, was nine years long. In other words, an individual who decided in 1982 to apply for the chance to organize a noncommercial river trip in the Grand Canyon could not expect to make that trip before 1991. No historical precedents for such a situation existed. For the first time wilderness had more friends than it needed.

The Grand Canyon allocation controversy raised the deeper question of what kind of use is most appropriate in a federally managed wilderness. One point of view regarded the large, motorized commercial trips as little more than outdoor parties. Beach volleyball and cold beer highlighted these trips. The customers neither expected nor wanted a wilderness experience. The whitewater rapids might as well have been located in an urban amusement park. The highly publicized and much photographed river trip that *Playboy* staged came to represent the problem in many minds.[59] The fact that this kind of Grand Canyon trip used part of the limited visitor quota, and in effect kept wilderness enthusiasts off the river, rubbed salt in the already tender wounds of noncommercial boaters.

In fairness, some commercial guides labored to create and interpret a wilderness experience for their clients. Ron Hayes of Wilderness World went so far as to invite a professional string quartet on some of his Grand Canyon trips and directed client attention to the complex relationships between wilderness and culture.[60] But such journeys were exceptional; and noncommercial river runners generally believed that their trips were more in keeping with the wil-

---

High Sierra?" *Not Man Apart,* 6 (1976), 10–11. A statement by one leading proponent of noncommercial use is Fred B. Eiseman, "Who Runs the Grand Canyon?" *Natural History,* 87 (1978), 82–93. The proceedings of a conference on the issue of commercial versus noncommercial use of wilderness and other public lands is available as Leon J. Buist, ed., *Recreation Use Allocation,* State of Nevada, Agricultural Experiment Station Publication R–149 (Reno, 1981).

58. Grand Canyon National Park, *Final Environmental Plan,* pp. 1–7.

59. Richard Fegley, "Riverboat Gambolers," *Playboy,* 24 (1977), 81–87.

60. Roderick Nash, "Mozart on the Rocks: A Grand Canyon Experiment in the Relationship Between Wilderness and Civilization," *Western Wildlands,* 4 (1977), 39–44.

derness character of the inner Grand Canyon than were commercial ventures. The corollary to this idea was the claim to a higher priority in the allocation of wilderness opportunities. Indeed, extremists argued that *all* noncommercial demands should be satisfied before any commercial passengers could take trips. This claim, that one group would get more from a trip than another, opened highly subjective questions of personal motivation and control into which the National Park Service has so far feared to tread in making Grand Canyon allocations. Still, this issue was a harbinger of those wilderness managers might one day be obliged to face. They could well be asked in the future to determine who among a horde of applicants was intelligent, sensitive, and skillful enough to be allowed the privilege of entering a wilderness. Wilderness entrance examinations, comparable to those used to select college students, may not be far around the corner (see below pp. 386–87).

As the history of the Grand Canyon illustrates, development, and then popularity, constituted the first two threats to wilderness. A third is only beginning to be recognized. It is, frustratingly, implicit in the solutions to the earlier problems. The managers have generally been too busy to realize it, but wilderness management is a blatant contradiction in terms.[61] By etymology and by tradition, wilderness is uncontrolled. *Wild* places and *wild* animals were those which man and his civilization did not plow, herd, log, settle, or otherwise control. Often the wild was beyond even the knowledge of man—mysterious, dark, risky and, in time, attractive for those reasons. The word management, in contrast, derives from the Latin *manus* ("hand") and literally means to handle.

The bureaucratic and then legal designation of wilderness areas began in subtle ways to erode the uncontrolled essence of wildness.[62] For all its benefits, the National Wilderness Preservation System might be regarded as a kind of zoo for land. Wilderness is exhibited in legislative cages, clearly mapped and neatly labeled. The unknown is known. Uncertainty decreases. So do risk and fear.

61. Roderick Nash, *Wilderness Management: A Contradiction in Terms?* "University of Idaho Wilderness Resource Distinguished Lectureship" (Moscow, Id., 1978). An early recognition of the intellectual dilemma involved here is Stephen H. Spurr, *Wilderness Management,* "Horace M. Albright Conservation Lectureship, VI" (Berkeley, Ca., 1966), p. 1.

62. This point has been recognized and analyzed by Yi-Fu Tuan in *Topophillia: A Study of Environmental Perception, Attitudes, and Values* (Englewood Cliffs, N.J., 1974), p. 112.

Trails, shelters, ranger patrols, and search-and-rescue teams further compromise wilderness. Perhaps the most erosive force on the way people perceive uncontrolled environments are the rules and regulations that recent popularity of wilderness has mandated. Because wilderness is a state of mind, the conditions under which one enters it are vital to the overall wilderness experience. Quotas, permits, lotteries, waiting lists, prescribed itineraries, and campsite assignments devastate the feeling of wilderness. For some persons just the knowledge that they visit a wilderness by the grace of, and under conditions established by, civilization can destroy the wilderness experience before it begins. There are many who have turned away forever from intensely managed wildernesses like the Grand Canyon and tried to find new frontiers in Alaska, Chile, and Nepal. Sociologists call the phenomena "displacement." But how long before the crowds, and, as a consequence, the rules, catch up? Only thirty years ago in 1952, a total of nineteen persons boated the Colorado River through the Grand Canyon. They needed no permit; there were no rules.

Unquestionably such good old days when society could afford to let wilderness be uncontrolled, are gone forever in places like the Grand Canyon and are clearly on the decline elsewhere. Robert Marshall may have been the last American able to dream of being Lewis and Clark and then find a blank space on the map (in Alaska's Brooks Range) to explore. Marshall, as we have seen, hoped to maintain this opportunity in a few "super wildernesses" but in the 1930s he had no conception of the numbers who would want to visit them. Even if one could be found, it would be futile today to attempt to manage a large wilderness for the kind of experience enjoyed by Powell or Marshall. The price of the popularity that saved wilderness is intense management. The alternative to such control is a level of recreational use that would quickly deprive anyone of having even a semblance of a wilderness experience. Unmanaged wilderness would indeed be loved to death.

The logic that leads to this reluctant conclusion might be illustrated by comparing wilderness recreation to tennis. Tennis players would prefer to play, when they wish, for as long as they wish. But the growing popularity of the game does not permit this luxury except on private courts. (An analogy here to the game reserves of medieval nobility is intriguing.) On public, tax-supported courts, comparable to wilderness on public lands, demand frequently exceeds available time and space. Management becomes necessary. There are sign-up sheets and limitations on the length and frequency of play. Court monitors (rangers) enforce the rules which nobody likes but everybody accepts. They realize that without management desperate players might squeeze onto a court. "Triples" would be common, and at times of peak demand a kind of volleyball-with-rackets with as many as twenty-five on a side is conceivable. Such a game might be enjoyable (as some experiences in heavily used, outdoor recreation areas are) but it would not be tennis. Players accept control, and control themselves, because they recognize that tennis is a game for two or four persons. So, out of respect for the integrity of the game, and with their own self-interest in mind, players follow the rules. They sign up, wait their turn, and vacate the court at the appointed hour in the understanding that when their chance arrives they will at least be able to play tennis.

Wilderness recreation is also a game that cannot be played at any one time and place by more than a few people. Solitude is not easily shared. Respect for the quality of the wilderness experience argues for acceptance of regulation. Just as with popular tennis courts, inconvenience and frustration are inevitable. But the rules at least insure that when one's turn arrives wilderness enthusiasts will find what they seek.

In two respects, however, tennis and wilderness recreation are not comparable. New tennis courts can be built, and popularity frequently argues for their construction. Wilderness can be reclaimed from civilization only slowly and seldom completely. For all practical purposes the wilderness that remains is all we will ever have, and it is already crowded. Construction of a separate but equal Grand Canyon is, of course, an absurdity. Secondly, the absence of control is not as integral a part of tennis as it is of wilderness. Management is annoying to tennis players; it can be totally disruptive to people seeking wilderness. The paradox of wilderness management is that the necessary means defeat the desired end.

CHAPTER 16

The International Perspective

> I personally am not very interested in animals. I do not want to spend my holidays watching crocodiles. Nevertheless, I am entirely in favor of their survival. I believe that after diamonds and sisal, wild animals will provide Tanganyika with its greatest source of income. Thousands of Americans and Europeans have the strange urge to see these animals.
>
> Julius Nyerere, ca. 1961

FROM 1854 to 1857 Sir St. George Gore, a British nobleman, vacationed in the wilderness of the upper Missouri River. Gore traveled through what later became Wyoming and Montana with 40 assistants, 112 horses, 24 mules, six yoke of oxen, a large pack of staghounds and greyhounds, and three milk cows. He shot 2,000 buffalo, 1,600 deer and elk and 105 bears.[1] From April 1909 to March 1910 ex-President Theodore Roosevelt vacationed in the wilderness of British East Africa. Roosevelt traveled through what later became the nations of Kenya and Uganda with 200 trackers, skinners, porters, gun bearers, and tent "boys." Roosevelt and his son shot, preserved, and shipped to Washington, D.C., over 3,000 specimens of African wildlife.[2]

In the half century between Gore's safari and Roosevelt's the United States changed from an exporter to an importer of wild nature. The changeover might be thought of as occurring in the 1890s when the American frontier officially ended and the cult of wilderness began (see Chapter 9). Previously, foreign tourists seeking wildness found a mecca in the trans-Missouri West. St. George Gore's trip exemplifies the efforts of wealthy and socially prominent Europeans to experience wild America while it lasted.

1. Francis Haines, *The Buffalo* (New York, 1970), pp. 146–47; Wayne Gard, *The Great Buffalo Hunt* (New York, 1959), pp. 62–64; F. George Heldt, "Narrative of Sir St. George Gore's Expedition, 1854–1856," *Contributions of the Historical Society of Montana,* I (1876), 128ff.

2. Theodore Roosevelt, *African Game Trails: An Account of the African Wanderings of an American Hunter-Naturalist* (New York, 1910); R. L. Wilson, *Theodore Roosevelt: Outdoorsman* (New York, 1971), pp. 172–202; Paul Russell Cutright, *Theodore Roosevelt: The Naturalist* (New York, 1956), pp. 186–224.

Contemporary Americans competed too closely with the wild to hear its call. Their relationship to it was that of transformers, not tourists, and they did their work well. By the time a later generation of Americans, represented by Theodore Roosevelt, became civilized enough to appreciate wildness, it had largely vanished from the American West. Africa became the new mecca for nature tourists like Roosevelt who were wealthy enough to import from abroad what had become scarce at home.

Thinking of wild nature as an actively traded commodity in an international market clarifies appreciation and largely explains the world nature protection movement. The export-import relationship underscores the irony inherent in the fact that the civilizing process which imperils wild nature is precisely that which creates the need for it. As a rule the nations that have wilderness do not want it, and those that want it do not have it. Nature appreciation is a "full stomach" phenomenon, that is confined to the rich, urban, and sophisticated. A society must become technological, urban, and crowded before a need for wild nature makes economic and intellectual sense. A Marxist formulation is tempting. There seems to be a social and economic classs of nature lovers whose national affiliations are not as strong as their common interest in enjoying and saving wilderness wherever it exists. These people organize, confer, correspond, and raise money for nature preservation. A social profile of their ranks would reveal an inordinately high proportion of scientists, writers, artists—people of quality and the affluence to pay for it.

More than a metaphor is involved in nature importing; it has an economic value.[3] Wildness is actually bought and sold and not for trifling amounts. Except in the case of trophies and the live capture of animals for zoos, nature does not physically leave the exporting country. The traded commodity is experience. The importers consume it on the premises. In addition, there are many armchair nature enthusiasts. Their eagerness to consume motion pictures, television specials, magazines and books about wildlife, and to

3. Norman Myers, "Wildlife of Savannahs and Grasslands: A Common Heritage of the Global Community" in *EARTHCARE: Global Protection of Natural Areas,* ed. Edmund A. Schofield (Boulder, Co., 1978), pp. 396ff. and Boyce Rensberger, *The Cult of the Wild* (Garden City, 1978), pp. 217–51, are important recent recognitions of the economics of world nature protection.

support nature philanthropy is an important form of nature importing. But wealthy tourists, following in the footsteps of Gore and Roosevelt, have been the mainstay of the nature business. Their willingness to pay heavily to see wild nature is a major factor in the economies of the nations where it still exists.

To extend the export-import metaphor, national parks and wilderness systems might be thought of as the institutional "containers" that developed nations send to underdeveloped ones for the purpose of "packaging" a fragile resource. Personnel sent to run the parks or to train native managers have a key role in the transfer of wildness for money.

Although less utilitarian arguments certainly do exist, in actual fact money is the most important reason for preserving nature in most cultures. As the scope of the Gore and Roosevelt trips suggests, nature exporting can be lucrative. It subsidizes nature preservation. Less developed countries can afford to maintain wildness, while necessarily restraining development, if the exportation of nature pays sufficient dividends. A poster intended for natives in Africa makes the point explicitly: "OUR NATIONAL PARKS BRING GOOD MONEY INTO TANZANIA—PRESERVE THEM." Local people are reminded, for instance, that an adult male lion in Amboseli National Park in Kenya generates $515,000 in tourist revenue over the course of its lifetime. For a poacher, the meat and skin might bring as much as $1,150.[4] On the basis of the revenue they generate by attracting tourists, lions or elephants may be the most valuable animals in the world, race horses included.

The tension between the nature exporters and the nature importers is historic and continuing. It should be clear that the exporters do not as a rule recognize the marketability of their product. Africans, for example, have lived with wild animals as long as they can remember. You cannot interest a Masai in seeing and photographing a giraffe any more than you can interest a New Yorker in a taxicab. Similarly, the restrictions on grazing and farming in an African park or preserve are as perplexing to the natives as a law that prevents a New Yorker from living in and using ten square blocks of midtown Manhattan would be. Not sharing the developed world's conception of the value of wild

4. Philip Thresher, "The Present Value of an Amboseli Lion" (unpublished manuscript, April, 1977), p. 1.

nature, the less developed world sees no reason not to continue to exploit resources in the accustomed manner. But as Tanzania's president Julius Nyerere's remark opening this chapter suggests, if incomprehensible foreign tourists want to travel thousands of miles just to *look* at wild animals, and especially if they spend money in the process, exporters will not protest.[5]

Exporting and importing nature also has a regional or *intranational* significance. The urban segment of a population may support preservation of wilderness in hinterlands, the inhabitants of which are indifferent or actively hostile. In the United States, the East and civilized islands in the West, like San Francisco, reached the nature importing stage several generations before the still-wild West. The first nature tourists came from these areas.[6] So did the first stirrings of the nature preservation movement. Henry David Thoreau and Theodore Roosevelt were Harvard men. John Muir, like Sir St. George Gore, came from Great Britain, and when he organized the Sierra Club in 1892 it was dominated by an elite from Berkeley and San Francisco.[7]

Parallels exists throughout the world. The concern in Tokyo protects what wildness remains on Japan's northernmost island, Hokkaido. Australia's outback is of primary interest to residents of Sydney and Melbourne. The Malaysian Nature Society has little support outside the nation's metropolis, Kuala Lumpur. The national parks of Norway and Sweden are the concerns of urban people in the southern portions of those countries. And, to return to the American experience, nature preservation efforts in Alaska have been led by outsiders from the rest of the United States. Robert Marshall, for example, was a classic nature importer, amply endowed with the money and free time to indulge his passion for wilderness during the depths of the Great Depression.

In stating this thesis graphically the economists' concept of marginal valuation is useful. The vertical axis in the figure below measures the value a society or nation attaches to an extra unit of the commodity or experience in question. The horizontal axis mea-

5. Quoted in Wolfgang Engelhardt, *Survival of the Free,* trans. John Coombs (New York, 1962), p. 112.

6. Earl Pomeroy, *In Search of the Golden West: The Tourist in Western America* (New York, 1957).

7. Holway R. Jones, *John Muir and the Sierra Club: The Battle for Yosemite* (San Francisco, 1965).

CHANGING ATTITUDES TOWARD NATURE AND CIVILIZATION WITH DEVELOPMENT

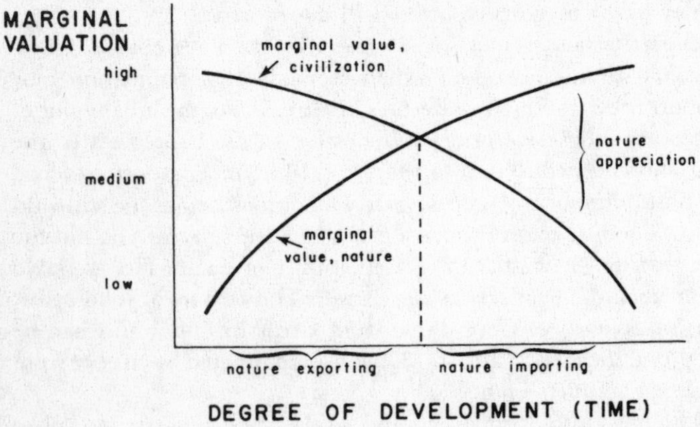

sures the degree of economic development in the society and is roughly equivalent to historical time. Read from left to right the graph shows what happens to the relative valuation of wild nature and civilization as a nation undergoes development. Initially the marginal valuation of civilization is much higher than that of wildness. Wildness at this stage is so abundant as to constitute a threat to the society. This condition favors nature exporting. With the passage of time, civilization becomes plentiful and nature scarce. The marginal valuation of each changes. After the curves cross, society values increasingly rare nature more than it values now plentiful civilization. Henceforth it is civilization that constitutes the threat to people's mental and physical well-being. This situation encourages nature importing. The widening vertical distance between the curves to the right of the graph may be taken to represent the growing amount of nature appreciation.

Until very recently traveling for pleasure almost always entailed movement from less civilized to more civilized areas. The trapper or farmer came out of the woods for a few days of fun in the biggest city available. If people traveled in the other direction their purpose was invariably to transform wilderness into civilization in the manner of the Pilgrims and the Mormons. No one went to New England or Utah in the early years for recreation. The intellectual revolution that made unmodified nature *per se* a mecca for travelers is the principal subject of this book. It depended upon the emergence of a group of affluent and cultured persons who resided in urban environments. For such persons wilderness could become an intriguing novelty and even a deep spiritual and psychological need. But the civilized conditions that cause interest in wilderness also destroy it. Travel was the solution.

If wild country no longer existed close to home, one could, given sufficient wealth and leisure, find it elsewhere. The procession of English tourists to the Alps was the first major instance of nature importing as a social and intellectual movement. Stimulated by the descriptions of Jean-Jacques Rousseau in the 1760s, and later by the new aesthetics of John Ruskin, English travelers crossed the Channel to find in France, Switzerland, and Italy what their homeland could not provide. By the middle of the nineteenth century, tourism had evolved into mountaineering. The decade after 1854 was the golden age, with the first ascents of 180 peaks in the Alps, including, in 1865, the Matterhorn.[8]

Englishmen of privileged social and economic backgrounds predominated in the new sport. Significantly the local people who lived in the Alps initially had no interest in mountaineering. The natives feared and hated the high country, avoiding it whenever possible. Only when it became apparent that money was to be made by assisting foreigners climb did the legendary alpine guide stride forth with rope coiled and hand outstretched. Even then, the attitudes of the importers and the exporters toward mountains remained far apart. What was pleasure for the visitor remained strictly business for the locals.[9]

8. The first nature tourists are well described in Bruce C. Johnson, "The Leader Must Not Fall: A Sociological Analysis of Mountain Climbing," (unpublished manuscript prepared in the Department of Sociology, University of California, San Diego, 1977), especially Chapter 2; Brian Dunning, "In the Beginning the English Created Mountaineering," *Mountain Gazette* (April 1973), 8; Gaven de Beer, *Early Travelers in the Alps* (New York, 1967); Ronald Clark, *The Victorian Mountaineers* (London, 1953); Claire Engle, *Mountaineering in the Alps* (London, 1971); and Arnold Lunn, *Switzerland and the English* (London, 1944).

9. Johnson, "The Leader Must Not Fall," especially chapter 4; Edward Whymper, *Scrambles Amongst the Alps* (Philadelphia, 1871), p. 36; Claire Engel, *A History of Mountaineering in the Alps* (London, 1950), pp. 23, 58, 63; Ronald Clark, *The Early Alpine Guides* (London, 1949).

The Alps had the advantage of proximity, but for the European importer of nature in the nineteenth century the western territories of the United States held special fascination. The New World still had real wilderness—unsettled country with wild animals and wild people. The difficulty and expense associated with travel on the American frontier acted as a filter for visitors. Importing wildness from North America remained for a half century a special treat reserved for royalty and the extremely rich. A growing number made the investment. One of the first was François René de Chateaubriand who in 1791 found New York state sufficiently wild to fire his romantic imagination (see above, pp. 49–50). His countryman, Alexis de Tocqueville, came forty years later and followed the fast-moving frontier all the way to Michigan to find wilderness. Tocqueville's remarks (above, p. 23) are a classic explanation of the nature exporting and nature importing perspectives.

As late as the 1870s almost all the nature tourists on the American frontier continued to be foreigners. Americans went west for science and discovery, for fur and gold, to fight Indians and secure homesteads. The foreigners were there for fun. Their pioneering was in wilderness appreciation. So Prince Maximilian traveled up the Missouri in 1833 strictly as a tourist. In this precamera age, he brought along a Swiss artist, Karl Bodmer, to record the sights.[10] The German Heinrich Balduin Möllhausen accompanied Duke Paul William of Württemberg in a similar capacity on an 1851 pleasure trip to the Missouri headwaters. The Duke, known as "the gypsy Prince," had traveled in the wild West as early as 1822, but the trip with the artist turned into a survival situation with Indian attacks and starvation. Subsisting on frozen wolf meat, Möllhausen still managed to return with some creditable paintings.[11] Sir William Drummond Stewart, heir of one of the oldest and wealthiest families in Scotland, returned to the American West repeatedly in the 1830s and 1840s. His retinue in 1843 consisted of some thirty "gentlemen," the same number of "hunters," and 120 horses and mules. Six years earlier, at the annual trappers' rendezvous, Stewart presented the legendary mountain man Jim Bridger

10. Harold McCracken, *Portrait of the Old West* (New York, 1952), pp. 71–76; Alexander Philip Maximilian, *Travels in the Interior of North America, 1832–1834*, ed. Reuben Gold Thwaites (Cleveland, 1906); John C. Ewers, *Artists of the Old West* (Garden City, 1973), pp. 76–97.

11. McCracken, *Portrait*, p. 126–28; Möllhausen, *Diary of a Journey from the Mississippi to the Coast of the Pacific*, trans. Mrs. Percy Sinnett (London, 1858).

with a full suit of armor. In their relation to wild nature, the men stood at opposite ends of the spectrum. Bridger was in the West to harvest the remaining beaver and profit from an expanding civilization.[12]

In the third quarter of the nineteenth century, what Earl Pomeroy calls "the Far Western hunter-tourist"[13] became increasingly common. The tales of Sir St. George Gore, as told by an uncle, inspired Windham Thomas Wyndham-Quin, the Fourth Earl of Dunraven, to import the wilderness of the West. In 1871 Dunraven hunted the Nebraska plains guided by Buffalo Bill Cody and Texas Jack Omohundro. Three years later Omohundro led the Earl through northwestern Wyoming. Dunraven harbored no illusions about his purposes. In one of the earliest instances of the use of the word, he calls himself a tourist. Hunting was not the primary reason for his trip but rather "the satisfaction of my curiosity and the gratification of my sight-seeing instincts."[14]

William A. Baillie-Grohman was the most persistent of all the late nineteenth-century importers of American nature. Beginning in the late 1870s, this wealthy English sportsman and alpinist made no fewer than thirty trips to the Far West and British Columbia. It is clear that he sought in North America what he could no longer find in Europe. For two decades Baillie-Grohman had hunted close to home, "killing my first deer in the Alps before I was ten years old." But the Old World could not satisfy his thirst for wildness. He longed "to make the acquaintance of the great Mountain System of the New World, the home of such lordly game as the grizzly, the bighorn, and the wapiti—the latter our own stag, produced on a wholly magnificent, one might say *American* scale."[15]

12. Mae Reed Porter and Odessa Davenport, *Scotsman in Buckskin: Sir William Drummond Stewart and the Rocky Mountain Fur Trade* (New York, 1963), pp. 213–45; Matthew C. Field, *Prairie and Mountain Sketches,* ed. Kate L. Gregg and John Francis McDermott (Norman, Okla., 1957), Gene Caesar, *King of the Mountain Men: The Life of Jim Bridger* (New York, 1961), pp. 153–54, 174, 186.

13. Pomeroy, *Golden West,* p. 77.

14. Earl of Dunraven, *The Great Divide: Travels in the Upper Yellowstone in the Summer of 1874* (1876; reprint, Lincoln, Neb., 1967), pp. xx, xxv.

15. William A. Baillie-Grohman, *Camps in the Rockies: Being a Narrative of Life on the Frontier, and Sport in the Rocky Mountains, With an Account of Cattle Ranches of the West* (London, 1882), pp. v–vi. A comprehensive account of Baillie-Grohman's North American experience is *Fifteen Years' Sport and Life in the Hunting Grounds of Western America and British Columbia* (London, 1900).

Baillie-Grohman's expeditions mark the concluding phases of the individualized safari in the West. Thereafter most tourists used the services of commercial travel companies such as those of Thomas Cook and Walter Raymond. But even on these standard tours, the West's great attraction was its wildness. Certainly no European would journey to Arizona or Wyoming in 1900 to see cities, museums, and churches. But Indians, the Rocky Mountains, Yosemite and the Grand Canyon were compelling. Nature, not civilization, was the actively traded commodity between America and its foreign visitors.[16]

Given the ambitions of a growing United States and the absence in the nineteenth century of an effective nature protection movement, the pleasure of nature tourists was inevitably transitory. Environmental conditions changed rapidly. In his account of 1882, Baillie-Grohman is overjoyed and overwhelmed with the wildness, the vastness, and the abundance of the region. Big game was plentiful, and the avowed object of his early trips was trophy hunting. Baillie-Grohman depicted the West as the mecca of the lover of wilderness. But his book of 1890 reflects the change brought about by the accelerating expansion of American civilization. Baillie-Grohman devotes a chapter to the careless slaughter of buffalo and elk. In his view, "railways, ranchemen [sic], and miners have taken possession of what was once the sportsman's paradise." The wildness relished by early tourists had vanished. "Many parts of Montana, Wyoming, and Idaho are still worth visiting for the sake of sport," Baillie-Grohman concluded, "but the old glory of those states is gone never to return."[17]

From this perspective national parks acquired importance as a means of keeping at least a symbol of a wild region's old glory alive. Significantly, the world's first national park, Yellowstone, protected a part of the northwestern Wyoming that Gore, Dunraven, Baillie-Grohman, and other foreigners prized. Moreover, the men responsible for conceiving of the national park idea and pushing it through Congress in 1872 were, without exception, nature importers from the eastern states. George Catlin, the first (in 1832) to advocate creation of a *nation's park* in the Rocky Mountains, was a Philadelphia artist. Cornelius Hedges, whose 1870 trip through the

16. For a discussion of the evolution of travel in the West from the expedition to the tour see Pomeroy, *Golden West*, Chapters 2 and 3.

17. Baillie-Grohman, *Fifteen Years'*, p. 26.

Yellowstone country led directly to the park movement, held degrees from Yale and Harvard. His colleague, Nathaniel P. Langford, had family roots in New York. Jay Cooke, the railroad entrepreneur who lobbied for the park, dominated eastern financial circles. In sharp contrast, the local residents of Montana and Wyoming remained suspicious about the park concept until it became clear that Yellowstone Park would attract money-spending tourists. The realization that the park might help, rather than hinder, regional development won over the locals.[18]

Predictably, foreign importers of nature from the American West were delighted with Yellowstone National Park. The Earl of Dunraven rejoiced that his favorite sporting ground was now protected for "all nations and all people."[19] The Earl's friend Moreton Frewen went even further. After a hunting trip to Yellowstone in 1878 (hunting was not prohibited in the park until 1883), Frewen attempted to use his contacts to persuade Congress to expand the park to include the lower elevation wintering ground of big game in the adjacent Wind River Basin. The idea made ecological sense, but no headway on Capitol Hill. Disappointed and fearful that the pressure of settlement would end wildlife and hunting, Frewen acted on his own. In 1879 he bought a large property on Wyoming's Powder River, built a ranch house complete with hardwood floors from England, and enjoyed wilderness hunting trips with his wealthy friends.[20] The same idea occurred to other nature importers. Baillie-Grohman reported in 1900 that a group of prominent Eastern and European sportsmen were organizing to purchase 50,000 acres in the Rocky Mountains, fence the land, build a $50,000 clubhouse, and hunt elk, deer, bear, and mountain sheep on their private nature preserve.[21]

Actions like those of Moreton Frewen or the friends of Baillie-Grohman might slow but could not reverse the trend favoring civilization over wilderness in the American West. Even large national

18. Since the second edition of this book, several new publications have appeared which present the early history of Yellowstone in detail: Aubrey L. Haines, *The Yellowstone Story* (Yellowstone National Park, 1977); Haines, *Yellowstone National Park: Its Exploration and Establishment* (Washington, D.C., 1974); and Richard A. Bartlett, *Nature's Yellowstone* (Albuquerque, 1974).

19. Dunraven, *Great Divide*, p. xxiii.

20. Moreton Frewen, *Melton Mowbray and Other Memories* (London, 1924), pp. 172, 176–77; Pomeroy, *Golden West*, pp. 79, 92.

21. Baillie-Grohman, *Fifteen Years'*, pp. 27–28.

parks such as Yellowstone were no substitute for the quality and quantity of wildness that St. George Gore experienced in the 1850s. Inexorably, a developing America was maturing and changing in the process from a nature exporter to a nature importer. While it lasted, the West's resource of unmodified nature had been systematically exploited by tourists from abroad and from the East. By the turn of the century the importers were looking for new frontiers, and the successor to the wild West was Africa.

Buffalo are an index to the change. By the time of Theodore Roosevelt's first western trip in 1883, the buffalo were making their last stand. Hunting, fencing, and the general expansion of settlement had reduced a population of from sixty to seventy-five million animals to a few hundred. The year 1883, in fact, saw the last commercial buffalo hunt on the Great Plains.[22] After a week's effort in the Dakota badlands, Roosevelt and his guide finally found one lonely buffalo to shoot, but the New Yorker was puzzled and saddened by the scarcity of game.[23] Anticipating the future, Roosevelt turned to ranching and, for wildness, to Africa.

Theodore Roosevelt's widely publicized 1909 safari to East Africa actually followed a well-beaten trail of nature importers from countries that had used up their wildness earlier than had the United States. The publicity surrounding the search of H. M. Stanley for David Livingstone in 1871 triggered a surge of interest in Africa as a dark, wild continent. As early as 1894 British authorities on hunting, such as Clive Phillips-Wolley, spotlighted Africa as the successor to India and the western United States as a sportsman's paradise. Bitterly, Phillips-Wolley told how meat hunting and disregard of game laws by local people had ruined opportunities in many parts of the world for "the alien who pays for his sport."[24] Similarly, Parker Gillmore returned to the American West in the 1870s and was shocked at the changes. "Alas! how altered, how changed, had the great Western continent become! West! farther

22. Gard, *Great Buffalo Hunt,* pp. 256–75; Tom McHugh, *The Time of the Buffalo* (New York, 1972). McHugh's estimation of the precontact population of buffalo is 30 to 100 million.

23. Wilson, *Roosevelt: Outdoorsman,* pp. 33–39; Cutright, *Roosevelt: The Naturalist,* pp. 38–42; Herman Hagedorn, *Roosevelt in the Bad Lands* (Boston, 1921), pp. 28–46. Roosevelt's relationship as an Easterner to the West, both as reality and idea, is treated in G. Edward White, *The Eastern Establishment and the Western Experience* (New Haven, 1968).

24. Clive Phillips-Wolley, *Big Game Shooting* (London, 1894), vol. 1, 1, 346–48.

west, still farther west, I pushed my way, but the game had gone to the spirit-land . . . grizzly bears, where they had once been numerous, had entirely disappeared and the weird voice of the wolf was unknown." Sadly Gillmore returned to his native England "wondering how I could kill time." The mail brought an answer in the form of an invitation to a year-long hunting trip in Africa. Without a moment's delay, Gillmore, the classic nature importer, agreed to a sporting adventure on the new frontier.[25] C. J. "Buffalo" Jones, the renowned American cowboy, responded similarly in 1910 when he left a West that had become "stale to [him]" for "other worlds to conquer" in Africa. Jones proposed to capture African lions and rhinoceros.[26] Even the vicarious wilderness adventurer gave up on the American West. Edgar Rice Burroughs led the way in 1913 by making Africa the locale of his enormously popular Tarzan sagas.

But it was increasingly clear from the American experience that even in Africa nature importing would not be possible for long without nature protection. The most sophisticated of the early calls to save wild Africa came from Abel Chapman, an English gentleman-hunter who began importing wildness from Norway and Spain before moving on, in 1899, to the dark continent. Chapman devoted an entire chapter of his book *On Safari* to the protection question. He began by noting the "abominable massacre" of the American buffalo in the 1880s and the destruction of Norway's reindeer herd in the following decade. His intent was to "make such barbarities impossible at least on British soil." Significantly, in view of the early date of his statement, Chapman clearly recognized the export-import situation and its importance to the economy of Africa. "As a simple matter of fact," he wrote in 1908, "the traveller-sportsman was (and still remains) the best customer of the Colony; while the game is still its best asset." Yet, ambivalently, he also admitted that game protection should not stand in the way of "the necessities of white settlement and colonization." Chapman's point

25. Parker Gillmore, *The Great Thirst Land* (London, ca. 1880), pp. 2–3. Similar statements are numerous. See, for example Frewen, *Melton Mowbray*, p. 207; C. G. Schillings, *In Wildest Africa* (New York, 1907), pp. 196–98, 203; and J. G. Millais, *Wandering and Memories* (London, 1919), pp. 219–20.

26. Robert Easton and MacKenzie Brown, *Lord of the Beasts: The Saga of Buffalo Jones* (Tucson, 1961), pp. 196–262. Zane Grey, who attended the farewell banquet for Jones, had written about him in *The Last of the Plainsmen* (New York, 1908).

was that many parts of Africa were unsuited to development and could be dedicated to "God's beautiful wild creatures." Chapman, to be sure, killed game, but in company with most of the importers of his era he defined himself as a sportsman and he supplied his own definition of that term: "One who loves the game as though he were the father of it."[27]

Theodore Roosevelt was in the vanguard of sportsmen who urged the conservation of wildlife and its habitat around the world. In 1909, the year he began his safari, Roosevelt published an introduction to William Baillie-Grohman's edition of a medieval hunting classic, *The Master of the Game.* He acknowledged that there were still a few remote places where one had to hunt in order to eat and where settlers had to "war against the game" in the manner of primitive man. "But," Roosevelt noted, "over most of the earth such conditions have passed forever." People who loved the wild as Roosevelt did realized that only their determination, and their money, stood between it and the pressures of an expanding technological civilization. "Even in Africa," Roosevelt stated in 1909, "game preserving on a gigantic scale has begun."[28]

The preservation of game animals in Africa is an excellent illustration of nature exporting and importing at work. Colonization made it easy. Developed nations found themselves in control of a huge area rich in wildness which had been exhausted at home. The logical next step was to protect nature in Africa so that it could be enjoyed by people from Europe. Efforts in this direction first appeared in England in the 1890s. By 1899 a series of general propositions had been drafted, and on May 19, 1900, seven European nations signed draft articles concerning nature protection in Africa. They proposed regulations on hunting licenses, closed seasons, and methods of capture. Schedules itemized species that would enjoy complete protection (the gorilla, giraffe, and chimpanzee are examples) and, invoking a philosophy repudiated by later ecologically minded preservationists, "noxious" forms of life that should be exterminated (crocodiles, dangerous monkeys, pythons). An attempt

27. Abel Chapman, *On Safari: Big-Game Hunting in British East Africa* (London, 1908), pp. 295–97, 300, 302. For the role of the sportsman in wildlife conservation in America see John F. Reiger, *American Sportsmen and the Origins of Conservation* (New York, 1975).

28. From Roosevelt's introduction to William A. and F. Baillie-Grohman, *The Master of the Game* (London, 1909), p. xxvi.

to assist elephants by controlling the ivory trade occupied a central part of the document.[29]

As a first step the English-inspired convention of 1900 was remarkably strict and comprehensive, but those same characteristics explain why it was never implemented. Few nations wished to be bound so tightly. Commerce and administrative convenience remained the dominant considerations. Moreover, this pioneering effort in international cooperation for nature protection suffered from what would become a chronic problem in this endeavor: no teeth. Given the world's political organization, it was naive to expect that one nation's telling another to be good would have much effect. After a few years of sporadic communication between bureaucrats in England, France, Italy, Germany, and Portugal, the grandiose plans of 1900 for protecting African wildlife died quietly. Their most important contribution was the establishment of the pattern whereby one country tried to encourage the protection of nature in another.

Parks and reserves proved more successful in African nature protection than sweeping and unenforceable resolutions. Here again all the momentum came from Europe and, later, from America, where the 1872 invention of the national park was attracting the attention of nature importers in many parts of the world. The case of Kruger National Park is South Africa is instructive. The prime mover was James Stevenson-Hamilton, an Englishman who in 1902 accepted the position of head ranger in the Sabi Game Reserve. This expanse of undeveloped low veld, rich in wildlife, received nominal protection from the South African Volksraad four years earlier, but there was no local support. "In those days," Stevenson-Hamilton noted, "to be shot was the sole end for which wild animals were supposed to exist."[30]

Stevenson-Hamilton did not know how to respond to such logic until he heard about the national park concept in the United States. Closed to hunting, the American parks reflected the attitude that moose, bear, and buffalo were more valuable as life forms than as targets. Stevenson-Hamilton resolved to convince South Africans that the same was true for lions, elephants, and giraffes. He sent to

29. Sherman Strong Hayden, *The International Protection of Wild Life* (1942; reprint, New York, 1970), pp. 36–39.

30. Stevenson-Hamilton, *South African Eden: From Sabi Game Reserve to Kruger National Park* (London, 1937), p. 112.

the United States for all the literature available on the national parks and studied the methods of their first director, Stephen T. Mather. Stevenson-Hamilton took special note of how Mather interested railroad companies in the parks by demonstrating their potential for attracting tourists. Finally, in 1926, the precarious Sabi Game Reserve became Kruger National Park. The telling argument, advanced by the Minister of Lands, Piet Grobler, was the financial success of the American initiative in nature protection.[31]

Only one other major national park was established in Africa earlier than Kruger and it also owed much to the American example. A catalytic event which lead six years later to the creation of Albert National Park in the Belgian Congo was the visit of King Albert of Belgium to the American West in 1919. The American scientists who accompanied Albert on parts of his journey, John C. Merriam and Henry Fairfield Osborn, Sr., made sure the king appreciated the scientific importance of national parks like Yosemite. In so doing the Americans practiced a favorite technique of nature importers: inspiration by good example.[32] Back in Europe, King Albert faced a dilemma. The American parks had inspired him to do something comparable in Belgium, but wilderness had disappeared from that country centuries before. In Africa, however, the wild was alive and well, and Albert ruled over part of it: the Belgian Congo.

At this point enters an American who knew the Congo as well as any white man and loved its remote interior as one of the last unmodified African environments. Carl Akeley was a taxidermist and designer of exhibits of large mounted animals at the American Museum of Natural History in New York. In 1910, just as Roosevelt's safari concluded, Akeley began extended field studies of the African elephant. His next project concerned gorillas and brought Akeley to the Congo. By 1922 he was convinced that without protection the few hundred remaining gorillas were doomed. Communicating with Belgian authorities, Akeley advocated the establishment

31. Ibid., pp. 113, 120.

32. New York *Times,* Oct. 19, 1919. Details of the tour of the Belgian royal family to Yosemite, the Grand Canyon, and other parts of the American West may be found in the *Report of the Director of the National Park Service to the Secretary of the Interior, 1920* (Washington, D.C., 1920), I, 19–20, and in Franz Ansel, *Le Grand Voyage du Roi des Belges aux Etats-Unis d'Amérique* (Brussels, 1921) and P. Goemaere, *A Travers l'Amérique avec le Roi des Belges* (Brussels, 1923).

of a sanctuary and a biological research station. John C. Merriam, who had been with King Albert in 1919, intervened on behalf of Akeley's ideas. On March 2, 1925, they bore fruit when a royal decree established Albert National Park.[33] Later expanded to six million acres, the park was unusual in emphasizing science rather than tourism. Since only trained researchers would be admitted, the reserve could not meet the needs of nature importing tourists. But as a nature sanctuary guarded from local exploitative pressure by a multinational board of scientists, Albert National Park provides classic evidence of the different perspectives underlying nature exporting and importing. In this case it was the idea that the world's last gorillas were safe that was the saleable commodity. For a scientist like Carl Akeley the park was almost a private reserve. It also became a cemetery. Akeley died in November 1926 on an expedition to the park he had done so much to create.[34]

The effectiveness of Carl Akeley and John C. Merriam in convincing Belgium to establish Albert National Park was not entirely circumstantial. Thanks to Yellowstone (1872), Yosemite (1890), the National Park Service Act (1916), the Forest Service initiatives in wilderness designation in the 1920s and 1930s and, later, the Wilderness Act (1964) and the Alaska National Interest Lands Conservation Act (1980), the United States has maintained a reputation as the world's foremost protector of wildlife and wilderness. Time and again the American example inspired preservationists in other countries. In Japan, for example, the first proposals for national parks followed the visits of nineteenth-century students and tourists to Yosemite and Yellowstone. Then, in 1914, a twenty-four year old Japanese student and mountaineer, Ryozo Azuma, called on John Muir at his ranch in Martinez. Depressed after the Hetch Hetchy defeat, Muir would have only a few more months to live, but he entertained Azuma for two days. Even though Azuma was already familiar with most of Muir's writings, he was overwhelmed by the visit. "The deep spiritual influence I had from John Muir," he later wrote, "has dramatically and decisively directed the way for

33. The reserve has now become Virunga National Park in Zaire and Volcanoes National Park in Rwanda.

34. Carl Akeley, *In Brightest Africa* (Garden City, 1923), pp. 249 ff. Mary L. Jobe Akeley, *Carl Akeley's Africa* (London, 1931) and her *Congo Eden* (London, 1951) and "Belgian Congo Sanctuaries," *Scientific Monthly*, 33 (October, 1931), 289–300, provide further detail.

my whole life."[35] What Azuma meant is that he went on to become a major interpreter of American life and institutions for the Japanese, writing two dozen volumes including a biography of John Muir. Azuma also worked with Tsuyoshi Tamura, who had visited Yosemite and met Stephen T. Mather. In 1931 Tamura pushed into law a bill creating a national park system for Japan. Azuma traveled over the world but returned to Japan only to lose his government job during World War II because he refused to remove from the walls of his office posters with photographs of parks and wilderness areas of the United States.

The idea of international collaboration to protect wild nature in the less developed parts of the world also had American roots. Following their 1908 triumph in publicizing conservation at a White House conference, Theodore Roosevelt and Chief Forester Gifford Pinchot called a North American Conservation Conference. At its February 1909 meeting the delegates resolved to work for a world conference the following September in Holland.[36] Before he left office, President Roosevelt sent invitations to fifty-eight nations, but his successor, William Howard Taft, dropped the project. But Paul Sarasin, a Swiss zoologist, continued the campaign for an international commission having a "mission to extend protection of nature to the whole world from the north pole to the south pole, covering both continents and seas."[37] In 1911 the Swiss government appointed a committee of internationally respected scientists and simultaneously issued a call for an International Conference for the Protection of Nature which convened in Basel in November 1913. Delegates from sixteen nations (not the United States) participated. Their initial resolves concerned the establishment of an information clearing house and a propaganda agency for nature protection everywhere in the world.[38] Everything collapsed six months later, however, with the outbreak of the First World War. Even in 1923, when

35. Maymie and William Kimes, "Ryozo Azuma, the John Muir of Japan," *Sierra, 64* (1979), 43. See also Tetsumaro Senge, "The Educational Contributions of National Parks in Japan," in Alexander B. Adams, ed., *First World Conference on National Parks* (Washington, D.C., 1962), pp. 139 and Ian G. Simmons, "Parks and Recreation in Japan," *Recreation News Supplement, 10* (1973), 26–30.

36. Gifford Pinchot, *Breaking New Ground* (New York, 1947), pp. 361–67. See also M. Nelson McGeary, *Gifford Pinchot: Forester-Politician* (Princeton, 1960), pp. 107–08.

37. As quoted in Max Nicholson, *The Environmental Revolution: A Guide for the New Masters of the World* (New York, 1970), p. 193.

38. Ibid., pp. 193–94; Hayden, *International Protection*, pp. 16–17.

Switzerland tried again with an international conference held in Paris, it was clear that Europe was not ready to think seriously about international nature protection when more basic human problems remained unsolved. Environmental preservation remained a full stomach phenomenon.

After Paul Sarasin, P. G. Van Tienhoven assumed leadership of the crusade to institutionalize international nature protection. Van Tienhoven, who was a Dutchman, organized in 1925 and 1926 committees for the international protection of nature in France, Belgium, and the Netherlands. On July 10, 1928, he established, under the auspices of the International Union of Biological Sciences, an International Office for the Protection of Nature based in Brussels. Its function was restricted to information-gathering and, like Paul Sarasin's committee, it eventually fell victim to the disruptions associated with another world war. For a few years, though, in the early 1930s, institutionalized global nature protection enjoyed its finest hour. At Paris in 1931 the Conseil International de la Chasse held an enthusiastic meeting centered on the conservation of birds throughout the world. In the same year Van Tienhoven organized an International Congress for the Protection of Nature. The delegates resolved that the rest of the world should resume the effort to save wild nature in Africa.[39]

Similar concern motivated the American Committee for International Wildlife Protection which took shape in 1931 in response to Van Tienhoven's initiative. John C. Phillips, a gentleman conservationist-hunter and brother of the American ambassador to Great Britain, chaired the committee; Harold J. Coolidge, Jr., was its first secretary and primary spokesman. These men and their board of directors were generally affluent, well-traveled, and connoisseurs of the beauty of wild nature wherever it existed in the world. Recognizing Africa as a threatened resource of wild nature, the committee produced a handsome special publication entitled *African Game Protection.* It listed the national parks and game reserves in Africa and discussed threatened species.[40]

The high point of institutionalized global nature protection before the Second World War came on October 31, 1933, when repre-

39. Second International Congress for the Protection of Nature, *Minutes* (Paris, 1932).

40. American Committee for International Wildlife Protection, *African Game Protection* (Cambridge, 1933).

sentatives of all the colonial powers in Africa plus observers such as P. G. Van Tienhoven and John C. Phillips convened in the House of Lords to open the London Conference for the Protection of African Fauna and Flora. After a week's deliberations, a nineteen-article convention emerged for final signing.[41] It expressed a determination to increase the number of national parks and what were termed "strict natural reserves." In contrast to the parks, where tourism but not hunting was allowed, the strict reserves banned all human visitation except that of qualified scientists under carefully regulated conditions. Such a policy obviously would not generate much revenue from nature tourism. For the Belgian delegates, at least, this had not been a concern previously. Their Albert National Park was closed to all but scientists, and the Belgians believed that tourism should be subordinated to the right of wild plants and animals to exist for their own sake.[42] This departure from the anthropocentrism normally present in nature protection was unusual. The other delegates insisted that enjoyment by people was the only legitimate reason for protecting nature. Most nature importers would have agreed. The concept of deriving pleasure merely from the knowledge that a place or species was protected had little support in 1933.

The London Convention went on to urge the protection with game laws of animals outside the parks and reserves. An attempt was made to regulate the trade in animal trophies. The signatories agreed to prohibit certain hunting methods such as the shooting of game from cars and airplanes. Two lists designated animals deserving total protection and those which should be killed only occasionally and under special licensing procedure. Unfortunately, when it came to enforcement the convention temporized badly. Local African authorities were accorded the right to set aside the restrictions for a variety of reasons. A clause that anticipated Alaskan policy allowed natives to continue hunting where they had hunted

41. American Committee for International Wildlife Protection, *The London Convention for the Protection of African Fauna and Flora* (Cambridge, 1935). The 1933 convention report is also reprinted and discussed in Hayden, *International Protection*, pp. 43–63, 177–93. A contemporary discussion is G. Dolman, "The Peril to Africa's Big Game—Why the Conference is Necessary," *Saturday Review*, *155* (1933), 463.

42. London Conference for the Protection of African Fauna and Flora, "Minutes, Nov. 1, 1933," in the files of the American Committee for International Wildlife Protection, New York.

before. In the end, the resolutions contained in the London Convention were not law but advocacy, and even that function crumbled as the Second World War approached.

The final act in the second surge of interest in international nature protection occurred in 1940 just before the European war became worldwide. The Pan-American Union provided the institutional mechanism for preservationists from the various American nations to meet in Washington, D.C. On October 12 a draft convention emerged. The Pan-American document reaffirmed the London Convention of 1933 but went further in its identification of the kinds of reserves that the contracting governments would attempt to establish. Along with national parks and what the Washington conferees called "strict wilderness reserves," the articles called for the establishment of national reserves where resource exploitation and preservation would theoretically coexist. Another new category went beyond the other three in completely prohibiting visitation even for recreational purposes.[43] The United States ratified the articles on April 23, 1941. Then came the war.

After the Second World War the movement for international unity that gave rise to the United Nations provided a favorable climate of opinion for the rebirth and growth of global nature protection. Once again a coterie of nature importers took steps to protect their interests in foreign countries. The Swiss took the lead by hosting a conference in Brunnen on June 30, 1947. A provisional International Union for the Protection of Nature emerged. On September 30 of the following year, Julian Huxley, the Director-General of UNESCO and a classic example of the British nature importer, engineered a meeting at Fontainebleau in France. Eighteen governments, seven international organizations, and 109 national nature protection organizations participated. On October 5, 1948, they completed a constitution. Its preamble defined the object of the new organization as nothing less than "the preservation of the entire world biotic environment." The stated reason behind this objective was the dependence of human civilization upon renewable natural resources. Yet it was clear that the Fontainebleau conferees had amenity values as well as practical considerations in mind. The second paragraph in the preamble set forth as axiomatic that "natural beauty is one of the higher common

43. Hayden, *International Protection*, pp. 62–66, 193–98.

denominators of spiritual life." The statement went on to stress the value of wild life and wilderness areas and to champion "national parks, nature reserves, . . . and wild life refuges." According to the constitution, there were "social, educational and cultural reasons" for protecting nature along with economic ones. The organization, known after 1956 as the International Union for the Conservation of Nature and Natural Resources (IUCN), attempted to cover both bases. But a utilitarian interest in "soils, water [and] forests" always seemed to be a means to the end of gaining wider support for the preservation of the wild places and wild things that delighted nature importers.[44]

Evidence for this slant of the IUCN appeared in its early and continuing emphasis on vanishing species and national parks. A Survival Service Commission emerged from the IUCN's 1949 conference at Lake Success, New York. Its work in documenting species led in 1966 to the first edition of the *Red Data Book,* a worldwide listing of threatened birds, animals, and later, plants. The format was loose-leaf to permit periodic updating if the status of a species improved or declined. To minimize the possibility of species extinction the World Wildlife Fund had been organized in 1961 in Switzerland. Although not formally affiliated, the Fund acted symbiotically with IUCN, raising money for IUCN projects and sharing a headquarters in Morges, Switzerland.[45] The caliber of the Fund's leaders and their money-raising capacities were impressive. Prince Bernhard of the Netherlands, first president of the World Wildlife Fund, obtained ten million dollars from a thousand select individuals. In return they received a print of a bald eagle and an invitation to tour East Africa or the Galapagos Islands. Significantly, most of the contributors began their interest in wildlife conservation on importing trips like these. Prince Bernhard's experience included several hunting safaris in Africa in the 1950s. On each successive visit he noted a decline in the number of animals. "Where once I

44. International Union for the Conservation of Nature and Natural Resources, *1973 IUCN Yearbook* (Morges, Switzerland, 1974), pp. 17–21; Nicholson, *Environmental Revolution,* pp. 194 ff.; Philip Street, *Wildlife Preservation* (London, 1970), p. 24.

45. Peter Scott, ed., *The Launching of a New Ark: The First Report of the President and Trustees of the World Wildlife Fund* (London, 1965) and Fritz Vollmar, ed., *The Ark Under Way: Second Report of the World Wildlife Fund* (Morges, Switzerland, 1978) detail the activity of the organization. Additional in-

saw thousands," the Prince recalled, "I found only a few hundred, then a mere handful of even the most common animals."[46] The response of this nature importer was to protect his pleasure through the World Wildlife Fund.

Encouraging the formation and maintenance of national parks and other kinds of nature reserves was the second major emphasis of the IUCN. Its Athens meeting in 1958 launched the International Commission on National Parks which, in turn, undertook the preparation of the *United Nations List of National Parks and Equivalent Reserves.*[47] The American, Harold J. Coolidge, and the IUCN's Secretary from Belgium, Jean-Paul Harroy, headed the effort. The first compilations were ready in time for the First World Conference on National Parks held in Seattle beginning on July 30, 1962. At this gathering of 145 delegates from 63 countries, which the IUCN organized, the themes of nature importing and exporting were much in evidence, as in the keynote address of the American Secretary of the Interior, Stewart L. Udall. Udall explained how his countrymen initially bemoaned the way in which resources like forests, game, and minerals were locked up in national parks. But later they discovered "that the income from providing services to visitor-tourists has equaled or surpassed whatever sums might have been gained exploiting these park resources." Udall predicted that with improvements in air travel, the nations of East Africa would find that "the world's travelers [to the parks] will add far more to their economic growth than would any alternate use of these lands." Later in the conference an entire session detailed the economic values of preserved wild nature. In fact, the economic argument had been one of the four "pillars" that the World Wildlife Fund and the IUCN saw as supporting global nature conservation. The other three ideological supports stemmed from ethical, aesthetic and scientific arguments.[48]

---

formation came from an interview wth Fred Packard, International Division, National Park Service, Washington, D.C., September 12, 1974.

46. "Royal Conservationist," *The New Yorker,* 50 (December 1, 1974), 42.

47. The most complete effort to date is Jean-Paul Harroy, ed., *United Nations List of National Parks and Equivalent Reserves,* 2nd ed. (Brussels, 1971). Supplements have been issued as IUCN Publications, new series, no. 27 (1973) and no. 29 (1974).

48. Adams, *First World Conference,* pp. 5, 98 ff. Elspeth Huxley, "The Four Pillars—A Summary of the Aims," in Scott, ed., *Launching of a New Ark,* pp. 151–54.

Neither the IUCN nor the World Wildlife Fund had the power to coerce sovereign states into protecting nature. More subtle means of persuasion had to be employed. *The Red Data Book,* the *United Nations List of National Parks and Equivalent Reserves,* and the First World Conference on National Parks endeavored to make nations proud of having national parks and protected rare species. It would be shameful, in the eyes of the world, the implicit argument ran, to destroy wildness needlessly just as it would be to wreck Chartres cathedral or the Taj Mahal. A truly civilized society protected its natural as well as its cultural treasures. If there was money to be made in the process from nature tourism, so much the better. Unless such arguments influenced people, the importers realized, their hopes of protecting nature in the less developed countries were slim.

Africa became the principal testing ground of these methods. Prior to the 1960s and the independence of the black African states, nature protection was exclusively the concern of white colonists. In British East Africa white game wardens like Blayney Percival and A. T. A. Ritchie, supported by the Society for the Preservation of the Fauna of the Empire, attempted to defend the shaky game reserves. The London Convention of 1933 raised hopes briefly, but when Colonel Mervyn Cowie returned to his family home near Nairobi in 1936 he found a hopeless situation. The native people simply ignored the reserves, and most of the colonial administrators did not care. The wildlife near Nairobi was vanishing rapidly. Cowie labored to arouse public opinion among the white settlers, and, on December 24, 1946, succeeded in securing the establishment of Nairobi National Park. Others followed, of which Tsavo (1948), Mount Kenya (1949), and the Serengeti (1951) were the most important. Cowie and his colleagues knew full well that these royal national parks were established by whites for whites. They were, in Cowie's words, "cultured persons' playgrounds." The natives had little interest in the parks; indeed, the idea of establishing parks and reserves in Africa in the first place had been to protect nature from the natives. For this reason the prospect of relinquishing the colonies to autonomous native governments frightened white preservationists like Cowie. "Less than a lifetime ago," he fumed in 1961, "the progenitors of these same people who shout for freedom were bargaining with my father to buy and eat his porters." It appeared unlikely to Cowie that the parks would survive independence, particularly with native populations rising as rapidly as their ambitions for a higher material standard of living.[49]

The same concern motivated the extraordinary German nature importer Bernhard Grzimek. An eminent zoologist and director of the Frankfurt Zoo, Grzimek had become aware in the 1950s that Africa, "the ultimate and last paradise of all our yearnings," was in trouble as far as wildness was concerned. He determined to do what he could to arouse public opinion throughout the world, reasoning in a manner strange to politicians and natives but familiar to nature importers that "Africa really belongs to all who take comfort from the thought that there are still wild animals and virgin lands on earth."[50] Although he did not take a leading role in its work, Grzimek used the same metaphor as the World Wildlife Fund: an ark, built by people who cared, to save wild animals from the rising flood of human numbers and aspirations.

On December 11, 1957, Grzimek and his son, Michael, took off from Frankfurt in a zebra-striped single-engine plane to try to save what they had come to love since their first trip to Africa six years before. Their target was the Serengeti Plain of Kenya and Tanzania and its amazing concentrations of grazing animals and predators. The Serengeti was a national park, but it existed mainly on paper. Maps and boundaries were vague, and no one knew how many animals used the range or what their migratory movements were. Moreover, as Alan Moorhead wrote in the introduction to Grzimek's account of the trip, African authorities "are decided that the interests of human beings are paramount, and that wherever human beings are in conflict with wild life it is the wild life that must go." The only hope in this "dismal story," Moorhead continued, is the small group of people "determined to make one final outcry before the Serengeti is irrevocably lost." If these nature importers who were "committed to the idea that human beings are not the only living creatures who have rights upon this earth" could "arouse not

49. Mervyn Cowie, *Fly Vulture* (London, 1961), p. 218; Cowie, "History of the Royal National Parks of Kenya" (unpublished manuscript, 1952); interview with Mervyn Cowie, Nairobi, April 11, 1975.

50. Bernhard Grzimek, *No More Room for Wild Animals* (New York, 1957), pp. 25, 13; John McDougall, "At Home with Grzimek: A Profile," *Africa Encounter, 12* (ca. 1975), 8–11; Harold T. P. Hayes, 'The Last Place," *The New Yorker, 52* (December 6, 1976), 62 ff.

only the interest but the conscience" of political authorities, the tide might be halted if not turned.[51]

This was the mission of the Grzimeks. They hoped that their flight and survey would concentrate international interest, and money, on East Africa. Their several trips, their book *Serengeti Shall Not Die,* their films, and, tragically, the crash and death of Michael Grzimek on January 10, 1959, while continuing the aerial inventory of wildlife did much to make Serengeti a familiar word in world nature appreciation circles. In addition, Bernhard Grzimek founded the Serengeti Research Institute, based in the national park, where a group of predominantly non-African scientists studied wildlife ecology. With a normal audience of thirty-five million Europeans, Grzimek's television specials raised large sums for the Institute and for international nature-philanthropy organizations such as Friends of the Serengeti. Much of the money became direct gifts (Grzimek did not hesitate to call them bribes) to the African governments. But despite his success as Europe's leading nature entrepreneur, Grzimek remained pessimistic. He hoped that in regard to nature conservation Africans would learn from "our mistakes and our sins." He realized, however, that as in Europe and America, the learning process might take generations. In the meantime, Grzimek worried whether the newly independent Africans would destroy the whole structure of nature protection "with one stroke of the pen."[52] As an archetypical nature importer, Grzimek understood that tourism was nature's best hope in Africa. I am "bringing you the tourists," he reminded Kenyans. "There were sixty thousand Germans in your country last year, and in this way I helped bring many thousands of marks into your country."[53] The end of the game meant the end of the tourists and the marks. Nobody, Grzimek explained, would come to Africa to see overcrowded villages and coffee plantations. Wild animals were money in the bank.

Julian Huxley shared Bernhard Grzimek's special concern for Africa. His 1961 report set forth in classic form the credo of the nature importer: "Africa's wild life belongs not merely to the local inhabitants but to the world, not only to the present but to the

51. As quoted in Bernhard and Michael Grzimek, *Serengeti Shall Not Die* (New York, 1960), p. 12.

52. Grzimek, *Serengeti*, pp. 173, 150–51.

53. Hayes, "The Last Place," p. 73.

whole future of mankind."[54] Huxley regarded the great African herds as one of the world's most valuable scientific resources, but he also stressed their cultural importance. To destroy Africa's wildlife would be comparable, in his view, to tearing down the Sistine Chapel or burning the Mona Lisa.

Fully aware that nature exporting and importing was the key to global nature protection, Julian Huxley explained that the main market for Africa's wildness was the citizenry of industrialized countries. Increasing numbers of Europeans and Americans, he wrote in 1961, will need to "escape . . . overcrowded cities, urban sprawl, noise, smog, boring routine, deprivation of contact with nature, and a general over-mechanization of existence." Huxley hoped that in time local African opinion could be enlisted on behalf of nature preservation, but, at least in the short run, he knew that nature protection would be the responsibility of foreigners. The Swahili word *nyama,* he noted, means both wild animals and meat. The great majority of Africans saw no value in wildlife other than as raw material for the stew pot or trophy salesroom. With independence in East and Central Africa just a few years away, Huxley also feared reaction against the strong aura of colonialism that surrounded the national park concept. Africans could not be blamed for regarding the national parks and game reserves as the playgrounds of white men because that is what they had always been. Huxley also heard Africans complain: "You white man have killed all your wolves and bears: why do you want us Africans to preserve our lions and elephants?" The implication was that Africa, too, should have a chance to modernize and industrialize.[55]

The Englishman used a concise formula to answer these objections: "Profit, Protein, Pride and Prestige." Tourists supplied the first; carefully managed game cropping the second. The two less tangible reasons derived from having something that the whole world admired. Shame also figured in Huxley's argument. The almost independent African nations wanted respect, and Huxley made it clear that "in the modern world . . . a country without a

54. Julian Huxley, *The Conservation of Wild Life and Natural Habitats in Central and East Africa* (Paris, 1961), p. 24. The same idea figured in most pleas for preservation. See, for example, E. B. Worthington, *The Wild Resources of East and Central Africa* (London, 1961) and Noel Simon, *Between the Sunlight and the Thunder* (London, 1962).

55. Huxley, *Conservation of Wild Life and Natural Habitats,* pp. 88, 93.

National Park can hardly be recognized as civilized." If Africans abolished their parks they would "shock the world and incur the reproach of barbarism and ignorance."[56] Since this was indeed a fear of many Africans, the point was persuasive. Huxley did not add that his own nation established its first national park only in 1949, centuries after its wildness vanished. Nor did he acknowledge that for more than fifty years the principal object of the national park movement in England was, in reality, Africa.

As Mervyn Cowie, Bernhard Grzimek, and Julian Huxley recognized, the key to saving wild nature in Africa lay in transferring a sense of responsibility from the white colonists to the new native leaders. With this express purpose in mind, the International Union for the Conservation of Nature launched its African Special Project in 1960. The first major achievement was the staging, in September 1961, of the "Symposium on the Conservation of Nature and Natural Resources in Modern African States." Known as the "Arusha Conference" for the city in Tanganyika (later Tanzania) where it met, the gathering had a clear task: nature importers wanted to encourage nature exporters. The highlight of the conference was the Arusha Manifesto signed by Julius K. Nyerere, Prime Minister of Tanganyika. It declared that Africans were concerned about protecting wild creatures and wild places for aesthetic as well as economic reasons. The conclusion of the manifesto acknowledged the export-import relationship by noting the stake of "the rest of the world" in Africa's wildness and soliciting international assistance in the form of "specialized knowledge, trained manpower and money."[57] On September 18, 1963, President Jomo Kenyatta of Kenya invited "other nations, and lovers of nature throughout the world" to help his newly independent government honor its pledge to conserve wildlife and wilderness.[58] These statements called the bluff of the nature importing nations. If they wanted another nation to save its wildlife for their enjoyment, they would have to make the sacrifices inevitably entailed by preserva-

56. Ibid., p. 94.

57. Gerald G. Watterson, ed., *Conservation of Nature and Natural Resources in Modern African States* (Morges, Switzerland, 1963), p. 13. For Nyerere's even more explicit commentary on nature protection and an insight into his personal opinion see the epigraph to this chapter.

58. Declaration by the President H. E. Mzee Jomo Kenyatta, September 18, 1963 (Files of the Ministry for Natural Resources, Nairobi, Kenya).

tion economically worthwhile. As Boyce Rensberger has understood,[59] is was a clear challenge to the developed nations to put up or shut up.

Words acquired substance as nature importers sought to protect their interests in Africa. The work of the African Wildlife Leadership Foundation with headquarters in Washington, D.C., is a case in point. Organized in 1961 in the aftermath of the Arusha Conference by Russell Train, a wealthy American safari enthusiast and environmentalist, the Foundation's purpose was "to provide the chance for education in management of wildlife to the men in whose hands its destiny has been placed." Its first undertaking was the College of African Wildlife Management located at the foot of Mount Kilimanjaro in Tanzania. The African students received professional training in park administration and wildlife ecology. Graduates of the college, such as David Babu, soon held most of the key park jobs in East Africa. A second foreign-supported college at Garova in Cameroon supports conservation education in French-speaking West Africa.[60]

Also interested in raising the public consciousness regarding nature protection, the African Wildlife Leadership Foundation joined with the East African Wild Life Society and the Elsa Wild Animal Appeal, two other predominantly non-African organizations, to sponsor the Wildlife Clubs of Kenya. Intended to interest African school children in wildlife conservation, the clubs feature films, lectures, essay contests and, as special treats, trips to national parks that most young Africans have never seen.[61]

Another way of training Africans in nature preservation methods was to finance their education abroad. Perez Olindo of Kenya is an example. The generosity of American nature importers enabled Olindo to complete a degree in zoology and wildlife management at Michigan State University. In 1966 his efforts earned him recognition from the Washington [D.C.] Safari Club as Conservationist

59. Boyce Rensberger, *The Cult of the Wild* (New York, 1978).

60. *African Wildlife Leadership Foundation News, 8* (Winter, 1973), ii, 12–13; Robinson McIlvaine, "Invisible Intangibles," *African Wildlife Leadership Foundation News, 9* (Spring, 1974), 1; interview with David Babu, Serengeti National Park, March 25, 1975; interview with Robinson McIlvaine, Nairobi, March 10, 1975; interview with Russell Train, Moab, Utah, August 10, 1972.

61. Hugh Russell, "Conservation Education," *African Wildlife Leadership Foundation News, 9* (Spring, 1974), 2–5; *Newsletter: Wildlife Clubs of Kenya* (Term III, 1974); interview with Sandra Price, Nairobi, March 25, 1975.

of the Year. Olindo was fully aware that not only scholarships and awards but the financial and political leverage needed to protect African animals came from outside Africa. Indeed, his repeated recourse to American and European contacts cost him political support, and ultimately his job, in nationalistic Kenya. But Olindo continued to encourage nature importing. In 1975 he told the Earthcare Conference in New York City that Americans frustrated in their attempts to establish a prairie national park in Kansas or Nebraska should transfer their efforts to the Serengeti Plains. Buy land in Africa, Olindo urged his American audience, and put it into a park.[62]

Though Olindo's idea had serious political obstacles to overcome, Americans could respond easily to the appeal of American television personality Bill Burrud for donations to purchase a helicopter to deter poachers in Tsavo National Park, Kenya, The idea originated in 1973 when Burrud talked with Ted Goss, Chief Warden at Tsavo. Goss said that poaching was wiping out the park's big game. Burrud responded by making a film, "Where Did All the Animals Go?" which appeared on American and Canadian television along with an appeal for donations for a spotlight-equipped police helicopter that could land right next to a kill and arrest poachers. Nearly $100,000 came in and in August 1973, the helicopter began its patrols. Most of the contributions were in small amounts. A note that accompanied one $5 donation simply said, "You can't xerox an elephant."[63]

Government-to-government aid also helped African nature protection in the period of transition from colony to independent nation. One form was the United States National Park Service's "International Short Course." Offered annually since 1965, the program has taken park leaders from seventy countries on both field and classroom exploration of the national park idea. Perez Olindo

62. Perez Olindo, "National Parks, Tourism and African Environment," *Kenya Past and Present, 1* (July, 1972), 3–9; Perez Olindo, "Preservationist Viewpoint," in *The Dilemma Facing Humanity,* ed. George Dalen and Clyde Tipton, Jr.; "Battelle Memorial Institute International Symposium 1" (Columbus, Ohio, 1974), pp. 24–26; Perez Olindo, "Park Values, Changes, and Problems in Developing Countries" in Hugh Elliott, ed., *Second World Conference on National Parks* (Morges, Switzerland, 1974), pp. 52–60; interview with Perez Olindo, New York City, June 7, 1975.

63. Interview with Ted Goss, Chief Warden, Tsavo West National Park, March 29, 1975; interview with Valeri Timbrook, Staff Assistant, Bill Burrud's Animal World, December 10, 1976; Daphne Sheldrick, *The Tsavo Story* (London, 1973).

participated in the 1965 seminar.[64] Another aid program found teams of park experts on loan to African governments. Frequently private donors facilitated these undertakings. In 1967, for instance, the Virgil and Judith Stark Foundation of New York financed the study of a potential park on Mount Kilimanjaro by U.S. National Park Service officers. In 1972, the government of Norway undertook an extensive aid program to Tanzania on behalf of the Kilimanjaro park plan. Recently the African Wildlife Leadership Foundation has collaborated with the Rockefeller Brothers Fund to send American park planners to every park and reserve in Kenya. Other governments support nature protection in Africa through the United Nations Food and Agriculture Organization, which has taken a special interest in the economics of game cropping and of tourism.[65]

Ruben J. Olembo, a scientist with the United Nations Environment Program and a member of Kenya's national parks board, summarizes the experience of his nation with nature exporting.[66] As an African in Kenya's public schools in the 1950s, Olembo remembers that his teachers told him that national parks and game reserves were white men's toys, symbols of hated colonialism. Everyone expected that the coming of independence (for Kenya in 1963) would mean the end of nature protection. Wildlife was a "bloody nuisance," an obstacle to development which should be removed quickly and completely. But in the early 1960s the big jets, crammed with tourists, began to arrive at Nairobi. The white people they carried were not colonists or businessmen anxious to exploit Africans. Many were not even hunters. The new breed simply wanted to *see* wild animals, and to the surprised but de-

64. "Representation in the First Seven Seminars of Administration of National Parks and Equivalent Reserves, 1965–1971" (unpublished staff paper, 1972), Records of the Division of International Park Affairs (National Park Service, Washington, D.C.); Barry S. Tindall, "National Parks in the World Community: An Overview of the United States Aid and Assistance," *Parks and Recreation, 18* (February, 1973), 24–29; interviews with Fred Packard, Bruce Powell, and Myron Sutton, Division of International Park Affairs (National Park Service, Washington, D.C.), September 12, 13, and 25, 1974.

65. U.S. National Park Service, *Kilimanjaro: Survey for Proposed Mount Kilimanjaro National Park, Tanzania, East Africa* (New York, 1967); interview with Leif Mattsson, Planner, Norwegian Foreign Aid Department, Marangu, Tanzania, March 13, 1975; John S. McLaughlin, *A Conceptual Master Plan for Shimba Hills National Reserve* (n.p., 1973); interview with Philip Thresher, Economic Planner, United Nations Food and Agriculture Organization, March 7 and April 11, 1975.

66. Interview with Ruben J. Olembo, Nairobi, Kenya, March 26, 1975.

lighted natives they would pay plenty for the privilege.[67] In Olembo's opinion it was this realization, not any newfound love of nature, that saved the parks in the early 1960s. Tourism, which rose through that decade to become the first or second source of foreign exchange in many African nations, also explains the 1968 African Convention for Conservation of Nature and Natural Resources. Thirty-eight African heads of state signed the document, which superseded the London Convention of 1933.[68] Significantly, the 1968 agreement was as much an African product as the 1933 was European. The exporters had learned what the importers long knew: the nature business was good business.

As a postscript to the African experience with nature protection, the 1974 comment of Lawrence Kinyua, a Kenyan schoolboy, is revealing. Concluding an essay for the wildlife club organized by his teachers, Kinyua wrote a prayer: "I would like the almighty God to bless our wild animals to increase more abundantly so that the affinity of tourists for our prospering country is increased."[69] Twenty years before the schoolboy Ruben J. Olembo had been taught that there was no value in colonial relics like game reserves and that they would disappear after independence. In two decades the economics of the world nature market had revolutionized some African attitudes. There was no guarantee that this would be enough. The future of wild nature in a nation whose population is doubling every twenty-five years is precarious. Even with Kenya's May 1977 ban on all sport hunting, many anticipate the end of the game as human ambitions encroach on open space.[70] There are not, after all, very many buffalo in Iowa or Kansas, but, then again, there was no massive, jet-propelled nature tourism to make buffalo contribute to the economies of these areas in the 1860s.

67. Philip Thresher, "Could Wild Animals Pay to Survive?" (unpublished manuscript, April, 1975); Thresher, "The Present Value of an Amboseli Lion." The studies are based on Thresher's computer-simulation model of the costs and benefits of wildlife viewing undertaken for the United Nations Food and Agriculture Organization.

68. Kai Curry-Lindahl, "The New African Conservation Convention," *Oryx, 10* (1969), 116–26.

69. Lawrence Kinyua, "Encounter with a Dead Elephant," *Wildlife Clubs of Kenya Newsletter* (Term III, 1974), 41.

70. Hayes, "The Last Place," pp. 52–113. Peter Beard, *The End of the Game* (New York, 1965); Boyce Rensberger, "This is the End of the Game," *New York Times Magazine* (November 1, 1977), 43, 136–48; Rensberger, *Cult of the Wild*, esp. pp. 201 ff.

Jet travel and the expansion of the clientele for wildness beyond a few aristocrats like Sir St. George Gore and Theodore Roosevelt have recently increased the leverage of the nature importers. Purveyors of nature tours, such as Questers of New York and Mountain Travel, based in California, have simplified the task of importing nature. The cost is still considerable, but apparently enough well-to-do nature lovers exist to fill dozens of trips. Hotels specializing in bringing civilized people and wildness together under comfortable circumstances—Treetops in Kenya and Tiger Tops in Nepal are famous examples—are solidly booked months in advance. Leaders of the nature travel industry are aware that the business they generate underwrites nature preservation and thereby ensures their own future. "Since tourism is an increasingly important source of revenue to countries around the world," declares Questers's president, Michael L. Parkin, "we believe that international . . . travel to wildlife sanctuaries and nature reserves will help encourage further conservation efforts."[71]

Yet even as nature tourism increases, doubts remain about its effectiveness in preserving wildness. Even nonhunting tourism is not always compatible with preservation. Those who can afford to import nature are, in general, older people unprepared to rough it in the wilds. They demand hotels, restaurants, roads, motorized vehicles, and small towns of supporting servants, all located, more often than not, inside the park or reserve.[72] This luxury tourism yields the biggest economic rewards for the nature exporters. Backpackers are notoriously low spenders, preferring self-sufficiency to service. Roadless wilderness does not generate much revenue, yet this kind of environment is precisely what some importers and most scientists accord the highest value. If the only reason for a park is to make money, restrictions on revenue-producing tourism, even in the cause of protecting nature, are unlikely.

A second argument against tourism as the mainstay of global nature protection centers is on the final distribution of the importers' money. Although local people are supposed to be compensated for what they forgo in income by *not* developing wilderness, the

71. Michael L. Parkin in the introduction to *Questers Directory of Worldwide Nature Tours, 1975* (New York, 1974), p. 2.

72. See, for example, Norman Myers, *The Long African Day* (New York, 1972). Another critical look at African nature tourism is Colin Turnbull, "East African Safari," *Natural History, 90* (1981), 26–34.

bulk of the tourist revenue goes to entrepreneurs from the developed world. The extreme examples are the cruise ships such as those Lindblad Travel sends to wild places throughout the world. The modest sums spent on shore by the passengers for souvenirs and postcards do not constitute a strong argument for protecting nature. The economics of land-based tours work out better for native people, but it is still foreign-owned airline companies, hotel chains, and travel agents who chiefly benefit. On a forty-four day, $3,600 trip on a wild river in Peru, Amazon Expeditions, headquartered in Erie, Pennsylvania, does not even buy its food locally. Each member of the trip is sent a bag of foodstuff before leaving the United States. The consumption of local goods and services is limited to a few nights' lodging and the services of a local truck and driver before and after the river trip. Hydropower developers wishing to dam the river can plausibly claim that nature importing does not constitute a viable economic alternative.[73] In addition, political disturbances, such as those of the late 1970s which closed all of Uganda and the Kenya-Tanzania border to tourists, could completely remove the protection to nature afforded by nature tourism.

The alternative, and the ultimate extension of nature importing, is outright ownership, or at least control, of important natural environments. Though it is unfair to think of international collaboration to this end as neocolonial, its purpose is much the same as that of the earlier European park promoters in South Africa, the Belgian Congo, and Kenya. The central concept of what might be thought of as an international park is found as early as 1834 in the statement of Andrew Reed and James Natheson regarding one of North America's scenic wonders. "Niagara," these tourists wrote, "does not belong to Canada or America. Such spots should be deemed the property of civilized mankind."[74]

Since Niagara Falls certainly did in the traditional sense "belong" to Canada and the United States, the logic behind this and many similar statements needs clarification. Apparently Reed and Natheson looked on Niagara as a scenic resource of value to all

73. Henry Pelham Burn, "Packaging Paradise: The Environmental Costs of International Tourism," *Sierra Club Bulletin, 60* (May, 1975), 25; Myers, "Wildlife of Savannahs and Grasslands," p. 395.

74. As quoted in Charles M. Dow, ed., *Anthology and Bibliography of Niagara Falls,* 2 vols. (Albany, 1921), 2: 1070–71.

mankind. By geographical accident the Falls happened to be in Canada and the United States, but this did not give these nations the right to destroy them. Every human being, now and for all time, had a stake in such treasures and individual nations must not be allowed to act unilaterally in regard to their future. Pressed to the logical conclusion, this line of reasoning would authorize the world community to intervene, forcibly if necessary, to halt the destructive activities of a country within its own borders. Institutionalizing this idea was extremely difficult since it touched upon the uniquely sensitive issue of sovereignty.

Moreton Frewen, the English aristocrat, anticipated the international park in the 1870s when he bought land in Wyoming to protect it from American frontiersmen. Recent world control of natural treasures began in 1956: Masai incursions upon Serengeti National Park, and the prospect of African independence, led nature conservationists like Bernhard Grzimek to propose to buy or otherwise arrange for the Serengeti to be made international property under the United Nations. Nothing came of the idea, but in the following decade the Sierra Club discussed the prospects for an Earth International Park, while Friends of the Earth preferred Earth National Park. In 1971 Wildlife Conservation International arranged with the government of Zambia to manage, under a twenty-five year lease, the Zambia International Wildlife Park. The Nature Conservancy, based in Arlington, Virginia, preferred to work by purchasing or receiving actual title to endangered natural environments. After two decades of concentration on the United States, the Nature Conservancy began in the mid-1970s to look into the acquisition of title to lands in foreign countries. In 1975 the Conservancy received a gift of 950 acres of pristine tropical rainforest on the Caribbean island of Dominica, leased to the Dominican government for management as a park.[75] Much broader in scope is the Man and the Biosphere Program (MAB) set in motion under the the auspices of UNESCO in 1970. Participating nations link appropriate sites into a worldwide network of ecologically significant

75. R. Michael Wright, "Private Action for the Global Protection of Natural Areas," in *EARTHCARE,* pp. 715–39; R. Michael Wright, "After God the Earth—Rainforest Preserved in Dominica, West Indies," *Nature Conservancy News,* 25 (Spring, 1975), 8–11; R. Michael Wright, Director, International Program, Nature Conservancy, to Roderick Nash, January 23, 1976.

environments. Science, not recreation, is served by MAB. Participation is voluntary, but the program generates pressure, if only that of world opinion, to keep reserved sites protected. At Stockholm in 1972 the United Nations Conference on the Human Environment gave full support of MAB.[76]

The other international gathering of nature protectors in 1972 occurred in northwestern Wyoming in honor of the centennial of Yellowstone National Park.[77] It was a pleasant experience for Americans, scarred as a society by the Vietnam War, political assassinations and the developing Watergate scandals. Delegate after delegate from around the world rose to credit the United States with inventing the national park.[78] A few speakers added that, in frankness, the American experience in preserving wilderness served as warning as well as inspiration. The 1913 removal of Hetch Hetchy Valley from Yosemite National Park (see Chapter 10) was an example of what not to do. So was the overcrowded condition of Yosemite Valley. But in general the gathering celebrated Cornelius Hedges, John Muir, and Stephen T. Mather as visionaries who anticipated human needs for nature and worked to institutionalize wilderness preservation. Thinking about the future, the four hundred delegates from eighty nations resolved that in the second century of national parks "the concept of world parks should be promoted." As a start the conference further resolved that "the nations party to the Antarctic Treaty should negotiate to establish the Antarctic Continent and surrounding seas as the first world park."[79] The United Nations would provide management of this unprecedented international wilderness.

76. International Co-ordinating Council of the Programme on Man and the Biosphere, *UNESCO MAB: Final Report* (Paris, 1971); Michel Batisse, "The Beginning of MAB," in *World National Parks: Progress and Opportunities,* ed. Richard van Osten (Brussels, 1972), pp. 178–79.

77. The proceedings are available as Hugh Elliott, ed., *Second World Conference on National Parks* (Morges, Switzerland, 1974). Related publications are Freeman Tilden, *National Parks Centennial, 1872–1972–Yellowstone, the Flowering of an Idea* (Washington, D.C., 1972) and *A Gathering of Nations: A Time of Purpose–In Commemoration of the Centennial Celebration of Yellowstone and the Second World Conference on National Parks* (Washington, D.C., 1973).

78. On this point see Roderick Nash, "The American Invention of National Parks," *American Quarterly, 22* (1970), 726–35. Another essay evaluates the evidence that Australia may have been the first nation to establish a national park: Roderick Nash, "The Confusing Birth of National Parks," *Michigan Quarterly Review, 19* (1980), 216–26.

79. Elliott, *Second World Conference on National Parks,* pp. 443–44.

Russell Train took the platform to offer another idea: the world heritage trust. Train explained it as an international extension of the national park concept. Certain natural features had such outstanding value "that they belong to the heritage of the entire world."[80] As examples Train cited Mount Everest, the Galapagos Islands, the Serengeti Plain, Angel Falls in Venezuela, the Grand Canyon of Arizona, and certain animal species like the mountain gorilla. Train's idea was to marshal the world's financial, technical, and managerial resources on behalf of these places and life forms.

Moving toward institutionalization of the world heritage idea, UNESCO drafted a convention in November 1972, and the United States became the first nation to ratify it on December 7, 1973.[81] Not until September 1978, however, did eleven nations actually place areas on the "World Heritage List." Yellowstone, Grand Canyon, Everglades, and Redwoods national parks are among the American listings. Forty-two countries have ratified the convention to date, and more areas will be added to the list, but the degree of protection obtained thereby is not great. The chronic problem is that national sovereignty is left unchallenged. Participating nations may delete areas listed at will or, for that matter, denounce the entire convention. There are no reprisals. What a nation does to nature within its own borders remains its own business as Principle 21 of the Declaration of the United Nations Conference on the Human Environment made clear in Stockholm in 1972.[82] Yet the world heritage concept does give more recognition than ever before to the international significance of natural environments and the international responsibility for their protection.

The economics inherent in trading wild nature are not, to be sure, the whole story. Other motives—some would say better or higher ones—exist for protecting the natural world, and the less developed nations may eventually evolve economically and intel-

80. Russell E. Train, "An Idea Whose Time Has Come: The World Heritage Trust, A World Need and a World Opportunity," in Elliott, *Second World Conference*, pp. 378–79. Train first raised the idea of a world heritage trust in 1965: Committee on Natural Resources Conservation and Development, *Report to the White House Conference on International Cooperation* (Washington, D.C., 1965), pp. 17–19.

81. UNESCO, *Convention Concerning the Protection of the World Cultural and Natural Heritage* (Paris, 1972).

82. Nicholas A. Robinson, "Environmental Laws and Conventions: Toward Societal Compacts with Nature," in Schofield, ed., *EARTHCARE*, pp. 513–45. The Declaration is reprinted there beginning on p. 771.

lectually to the point where nature protection is more than a business. In the meantime preservation of the world's remaining wilderness will depend as it has depended since its beginning a century ago, on the exporting and importing of an increasingly rare commodity.

Epilogue

THE idea that we are entering a new millennium is, of course, a contrived, Christian way of marking time passages. But it still affords a badly needed invitation to ponder the big picture of historical change. Just the idea of a thousand years should challenge us to move beyond our chronic myopia and lift our eyes to the far horizons of planetary possibility.

As for wilderness, we have seen it as the unrecognized and unnamed environmental norm for most of the earth's history, created as a concept by civilization, thereafter widely hated and feared, and quite recently and remarkably, appreciated. Relative scarcity helped wilderness gain value, but there was a price to pay: wilderness is now an increasingly endangered geographical species. The spectrum of environmental conditions has been tilted sharply toward the civilized end.[1] Only about 2 percent of the contiguous forty-eight American states is legally wild—the same amount that is paved! Much of the American landscape has been modified to some degree. But in fact the United States is a *leader* in the establishment of national park and wilderness areas and is only a little more than a century beyond its frontier era. In other, older nations (Japan, for instance, or France), environmental control is near total. At least in the temperate latitudes, we are dealing with remnants of a once-wild world, and we face irreversible decisions about their future on a planet that suddenly seems small and vulnerable.

There are some certainties out there. Unless it is sharply restrained, civilization will continue to modify the Earth's environment. Wilderness will be a casualty of this process; indeed, it could disappear. For perspective, consider that just a little over a century ago scholars were documenting the end of the American frontier. Wild Indians were still a "problem," and personal transportation meant horses. Today there are four *times* as many of us on the planet. We are armed with an increasingly potent technology, and our ambitions are on the rise as well. Recent observers such as William McKibben and Carolyn Merchant are raising the prospect of "the end of

1. See above, p. 6, for the "spectrum" idea.

nature" and the "death of nature" or are calling, with John Terborgh, for a "requiem for nature."[2] What they mean is that the conditions that nurtured us for millions of years through the course of our evolution are disappearing. What this implies is no more wilderness.

There are two ways of thinking about how this might occur. One is *the wasteland scenario.* It anticipates human growth and environmental modification to the point of disfunction and breakdown. Civilization proves, as some now fear, to be cancerous and unsustainable. We end up with a ravaged planet—paved, poisoned, and populated by remnants of a desperate species that have brought their ecosystem crashing to its knees. Or perhaps, in a thousand years, the earth has been used up and discarded. A vanguard of humans, no wiser for historical experience, moves on through the stars in search of new frontiers to plunder. Except in the very long, post-civilization run, there is no place for wilderness in this nightmare future. It dies with the prophesied whimper or maybe with the big bang of a nuclear war.

The *garden scenario* is another possible future.[3] Imagine a thousand years from now, human control of nature is also total, but this time it's beneficent. The environmentalists have been heard: we occupy a bounteous, beautiful, sustainable garden. The fertility of the soil is well maintained; carefully managed rivers flow clean and pure. Population is not a concern because technological breakthroughs

2. Bill McKibben, *The End of Nature* (New York, 1989); Carolyn Merchant, *The Death of Nature* (San Francisco, 1980); John Terborgh, *Requiem for Nature* (Washington, D.C., 1999). Books that make a similar statement are Norman Myers, *The Sinking Ark: A New Look at the Problem of Disappearing Species* (New York, 1992); Neil Evernden, *The Social Creation of Nature* (Baltimore, 1992); Jonathan Schell, *The Fate of the Earth* (New York, 1982); David Quammen, *Flight of the Iguana: A Sidelong View of Science and Nature* (New York, 1998); Edward O. Wilson, *The Diversity of Life* (Cambridge, Mass., 1992); Paul R. and Anne H. Ehrlich, *Extinctions: The Causes and Consequences of the Disappearance of Species* (New York, 1981); Beverly Peterson Stearns and Stephen C. Stearns, *Watching, from the Edge of Extinction* (New Haven, 1999); and R. Edward Grumbine, *Ghost Bears: Exploring the Biodiversity Crisis* (Washington, D.C., 1992).

3. In earlier editions of this book I discussed proponents of Earth as a garden: see above, p. 241 ff. For representative recent statements see Wendell Berry, *The Unsettling of America: Culture and Agriculture* (San Francisco, 1986); William Ashworth, *The Left Hand of Eden: Meditations on Nature and Human Nature* (Corvallis, Oreg., 1999); Michael Pollan, *Second Nature: A Gardener's Education* (New York, 1991). Peter M. Vitousek, et. al, "Human Domination of the Earth's Ecosystem," *Science*, 277 (1997), 494–99 is a revealing report.

enable people to live pole-to-pole: in the deserts, under the sea, in the air. Many people have followed the advice of the neopastoralists and left the cities to live on either real or "hobby" farms. Some eat what they grow or gather; of course, they meet their neighbors on the ridge tops doing the same thing. It's a planet-wide extension of Europe! But out there in the *fourth* millennium we conceivably control weather, genetic codes, ecosystems, evolution. New Noahs, our species determines who boards the ecological ark, and there isn't much room for "wildēor" or "self-willed land" after the satisfaction of human demands.[4] The gardeners of the planetary Eden have been efficient in weeding out forms of life incompatible with our tastes and needs. It's ecosystem management on a planetary scale. Inconceivable? Think about it. Television, computer communication, and moon walks were just as fanciful to people in 900 or even 1900. Don't bet that in another thousand years wildness will be protected by the *lack* of human capability to control nature.

Defenders of wilderness have traditionally considered proponents of environmental planning and management as fellow travelers if not comrades in arms. But a second look is disturbing. Wilderness is in just as much trouble in the planetary garden as it is in the wasteland. The problem, of course, is that pastoralism is a form of control. Wilderness, remember, began where the Garden of Eden ended.[5] "Good" kinds of human habitat expansion and "smart" or "sustainable" kinds of growth are just as invasive of wilderness as the bad kinds. A planet saturated, however wisely, by civilization has no place for wilderness and the nonhuman beings that live there.

Discouraging as these possible futures are to those who care for wildness on Earth, there is a third vision. I call it *Island Civilization*.[6] It envisions high technology actually *reducing* the impact of civilization. The key is implosion. A thousand years from now human beings (hopefully fewer of them) could occupy several hundred concentrated "habitats" ("cities" cannot begin to describe the new living

4. Recall the discussion of the derivation of the word "wilderness," pp. 1–2 above and in the preface.

5. See above, p. 15.

6. Although I touched on this subject in the third (1982) edition of the present book and used the phrase "beneficent forms of centralization" (p. 383 in the 1982 edition), my most complete statement is "Island Civilization: A Vision for Planet Earth in the Year 2992," *Wild Earth,* 1 (1992), 2–4. See also my "Afterword: Nature and Civilization—A Biocentric Solution" in William Henry Jackson and John Fielder, ed., *Colorado: 1870–2000* (Englewood, Colo., 1999), pp. 219–23.

arrangements that tomorrow's motivated planners might create). Integrated into each of them would be enormously efficient, closed-circle technologies for producing food, water, and energy, and for disposing of waste. The rest of the planet, indeed almost all of it, would be left alone, uncontrolled, and wild. Instead of dominating Earth, people and their works would occupy small niches in an interconnected, wild ecosystem.[7] Instead of islands of wildness (or parks) in a civilized matrix, it is *civilization* that is contained. Boundaries, in other words, would be drawn around the technological human presence, not around wild nature.

As I imagine it there would be no need for terrestrial interconnections like roads, rails, or wires among the self-sufficient habitats of the future. New technologies far beyond our present imagining would permit their residents to travel without environmental impact to other human communities and to live the kind of stimulating life that comes from well-designed proximity to other people. Island Civilization should not raise images of New York housing projects; think about Greek city-states, medieval monasteries, pueblos of the Southwest, the best of malls, and redesigned inner cities. It means clustering on a planetary scale—building in rather than building out, controlling civilization instead of wilderness.

The beauty of Island Civilization is that it permits humans to fulfill their evolutionary potential while not compromising or eliminating the chances of other species fulfilling theirs. Of course there is some reduction in accustomed human freedom. Just as with John Locke's *social* contract, humans give up some options—to live in sprawling suburbs, for instance, or to herd cows on vast ranches—out of respect for the existence rights of other members of the larger natural community. I think of this as an *ecological* contract: natural rights extended to the rights of nature. Conservation biologists see their

7. An early vision of this kind of occupation of the planet is Paul Shepard, *The Tender Carnivore and the Sacred Game* (New York, 1973), p. 237 ff. Representative later statements include Shepard's *Traces of an Omnivore* (Washington, D.C., 1996) and *Coming Home to the Pleistocene* (Washington, D.C., 1998); Reed Noss and A. Y. Cooperrider, *Saving Nature's Legacy: Protecting and Restructuring Biodiversity* (Washington, D.C., 1994); Michael Soulé, *Conservation Biology: The Science of Scarcity and Diversity* (Sunderland, Mass., 1986); Dave Foreman and Howie Wolke, *The Big Outside* (Tucson, Ariz., 1992); Ernest Callenbach, *Bring Back the Buffalo: A Sustainable Future for America's Great Plains* (Washington, D.C., 1995). The entire run of the journal *Wild Earth,* particularly descriptions of "The Wildlands Project," testify to academic and activist interest in this possible future.

dreams come true. The frontier reappears, but this time it's permanent. Rivers, full once again with salmon, run unimpeded by dams, and buffalo roam unfenced plains. As they were ten or fifteen thousand years ago, before herding and agriculture, humans are once again good neighbors in the biotic community.[8]

But what, the question always seems to be, are your options if you don't want to live on densely populated islands in a matrix of wildness? The short response is that if you want to live a highly technological lifestyle, you would not have a choice. The motivation for Island Civilization is an expanded environmental ethic that functions as a restraint on human freedom in regard to nature, just as our present social ethic limits our relationships with other people. Slavery, for instance, is now unacceptable in most of the world's societies. A thousand years from now I hope that the unconditioned ownership and abuse of nature will have been similarly outmoded.

One of the most compelling reasons for Island Civilization is that it respects the existence rights of the other species occupying this planet. Another is that it assures the continuation of wilderness, and not just as a hand-off museum. People living on the island habitats could leave them to enjoy minimum-impact vacations in the surrounding wild matrix. They could even *live* out there—for a while or forever. The proviso is that they would have to do so as wilderness people. I am assuming here that human integration into an environment that remains wild works only as long as people are wild, too. That means camping: a resumption of the ancient, pre-pastoral, hunting and gathering ways. Humans of the distant future could choose (perhaps on an annual basis) between ways of life centered around computers or campfires.[9] There are exciting possibilities for existences divided between quality wilderness and quality civilization. Isn't this one way to approach Henry David Thoreau's preferred "half-cultivated" or "border" life? The trick, Thoreau knew, was to find a way to live "to secure all the advantage [of civilization] without suffering any of the disadvantage."[10]

8. Recall the discussion of the impact of herding and agriculture on human attitudes toward nature in the introduction of this book, pp. xi–xiii.

9. For anticipations of this idea see the work of Gary Snyder and Paul Shepard, see above, pp. 246–47 and 383–84.

10. For references to and discusssion of Thoreau, see above, pp. 92–93; also review the proponents of a balanced lifestyle in ch. 13.

I have obviously not done more here than paint in very broad, visionary brush strokes (and I don't know exactly *how* to make the dream come true), but Island Civilization seems to me worth considering as one way of fitting increasingly technological human beings into the rest of nature. People would not be masters or "stewards" or even "eco-managers" but, following Aldo Leopold, plain members and fellow citizens of the community of life. It permits us to do our increasingly sophisticated thing as a species while respecting the opportunity of all other species to do theirs.

Island Civilization obviously focuses on the extremes of the spectrum of environmental conditions.[11] It challenges the classically American idealization of the "middle" or pastoral landscape as it has been celebrated in art, letters, and planning for three centuries.[12] Rural conditions were said to offer the best of both the wild and the civilized worlds. But isn't it conceivable that the rural option has been, in fact, the *worst* of both worlds, lacking both those campfires and computers? Paul Shepard, for example, argues that "peasant existence is the dullest life man ever lived," and there are abundant critiques of isolated ranch existence and suburbia on the same grounds.[13] The alternative, implicit in the idea of Island Civilization, is to offer each person the option either of returning to the hunting way of life they lived for millions of years or of passing into a beneficent form of highly technological concentration that may be our best bet for living millions more.

An imploded human presence is one way to save wilderness. But why, in the end, give a damn? Why not open the throttles on planet-scale control of life and the environment? Isn't it conceivable that the need for the wild is a transitory, frontier-related enthusiasm that Americans will eventually outgrow, as other older cultures already have? The wilderness experience, like the horse and buggy, might already be a quaint historical artifact—charming but inessential to a society whose needs and perceptions have changed. In this possibility is the greatest sadness for wilderness advocates: working so hard to protect something posterity will find irrelevant. These questions bring us back full circle to an examination of Thoreau's axiom about

11. See above, pp. 6–7.

12. One study of the pastoral tradition is Leo Marx, *The Machine in the Garden: Technology and the Pastoral Ideal in America* (New York, 1964).

13. Shepard, *Tender Carnivore,* p. 242. For post-suburban visions see, for example, Peter Calthorpe, *The New American Metropolis* (Princeton, 1993).

wildness being the preservation of the world.[14] What is the contemporary and future meaning of this idea?

A starting point for this discussion might be the criticism leveled at wilderness in the concluding years of the twentieth century. Some of it is essentially an extension of old-style pioneer bias salted with large doses of digitally fueled technological optimism. The message is that wilderness still "lurks" out there, and civilization can't relax its guard. Added to this is the reasoning that expanded control and exploitation of nature is necessary if the entire human population is to enjoy the "good life" of well-to-do people in the first world.[15] Objections that there are already too many humans making too many demands on natural systems are met with cries of racism and "environmental justice." Moreover, the optimists add, our ingenuity is capable not only of solving all environmental problems but, if we need it, of creating surrogate wilderness. Walls can be built for rock climbers, artificial rapids for river runners, and mazes for people who like to, on occasion, get lost.[16] The possibility of engineering genetic codes opens astonishing new vistas for human ingenuity and human intervention. If you miss wild creatures, why not just create them, as explained to great popular acclaim in Michael Crichton's *Jurassic Park?* And, some believe, the future can always fall back on the virtual reality of the computer screen. A digital "wilderness experience" is just a point and click away.

The basic rebuttal is that nothing technology creates can ever be wild, and that wildness is likely to have increasing value in an older and more complex civilization. At least the present should consider its responsibility to allow the future to experience the past. At the most basic level, wilderness preservation means keeping options open. Rather than inheriting one from us, let posterity decide if it wants to occupy a controlled, developed, and biologically impoverished planet.

Other recent critics of wilderness come from within the "green"

14. See above, p. 84.

15. For example, see Mark Dowie, *Losing Ground: American Environmentalism at the Close of the Twentieth Century* (Cambridge, Mass., 1995); Ron Arnold, *Undue Influence: Wealthy Foundations, Grant-Driven Environmental Groups, and Zealous Bureaucrats That Control Your Future* (Bellevue, Wash., 1999); Gregg Easterbrook, *A Movement on the Earth: The Coming Age of Environmental Optimism* (New York, 1995).

16. A major early statement in the discussion was Martin Krieger, "What's Wrong with Plastic Trees," *Science, 179* (1973), 446–54.

camp and bear some intellectual kinship to the garden earthers previously noted. They base their argument on the assumption that wilderness and its preservation accentuates the human/nature dualism that lies at the root of so many environmental problems. Such scholars as William Cronon and J. Baird Callicott allege that designated wilderness, national parks, and even the idea of wilderness are unnatural, irrelevant, old-fashioned, and elitist.[17] A better environmental model, they contend, would be one that does not exclude people and their civilization from nature. Wilderness is not helpful, in other words, in the quest for the integration of human beings and all the other beings.

The rejoinder should begin with the thought that it is technological power and human greed, and not the idea of wilderness and wilderness preservation, that separate people and nature. Sure humans are "natural," but somewhere along the evolutionary way from spears to spaceships they dropped off the biotic team and, as Henry Beston recognized, became cosmic outlaws. Maybe, as suggested at the start of this book, it was twelve thousand years ago when herding and agriculture replaced hunting and gathering.[18] Or did it start late in 1999, when the human population topped six *billion* (and counting, at the rate of about ten thousand new human lives each hour)? Perhaps the parting of the ways has something to do with global climate change or with a human-caused rate of species extinction thousands of times higher than historical norms.[19] The reality is that as the twenty-first century begins, civilized humans are no longer thinking or acting like a part of nature. Or, if we are, it is a cancerous one, growing so rapidly that it endangers the larger

17. The mid-1990s saw an intensification of the debate over the meaning and value of wilderness reminiscent of the years preceeding the Hetch Hetchy decision (1913) and the Wilderness Act (1964). The opening salvo came from environmental historian William Cronon: "The Trouble with Wilderness; or, Getting Back to the Wrong Nature" in Cronon, ed., *Uncommon Ground: Toward Reinventing Nature* (New York, 1995). Cronon published a shorter, but much more visible statement, as "The Trouble with Wilderness," *New York Times Magazine*, Aug. 13, 1995), 42–43. Representative debate on the issue can be found by various authors in the journal *Wild Earth, 4* (1994–95) and *Wild Earth, 6* (1996–97). The most convenient source of these and of many other writings on the wilderness theme is J. Baird Callicott and Michael P. Nelson, eds., *The Great New Wilderness Debate* (Athens, Ga., 1997)

18. See above, pp. xi–xiii.

19. McKibben, *End of Nature;* Myers, *Sinking Ark;* J. H. Lawton and R. H. May, eds., *Extinction Rates* (Oxford, 1995);

whole. It is hard to deny that our species has become a terrible neighbor to the thirty million or so other species sharing space on this planet. How many of them would applaud an endangered species act for *us?* Right now we desperately need a "time out" to learn how to be team players once again. We need to learn how to live responsibly in the larger neighborhood called the ecosystem, and the first requirement is to respect our neighbors' lives.

What wilderness provides is precisely this "time out" from the civilized juggernaut. Its presence reminds us of just how far we have distanced ourselves from the rest of nature. Wild places, remember, are uncontrolled, "self-willed," where the "wildēor" are.[20] We didn't make wilderness; it made us. In it we stand naked of the built and modified environment, open to seeing ourselves once again as large mammals dependent (at the real bottom line) not on our technological cleverness but on the health of our habitat. This is where wilderness assumes not only ecological but ethical value. Because this is country we don't own or use, we are open to perceiving its intrinsic value. The concept of wilderness helps our kind better understand the rights of other kinds to a place in this planet's community of life; the actuality of wilderness provides that place. By definition we don't dominate wilderness, and so it suggests the importance of sharing, which was, after all, the basis of the ethic of fair play that we did not learn very well in kindergarten. On a species level, fair play or unselfishness seems to many to be the key to effective global environmentalism. This kind of ecocentrism is not "against" humans; it transcends them and subsumes their interest in that of the larger whole.

What William Cronon and those of his persuasion think is " the trouble with wilderness"[21] relates to the fact that arguments for its appreciation and preservation have traditionally been cast in anthropocentric and utilitarian terms. The association of wilderness with national pride, with spirituality and beauty, and with nostalgia for a vanishing frontier all had an obvious human slant. So, of course, does the philosophy of "recreation."[22] This book endeavors

20. See the introduction, above, and pp. 1–7.

21. Cronon, *Uncommon Ground,* p. 69

22. It gives me pleasure here to recognize my father, Jay B. Nash, formerly a department chairman at New York University, whose *Philosophy of Recreation and Leisure* (St. Louis, 1953) capped a career devoted to defining and planning a major component of modern life. His service on the Outdoor Recreation Resources

to demonstrate that Americans began to do something for wilderness when they perceived that it could do something for them. Even the recent discussion of wild nature as a safe-deposit box for other species can have a strong utilitarian connotation. We know it best as the cure-for-cancer argument. No apologies necessary here! Instrumental values like scenery, recreation, and economics (tourists spend money) worked well as the nineteenth-century foundations of wilderness appreciation and motivated the early preservation efforts. But Cronon should be more aware that in the last quarter-century a new biocentric or ecocentric rationale for the meaning and value of wilderness has gained an impressive following among both philosophers and activists.[23] Human interests led the wilderness charge in the last century, but respect for nonhuman life and for ecological processes will assume increasing importance in the next one.

This ecocentric argument for wilderness centers on the proposition that human interests are not the paramount concern. Wilderness is not *for* us at all. We should allow it to exist out of respect for the intrinsic values of the rest of nature and particularly for the life forms dependent on wild habitats. The idea of integrating humans and nature is acceptable to a degree, but it doesn't work with a powerful, growth-crazed, technological civilization or with creatures who cannot coexist peacefully in controlled and modified environments. Keeping human hands off of some environments demonstrates an encouraging capacity for self-restraint on the part of a species notorious for its excesses and greed.

Wilderness used to be undiscovered or passed-over land. But in the light of our present capacity for modifying nature, we must understand that the existence of wild country reflects self-imposed ethical restrictions on our capacity to control, exploit, destroy, and grow. As such, wilderness is the best physical and intellectual environment for learning that, if sustainability is a concern, less can in-

---

Review Commission, established by Congress in 1958, was one of the influences on my decision to begin a study of the cultural significance of the American wilderness two years later.

23. In fairness to Cronon, his longer essay, but not the *New York Times* piece that many of his critics quote, recognizes that wilderness is a "corrective to human arrogance" and "an important vehicle for articulating deep moral values regarding our obligations and responsibilities to the nonhuman world": Cronon, *Uncommon Ground*, p. 87. His conclusion, however, must be that these ideals can best be furthered in an inhabited, gardenlike environment.

deed be more. We do belong, but not everywhere. To choose not to inhabit part of the planet demonstrates that we have finally understood what the ecologists have been trying to tell us for a century: that we are members, not masters, of the life community.

Just as fences and dams once proudly testified to our ability to control nature, the protection of wild country now symbolizes our determination to control civilization. The frontier has had its day in the sun. Pioneer, growth-oriented attitudes worked well when the human presence was relatively small and nature seemed vast and inexhaustible. But the evolutionary tide has turned. Growth has turned out to have ironic or self-defeating consequences. The environment is vulnerable. As the new millennium opens before us, it's time for new frontiersmen who understand that what really needs to be conquered is not nature but ourselves. Wilderness can be an intellectual and a biological starting point for putting human needs into ecological balance with those of our fellow travelers on spaceship Earth.

In the 1980s and 1990s, as environmental ethics gained attention, many defenders of wilderness shifted to this kind of biocentric, ethical argument under banners such as "deep ecology," "environmental ethics," "conservation biology," and "rewilding."[24] The common denominator is respect for the existence or intrinsic rights of other species and of ecological processes. Ethics, many now believe, must be extended beyond the human-to-human level to include our species' relationship to nature. As I detailed in *The Rights of Nature: A History of Environmental Ethics* (1989), the roots of this ethical expansion in American culture run back to the natural rights tradition, Thoreau, John Muir, the science of ecology, and especially Aldo Leopold and his "land ethic." By the end of the twentieth century, philosophers and theologians had begun to recognize the ethical relevance of the environment in general and of wilderness in particular. There was growing realization that of all the forms of pollution,

24. I have described the emergence of the concept that nature should be included in the moral community in *The Rights of Nature: A History of Environmental Ethics* (Madison, Wisc., 1989). The documentation in this book suggests the very large literature that has accumulated around this idea. Representative titles are Bill Devall and George Sessions, *Deep Ecology: Living As If Nature Mattered* (Salt Lake City, 1985); Carolyn Merchant, *Radical Ecology: The Search for a Liveable World* (New York, 1992); and Christopher D. Stone, *Earth and Other Ethics: The Case for Moral Pluralism* (New York, 1987).

that of the *mind* was the most serious. Correcting it meant changing values and attitudes, and wilderness was of major help here not only ecologically but intellectually as well. Its preservation is not only one of the best ideas American culture ever had; it may be a better one than we ever knew.

When Thoreau wrote in 1851 about wildness being the preservation of the world, he did not mean merely the human component. People could benefit from wilderness, of course, but nonhumans were also part of the picture. "What we call wildness," Thoreau explained a few years later, "is a civilization other than our own."[25] At the heart of the new, ecocentric rationale for wilderness is respect for this larger community of life and process. So wilderness preservation has become, finally, a gesture of planetary humility.

25. As quoted and discussed in Nash, *Rights of Nature,* p. 37.

Bibliography

In the earlier editions of this book I included detailed bibliographies, but I will not reprint them here. Some parts of them are now dated; however, the original references do appear unchanged in the footnotes. Consequently, I am providing here only a simple alphabetical listing of the central work in the study of wilderness. The emphasis is on wilderness-focused publications, mostly of recent vintage since older work is acknowledged in the text. I will not attempt to sort out the vast literature concerning "environment." Generally, I will not list work which fall into the category of "nature writing" or those whose focus is on a particular place. Very few periodical articles appear, but serious students of wilderness would do well to examine the entire runs of journals such as *Wild Earth, Conservation Biology, Environmental Ethics, The Environmental Professional, Orion, Wilderness,* and *Environmental History* (formerly *Environmental History Review* and *Forest and Conservation History*). I am confident that the books listed, and *their* references, will open most of the relevant doors.

Allin, Craig. *The Politics of Wilderness Preservation* (Westport, Conn., 1982).

Baldwin, Donald Nicholas, *The Quiet Revolution: The Grass Roots of Today's Wilderness Preservation Movement* (Boulder, Col., 1972).

Botkin, Daniel B. *No Man's Garden: Thoreau and a New Vision for Civilization and Nature* (Washington, D.C., 2001).

Brooks, Paul. *Roadless Areas* (New York, 1964).

Brower, David. *For Earth's Sake: The Life and Times of David Brower* (Salt Lake City, 1990).

Carroll, Peter. *Puritanism and the Wilderness: The Intellectual Significance of the New England Frontier, 1629–1700* (New York, 1969).

Chase, Alston. *Playing God in Yellowstone: The Destruction of America's First National Park* (New York, 1986).

Clough, Wilson. *The Necessary Earth: Nature and Solitude in American Literature* (Austin, 1964).

Coates, Peter. *Nature: Western Attitudes Since Ancient Times* (Berkeley, 1998).

Cohen, Michael P. *The Pathless Way: John Muir and the American Wilderness* (Madison, Wisc., 1984).

Cronon, William. *Changes in the Land: Indians, Colonists and the Ecology of New England* (New York, 1983).

———, ed. *Uncommon Ground: Toward Reinventing Nature* (New York, 1995).
Ehrenfield, David. *The Arrogance of Humanism* (New York, 1978).
Ekirch, Arthur A., Jr. *Man and Nature in America* (New York, 1963).
Elbers, Joan S., comp. *Changing Wilderness Values, 1930–1990: An Annotated Bibliography* (Westport, Conn., 1991).
Evernden, Neil. *The Natural Alien: Humankind and the Environment* (Toronto, 1985).
———. *The Social Creation of Nature* (Baltimore, 1992).
Fairchild, Hoxie Neale. *The Noble Savage: A Study in Romantic Naturalism* (New York, 1928).
Foreman, Dave. *The War on Nature* (forthcoming).
Foreman, Dave and Howie Wolke, *The Big Outside: A Descriptive Inventory of the Big Wilderness Areas of the United States* (Tucson, Ariz., 1992).
Fox, Stephen. *The American Conservation Movement: John Muir and His Legacy* (Madison, Wisc., 1985).
Frome, Michael. *Battle for the Wilderness* (New York, 1974).
Fussell, Edwin. *Frontier: American Literature and the American West* (Princeton, 1965).
Gilligan, James P. "The Development of Policy and Administration of Forest Service Primitive and Wilderness Areas in Western United States" (unpublished Ph.D. dissertation, University of Michigan, 1953).
Gisel, Bonnie Johanna, ed. *Kindred and Related Spirits; The Letters of John Muir and Jeanne C. Carr* (Salt Lake City, 2001).
Glover, James. *A Wilderness Original: The Life of Bob Marshall* (Seattle, 1986).
Glacken, Clarence J. *Traces on the Rhodian Shore: Nature and Culture in Western Thought from Ancient Times to the End of the Eighteenth Century* (Berkeley, 1967).
Gomes, Mary E. and Allen D. Framer. *Ecopsychology: Restoring the Earth, Healing the Mind* (San Francisco, 1995).
Graber, Linda. *Wilderness as Sacred Space* (Washington, 1976).
Graf, William L. *Wilderness Preservation and the Sagebrush Rebellions* (Savage, Md., 1990).
Hagen, Joel B. *An Entangled Bank: The Origins of Ecosystems Ecology* (New Brunswick, N.J., 1992).
Harvey, Mark W. T. *A Symbol of Wilderness: Echo Park and the American Conservation Movement* (Albuquerque, N.M., 1994).
Hays, Samuel P. *Beauty, Health and Permanence: Environmental Politics in the United States, 1955–1985* (New York, 1987).
Hays, Samuel P. *Conservation and the Gospel of Efficiency: The Progressive Conservation Movement, 1890–1920* (Cambridge, 1959).

Hazard, Lucy Lockwood. *The Frontier in American Literature* (New York, 1927).

Hendee, John, Robert C. Lukas, and George H. Stankey, eds. *Wilderness Management* (Golden, Col., 1990).

Huth, Hans. *Nature and the American: Three Centuries of Changing Attitude* (Berkeley, 1957).

Ise, John. *Our National Park Policy: A Critical History* (Baltimore, 1961).

Keiter, Robert B., ed. *Reclaiming the Native Home of Hope: Community, Ecology, and the West* (Salt Lake City, 1998)

Kellert, Stephen R. and Edward O. Wilson. *The Biophilia Hypothesis* (Washington, 1995).

Lewis, W. R. B. *The American Adam: Innocence, Tragedy and Tradition in the Nineteenth Century* (Chicago, 1955).

Martin, Calvin Luther. *In the Spirit of the Earth: Rethinking History and Time* (Baltimore, 1992).

Marx, Leo. *The Machine in the Garden: Technology and the Pastoral Idea in America* (New York, 1964).

McGregor, Robert Kuhn. *A Wider View of the Universe: Henry David Thoreau's Study of Nature* (Urbana, Ill., 1997).

Meine, Curt. *Aldo Leopold: His Life and Work* (Madison, Wisc., 1988).

Meredith, Robert. *The Environmentalists' Bookshelf: A Guide to the Best Books* (New York, 1993).

Mitchell, Lee Clark. *Witnesses to a Vanishing America: The Nineteenth-Century Response* (Princeton, 1981).

Mitman, Gregg. *The State of Nature: Ecology, Community and American Social Thought, 1900–1950* (Chicago, 1992).

Nash, Roderick Frazier., ed. *American Environmentalism: Readings in Conservation History* (3d ed., New York, 1990).

———. *The Rights of Nature: A History of Environmental Ethics* (Madison, Wisc., 1989).

Nicholson, Marjorie Hope. *Mountain Gloom and Mountain Glory: The Development of the Aesthetics of the Infinite* (Ithaca, N.Y., 1959).

Noss, Reed F. and Allen Y. Cooperrider, *Saving Nature's Legacy: Protecting and Restoring Biodiversity* (Washington, D.C., 1994).

Oelschlaeger, Max. *The Idea of Wilderness: From Prehistory to the Age of Ecology* (New Haven, 1991).

———, ed. *The Wilderness Condition: Essays on Environment and Civilization* (San Francisco, 1991).

Pearce, Harvey. *The Savages of America: A Study of the Indian and the Idea of Civilization* (Baltimore, 1965).

Quammen, David. *Flight of the Iguana: A Sidelong View of Science and Nature* (New York, 1998).

Richardson, Elmo R. *The Politics of Conservation: Crusades and Controversies, 1897–1913* (Berkeley, 1962).
Richardson, Robert D. *Henry Thoreau: A Life of the Mind* (Berkeley, 1986).
Riesner, Mark. *Cadillac Desert: The American West and Its Disappearing Water* (New York, 1986).
Rolston, Holmes. *Philosophy Gone Wild: Essays in Environmental Ethics* (Buffalo, 1989).
Ronald, Ann. *Words for the Wild* (San Francisco, 1987).
Rothenberg, David. *Wild Ideas* (Minneapolis, 1995).
Runte, Alfred. *National Parks: The American Experience,* 3d ed. (Lincoln, Neb., 1997).
———. *Yosemite: The Embattled Wilderness* (Lincoln, Neb., 1990).
Sanford, Charles A. *The Quest for Paradise: Europe and the American Moral Imagination* (Urbana, Ill., 1961).
Sax, Joseph. *Mountains without Handrails* (Ann Arbor, 1980).
Schmitt, Peter J. *Back to Nature: The Arcadian Myth in Urban America* (New York, 1969).
Schrepfer, Susan R. *The Fight to Save the Redwoods: A History of Environmental Reform, 1917–1978* (Madison, Wisc., 1983)
Sellars, Richard West. *Preserving Nature in the National Parks: A History* (New Haven, 1997).
Shabecoff, Philip. *Fierce Green Fire: The American Environmental Movement* (New York, 1993).
Shepard, Paul. *Man in the Landscape: An Historic View of the Esthetics of Nature* (New York, 1967).
———. *Nature and Madness* (San Francisco, 1982).
———. *Traces of an Omnivore* (Washington, D.C., 1996).
———. *Coming Home to the Pleistocene* (Washington, D.C., 1998).
Smallwood, William Martin. *Natural History and the American Mind* (New York, 1941).
Smith, Henry Nash. *Virgin Land: The American West as Symbol and Myth* (Cambridge, Mass., 1950).
Soulé, Michael and John Terborgh, eds. *Continental Conservation: Scientific Foundations of Regional Reserve Networks* (Washington, 1999).
Soulé, Michael. *Conservation Biology: The Science of Scarcity and Diversity* (Sunderland, Mass., 1986).
Soulé, Michael and Gary Lease, eds. *Reinventing Nature? Responses to Postmodern Deconstruction* (Washington, D.C., 1994).
Swain, Donald C. *Federal Conservation Policy, 1921–1933* (Berkeley, 1963).
Udall, Stewart. *The Quiet Crisis* (New York, 1963).
Terborgh, John. *Requiem for Nature* (Washington, D.C., 1999).

Thomas, Keith. *Man and the Natural World: A History of the Modern Sensibility* (New York, 1983).

Tobias, Michael. *A Vision of Nature: Traces of the Original World* (Kent, Ohio, 1995).

Turner, Frederick. *Beyond Geography: The Western Spirit Against the Wilderness* (New York, 1980).

———. *Rediscovering America: John Muir in His Time and Ours* (New York, 1985).

Turner, Jack. *The Abstract Wild* (Tucson, Ariz.,1996).

Williams, George H. *Wilderness and Paradise in Christian Thought* (New York, 1962).

Williams, Raymond. *The Country and the City* (New York, 1973).

Wilson, Edward O. *Biophilia: The Human Bond with Other Species* (Cambridge, Mass., 1984).

———. *The Diversity of Life* (Cambridge, Mass., 1992).

Worster, Donald. *Nature's Economy: The Roots of Ecology* (San Francisco, 1977).

Zeveloff, Samuel I., Mikel Vause, and William H. McVaugh, eds. *Wilderness Tapestry: An Eclectic Approach to Preservation* (Reno, Nev., 1992).

Index

Photo: Charles A. Cagara

Roderick Frazier Nash, a descendant of the Canadian river explorer Simon Roderick Fraser, has made wilderness the focus of both his professional and his recreational life. Nash joined the faculty of the University of California, Santa Barbara in 1966, where he offered the nation's first courses in environmental history. He also organized and chaired one of the first interdisciplinary undergraduate majors in environmental studies. In addition to *Wilderness and the American Mind,* Nash has written several other books, including *The Rights of Nature: A History of Environmental Ethics* (1989), which has been translated into six languages.

Nash was also one of the first commercial river guides in the American West, and he drew on his experience navigating legendary whitewater rivers to write *The Big Drops* (1989). He retired from teaching in 1995 to focus on whitewater boating, powder skiing, and ocean cruising. He continues to be a passionate advocate for environmental responsibility and wilderness preservation.

133 - Muir
lobbying
for Nat'l forest